ITALIAN
POPULAR COMEDY

A STUDY IN THE
COMMEDIA DELL'ARTE, 1560–1620
WITH SPECIAL REFERENCE TO THE
ENGLISH STAGE

By K. M. LEA

VOLUME II

OXFORD
AT THE CLARENDON PRESS
1934

OXFORD
UNIVERSITY PRESS
AMEN HOUSE, E.C. 4
London Edinburgh Glasgow
Leipzig New York Toronto
Melbourne Capetown Bombay
Calcutta Madras Shanghai
HUMPHREY MILFORD
PUBLISHER TO THE
UNIVERSITY

PRINTED IN GREAT BRITAIN

ITALIAN
POPULAR COMEDY

CONTENTS

VOLUME II

Part III

THE CONTACTS AND COMPARISONS WITH ELIZABETHAN DRAMA

Appendixes

PART III
THE CONTACTS AND COMPARISONS WITH ELIZABETHAN DRAMA

CHAPTER VI

THE COMMEDIA DELL'ARTE AND THE ENGLISH STAGE

Possible solutions to the problem of effecting a compromise between actor and poet in the production of drama. Comparison of the Italian and English methods in the sixteenth century. Contacts between the English and Italian stages: comments of English travellers; English players on the Continent; Italian players in England; travelling mountebanks; Amateur Italian plays in England; Italian musicians at Court; scholars and artists in the patronage of the nobility; merchants and commercial agents in the City. *References* to the Commedia dell'arte in English literature. Extent of the practice of *improvisation* and recognition of the uniqueness of the Italian method. Introduction of Italian *masks* into English drama: the Dulwich Plot; Jigs. General use of Character types compared with the more specific imitation of the figures of the Commedia dell'arte: Pantaloons; Pedants; Bravos; Zanni clowns, Italian 'lazzi' parallel to the patter and horse-play of Elizabethan clowns. Tricks of uncertain origin common to the English and Italian stages: the forces of Hercules; 'Jig' motifs. The importation of *plot material*. Allowance made for the spread of Italianate styles through the plays translated and adapted from the Commedia erudita. Consideration of the plays in which the Italian style of construction and characterization cannot be accounted for by literary sources: The Wit of a Woman; Englishmen for my Money; Jack Drum's Entertainment; Ram Alley; Greene's *Tu Quoque*; The Hog hath lost his Pearle. Allowance for direct and indirect literary sources of the Italian style of *Shakespearian* drama. Parallels to the *Merry Wives, The Comedy of Errors*, and the *Tempest* in the Commedia dell'arte traditions. *General estimate* of the connexions between the Commedia dell'arte and Elizabethan drama. Conclusion.

EVERY now and then the struggle between the claims of literature and the stage which is involved in the production of drama comes to the surface. The quarrel between Ben Jonson and Inigo Jones over the relative importance of poetry and scenery in the Court Masque is the test case for the Jacobean period, and for the twentieth century, Mr. Gordon Craig's proposal of the Über-Marionette as the ideal expression of the Art of the Theatre.

Of the many ways of adjusting a compromise there is first the agreement to differ. Milton is content to write *Samson Agonistes* and Shelley *Prometheus Unbound* with no intention of stage presentation: the producer concentrates upon the spectacular appeal of masque and ballet. Cases of such extreme independence hardly come within the scope of drama; the poet who ignores the values of representation is only by courtesy a dramatist, and the stage production must suffer from the lack of the permanence ensured by literary form. More common is the yield under protest. The tussle over cuts and adaptations goes on silently until one party gives in. The poet submits to a stage version or the actor does his best with a speech which is ineffective in delivery.

Theoretically it is the actor-poet who should solve the problem by uniting the opposing interests. The achievements of Shakespeare, Molière, and, in a less degree, of Ruzzante, support this theory, but even with the greatest the fusion is not always complete. The external division is abolished but the struggle becomes an internal one between inevitably conflicting tendencies. There are occasions when Shakespeare ignored his experience as an actor and wrote poetry, and others when the poet in him failed to justify passages which, as an actor, he knew would satisfy the cravings of a popular audience.

There is no rule for the concessions due between poet and player. Possibly it is not to be wished that there should be. It might be argued that the complexity makes for a finer tension. But while to a great and strenuous genius the conflict may be stimulating, to weaker faculties it is a strain. The list of entertainments for a London season compared with whatever can be salvaged of the total stage production for any given period suggests how heavy a price of second, third, and fourth rate 'shows' must be paid for one play worth preserving in literary form for another generation. The dual nature of drama makes it peculiarly difficult to find for it a true critical focus. At the moment of production the advantage is all on the side of the stage element, but as soon as the production is forgotten the literary qualities come to their own and gain yearly. The fact that it is comparatively rare for both crises in the life of a play to occur within the experience of an individual tends to dislocate the judgement.

Without estimating their artistic merits, therefore, we may consider the chief aspects of the conflict between the claims of the stage and the claims of literature in the drama of the Renaissance. Italian playwrights recognized the embarrassment of two masters and distinguished between Commedia erudita and the Commedia dell'arte or improvisa. In the first tradition plays were produced which neglected dramatic possibilities for the sake of an academic convention: in the second by vigorous reaction, professional comedians developed a style of drama which was completely independent of literature. The intercourse and interaction between the two types which has been traced in the preceding study modifies but does not change the essential distinction between them. It might be hazarded that it was for lack of a co-ordinating genius that all the literary and theatrical talent failed to produce a national Italian drama. Certainly Ruzzante was of the Shakespearian blend, but he lacked the comprehensiveness of soul.

The attempts made by English playwrights to solve the fundamental problem are less easily classified. Plays as stiffly academic as any Commedia erudita on the one hand, and on the other, dumbshows in which the player took leave of the poet, were produced, but these extremes leave untouched the mass of drama in which we are conscious that the give and take between actors and poets makes for its continual inequality and its occasional greatness. When it is considered that about a quarter of some two or three thousand plays produced between the accession of Elizabeth and the closing of the theatres[1] seem to have survived and how few of those that attained any printed record are of first-rate quality, and again that of this remnant even fewer are still stageworthy, it is not unfair to suppose that the proportion of good drama to bad was much the same in the sixteenth century as in any other period of dramatic productivity. We are apt to regard the Elizabethan-Jacobean period as a golden age for poetic drama, but it is evident that the poet had his own way in spite, rather than because, of his circumstances. The assumption that a popular audience found poetry any more acceptable in the sixteenth than in the twentieth century is challenged by a study of the record of Henslowe's experience of popular taste. For every magnificent soliloquy in *Tamburlaine* or *Dr. Faustus* Marlowe threw in the sop of an episodic sensation, and when the poet was empty-handed the producer saw to it that comic additions

[1] See Greg, *Henslowe's Diary*, vol. ii, p. 146. It is reckoned that roughly 650, excluding masques, belonging to the period 1557–1642 are extant, and that the total production was about 2,500.

were supplied. It is enough to compare the impressions left by a stage presentation and a private reading of *Hamlet* or the *Tempest* to see that their popularity is more likely to have been due to their vigorous dramatic and spectacular qualities than to the poetry of the conception and expression. The more often Elizabethan plays are put to the test of production the easier is it to realize how much attention was paid to the theatrical demands. Now that the literary sources have been discussed exhaustively for a century and a half the possibility of non-literary influences are being explored. While evidences of the stage conditions, of the composition of the particular companies, and their relation with the playwright who supplied them, and of methods of collaboration and revision are being assembled, it is worth while inquiring whether English actors and dramatists found any use for the method and material of the contemporary Italian stage in attempting to solve their fundamental problem. Although it must be confessed that the evidence is scanty and the influence will be found to be largely negative, the mere comparison may help towards a clearer idea of the nature of the Elizabethan dramatic compromise, for in studying the development of a technique even rejections can be instructive.

ENGLISHMEN IN ITALY

There were various opportunities for Elizabethans to become acquainted with the fashions of the contemporary Italian stage. A few notices survive of the way in which travellers in Italy, residents in Paris, and more particularly English players touring on the Continent came across Italian actors. Other records, scanty but distinct, prove that foreign players acted to provincial, city, and court audiences in England, and that Italian plays were produced by musicians and dilettanti at the English, as well as at the Bavarian court.

Playhouses were not among the public buildings that Bacon recommended his model traveller to inspect, but the author of a 'description of the estate of Italie in the yeare 1592', remarks that the pleasures of the Duke of Mantua are infinite 'in Tyltinge, Turnaye, Barryers & setting out of Comedyes, for all wch pastymes he hath buylt in his pallace at Mantua a fayre Amphitheatre being by reason of his youth given to more delights then all the Dukes of Italye'.[1] Fynes Moryson did not fail to observe 'the theatre for Comedies'[2] in the duke's palace in Florence and described how in the

'tyme of Carnavall all cittyes use to have publike comedies acted by the Cittizens, and in Florence they have a house where all the yeere long a Comedy was played by professed players once in the weeke and no more, and the partes of wemen were played by wemen, and the cheefe actours had not their parts fully penned, but spake much extempory or upon agreement betweene themselves, espetially the wemen, whose speeches were full of wantonnes, though not grosse baudry (which the Italians like, but neede no such provocation) and their playes were of amorous matters, never of historyes, much lesse of tragedies, which the Italian nature too much affects to imitate and surpasse. And one Lucinia a woman player, was so liked of the Florentines, as when shee dyed they made her a monument with an Epitaphe. Also not only in Carnavall but all the yeare long, all the Markett places of great Cittyes are full of Montebankes, or Ciarlatanes, who stand upon tables like stages, and sell their oyles, waters and salves, drawe the people about them by musicke and pleasant discourse like comedies, having a woman and a masked foole to acte these partes with them.[3]

Another Englishman who was in Flanders and Italy in 1610 notes that the Duke of Mantua 'is much delighted with Commedies and Mistresses'.[4] Finding himself in 'Vennice the 13th of May Eng. stilo: being Sonday' he continued in his rough journal 'Heare in the Quadrangle belowe are manie Montibanks which on a Scaffold doo sett rich Cabinets: and doe shew waters Oyles and Oyntments of great Raritie: and by Musicks wooment and good words promising woonders: doo persuade manie to buie of them.'[5]

   Coryat's description of the famous scene in the Piazza S. Marco is more circumstantial:

I hope it will not be esteemed for an impertinencie to my discourse, if I next speake of the Mountebanks of Venice, seeing amongst many other things that doe much famouse this citie, these two sorts of people,

[1] MS. Lans. 775. f. 128. Finished 6 March 1595.
[2] Itinerary (1617), pt. i. ch. 2, p. 150.
[3] Shakespeare's Europe, unpublished chapters of Fynes Moryson's Itinerary, edited from a manuscript in Corpus Christi College, Oxford, by C. Hughes, p. 465.
[4] MS. Sloane 682. f. 54.
[5] Ibid., f. 19.

namely the Cortizans & the Mountebanks, are not the least: for
although there are Mountebanks also in other Cities of Italy; yet
because there is a greater concurse of them in Venice than elsewhere,
& that of the better sort & the most eloquent fellowes; & also for that
there is a larger tolleration of them here then in other Cities (for in
Rome etc. they are restrained from certain matters as I have heard
which are heare allowed them) therefore they use to name a Venetian
Mountebanke for the coryphaeus & principal Mountebanke of all
Italy: neither doe I much doubt but that this treatise of them will be
acceptable to some readers, as being a meere novelty never before heard
of (I thinke) by thousands of our English Gallants. Surely the principal reason that hath induced me to make mention of them is, because
when I was in Venice, they oftentimes ministered infinite pleasure
to me.

After considering an etymological point, he proceeds to
describe the scene in front of S. Marco:

These Mountebanks at one end of their stage place their trunke, which
is replenished with a world of new-fangled trumperies. After the whole
rabble of them is gotten up to the stage, whereof some weare visards
being disguised like fooles in a play, some that are women (for there are
divers women also amongst them) are attyred with habits according
to that person that they sustaine; after (I say) they are all upon the
stage, the musicke begins. Sometimes vocall, sometimes instrumentall,
and sometimes both together. This musicke is a preamble and introduction to the ensuing matter: in the meane time while the musicke
playes, the principall Mountebanke which is the Captaine and ring-
leader of all the rest, opens his truncke, and sets abroach his wares;
after the musicke hath ceased, he maketh an oration to the audience of
halfe an houre long, or almost an houre. Wherein he doth most
hyperbolically extoll the virtue of his drugs and confections . . .
Though many of them are very counterfeit and false. Truely I often
wondred at many of these naturall Orators. For they would tell their
tales with such admirable volubility and plausible grace, even extempore, and seasoned with that singular variety of elegant jests and witty
conceits, that they did often strike great admiration into strangers that
never heard them before: and by how much the more eloquent these
Naturalists are, by so much the greater audience they draw unto them,
and the more ware they sell. After the chiefest Mountebankes first
speech is ended, he delivereth out his commodities by little and little,
the jester still playing his part, and the musicians singing and playing
upon their instruments. . . . I have observed marveilous strange matters
done by some of these Mountebanks. For I saw one of them holde

a viper in his hand, and play with his sting a quarter of an houre together, and yet receive no hurt; though another man should have been presently stung to death with it. He made us all beleeve that the same viper was linealy descended from the generation of that viper that lept out of the fire upon S. Pauls hand, in the Island of Melita now called Malta, and did him no hurt; and told us moreover that it would sting some, and not others. Also I have seen a Mountebanke hackle and gash his naked arme with a knife most pittifully to beholde, so that the blood hath streamed out in great abundance, and by and by after he hath applied a certain oyle unto it, wherewith he hath incontinent both stanched the blood, and so thoroughly healed the wounds and gashes, that when he hath afterward shewed us his arme againe, we could not possibly perceive the least token of a gash.[1]

There was another blind fellow, noticed by Coryat, who sang extemporal songs and made a pretty kind of music with two bones between his fingers.

Robert Dallington recommends that the English traveller should spend some time in Florence to acquire the best Italian under the direction of a reader, and recommends he 'shall not read any booke of Poetrie at the first, but some other kind of stile, and I think meetest some modern Comedie'.[2] It was probably with a less innocent intention that Coryat took the opportunity of visiting a Venetian playhouse and decided that it was

Very beggarly and base in comparison with our stately playhouses in England; neyther can their actors compare with us for apparell, shewes & musicke. Here I observed certain thinges that I never saw before. For I sawe women acte, a thing that I never saw before, though I have heard that it hath sometimes been used in London, & they performed it with as good a grace, action, gesture & whatsoever convenient for a Player, as ever I saw any masculine actor. Also their noble and famous Cortezans came to this comedy, but so disguised that a man cannot perceive them.[3]

We have no record of Whetstone's actual travels but the description printed in February 1582 of the performances of Mountebanks and of improvising comedians that he witnessed 'in a most noble Italian Gentleman's Pallace this Christmas twelve moneths past' show that he was perfectly

---

[1] Coryat's *Crudities*, ed. MacLehose, 1905, vol. i, pp. 410–12.
[2] *A Method of Travell shewed by* *taking a View of France as it stoode in* *1598.* Sig. B 3.
[3] Coryat, op. cit., i. 130.

acquainted with both kinds of professional entertainers. Towards the end of the Thyrde Dayes Exercise

when Supper was done, the Queene Aurelia, & the most Honourable of the Companie had taken their places uppon a Scaffolde made for the nonce, there mounted a Mountebanke, his necke bechayned with live Adders, Snakes Eau'ts, & twentie sundrie kinds of venemous vermines, whose mortall stinges were taken away by Arte, and with him a Zanni, and other Actors of pleasure: who presented themselves with a single desire, to recreate Signior Philoxenus, & his worthie companie: & not with the intent of common Mountebanckers to deceyve the people with some unprofitable Marchandize.

The serpents inspire one old man to a tirade against women's tongues which leads to a dispute;

By this time the Mountibanck, with describing the quallities of his Vermin, & the Zanni in showing the knavish conditions of his Maister, had wasted a good part of the night, & wearyed the most part of the company, so that desyre of repose, summoned them to their lodgings.

On the 'Fyfth Evening'

By that time Supper was done, certayne comedians of Ravenna presented their services to Signior Philoxenus & his honourable companie, who are not tide to a written device, as our English Players are, but having a certayne groundes or principles of their owne, will, Extempore, make a pleasaunt showe of other men's fantasies: so that to try the quickness of the Gentlemen & Gentlewomens wittes, to give the Comedians a Theame Signior Philoxenus demanded the meaning of certaine questions.

After debating a little over the riddling definitions of such abstractions as Inconstancie, Dissimulation, Ignorance, Chastytie, and Beautie,

Signior Philoxenus stopped his digression & commaunded the Comedians to bethinke themselves of some action, that should lyvelie expresse the nature of Inconstancie, Dissimulation, Ignorance & the rest of the passions, before named: which charge being given, while the Actors were attiring themselves, for the Stage, Queene Aurelia, & her Attendaunts took their places, with such advauntage, as every Gentleman, had lyberty, to devise with his Mistresse.

After the Comedians had put themselves in order, they patched a Comedy together, & under the resited names, showed some matter of Morallytie, but a greate deale of mirthe: who with their pastime kept the companie up so long, as drowsie sleepe, which delighteth in nothing but scilence, arrested ye greater part of them, & carried them close prisoners, unto their chaumbers.[1]

News-letters from Italy in 1584/5 announce the rehearsal of the grand tragedy of which the Venetian Academicians intend to give three performances at Vicenza during the Carnival.[2] There is a notice of the performance of Pino da Cagli's comedy *Li Ingiusti Sdegni* in the same theatre at Whitsuntide in the following year.[3] Letters from Venice dated 2 March 1584/5 mention a pastoral acted at the palace.[4] Successive packets from Rome report the preparation and the success of a 'pretty comedy in the house of the Duke of Soria at which there were present the Cardinals San Sisto, Vastavillano and Ezza(?) with many ladies and gentlemen of Rome'. There had been other entertainments at the house of Gio. Giorgio Cesarini and the whole week had been spent in festivities and comedies.[5] Carnival in Florence that year was celebrated 'according to the old usage, the races have been run this week, plays acted and continual festivities, with no less dulness (*freddezza*) than usual'.[6] If the Florentines were apathetic, the Spanish Governor of Milan and his Japanese guests and the Jesuit Fathers roared over a comedy of the *Gelosi* a few months later:

> Con l'ultimo di Milano s'intende . . . che era stata fatta una comedia al Gov^re dalli Comici Gelosi, con la presenza dalli 4 Sig^ri Giapponesi quali (*me: ne?*) recevettero così gran piacere, con quelli padri Giesuiti, che se gli sarebbono cavati li denti, tanto ridevano di cuore.[7]

It was the skill of Italian professionals that had delighted the English Ambassadors to the French Court some years before. In February 1571 the company of Taborino and next month the *Gelosi* were in Paris, and on 4 March Lord Buckhurst, who had come over to congratulate Charles IX on his wedding, was entertained by Louis Gonzaga, Duke of Nevers, 'with a comedie of Italians that for the mirth and handling thereof deserved singular commendacion'.[8]

---

[1] *Heptameron of Civill Discourses,* 3 Feb. 1582. Sigs. Liiiv; Miv.

[2] *State Papers, Foreign, Newsletter,* lxxii, 7. 23 Feb. 1584/5.

[3] Ibid., xcv, 31. 10 May 1586, Venice.

[4] Ibid., lxxviii, 27 Feb.–9 March 1584/5.

[5] Ibid., lxxii, 6, 10. 27 Feb.–9 March 1584/5.

[6] Ibid., lxxii, 8. 1584/5, p. 289.

[7] Ibid., lxxii, 23. 31 July–10 August 1585. Venice, 10 August.

[8] Ibid. (1569–71), p. 413.

In the summer of 1572 Edward Clinton, Earl of Lincoln, was sent to Paris to ratify the League with France, accompanied by a great train of noblemen, 'the Lords Dacres, Rich, Talbot, Sands and others'. Sidney and Brysket were also in Paris at that time. On 18 June Clinton wrote to Burghley:

On frydaye last I was sent for, to come to Madryll to the King ... we were lodged in the Kyng's howse theare, & hadd greate enterteynement wheare we remayned frydaie & Satterdaie in wch tyme the Kynge used suche familier enterteynemente as he tooke me wythe hym after his supper to walke in his parke, & he played at the tennys in the fyldes at randon with the noblemen, and carried me late to his pryvie chamber and did talke wythe me vearie pryvatelye. he hadd some pastyme showed him by Italian players whiche I was at wth him. . . . The Kyng upon Sondaye last towlde me that bothe his brethren (for the greate honor they beare to her Matie) dyd desyer to have me, and bothe her Ma^{ts} Imbassad^{rs}, & the Noblemen & Gentlemen of my companye, to dyne with theym upon Tewsdaie & Wensdaie next followinge that ys to saye wythe monsieur upon tewsdaye at his howse in parris, and wth the duke dalaunson upon wensdaie, wch thing the Kyng desyred that I wolde doo, and afterwards bothe Monsieur and the duke theamselves desyred me to doo the same. So that uppon tewsdaye we dyned wythe Monsieur, who sent for us twoo of the brethren of Monsieur de Momeransie, & Lansack & Larshaunt & dyvars other. And at oure comynge the Duke & his brother dyd mete us wythowt his greate Chamber dore accompanied with the Duke monpanser & his sonne prince Dolphyn, & the Duks de Nevers & bulleyn, and Domall and Guyse, and the Marshall de Cossie and danvyle and mons^r de merrew and torrey, who all dyned wyth hym. At after dynar, Mons. and his brother brought us to a chamber wheare was veary manie sorts of excelent musycke. And after that he hadd us to an other large chamber, wheare there was an Italian playe, & dyvars vawtars & leapers of dyvars sorts vearie excelent. And thus that daye was spent untyll yt was somewhat late.[1]

In a letter to Burghley of the same date Sir Thomas Smyth describes Tuesday's entertainment: after the music followed

an Italian Comedie wch eandid vaulting w^t notable supersaltes, & through hoopes, and last of all the Antiques, of carying of men one uppon an other wch som men call Labores Herculis, These things may better be declared by word of them that saw & can skill of it, then by writing especially of me. . . .

[1] 18 June 1572. MSS. Cott. Vesp. F. vi. f. 95 (old numeration 91).

Of Wednesday's entertainment he writes:

After dynner Monsieur and the Duke brought my Lord *Ad*^{all} &
us into a Chamber somewhat more fresh, where we heard excellent
musique both of voice & virginalls, & of voice & violls as the daie
before, And the Duke shewed unto us he had provided for us a
comedie, & som Eskrymeurs to shew us pastyme. But he saw the day
was so hote & the place, that he feared he should do us more displeasure
& grief, w^t heate, then pleasure.[1]

These were not the *Gelosi*, for they were in Milan and
Genoa that summer, but either the comedians with *Ganassa*
who was in France at least from August to October for the
marriage of Henry of Navarre with Marguerite of Valois,[2] or
the company, or companies, led by Anton Maria and Soldino.
On 25 March Soldino was paid on behalf of eleven actors
for acrobatic feats and a comedy at Blois; two days later
Anton Maria Venitiano received '25 livres en testons a XII
sols par livre' for himself and his nine companions. A joint
payment on 11 April shows that at least on one occasion the
companies were amalgamated.[3]

The performance of the company criticized by Robert
Dallington must have been before 1598, but cannot be more
precisely dated. Commenting upon the lack of ceremony
observed by the French King he reminds his reader,

You saw here in Orleans, when the Italian Commedians were to play
before him, how himselfe came whifling with a small wand to scowre
the coast, and made a place for the rascall Players (for indeed these
were the worst company, and such as in their owne Country are out
of request) you have not seene in the Innes of Court, a Hall better
made: a thing, me thought, most derogatory to the Maiesty of a King
of France.[4]

It was for politic reasons that Dr. Hawkins told Antony
Bacon that after the taking of Amiens early in 1597 the
French were 'attending only to their sports, called Com-
medianti out of Italy',[5] and that Winwood informed Cecil

---

[1] 18 June 1572. MSS. Cott. Vesp. F.
vi. f. 99–100.

[2] Tresorie de l'espargne. Vol. iii,
f. 3529. (Bib. Nat. de Paris. Fonds
Clairambault 233.) Quoted Baschet,
op. cit., p. 43.

[3] Idem, ff. 3153–4, 3238. Baschet,

op. cit., pp. 33–8.

[4] *Method of Travell*, 1598. Sig. H. 4 v.

[5] Venice. 18/28 March 1596/7.
Birch, *Chronicles of the Reign of Queen
Elizabeth*, ii. 306, quoting from the
papers of A. Bacon at Lambeth Palace
Library, vol. iv, f. 42.

from Paris on 7 July 1602 that, 'upon Thursday last, certain
Italian comedians did set up upon the corners of the passages
of this towne that that afternoone they would play *L'Histoire
Angloise contre la Roine d'Angleterre*.[1] In the satirical verse-
letter dated from Paris, September 1608, Lord Herbert of
Cherbury comments upon the Italian plays in which women
play as boys.[2]

ENGLISH ACTORS ABROAD

It would be more interesting to us if the impressions of the
English actors who went abroad had been recorded. With
the vivid touch in the preface to *An Almond for a Parrat*
(1590), where Nashe represents the 'famous Francatrip
Harlicken' at Bergamo inquiring whether he knew 'any such
Parabolano here in London as Signior Chiarlatano Kempino',[3]
we are bound to allow for the colouring of fiction. But for
the scene in the *Travailes of the Three English Brothers*,[4] in
which Kemp agrees to play a part with the Italian Harlaken
before Sir Anthony Shirley in Venice, there is a core of fact
in the records which make it practically certain that Kemp
crossed the Alps in 1601. In the diary of William Smith of
Abingdon there is interpolated an entry for 2 September
1601 which reads:

Kemp, mimus quidam, qui peregrinationem quandam in Germaniam
et Italiam instituerat, post multos errores, et infortunia sua, reversus:
multa refert de Anthonio Sherley, equite aurato, quem Romae (legatum
Persicum agentem) convenerat.[5]

It is due to the imperfection of the itineraries which can
be but fragmentarily reconstructed that we have to conjecture
the occasion of such meetings as well as the effect which the
intercourse may have had upon their art. It is tantalizing for

[1] Winwood, *Memorials*, i. 425.

[2] Ed. Moore Smith, p. 16.

[3] Ed. cit. iii. 342.

[4] 'The Travailes of the Three English
Brothers Sir Thomas, Anthony, Mr.
Robert Shirley. Play'd by her Maiesties
servants. Printed for John Wright . . .
1607.' The reference to the plot of
England's Joy gives us 1601/2 as a date
a quo. See *infra*, p. 381.

[5] MS. Sloane 414. f. 56. Although

this entry is not in the same hand as the
rest of the diary Sir E. K. Chambers
does not appear to doubt its authenticity.
(See *Eliz. Stage*, ii. 326.) The central
fact of Kemp's journey into Italy is
corroborated by other references. See
Nine Daies Wonder (1600), reprinted by
the Camden Society, 1840, pp. 20-2,
and *Pilgrimage to Parnassus*, pt. iii,
Act IV, sc. iii.

instance to know so much of the movements of Italian players in Italy and so little of them in Germany, so much of English players in Germany and so little in Italy; or again to know that there were English acrobats in Madrid on 11 January 1583, and that sometime in that year *Ganassa's* troop was also in Spain playing at Seville. Between the visits of Italian comedians to Paris in 1597 and 1599 English players rented the Hôtel de Bourgogne during the summer of 1598. In 1604 the succession and possible coincidence of travelling players in Paris was considerably closer. The *Gelosi* must have left sometime in May to reach Lyons where Isabella Andreini died on 11 June.

From a letter from Loreden to Carleton on 14 March 1603/4 describing the disturbance occasioned by the Welshmen who would insist upon entertaining the English players, and the mention of a warrant to one Browne, an English comedian, for transporting 'dogges, Beares and Apes', in Sir Thomas Parry's dispatch of 11 August it appears that the English actors who played before the Dauphin at Fontainebleau on 18 September had been in France for some time.[1]

Fynes Moryson observed that in England

All Cittyes, Townes and villages swarme with Companyes of Musicians and Fidlers, which are rare in other Kingdomes. The City of London alone hath foure or five Companyes of players with their peculiar Theaters capable of many thousands, wherein they all play every day in the weeke but Sunday, with most strang concourse of people, besydes many strange toyes and fances exposed by signes to be seene in private houses, to which and to many musterings and other frequent spectacles, the people flocke in great nombers, being naturally more newe-fangled then the Athenians to heare newes and gaze upon every toye, as there be, in my opinion, more Playes in London then in all the partes of the worlde I have seene, so doe these players or Comedians excell all others in the worlde. Whereof I have seene some stragling broken Companyes that passed into Netherland and Germany, followed by the people from one town to another, though they understoode not their wordes, only to see theire action, yea marchants at Fayres bragged more to have seene them, then of the good marketts they made. Not to speake of frequent spectacles in London exhibited to the people by Fencers, by walkers on Ropes, and like men of activity. . . .[2]

[1] See F. Yates, *Review of English Studies*, Oct. 1925.

[2] Fynes Moryson, *Itinerary*, 1617, p. 476.

The unique record which survives of Italian professional comedians in Germany gives us a most likely case of coincidence. In the accounts of the household of Maurice of Hesse-Cassel for 1597/8 after the item of white clothes for the clown occurs the entry of payment to an Italian Zanni and his companions:

> Dem welschen Jan und seiner Bereitern zweimal, summa . . . 150 Thlr.[1]

The nationality of the first clown is not specified, but he was probably one of the companions of Robert Browne and John Webster, who belonged to the household at least between 1596 and 1598.[2]

ITALIAN PLAYERS IN ENGLAND

Attempts to identify the Italian players who appear from time to time on this side of the Channel are also hampered by the imperfection of such lists and itineraries as are now available. Even if we were to discover the *personnels* of the companies we should still be uncertain of their repertories; and again, could we know the titles of their plays the nature of improvised comedy puts it beyond hope that we should ever be able to make more than a most tentative reconstruction of their dramatic effect.

The earliest record of foreign players which might refer to 'comici dell'arte' is the entry in the Chamberlain's accounts in Norwich 1546/7:

> Itm gof in reward on the Sonday beyng sent Jamys Evyn to certen Spanyards & Ytalyans who dawnsyd antycks & played dyvrse other feets at the Comon Halle before Mr Mayor & the coĩalte 13/4
> Itm for a fferkyn of bere for them etc. . . . 9d.
> Itm to dyvrs men yt removyd the tabyles trustylls & fforymes & set them agayne when all thyngs was don . . 3d.[3]

In 1573 it is again in the provinces that we find traces of 'Italyans' who were paid five shillings at Nottingham on

---

[1] A. Cohn, *Shakespeare in Germany* (1865), p. 445.
[2] *Elizabethan Stage*, ii. 278-9.
[3] Norwich Chamberlain's Accounts.

Henry VII-Ed. VI, 1546/7. See J. Tucker Murray, *English Dramatic Companies*, ii, p. 363.

4 or 14 September 'for serteyne pastymes that they shewed before Maister Meare and his brethren'.[1]

These were probably the Italian Players whose permit 'to make shewe of an instrument of strange motions within the Citie' was the subject of two letters belonging to 1573, but otherwise undated, sent by the Privy Council to the Lord Mayor of London.[2]

In the Revels Accounts for February 1573–November 1574 are charges 'ffor The Ayrynges, Repayryngs, Translatynges, preparing, ffytting, ffurnishing, Garnishing Attending, & setting foorth, of sundry kyndes of Apparell propertyes & ffurnyture for the Italyan players that ffollowed the progresse & made pastyme fyrst at Wynsor & afterwardes at Reading'. Some properties are distinctive:

Itm̄ for Ladles & Dishes to beare the lightes at wynsor for
 the Italyans & for payntyng & garnishing of them with
 Rewardes given to dyvers whose Necessaryes & services
 were then used . . . . xj^s vj^d
Itm̄ for preparacons etc at Reading the xvth of July 1574
 aº R.R.F. xvj^{to}

Gold Lether for cronetes	iii^s	iiij^d
Thred & sheperdes hookes		xiiij^d
Lamskynnes for Shepperds		iiij^d
Horstayles for the wylde mannes garment . . .	iiij^s	viij^d
Arrowes for Nymphes		vj^d
Lightes & shepperdes staves		vij^d
Hoopes for Garlandes		iiij^d
Pottes for the Paynter		ij^d
Pack thredd ii^d, Glew iii^d, Lyne iiij^d, Tacks ii^d, Wyer iiii^d & Coles iiii^d		xix^d
Plates for the Candelstickes	iiij^s	
Wyer to hang the lightes		xvj^d
Baye Leaves & flowers		xii^d
for paynting sundry devices	ii^s	
Rewardes for vi Taylers there	vj^s	
Howseroome for the stuf	v^s	
The hyer of A Syth for saturne		iiij^d
Cariage of Stuf fro(m) Reding	ii^s	vj^d
The hier of A Trunk	ii^s	vj^d

[1] Nottingham Chamberlain's Accounts, ibid. ii. 374. [2] Acts of Privy Council 1573, pp. 131–2.

sundry Necessaries & Rewardes disburced by John drawater
   there . . .
under the heading of 'The hyer of apparrell'
Thomas Clatterbooke for hier of iii devells cotes & heades &
   one olde mannes fries cote for the Italian prayers [sic] at
   Wynsor .   .   .   .   v^s 1

Possibly the 'Marryners whissell' and the 'sack for the
players' hired later were also for the foreign actors.[2] Sir
E. K. Chambers suggests that these were the 'comedie
players' about whom the Privy Council wrote to the Cor-
poration on 22 July 1574,[3] and probably those who provoked Thomas Norton's remonstrance against the 'unchaste,
shamelesse & unnaturall tomblinges òf the Italion Woemen'
in November.[4] The entry in the municipal accounts of
Dover of 10s. paid to 'the Italian Tumblers or players'[5] is
only dated for the year 1574/5 and does not help us to know
whether they were arriving or leaving the country.

The magnificent display of fireworks presented to the
Queen at Kenilworth in 1575 may have been engineered by
the Italian pyrotechnician recommended to Leicester by
Killigrew in May.[6] There was in the Earl's service that
summer at least one other Italian entertainer of whose acrobatic feats Robert Laneham's description seems almost as
lively as the actual performance. On Thursday 14 July
between the bearbaiting and the fireworks, he relates how

within allso, in the mean time, waz thear sheawed before her Highness,
by an *Italian*, such feats of agilitie, in goinges, turninges, tumblinges,

---

[1] *Documents relating to the Office of Revels in the time of Queen Elizabeth*, ed. A. Feuillerat, 1908, pp. 225-8.

[2] Ibid., p. 236, ll. 24-5. 1574/5.

[3] Acts of the Privy Council 1574.

[4] MS. Add. 32, 379, f. 37 v. (now 41 v.), 'an exhortaĉon or rule sette downe by our Mr Norton sometyme remem-brauncer of the Cittie'. Dated Nov. 1574 by a reference to the Lord Mayor as James Hawkes on f. 35 v. (now 39 v.). 'And we here owte of place that should before have bene spoken. the pñte time requirethe yoᵂ have good care and use good meanes towchinge the contagion of sickenes that the sicke be kept from the whole that the places of persons infected be made plaine to be knowen and the more releeved that sweetenes & holsomnes of publique places be provided for, that unnecessarie and scarslie honeste resorts to plaies to showes to thoccasion of thronge and presse, except to the servyse of God, and especiallie (to) the assemblies to the unchaste, shamelesse and unnaturall tomblinges of the Italion Woemen maye be avoided and offend God & honestie is, not to cease a plague.'

[5] Tucker-Murray, op. cit., p. 261.

[6] H.M. Com. Report of the Pepys MSS., p. 178.

castinges, hops, jumps, leaps, skips, springs, gambaud, soomersauts, caprettiez & flights; forward, backward, sydewize a doownward, upward & with sundry windings, gyrings, & circumflexions; allso lightly, & with such easines, as by mee in feaw words it iz not expressibl by pen or speech, I tell yoo plain. I bleast me by my faith to behold him, & began to doout whether a waz a man or a spirite, & I ween had doouted mee 'till this time, had it not been that anon I bethought me of men that can reazon & talk with too toongs, & with too parsons at onez, sing like burds, curteiz of behaviour, of body strong, & in joynts so nymbl withall, that their bonez seem az lythie & plyaunt az syneuz. They dwel in a happy lland (az the Book tearmz it), four moonths sayling Southward beyond *Ethiop.* Nay, *Master Martin*, I tell you no jest: for both *Diodorus Siculus*, an auncient Greek Historiographer, in his third book of the Acts of the olld *Egypticians*; and also from him, *Conrad Gesnerus* a great learned man, and a very diligent Writer in all good arguments of oour time (but deceased), in the first chapter of his *Mithridates*, reporteth the same. Az for thiz fellow, I cannot tell what too make of him, save that I may gesse hiz bak be metalled like a Lamprey, that haz no bone, but a lyne like a Lute-string. Well, Syr, let him passe & his featz, and this dayz pastime withall, for heer iz az mooch az I can remember mee for *Thursdaiz* entertainment.[1]

The chapter on 'Saltatori' in the *Piazza Universale* (1585) may help us to identify this acrobat. Garzoni enumerates ninety-two of the most sensational leaps, and mentions by name nineteen famous tumblers of his day. Among them is Soldino of Florence in whose favour we are biased by the fact that he was one of the leaders of the company which the Earl of Lincoln is most likely to have seen in 1572.

In 1576 there were Italian Players at Court collaborating with Alfonso Ferrabosco, who is probably the Queen's favourite Bolognese musician referred to about this time by Zuan Falier.[2] The entry of payment for a play at Court 'To Alfruso Ferrabolle and the rest of the Italian players' contains an obvious scribal error.[3]

Gascoigne had probably some such entertainment in mind when in the Prologue to the *Glasse of Government* printed in 1575 he referred to 'Italian toyes' that 'are full of pleasaunt sporte', and when he mentioned 'These Enterludes, these

---

[1] Reprint: 1907, p. 18.   [3] Chambers, *Eliz. Stage*, iv, p. 150.
[2] *State Papers, Venetian*, vii. 527.

newe Italian sportes' in the *Stele Glas* for which he dated the dedicatory letter 15 April 1576.

The notice of an Italian play given before the Council at Durham Place in April 1577,[1] the item in the Chambers accounts for 1577/8 of 'a mattres hoopes and boardes with tressells for the Italian tumblers',[2] and permission granted Drusiano Martinelli by the Privy Council to play in the city between January and the first week of Lent 1578,[3] in spite of the plague prohibitions, point to the visit of at least one, probably two, or even three successive companies. It has been suggested that the *Gelosi* who performed frequently at Blois and in Paris between January and October 1577 may have crossed the Channel before they made their way back to Florence. But little that we know of the movements and *personnel* of this company fits this theory. Although they do not appear to have accompanied Henry III when he left Blois on 23 April for Amboise, Chenonceaux, Tours, and Poitiers, they would hardly have had time to visit England before their reappearance in Paris on 18 May. Towards the end of July (27th) the Parisian civic authorities forbade the performances of the *Gelosi*, and in spite of their letters patent it was not until the beginning of September by special Royal permission that they were allowed to give their comedies at the Hôtel de Bourbon. The Chamber Accounts give no precise date for the provision of properties for the tumblers; the *Gelosi* might have tried their fortunes in London in August, but it is not likely that so finished a company would be described merely as tumblers. In October they were still in Paris in high favour with the king, who writes to Sr de Bellièvre:

Monsieur jay accordé aux commédiens de avoir ce quilz avoient à Bloys, je veux qu'ainsi soit faict et qu'il n'y ait pas faulte, car j'ay plaisir à les oÿr je n'ay eu oncques plus parfaict.[4]

How much longer they stayed does not appear. The reasons for doubting that they were the players allowed by the Privy Council for the first few months of 1578 are negative but strong. The Drousiano in whose name the licence was granted can only be Drusiano Martinelli, who was associated

---

[1] Chambers, *Eliz. Stage*, iv, p. 80.   [3] Ibid., iv, p. 152.
[2] Ibid., ii, p. 262.   [4] Baschet, op. cit., p. 76.

with many different companies, but never, I think, with the *Gelosi*. We know nothing of him before this date: on his next appearance in July 1580 he is trying to persuade the Duke of Mantua to patronize a new company. But Lanfranco Turino reported privately that beyond Angelica (the wife of Drusiano) and some fine vaulters it was not good.[1] In 1587 Drusiano left the *Confidenti* in Spain,[2] in 1595 he served the Duke of Mantua with the *Uniti*,[3] and in 1600/1 he went into France with the *Accesi*.[4] He may have played the part of Arlecchino,[5] but his fame as an actor was covered by that of his brother Tristano, and his identity as a conductor behind the reputation of his wife, who is possibly the 'nimble tumbling Angelica' to whom Marston refers in the *Scourge of Villany* (1598).[6]

The licence to Drusiano's players is the last satisfactory record of a regular Italian company in England, but by 1591 the visits of Italian comedians were evidently common enough for spies to choose the habit of tumblers as a safe disguise. In July 1591 Weston reports to Francis Bacon 'a devise of Italian espiales & intelligencers to come shortly in the habite & colo^r of Tumblers (hayw [Haywoods] report). Y^e was accownt of [secresie—successe?] in frawnce (hay rep.) (x August) The tenth of Awg^t holdeth for meeting in the Clynke'.[7] Whether these supposed players ever reached their sinister destination I do not know. Saintmann (alias Sterrell) has heard nothing of 'the Italian who is in the plot' in October, but this may refer to another conspiracy.[8]

The possibility of international companies of French and Italian composition tempts us to mention that at Ipswich in 1569, 7s. 8d. was paid to 'certen strange players';[9] that in 1580 a French tumbler visited the town;[10] that in 1600 a Frenchman was to 'dooe feates upon a rope', before the

---

[1] *Giorn. Stor.* xviii, p. 169. Compare ch. v, pp. 274.

[2] Rasi, op. cit., ii. 104.

[3] D'Ancona, op. cit., ii. 519. Compare ch. v, pp. 277.

[4] Baschet, op. cit., p. 108. Compare ch. v, p. 278.

[5] Compare ch. v, p. 276.

[6] *Eliz. Stage*, ii. 263, n. 4.

[7] *State Papers, Domestic*, xii. 239, 114.

[8] Ibid., 240, 34 and 241, 10. See also 241, 44; 243, 118.

[9] H.M. Commission Reports, ix, p. 249 b. Chamberlain's Accounts.

[10] Ibid., p. 250.

Queen, 'in the Conduit Court';[1] and that in 1616 Jeronimo Galt and John de Rue calling themselves French tumblers presented themselves at Norwich 'to shewe rare feats of Activity with dancinge on the Ropes pformed by a woman and also a Baboone that can do strange feats', with a licence dated 13 Eliz. (1571) and 1616 which was considered insufficient.[2]

The remaining notices of specifically Italian entertainments refer to isolated performers, jugglers, mountebanks, and puppet-shows. On 17 May 1602 there is at court a Sicilian juggler who works wonders at cards, and gets much from credulous women.[3] On 17 March and 13 April 1600 two pounds was bestowed upon an unnamed comedian 'at his highnes comand' from Prince Henry's Privy Purse.[4]

MOUNTEBANKS.

Though not every mountebank was, but since any mountebank might be, a player, it is perhaps as well to give references to their performances the benefit of the doubt. The term 'mountebank' covers many activities. Originally it denotes a charlatan who mounts his bench in the piazza to cry his wares: Whetstone has a marginal explanation 'mountibanks of Italie are in a maner as English Pedlers'; Jonson glosses the word by 'quacksalver'.[5] Kemp was referred to as 'Sr Chiarlatano'. In *Hans Beer-Pot* the terms are used as synonyms:

> I thinke the Seriante is grown mountebancke
> To cling by shifts, hey passe, passe,
> Italian grown; a sharking charlatan.[6]

In the First Antimask at Gray's Inn in 1594 a Mountebanck and his disciples, 'fellow artists of several nations all famous for their bante', challenged the mad Greek Paradox.[7]

---

[1] Sydney Papers, ii. 194.

[2] Mayor's Court Book, Norwich, 9 Oct. 1616. Tucker Murray, op. cit., ii. 342.

[3] *State Papers, Domestic*, xii. 284, 14.

[4] Ibid., xiv; lvii, 87. Thaccōptesof Sr David Murrey for money receavd and disbursed for and out of the Prince his Privie Purse.

The quality of the 'poore stranger Italian' who was given two pounds on Nov. 10th, or of 'Daniel the Italian' who received six pounds on January 9th 1609/10, is not stated.

[5] *Volpone*, II. i.

[6] *Hans Beer-Pot his Invisible Comedie of See Me & See Me Not*, Daubridgcourt Belchier. 1618. Sig. Dv.

[7] *Gesta Grayorum*, pt. ii.

Given a Zanni, or apprentice loud in attendance who sings songs when the master quack has exhausted his extravagances, it is easy to see how the succession of speech and song with the possibilities of repartee might assume a dramatic form.[1] It appears from the terms of the licence granted to Zoppino and Martinelli appointing them Directors over all the

Comici, mercenarie, Bagatellieri, Saltatori che vanno sulla corda, che monstrano mostri et edifici et simili cose e Zarlattani che mettano banchi per le piazze per vendere ogni unguenti, pomate, lituari, controveleni, bolli, moscardini, acque muschiate zibetto, muschio, istorie, et altre cose stampate, ongia della gran bestia, et che mettano cartelli per medicare, et simile sorta di gente,[2]

that mountebanks were closely associated with the 'comici' and passed with that miscellaneous crowd of tumblers, itinerant musicians and puppet showmen who filled up the lower ranks of the profession. The piazza scene in *Volpone* shows how easily the charlatan's bench might become the stage for improvising comedians.[3] When Volpone as a mountebank doctor has delivered his harangue dispraising the 'rabble ciarlatani' and advertising his own oils and drugs, and Nano as his Zan Fritada has given two songs extempore, Celia looks out of the window and throws him her handkerchief. Corvino rushes out to interrupt their conversation, shouting,

> Spight o' the Devil, & my shame! Come down here;
> Come down: No house but mine to make your scene?
> Signior Flaminio, will you down, sir? down?
> What, is my wife your Francescina, sir?
> No windows on the whole Piazza, here,
> To make your properties, but mine?

---

[1] It is characteristic of Coleridge that from chance observation and cloudy speculation he should have lighted on the historical truth. Raysor, in his edition of *Coleridge's Shakespearean Criticism*, ii. 8, cites a note of the lecture delivered on 5 February 1808:
'Mr. C., in Italy, heard a quack in the street, who was accosted by his servant smartly; a dialogue ensued which pleased the mob; the next day the quack, having perceived the good effect of an adjunct, hired a boy to talk with him. In this way a play might have originated.'

[2] T. Martinelli to Strigi. From Fontainebleau 10 Oct. 1613. Cf. Grant to 'Zoppino', 14 March 1580. D'Ancona, op. cit., ii. 474. 'Instrutti dell'informatione che ha il giocondo nostro Filippo Angelone di tutti li comici mercenarj Zaratani et cant' in banchi ...'

[3] See W. Smith, *The Commedia dell'arte*. Ottonelli, op. cit., p. 455.

He sees himself in the appropriate role of the 'Pantalone di Besogniosi' and visualizes the situation as part of a performance of the Commedia dell'arte.

Although Jonson might have found all the names which give local colour to the scene in Garzoni's description of the Piazza of S. Marco, it is tempting to wonder whether it was not more than a personal connexion that led him to call his mountebank Scoto of Mantua. Zan Fritada, Flaminio, Franceschina and Pantalone were common masks, but Scoto was more distinctive. In addition to the allusion in *Jack Wilton* to 'Scoto, that dyd the jugling tricks before the quene',[1] Dr. McKerrow quotes from two pamphlets, *The Defensative against supposed Prophecie of Henry Howard, Earl of Nottingham* (1583) and J. Harvey's *Discoursive Problem concerning Prophecies* (1588). In the second Scoto is coupled with the well-known Juggler Feates as a typical member of the 'foisting crue';[2] in the first the mention is more detailed.

I was present myselfe when divers Gentlemen & noblemen, which undertooke to descry the finest sleights, that Scotto the Italian was able to play by leger du main before the Queene: were not withstanding no lesse beguiled then the rest: that presumed lesse uppon theyr own dexteritie & skyll in these matters.[3]

Scotto's visit must have taken place between 1576 and 1583. In the postscript of a letter written on 25 March 1576 Dr. Dale informs Burghley that in Paris,

There is one Scotto an Italian that playeth such knackes as Feates doth uppon the Cardes who commeth to showe the Quenes Matie sum of his toyes, he hath been made [much] of in this court, & maketh himself a iolye fellow.[4]

His visit may be dated more precisely if he is to be identified with the Sr Scoto mentioned by Cobham on 20 February 1579/80:

Fard^{er} the said partie wryteth to me from Maestricht that the Prince of Parma expecteth the prophecies of (m) Sr Scoto the Italyane, who hath ben in England & maketh the Prince believe there shalbe great news from thence yer it be longe the wch prophecies are founded upon the present preparations.[5]

---

1 Ed. cit. ii, p. 252.
2 Sig. Hv.   3 Sig. Y iiiv–iv.
4 *State Papers, Foreign*, 1576, 691.

5 *State Papers, Foreign*, 78, 4. The letter from Maestricht was dated Feb. 8. It is the 'S^r' rather than the single 't' of

Scotto came over to England as a juggler, but in Italy he was closely associated with the professional comedians. A letter dated 11 March 1602 from P. Vinta to his brother Belisario, the chief secretary to the Grand Duke of Tuscany, mentions 'Dionisio detto lo Scotto Mantovano' as the first of three leading charlatans whose performances as mountebanks and street comedians were to be prohibited during the octave of Easter.

Questa mattina a hora 17 in circa feci precetto all' Canta in Banchi esistenti in Fiorenze che si riducano a tre capi et tre squadre, una di Dionisio d° lo Scotto Mantovano, una di Marsilio Savino Venetiano, et una di Decio Albani da Siena, che non ardissino per tutta l'ottava della Pasqua di Resurez: montar in Banco ne recitare, o far recitar Commedie in Piazza, o strade, et luoghi publici della Città, ne anco in alberghi, hosterie, o altro luogo di essa con interveno di Zanni, o strioni infami et donne disoneste et lascive sotto pena del mio arbitrio. . . .[1]

He appears to have been a free lance, but lack of a full company would not have prevented him from giving a dramatic performance.

In 1630 F. Nicolini was licensed as a miscellaneous performer, 'to dance on the ropes, to use interludes and masques and to sell his powders and balsams'.[2] The Italian mountebank who was tried in 1617 for poisoning a patient,[3] may have been the Italian who received nine shillings from the Mayor of Coventry for the old trick of 'thrusting himself through the side to make experiment of his oyle' the year before.[4] From the fact that they showed an 'Etalion motion',

---

'Scoto' that makes it a little doubtful whether it is to the juggler that Cobham is referring. In 1582 he mentions the Count Alandi Scoti, but he evidently had not been to England. (*State Papers, Foreign*, 394.) Another Conte Paulo Emilio Scoto was murdered in 1585 (*State Papers, Foreign*).

[1] Arch. di Stato Florence Fa 908. c. 103. 1600, 2 May. Venice,

Che sia commesso di ordine di questo Conseglio al *Scoto* montà in banco, et così alli altri montà in banco...non debbano nell'avenire far, nè far far comedie in banco di alcuna sorte, nè in Piazza di

S. Marco, nè in altro luogo di questa città. See Sforza, *F. M. Fiorentini ed i suoi Contemporanei lucchesi.*—(1879). Appendix E. Compare G. B. Andreini's *Lo Schiavetto* (ed. 1600), p. 100, where there is mention of 'Scoto e Fortunato . . . ceretani ceretanissimi'.

[2] E. Chalmers, *Supplemental Apology* (1799), p. 209 n. 2.

[3] *State Papers, Domestic*, xiv. 93, 123.

[4] Wardens' or Chamberlains' Accounts, 27 Nov. 1616. Tucker Murray, op. cit., ii. 247. Cp. Garzoni, op. cit., p. 757.

it does not follow that the players who were paid at Leicester in 1619 were foreign.[1] In 1623 Barth. Cloys,[2] and in 1635 T. Maskell were licensed;[3] and in 1632 William Costine, Thomas Hunter, and Henry ffussell with their assistants exhibited an 'Italian motion with divers and sundry storyes in it' at Coventry.[4] It is recorded that at Norwich in 1639 'Robert Browne & George Hall did this day [9 October] exhibit a lycense from Sr Henry Herbert, Master of the Revells to shewe an Italian Motion because he sayeth his motion is noe Italian motion but made in London this Court thinks fitter not to suffer them to shewe'. Presumably the 'Larzeus Colleretto who wished to shew a monster on Dec. 1st was a foreigner.[5]

AMATEUR ITALIAN PLAYS IN ENGLAND.

Courtiers who had a taste for Italian drama were not entirely dependent upon travelling professionals. There is among the Pepys Manuscripts a note from Petruccio Ubaldini to the Queen explaining that the delay over the Italian Comedy in which Claudio Cavallerizzo and Alfonso Ferrabosco had asked him to perform was due to the difficulty of collecting a cast.

Sacra Ser^ma M^tà.

Perche i giorni passati io haveva promesso à Ms Claudio Cavallarizzo, e à Ms Alfonso Ferrabosco, d'esser contento di recitar ad una piacevol Comedia Italiana; per compiacere alla M^ta Vra et non si trovando di poi altri, che tre ò quattro, che fusser contenti d'accettar tal carico; ho voluto che l'Altezza V^ra conosca da me stesso il pronto animo, ch'io ho per la mia parte di servirla, et di compiacerla in ogni attione, che mi sia comandata, ò da lei, ò in suo nome, non solamente come servitore giurato, ch'io gli sono; ma come desiderosiss: di far conoscere, che la divotione, ch'io porto alle sue Reali Qualità, supera ogn'altro rispetto; desiderandogli io contentezza, et felicità non meno, che qualunque altro suo servitore gli desideri. . . .[6]

---

[1] Ibid., ii, p. 313. Chamberlains' Accounts.

[2] Ibid., ii, p. 250. Coventry Chamberlains' Accounts, year ending 20 Nov. 1624, 'for shewing a musicall organ with divers strang and rare motions'.

[3] Ibid., ii, p. 358. Dec. 1635. Mayors' Court Book, Norwich.

[4] Ibid., ii. 251. [5] Ibid., ii. p. 359.

[6] Pepys MSS. Magdalene College, Cambridge.

Original Papers of State under ye Hands of several Emperors, Kings, Queens & Princes, Principal Ministers, Great Officers, & other Persons of Note before, in, & since the time of Queen Elizabeth. . . . Vol. 2502, t. ii, f. 663. (Endorsed 'to Q. Elizabeth:

It is most tantalizing that the signature and possibly the date of this note has been worn away from the foot of the page. As Sir E. K. Chambers suggests it may refer to the play on 27 February 1576, but the entry of payment on this occasion to 'Alfonso Ferrabolle and the rest of the Italian players' reads more like a reference to professionals than to the amateurs whom Ubaldini was trying to collect. After examining the movements of the three actors who are mentioned we are left with a choice of any date between 1562 and 1578, excepting for some months in 1564 and 1569/70, and with a bias of probability in favour of 1565.

Petruccio Ubaldini was not a musician, as whoever endorsed the note to the Queen had 'supposed'. He visited England in 1545 and again in 1551; by 1562 he appears to have decided to settle in this country, trying to make a living by transcribing, illuminating, and translating. This was a gentlemanly employment but not lucrative, so that in 1574 and again in 1578/9 he was seriously in debt. With the exception of a possible visit to Ireland in 1580, Ubaldini seems to have remained in England until the end of October 1586,[1] when he was granted a passport to go into the Low Countries. His *Discrittioni del Regno di Scotia et delle Isole sue Adjacenti* was published at Antwerp in 1588, but he must have returned to England that winter for at the New Year (March 1588/9) he gave the Queen a 'boke of Italian'.

There is nothing in this record to help date the proposal for a comedy, though the fact that in 1577 Ubaldini dedicated to Elizabeth his account of *Le Vite e fatti di sei Donne Illustre* and at the New Year received gilt spoons in return for 'a boke of Italian, with pictures of the lyfe and meta- morphoses of Ovid',[2] leads Sir E. K. Chambers to connect this note with the 1576/7 performance.

The travels of Alfonso Ferrabosco are more helpful in providing us with one or two eliminations. In 1562 he was established as the Queen's musician with a yearly pension of one hundred marks.[3] In 1564 he was for some time with

Ubaldino an Italian
Musitian, I suppose')
The large sheet of paper has been fingered so that the signature is lost; at the foot of the page it is possible to make out

'Humilliss[i .. mamente ?]' but no more.
[1] See *Dict. of Nat. Biography*.
[2] Nichols, *Progresses*, iii, p. 105.
[3] Cunningham, *Revels Accounts* (1842), p. xxviii.

Cardinal Farnese in Rome and was due to return to England at the end of June.

From the reference to the death of his father Domenico Maria Ferrabosco, which took place in 1574, it appears that a letter addressed to Leicester on 23 October is misdated for October 1564 by the omission of a stroke from the Roman numeral. It is not therefore evidence that he was back in London by the autumn as it has generally been supposed.[1] He was in England at any rate by February 1565.[2] On 10 September 1567, after thanking Cecil for his pension, he urges that it should be secured in the event of the Queen's death and made transferable to his heirs.[3]

Later in the month he is concerned to reinstate himself at Court, protesting that the reasons for his visits to the Ambassador of France have been misrepresented to the Queen.[4] For October and December there are two letters to Sussex reiterating his innocence of the more serious charge of having assassinated a young foreigner, a follower of Sir Philip Sidney.[5] Early the next year Ferrabosco obtained leave to go into Italy, promising to return as soon as he had settled his affairs.[6] In Paris he was robbed and delayed by one who had been page to Sir Charles Howard,[7] and once in Bologna was refused the Papal licence to leave the country again.[8] He forced a return and so forfeited his property.[9] In 1572 he took part in a Masque at Whitehall before the Queen and the Ambassador of France.[10] In 1578 he went into Italy again. Cobham in Paris worked for his return, and on 11 February 1579/80 bade Walsingham tell Elizabeth that he had dealt with the Queen Mother who had sent to Rome

[1] Brit. Mus. MS., Titus B. VII. c. 48. See *Musical Antiquary*, iii and iv.

[2] Titus B. VII. f. 358.

[3] *State Papers*, xliv, No. 4. See also Arkwright, *Rivista Musicale*, 1897, p. 10.

[4] Titus B. VII, p. 344. 26 Sept. 1567 (endorsed 1577), London to Cecil. Lans. 25. See *Zeitschrift für internat. Musik. Gesellschaft*, 1906/7, p. 272.

[5] 13 Oct. 1567. Titus B. VII, p. 231 and 309. 29 Dec. 1567.

[6] 22 March 1568 to Cecil from Court. Hatfield MS. Report, pt. i, p. 462,

Document 1284.

[7] 25 June 1569. *State Papers, Foreign*, 1569, No. 308.

[8] *State Papers, Foreign*, 1570, No. 1293.

[9] 23 Oct. 1574 (in error 1564), London. Titus B. VII. f. 48.

In the catalogue of MSS. destroyed in the fire at Turin in 1912 there is record of a pamphlet entitled: 'Dell'Historia d'Altimauro composta per Alfonso Ferrabosco' dedicated to his patron Carlo Emanuele I da Savoia.

[10] Feuillerat, pp. 159, 160.

to procure the deliverance of Alfonso,[1] but he had left England for good and ended his life in the service of the Duke of Savoy.[2] Ferrabosco had evidently kinsmen in England: in January 1576 a brother of Mr. Alfonso was hurt at Southwark,[3] but it was to Gomer van Awsterwyke, a fellow musician, that he left the charge of his children. This friend was burdened with the care of them for eleven years, for the Queen regarded them as hostages for Alfonso's return and refused to let them leave the country in 1584. At last in 1589, hearing that Ferrabosco was dead, he ventured to ask for a lease in reversion to relieve him of his expense.[4] They were brought up in the family tradition: the younger Alphonso had charge of Prince Henry's musical education, and in 1624 Henry in the third generation belonged to the King's music.

The identification of the third actor narrows the field. It is common to refer to Ms Claudio as though 'Cavallarizzo' were his surname, but the phrase 'Sig. Claudio suo Cavaglierizzo' used by Thommaso Baroncelli in writing to the Earl of Leicester from Antwerp on 21 February 1565 justifies the translation offered in the calendar of the Pepys Manuscripts which reads, 'Claudio, your master of horse'.[5]

In this case the professional title was doubly appropriate, for this was Claudio Corte of Pavia, author of *Il Cavallerizzo*, a treatise upon horsemanship which was, after Grisone, the standard work of the period. His book is a substantial composition with ample digressions showing an impressive muster of classical examples and modern instances. In the first part he deals fully with the origin, nature, anatomy, and breeding of the horse, in the second with the art of riding in all its branches; only with the third does he reach the titular subject and M. Prospero asks his friend Claudio what of 'il Cavallerizzo' himself. Here Corte adopts the dialogue

---

[1] *State Papers, Foreign, France,* iv. 15.
[2] G. Livi, *Musical Antiquary,* iv, pp. 129–33. See also *State Papers, Rome* (edited by Rigg), 2077, f. and g. 5 Aug. 1578. Ferrabosco and an Englishman set out from Paris to Bologna and are to be watched (Doc. 922). They are supposed to be bringing pensions to the Queen's adherents in Venice (Doc. 984).

[3] Acts of the Privy Council.
[4] 8 May 1589. Hatfield, pt. iii. 869. Cecil Papers. Petitions iv. 992.
[5] Pepys, i. 545. Cavallarizzo is also used as the Italian form of address to Leicester as Master of the Horse to Elizabeth. In other letters M. Claudio is mentioned as 'il Cavallarizzo'.

form and expatiates on his ideal of a 'cavallerizzo' revealing
the influence of Castiglione in his generous conception of a
master of horse as versatile and urbane as the Corteggiano.
His virtuosity draws an admiring comment from Prospero:

Non dite piu oltra circa questo di gratia, che m'havete si persuaso, che
io ne resto quietissimo, et contento; et in ciò havete dimostrato non
essere meno Oratore, et Rettore, che cavalcatore degno della grande
Elisabetta Regina d'Inghilterra, et d'havere per gran Scudiere, et
patrone il non mai à bastanza lodato Conte di Lancastro Milort
Roberto.[1]

In 1584, at the instance of Mr. Henrie Mackwilliam,
T. Bedingfield published a useful summary of Corte's second
book 'brieflie reduced into certeine English discourses to the
benefit of Gentlemen and others desirous of such knowledge'. Nothing of the erudition or idealism of *Il Cavallerizzo* survives in this simple *Art of Riding*.

Two editions of *Il Cavallerizzo* were published in 1573,
the one in Venice dedicated to Cardinal Alessandro Farnese,
the other in Lyons with its prefatory letter to Charles IX
dated precisely 'Di Leone 10. di Giugno, 1573'.[2] Both are
described as enlarged and revised, but they differ so considerably that one might suppose that Corte had rewritten
rather than transcribed his manuscript, freely adapting himself to the tastes of his different patrons. The Lyons edition
as the larger might be regarded as the later were it not for
the letter prefixed to the third book dated 'Parigi il terzo di

---

[1] Venetia, 1573, f. 131. The puzzling
use of 'Lancastro' which prevails in the
Venetian edition may be disregarded as
the error of a foreign scribe or com-
positor after comparison with the
corresponding passages in the Lyons
edition where Milort Roberto is cor-
rectly styled 'Conte di Lecestre'. See
Venetia, f. 16 v, and compare Lyons,
f. 20.

[2] (1) Il Cavallerizzo di Claudio Corte
da Pavia Nel qual si tratta della natura
de' Cavalli, delle Razze, del modo di
governarli, domarli, e frenarli. Et di
tutto quello, che à Cavalli, e à buon
Cavallerizzo s'appartiene;
Di nuovo dell'Auttore stesso corretto

ed emendato, ed aggiuntovi di molte
cose necessarie, che nella prima impres-
sione mancavano.
     In Venetia, Appresso Giordano
Ziletti M DL XXIII.
     (2) Il Cavalerizo di Messer Claudio
Corte di Pavia Nel quale si tratta della
natura de' Cavalli del modo di domargli,
e frenargli, et di tutto quello, che à
Cavalli, et à buon Cavalerizzo s'appartiene.
Accresciuto, emendato, ed ornato di
utilissime cose molto piacevoli.
     In Lyone appresso Alessandro Mar-
silij 1573, p. 162 'Il fine. Laus Deo.
Stampato in Lione per Pietro Roussin.'

di Maggio del 1571'. The corresponding letter to Farnese
in the Venetian edition is undated. The exact relationship
of the two versions does not affect this argument and we may
take advantage of the passages peculiar to each as well as of
those common to both to recover some notion of the author's
capacity and career.

Claudio came of a family of famous riders. His father
'M. Gio. Maria della Girola, così detto, ma de' nobili in
Corte di Pavia', nephew and pupil of that M. Evangelista di
Corte whose fame he believes will never wither, was master
of the horse to Isabella of Aragon, daughter of Alfonso of
Naples and Duchess of Milan, in the days when horses were
really good and 'cavallerizzi' well paid and esteemed.
Claudio was brought up as a page in her household together
with some five and thirty boys, all noble and some of almost
princely stock, among whom was the Commendatore Fra
Prospero Milanese,[1] who appears as interlocutor in the third
book. At the death of Isabella he passed into the service of
Signor Vespasiano, son of Prospero Colonna and father of the
Principessa Isabella di Sulmona.[2]

His expressions of gratitude for the patronage of the
Farnese and of French nobility and royalty serve as an
advertisement with which to meet the slander of his rivals.
'Ma che?' he goes on, scornful and triumphant, 'Non servo
io hora la Magnanima Elisabetta, gran Regina d'Inghilterra
con quel stipendio, et honorato grado, che ciascun può
sapere? et à me non tocca dire? Volendo così il mio gran
Mecenate, delitie del mondo Milort Roberto, Conte di
Lancastro . . .' to his most Christian Majesty it is phrased
discreetly 'col consenso però del Sommo Pontefice, e gran
Vicario di Christo Pio Quarto'.[3]

Leicester is praised so often that at last Prospero checks
the panegyrist gently and elicits a tribute to Darnley as the
next most perfect Cavallerizzo. He is as spirited as he is
handsome, and now as the husband of the Queen of Scots is
not merely princely but royal.

In answer to Prospero's question Claudio explains that he

---

[1] Venetian ed., sigs. a 3 v and a 4, cp.   E and E v.
Lyons, sig. ***2.   [3] Venetian ed., sigs. a 3 v and a 4;
[2] Venetian ed., f. 14. Lyons, sigs.   Lyons, sigs. **2 and 2 v.

had met 'Milort d'Arli' at the English Court and admired his skill on horseback: 'Ma durò poco, che se ne passò in Scotia, dove essendo Simpathia grande tra lui, e la Regina, divenne, come io v'ho detto, suo marito.'[1]

Claudio was not long at the English Court himself. Commenting upon the handsome rewards from Elizabeth and the Earl, to each of whom he had presented a book, Prospero asks why he made so short a stay, not more than six months, he has heard. That is too long a story, says Claudio evasively.[2] He was much impressed by the pace and docility of the ordinary English hackneys, but the strength and intelligence of the royal stud amazed and delighted him.

Non era cavallo nella cavallerizza di Londra, dov'io gia fui principale, et vi hebbi da trenta cinque in quaranta cavalli elletti d'amaestrare et far governare, che non intendesse à cenno il suo curatore. Tutti si lasciano strigliare, e governare, per feroci, et grandi, che fossero, senza cosa alcuna in bocca, et senza attacco alcuno, et essendo col capo alle magnatore dislegati sentendosi chiamare si rivoltavano, et andavano verso il curatore, et cosi dislegati radoppiavano nelle lor poste con si bell'aere, che haureste detto, non farebbono meglio sotto un buon Scudiero.[3]

While he was in charge of the royal stables, with the help of his pupil M. Bernardino Menci of Perugia he broke in two fine horses, a roan with a flowing mane called Scapigliato and a starred bay, 'lo Stella'.[4] He also picked up an English expression and explains gravely, 'Nel parar à salti con calci devete usar questa op op op. La qual voce non vuol dir altro che de bout de bout: cioè Su su, leva leva, alto alto in Italiano'.[5]

The allusion to Darnley's departure from the English to the Scottish Court fixes Claudio's visit as a little before the middle of February 1565. This date is confirmed by two letters in the Pepys Collection. In April 1564 Gurone, an agent in Rome known to Antonio Bruschetto, the father of Spenser's friend Lodovic Bryskett, added as a postscript to Spinola in London: 'Il Cavallarizzo si mandarà al piu presto che sara possibile'.[6] In the following June Sebastiano

---

[1] Venetian ed., f. 127.   [2] Ibid., f. 118 v.
[3] Lyons ed., f. 20, cp. Venetian ed., f. 16 v.   [4] Lyons ed., f. 22.
     [5] Ibid., f. 91 v.   [6] Pepys, i. f. 126.

Bruschetto instructs Spinola to explain to the Earl that M.
Claudio, who was due to leave Rome on the 18th, has been
arrested by a man to whom he had recommended a horse,
and it is suspected that the delay was contrived by Cardinal
Farnese, who was annoyed with Leicester's friends for persuading Alfonso Ferrabosco to return to England with
'il Cavallarizzo'.[1]

Clinching the identification of this Claudio with the Corte
of Pavia there is the mention in the third book of *Il Cavallerizzo*,[2] 'il mio Signor Alfonso Ferabosco gentilhuomo
compitissimo: il quale veramente hà piu virtù che la Bettonica:
ma nella Musica, e massime di canto è senza pare'.

A chance reference to a Zanni 'che disse . . . di se stesso
nella Comedia, sanno scrivere ma non leggere'[3] is of interest
in this connexion and may perhaps indicate Claudio's familiarity with the Commedia dell'arte. Unless he returned
to the service of Leicester after 1573 the most likely date for
his performance with Ubaldini and Ferrabosco would be the
spring of 1565.

ITALIAN MUSICIANS AT COURT

If numbers count for anything Ubaldini should have had
little difficulty in finding performers. All the Tudors were
served by Italian musicians.[4] Of the group of eight whose
names occur first in the Audit Office Declared Accounts in
1547, Albret, Frauncisco and Vinsent de Venytia, Ambrose
de Myllane, Anthony Maria, Piero Guy, Mark Anthony
(sackbut) and Marc An^{io} (Galliardello, violinist), at least four
are known to have continued into the service of Elizabeth.
Possibly it was from among these that Julyan chose the 'three
Etalyans' with whom he made a challenge in 1550.[5]

Fabricio, son of Luys Denti, a Neapolitan whom Henry
VIII had hoped to attract into his service, was recommended
to Leicester as one for whom, in the estimation of Sir Thomas

[1] Rome, 13 and 24 June 1564. Ibid.,
i. ff. 167, 175, 179.
[2] Lyons, f. 147 v.
[3] Ibid., f. 138 v.
[4] Unless separate references are given
the following facts are taken from the

List of the King's Musicians published
from the Audit Office Declared Accounts in *Musical Antiquary*, i–iv.
[5] *H. MSS. Commission Report*, xii,
App. IV, p. 55.

Challoner, who had heard him play at Barcelona in March 1564,[1] 'entertainment of four hundred crowns would not be excessive'. The name of Anthonie de Chountie who played the virginals recurs with various spellings for fifteen years.[2] Ranaldo Parradiso was at Court for three years (1567–70), Ambrosio Grasso of Pavia, who was drowned at Windsor in 1582, for four. Other musicians who served into the second, or like the Ferraboschi the third, generation may be grouped into families. In 1559 there were two Galliardelli and two de Comy brothers as violinists. The Caesar Galliardetto, who took the place of Mark Anthony Galliardello, reappears as 'Galliardello' in subsequent entries. When Innocent de Comy died in 1602 the place was given to his son Anthonie; another George de Comy is probably to be identified with the George de Combre of Cremonde (Cremona?) whose name occurs in 1547.

Four and possibly five of the Milanese family of Lupo were royal musicians. The violinist who appears as 'Ambrose de Myllane' in 1547 is entered as 'Ambrose de Myllane alias Lupo' in 1587/8. Petro was a violinist for thirty-nine years, Joseph for forty-five. Each had a son Thomas in the royal service. In 1611 Horatio Lupo succeeded Warren as violinist.

The Bassani were even more numerous. In 1549 'Lewes, Anthony, Jasper and John Bassyam, mynstreles', are mentioned;[3] in the Estate Book for 1552 is entered a payment of £183 6s. 8d. to 'fower brethren Venetians. vz. John, Anthonie, Jasper & Baptist'. A fifth, Augustine, was paid separately.[4] In 1565 the Lewes of 1549 returns as Ludovico to make up the six. In 1604, when Augustine's place was taken by Clemente Lanyer, an Andrea Bassano who had offered a New Year's gift of perfumed gloves in 1600[5] is mentioned as a maker and repairer of musical instruments. Thomas Bassano was granted the place of the musician John

---

[1] Pepys MS. cit. i. 207.

[2] This surname seems to have troubled English clerks; in the Declared Accounts it occurs as de Chontye; Countie; Counte. Stow, in the Establishment Book (1552 page 591) has 'Chountie', the 'Anthonny Comities the Quenes Maties servant' living in the Tower Ward in 1567 is no doubt the same person. (MS. Lans. x. 5.)

[3] *Musical Antiquary* cit.

[4] Stow, op. cit., p. 571.

[5] Nichols, op. cit., vol. iii. 24/5, 1599/1600.

Phelps in 1615.[1] Four others appear in commercial concerns: Arthur, Edward, and Scipio in 1604 over the transport
of calf-skins;[2] Paul in 1618 pleading that the petition of
certain fishmongers made against him over the question of
some lobsters is 'frivolous and unfounded'.[3]

Nor was it only in the Queen's household that foreign
artists sought a place. In 1564 a lute-player from Bologna
was privately recommended to the Earl of Leicester.[4]
Among the Manuscripts of the Marquis of Bath there is 'An
Entertainment for Noblemen, Knights & Gentlemen of
Worth. Prepared of an Italian, consort of strange musique,
consisting of nine instruments, musically concorded with
Italyan voyces, very delectable for all such persons of honour,
worship & worth as will vouchsafe their presence to hear
the same', dated 1612.[5] In the Delawarr papers is note of
a payment of £150 to Italian musicians.[6]

ITALIAN EXILES

There were no regular Italian Ambassadors during Elizabeth's reign, but from the State Papers and Italian archives
we may collect some fugitive details about State visitors,
spies, informers, poisoners, and exiles who sought tutor-
ships, monopolies, and benefices in recognition of their
various treatises and inventions. A few like Bruno, Florio,
and Gentili were well entertained; others probably became
facetious with poverty and despair like the Citolino who sent
the Queen an inventory of his goods, which were these:

> A great cupboard full of warm promises,
> A great chest full of good hopes,
> A great purse full of emptiness,
> Certain broken glasses and such like.

The Archbishop of Canterbury had given him reason to hope
for a prebend in the diocese of Winchester, but it had been
given to some one else; he would wait for another had he any
time to wait, but he is old, needy, and diseased.

---

[1] *State Papers, Domestic*, xiv. 81, 37.
[2] Ibid., 8 Nov. 1604, vol. x. 4 Sept.
1598. Ibid., vol. xii. 268, 48.
[3] Ibid., xiv. 98, 4.
[4] Pepys MS. i. 167, p. 24.

[5] *H. MSS. Commission Report on the
MSS. at Longleat*, vol. ii, p. 62.
[6] Ibid., MSS. of Lord Delawarr, iv.
301.

'A bira et odio libera nos Domine.' When her Majesty
pleases to provide for him the Muses who sit in a corner of
Parnassus their heads on their knees will rise up again
joyfully.[1]

ITALIAN MERCHANTS

The Italianate taste of the Court encouraged the patronage
of scholars, literati, artists, commercial and political agents:
but in the City the foreign merchants, brokers, factors, and
tradesmen were solidly established and therefore more
suspiciously regarded. According to Rye there were 4,631
aliens in London in 1571. An undated slip in the Lansdowne Manuscript (xxxii, 11) estimates 3,909, and the
churches to which they belong as, French 1,149, Italian 66,
English 1,043, Dutch 1,384, no church 287. Taking warning by the error in the addition, we may take this as a very
rough computation. The minority of the Italian may perhaps
be accounted for by the fact that 'Italian Church' presumably
means those Protestants to whom Michelangelo Florio,
G. Ferlito,[2] and Ascanio Balliano[3] ministered.

Two other lists among the Lansdowne Manuscripts, one
endorsed 'Strangers in London (and Westmins) 1567 and
1586', and the other 'Strangers in London not coming to
church 1581', give us the names, the parishes, and in many
cases the years of denization of Italians.[4]

The letters which Sr Gargano has recently salvaged from
the Florentine Archives give, as it were, a transverse section
of this colony. The racy correspondence of Paolo Gondola
takes us behind the scenes in the household of Nicolò de
Gozzi, a mean shrewd man but one of the best accredited
merchants in London. Gondola lived with Gozzi for two
years working to establish a commercial footing for himself

---

[1] 14 Aug. 1573. MS. Lans. 17, 6.
The signature 'Il Citolino Inglese de la
bira in fuori' gives no indication
whether he should be identified either
with the Alessandro Citolyn suggested
as a tutor for Prince James in 1574
(*Cal. Scott. State Papers*, iv. 680) or with
the Paolo Citolino who petitioned for
the reversion of an estate in 1590.
(*H. MSS. Commission Report*, iv, p. 49.)

(Salisbury Papers.) A certain A. Citolini
published a work entitled *Typocosmia*
which is discussed in *La Critica*, 1923/4.
See also Gentili's edition of the works of
G. Bruno, p. 53, for a bibliography.

[2] Pepys, p. 139.

[3] Gargano, *Scapigliatura Italiana a
Londra sotto Elisabetta & Giacomo*, i,
p. 172. p.

[4] Lans, x. 5; xxx. 10.

and his friend Gualtari Panciatichi of Florence. He was an energetic business man and a Catholic ardent to the point of risking arrest for attending Mass. But if he was an angel abroad, in the home he was the proverbial devil and had all de Gozzi's dependants by the ears. One clerk, Mario Berti, was dismissed at Gondola's complaint, with another, the more virtuous Orazio Franciotto, he was continually quarrelling over the beer; Mannelli he introduced to the taverns and stews and laughed at his innocence; he described to Panciatichi with some relish how he dealt with a fourth:

He (Piero) has become prouder than Lucifer; but I will tame him with a stick. The other night as I lay in bed I had a sudden whimsy to go & give him a whacking: so I dressed & took a rod that I had in pickle for him & my dagger. I only put on my jerkin & hose, nothing else, & I went down to the kitchen, but he had gone to bed & I could not find him; but never mind, the time will come when I'll get hold of him.

Such ructions might be kept private, but Gondola's love affairs seem to have been conducted more publicly through 'nostro Gioanna', the hostess of the 'Dolphin'. There was a certain young lady in the country who heard that Gondola was to leave England within a fortnight,

and as soon as she heard of this, she took leave of her mother, but without her father's knowledge, & rode off with two servants intending to follow me, so I am told, & they say that all the way she wept & tore her hair. And when she arrived in London she sent her man to seek me, & when he failed to find me he reported that I had gone away. But she would not believe him, & came to the 'Dolphin' weeping & prayed our Gioanna for the love of God to tell her the truth. She told her that it was a false report & came at once for me beseeching me for God's sake to go & see her. And when I arrived you cannot imagine the kisses & caresses she gave me.

He hopes she will stay in London a week longer, without the knowledge of her father who is in the City, so that they may become even more intimate. She is beautiful and fat, of good birth, spirited, and with plenty of money.

Such letters are worth many official lists as a means of suggesting the ways by which Italian ideas might permeate English society when Elizabethan dramatists could glean

Italian stories and study Italian types without going farther than the 'Elephant', where Vanni, another of Gondola's companions, haunted, and other taverns in the south suburbs.

REFERENCES TO THE COMMEDIA DELL'ARTE IN ELIZABETHAN LITERATURE

THE MASKS.

Frequent references put it beyond doubt that English audiences knew at least enough of the Commedia dell'arte to make it a safe subject for allusion. The uses of the names of the chief masks in their anglicized forms of Zany, Pantaloon, and Harlaken, are tests of the accuracy and familiarity of their knowledge of Italian popular drama. Nashe describes the representations of foreign comedians as consisting of 'Pantaloun, a Whore, and a Zanie'.[1] Heywood in the *Apology for Actors* proposes 'to omit all the Doctors, Zawnyes, Pantaloones, Harlakeenes, in which the French, but especially the Italians, have been excellent',[2] and in the preface to the *General History of Women* shows his acquaintance with the methods of the popular dramatists by a comparison.

It may likewise be objected, why amongst sad & grave Histories, I have here & there inserted fabulous jeasts & tales, savouring of Lightnesse? I answer, I have therein imitated our Historical & Comical Poets, that write to the Stage; who, least the Auditorie should be dulled with serious discourses (which are meerely weightie & material) in every Act present some Zanie with his Mimick action, to breed in the less capable, mirth and laughter; for they that write to all must strive to please all.[3]

Specific references show that the mention of the masks recalled the actualities of the 'Commedia Improvisa'. Valentine's memory of 'your spruce Pantaloun' who 'howles like a whelpe in a taverne; yet at the sight of cold yron runs, as if he had seen a seriant' in *The Honest Lawyer*;[4] Bartley's comment in *The Miseries of Inforst Marriage* as Ilford imitates a city father proposing a match with a neighbour's child, "sfoot, the Knight would have made an excellent Zany in an

---

[1] *Piers Penilesse*, ed. McKerrow, vol. i, p. 215.
[2] Ed. 1612, sig. E 2 v. For arguments in favour of 1608 as the date of composition see *Elizabethan Stage*, iv. 250.

[3] Ed. 1624. Preface to the Reader.
[4] Acted by the Queenes Maiesties Servants. Written by S. S., London, 1616, p. 4 r.

Italian Comedy',[1] and Ferdinando's advice to Alvarez, who
is to play a father in the comedy inset in *The Spanish Gipsy*,
to 'Play him up high: not like a Pantaloone',[2] would only
have occurred to playwrights who had seen performances of
the Commedia dell'arte. Hobson's description of his apprentices who 'peepe like Italian Pantelownes Behind an arras',[3]
and Macilente's scornful simile,

> He's like a Zany to a tumbler
> That tries tricks after him to make men laugh,[4]

would have little point for an audience unacquainted with the
peculiar arts of the foreign players.

Other references are so generalized that we glean nothing
from the casual usage beyond the impression of familiarity
with the objects to which they refer.

Florio in 1611 explains *Zane* as 'the name of Iohn in some
parts of Lombardy, but commonly used as a silly Iohn, a
simple fellow, a servile drudge or foolish clowne in any
comedy or enterlude play'. *Zanada* is a 'foolish trick of a
Zane' and *Zanni* is given as a synonym for 'Attelani . . . men
that with foule mouthes, unseemly speeches, disfigured faces,
minicke gestures and strange actions professe to procure
laughter'. It might also be used for 'crossebiting or cunny
catching knaves'.[5]

The word as Nashe uses it in *Jack Wilton* means no more
than a servant: 'A noble & chaste matron called Heraclide
& her Zanie . . . his simple Zanie Capestrano'.[6] In *Blurt,
Master Constable*, Middleton has the same usage: 'Lady
Imperia, the Artizan's Zani hath brought you this letter'.[7]
Drayton imagines Cupid as the Zany of Venus 'carrying her
boxes' and

> often sent
> To knowe of her faire patients how they slept.[8]

To this primary meaning there is often added a scornful

[1] George Wilkins, 1607.
[2] Act II, sc. iv.
[3] *If You Know Not Me You Know Nobody*, pt. ii.
[4] *Everyman Out of his Humour*, IV. i.
[5] *Queen Anna's Newe World of Words* (1611).
[6] Ed. cit. i, pp. 287, 295. See also pp. 288, 296.
[7] Ed. 1602. Sig. E 2.
[8] *Muses Elizium* (1630). Nimphall vii, p. 60.

comment. Brabant in *Jack Drum's Entertainment* speaks
slightingly of the other lovers:

> these are my zanyes, I fill their paunches,
> they feed my pleasures, I use them as my fooles.[1]

In *Law-Trickes* Day describes Learning who has lost his
wits,

> And ever since lives Zany to the world,
> Turns Pageant-Poet, toyler to the presse,
> Makes himselfe cheape, detested, hist & stale,
> To every bubble & dull Groome.[2]

In Berowne's estimation the 'slight Zany' is classed with

> some carry-tale, some please-man . . .
> Some mumble-news, some
> trencher-knight, some Dick
> That smiles his cheek in years, & knows the trick
> To make my lady laugh when she's disposed.[3]

Zanni's habit of imitating his master gives point to Drayton's
repeated synonym 'Apes and Zanies':[4] and explains the
Captain's comment in *Northward Hoe* that

> Your Norfolke tumblers are but Zanyes to connicatching punckes;[5]

and also indicates Matilda's gesture in *The Bashful Lover*,
when he asks to be given leave

> at distance
> To Zany it.—Sir, on my knees thus prostrate
> Before your feet.[6]

And there is no need to suppose that Dekker's parenthesis,

> The Cannon (Thunders Zany),[7]

Massinger's comment, 'Thie courtship as absurd as any
Zanies',[8] and the comparisons of Mosca and Malvolio: 'Such
sparks are the true Parasites, others but their Zanies',[9] 'These

---

[1] Sig. C 2.   [2] 1608. Sig. B.
[3] *Love's Labour's Lost*, v. ii, ll.
463–5.
[4] In the verses prefixed to the
Crudities Drayton addresses Coryat as
'The Fowler' who
> doest shew us shapes,
And we are all thy Zanies, thy true apes.
And in *Poets and Poesie* (1627), his
countrymen are reproved for being

'Very Apes & Zanies . . .
Of everything they doe heare & see.'
[5] Ed. 1607. Sig. F 2.
[6] Massinger, v. iii.
[7] *The Whore of Babylon* (1607). Sig.
K 3 v.
[8] *The Parliament of Love*, Malone
Soc., reprint p. 14, l. 450.
[9] *Volpone*, III. i.

set kind of fools' who are 'no better than fools' Zanies',[1] were intended to call to mind any definite performance. Evidently the word had been adopted as a convenient synonym for 'mimic'.

PANTALONE.

Reference to Pantalone is often hardly more specific than Sir Thomas Browne's mention of 'Pantaloones and Anticks'.[2] Freshwater turns upon Gudgin the servant with,

Thou Platalone [*sic*] be silent.[3]

Lucentio, thinking of Gremio, explains the purpose of his disguise to Bianca to 'beguile the old pantaloon'.[4] On other occasions, however, a nicer sense of the original character survives. Heywood thinks of Pantalones as 'usurers that have unthrifty sons'.[5] Jacques has a vivid memory of them as lean, spectacled old men who shuffle to and fro in slippers grasping their pouches.[6]

The indiscriminate use of the term 'Magnifico' and the proper name of 'Pantalone' for the chief old men of the Italian *scenari* tends to make us careless of the distinction which is more often observed by English writers. The impromptu comedy as cast by the Herlaken in the *Travailes of the Three English Brothers*, as well as 'an old Pantaloune', 'Some jealous coxcombe', and his wife, is to have a Magnifico to settle the difference between them. This distinction makes it doubtful whether in Gabriel Harvey's description of a Magnifico in *Speculum Tuscanismi* we are justified in recognizing a Pantalone or even a Venetian, though the figure might be a pen-portrait of the stage Magnifico as he was sketched by Callot.

---

[1] *Twelfth Night*, I. v. 95.

[2] *Religio Medici*, Everyman edition, p. 46.

[3] *The Ball*, Chapman and Shirley (1639). Sig. A 4 v.

[4] *Taming of the Shrew*, III. i. 37.

[5] *Apology for Actors*. Sig. F 3 v and F 4.

[6] *As You Like It*, II. vii. 157–63. As Mr. Isaacs has pointed out Pantalone is not the only figure from the Commedia dell'arte in Jacques's memory. The *Lover*,

'Sighing like furnace with a woful ballad
Made to his mistress' eyebrow,'
and the soldier
'Full of strange oaths, and bearded like
   the pard,
Jealous in honour, sudden and quick in
   quarrel,
Seeking the bubble reputation
Even in the cannons mouth,'
may also have strutted before Shakespeare's memory as the Inamorato and the Spanish Captain of the Italian stage.

Harvey visualizes

For life *Magnificoes,* not a beck but glorious in *shew,*
In deed most frivolous, not a looke but Tuscanishe allwayes.
His cringing side necke, Eyes glancing, Fisnamie smirking,
With forefinger kisse & brave embrace to the footewarde.
Large-belled Kodpeasd Doublet, unkodpeased halfe hose
Strait to the dock, like a shirte, & close to the britch, like a diveling.
A little apish Flatte, cowched fast to the pate, like an Oyster
French Camarick Ruffes, deepe with a witnesse, starched to that
    purpose.
Every one A per se A, his termes & braveries in Print,
Delicate in speech, Queynt in araye: conceited in all poyntes:
In Courtly guyles, a passing singular odde man,
For Gallants a brave myrrour, a Primerose of Honour,
A Diamond for the nonce, a fellowe perelesse in England.[1]

Harvey was evidently intending to satirize the Italianate
Englishman. The Letter Book preserves a first draft of this
passage[2] which was presented in 1580 as a 'bold satyricall
Libell, lately devised at the instance of a certayne worthy
Hartefordshire Gentleman, of myne olde acquaintance "In
Gratiam quorundam Illustrium Anglofrancitalorum, hic et
ubique apud nos volitantium. Agedùm verò, nostri homines,
tanquam tuam ipsius cutem", and printed as part of *A gallant
familiar letter, containing an Answer to that of M. Immerito
with sundry proper examples, and some Precepts of our English
reformed Versifying'.

Later on in a defensive note Harvey explains that a
'company of special good fellowes would needs forsooth
very courtlye persuade the Earle of Oxforde that some
in these Letters, and namely the Mirrour of Tuscanismo,
was palpably intended against him', but the author denies
this and says that the Earl wisely took no notice of the
slander.[3]

The description of Brabantio as a 'magnifico' in *Othello*
is appropriate without any thought of the Italian comedy, but
his position as a frantic father is so like that of Pantalone that

---

[1] See Grosart's edition of Harvey's
Collected Works, i. 84.
[2] *Letter Book,* ed. E. J. L. Scott,
Camden Society, 1884, p. 98. This
reads for 'shew', 'shewte', for 'Tuscanishe',

'Italish'; for 'Flatte', 'hat'.
[3] Grosart, i. 183. On other occasions
Harvey uses 'magnifico' as the accepted
title of an Italian gentleman. See
Grosart, ii. 220; *Letter Book,* p. 174.

we can hardly avoid the double allusion.[1] The mingled association makes it worth recording two more questionable references in Elizabethan Drama. Lollio in *The Changeling* speaking of the crazy Antonio says, 'He will hardly be stretcht up to the wit of a Magnifico'.[2] In the *Hog hath lost his Pearl* young Lord Wealthy asks, 'How, father! is it not possible that wisdom should be found out by ignorance? I pray, then, how many magnificoes come by it?' Old Lord Wealthy replies, 'They buy it, son, as you had need to do.'[3]

Arlecchino was known chiefly for his grimaces. The Page in the *Isle of Guls* remarks:

I can compare my lord & his friend to nothing in the world so fitly as to a couple of water buckets for whilst hope winds the one up, dispaire plunges the other downe, whilst I like Harlakenes in an Italian comedy, stand making faces at both their follies.[4]

The reference to the *French Herlakeene* in 1604 seems to be further particularized. The first scene of the third act of Marston's *Malcontent* in which it occurs does not appear in Dyce's copy but only in the edition published in the same year as 'Augmented by Marston. With additions played by the King's Maiesties Servants. Written by Ihon Webster. 1604.' It may therefore be an allusion to a recent performance of foreign players in London. The difficulty of reconciling the separate masks in Nashe's mention of 'Francatrip' Harlicken' has been discussed already in another connexion. The name of Franceschina, which is rightly given to the waiting-maid in *Volpone*, may have been chosen again by Marston in the *Dutch Courtezan* at its accepted Italian significance.

The disparaging tone in the majority of contemporary allusions to the Commedia dell'arte is reinforced by the attitude of superiority taken up by Elizabethan critics. Englishmen are warned repeatedly what they are to expect from foreign players. Whetstone, writing the Dedicatory Letter to *Promos and Cassandra* on 29 July 1578, says, 'For at this daye, the Italian is so lascivious in his comedies, that

[1] *Othello*, I. ii. 12.   xi, p. 453.
[2] *Changeling*, i. 2.   [4] Act II, sc. i. Ed. 1633. Sig. C 4 v.
[3] II. ii. 31–3. Dodsley (1875), vol.

honest hearers are greeved at his actions'. It must be admitted that most of the interests of the popular stage are covered by Gosson's summaries of the comedies which the Devil sends out of Italy to corrupt those who cannot read Italian baudry:

> The groundworke of commedies is love, cosenedge, flatterie, bawderie, slye conveighance of whordome; the persons, cookes, queanes, knaves, baudes, parasites, courtezannes, lecherous olde men, amorous young men with such lyke of infinite varietie.[1]

The substance of this condemnation of neo-classical comedy is to be found in Northbroke's treatise on *Dicing, Dancing, Vaine Playes or Enterludes* (1577) or again in Stubbes's *Anatomie of Abuses*.[2] For a more charitable survey we might take Heywood's account of comedy which is a matter

> pleasantly contrived with merry accidents, & intermixt with apt & witty iests, to present before the Prince at certain times of solemnity, or else merrily fitted to the stage. And what then is the subiect of this harmelesse mirth? either in the shape of a clowne, to shewe others their slovenly & unhansome behaviour, that they may reforme that simplicity in themselves, which others make their sport, lest they happen to become the like subiect of general scorne to an auditory, else it intreates of love, deriding foolish inamorates who spend their ages, their spirits, nay themselves, in the servile & ridiculous imployments of their Mistresses: & these are mingled with sportfull accidents, to recreate such as of themselves are wholly devoted to Melancholy. . . . Sometimes they discourse of Pantaloones, usurers that have unthrifty sonnes, which both the fathers & the sonnes may behold to their instructions: & sometimes of Curtezans, to divulge their subtleties & snares, in which young men may be intangled.[3]

But Heywood was not thinking exclusively of foreign plays; in the Prologue of *A Challenge for Beautie* he observes that

> The Roman & Athenian Drammaes farre
> Differ from us, and those that frequent are
> In Italy & France, even in these dayes,
> Compar'd with ours, are rather jigges than Playes:
> Like of the Spanish may be said, & Dutch,
> None verst in language, but confesse them such.

---

[1] *Playes Confuted in Five Actions.* Stat. Register, 1582. Action II. Sig. C4.
[2] S.R. 1583, p. 144. See *Eliz. Stage*,
iv, p. 223.
[3] *Apology for Actors*, pr. 1612. Sig. F 3v and F 4.

In 1608 Coryat had found a Venice playhouse 'very beggarly & base in comparison of our stately playhouses in
England: neyther can their actors compare with us for
apparell, shewes & musicke'.[1] Nashe, no squeamish
moralist, did not mince matters in remarking that

Our Players are not as the players beyond the sea, a sort of squirting
baudie Comedians, that have Whores & common Curtizans to playe
womens partes, & forbeare no immodest speech, or unchast action
that may procure laughter, but our Sceane is more statelye furnisht
than ever it was in the time of Roscius, our representations honourable
& full of gallant resolution, not consisting like theirs of Pantaloun,
a Whore, & a Zanie, but of Emperors, Kings & Princes.[2]

EXTEMPORE ACTING

The scene in the *Travailes of the Three English Brothers*, in
which Sir Anthonie Sherly requests Will Kemp to play a
part with the Italian Herlaken who has called to offer a performance, suggests what the practice of travelling players
may have been. Kemp objects that he is somewhat hard of
study but 'if they invent any extemporall merriment, ile put
out the small sacke of witte I ha' lefte in venture with them'.
Herlaken's company consists of himself and his wife; and
Kemp has with him only his boy, but Sir Anthonie assures
him that he looks not 'for Schollership nor Arte, But harme-
lesse mirth' and leaves them to cast the parts.

Harl. Marry Sir, first we will have an old Pantaloune.
Kemp. Some iealous Coxcombe.
Harl. Right, & that part will I play.
Kemp. The iealous Cox-combe.
Harl. I ha plaid that part ever since.
Kemp. Your wife plaid the Curtizan.
Harl. True, & a great while afore, then I must have a peasant to
my man, & he must keepe my wife.
Kemp. Your man, & a peasant, keepe your wife, I have knowne
a Gentleman keepe a peasants wife: but 'tis not usuall for a peasant to
keepe his maisters wife.
Harl. Oh 'tis common in our countrey.
Kemp. And ile maintaine the custome of the country.
[offers to kisse his wife]
Harl. What do you meane sir?

---

[1] Op. cit., i. 386.   [2] *Pierce Pennilesse*, ed. cit. i. 215.

Kemp. Why to rehearse my part on your wives lips: we are fellowes, & amongst friends & fellowes you knowe all things are common.

Harl. But she shall bee no common thing, if I can keepe her severall:
then sir we must have an *Amorado* that must make me Cornuto.

Kemp. Oh for love sake let me play that part.

Harl. No yee must play my mans part, & keepe my wife.

Kemp. Right, & who so fit to make a man a Cuckold, as hee that
keepes his wife.

Harl. You shall not play that part.

Kemp. What say you to my boy?

Harl. I, he may play it and you will.

Kemp. But he cannot make you iealous enough?

Harl. Tush I warrant you, I can be iealous for nothing.

Kemp. You should not be a true *Italian* else.

Harl. Then we must have a Magnifico that must take up the
matter betwixt me & my wife.

Kemp. Any thing of yours, but Ile take up nothing of your wives.

Harl. I wish not you should, but come, now am I your Maister.

Kemp. Right, & I your servant.

Harl. Lead the way then.[1]

That Kemp is represented as able to take the part in a
true extempore comedy while he is in Venice shows that
English actors were acquainted with the Italian methods
of improvisation but does not prove that those methods were
practised in England. Contemporary critics take care to
contrast the English and Italian technique. Whetstone
speaks of the comedians of Ravenna as 'not tide to a written
device, as our English Players are'. Gosson believes that
'if any goodness were to be learned at Playes it is likely that
the Players themselves which committ every syllable to
memory should profitte most'.[2]

In *The Case is Altered*, Sebastian in Milan inquires about
the drama of Utopia and asks,

And how are their plays? as ours are, extemporal?

And Valentine replies,

Oh no; all premeditated things, & some of them very good, i' faith.[3]

It is generally taken that Jonson has in mind the English
stage.

[1] 1607. Sigs. E 4 and F.   [2] Op. cit. Sig. C 4.   [3] Act II, sc. iv.

The only signs of emulation are for the convenience of improvisation. Old Jeronimo reminds his companions that

> The Italian comedians are so sharp of wit,
> That in one hour's meditation
> They would perform anything in action.

And Lorenzo replies

> I have seen the like
> In Paris 'mongst the French tragedians.[1]

In the *Spanish Gipsey* the supposed comedians offer a repertory of some five or six plays and propose a merry tragedy of *Cobby Nobby*. Ferdinand hints that if they could play extempore they might provide a more suitable entertainment:

> So, so, a merry tragedy! There is a way
> Which the Italians & the Frenchmen use;
> That is, on a word given, or some slight plot,
> The actors will extempore fashion out
> Scenes neat & witty.[2]

It is to be regretted that the Catholic priest who gives a synopsis of Anthony Munday's career in the *True Report of the Death & Martyrdome of M. Campion*, . . .1581, after telling us that he was once a stage-player, should deliberately 'omit to declare how this scholler, new come out of Italy, did play extempore: those gentlemen & others that were present can best give witness of his dexterity, who, being wery of his folly, missed him from the Stage'.[3] Munday's experiment was in imitation of the Commedia dell'arte and should be distinguished from the improvisation practised by English actors.

Falstaff's call for 'a play extempore', damped at first by Hal's retort, 'Content; and the argument shall be thy running away', revived at the prospect of the Prince's interview with his father, and the sight of Sir John, crowned with a cushion, mimicking Henry, wrung from Mistress Quickly a doubtful compliment: 'O Jesu! he doth it as like one of

---

[1] *Spanish Tragedy*, II. iv.
[2] Act IV, sc. i, l. 161.
[3] *A true Report of the death & martyrdome of M. Campion Jesuit & prieste.* Compare *L'Histoire de la Morte que le R. P. Edmonde Campion prestre de la Compagnie du nom de Jesus et autres on souffert. . . .'* Traduit d'Anglois et François, a Paris chez Guillaume Chandiere, 1582. Sigs. D 4v. and E r.

these harlotry players as ever I see.'[1] This was sheer mid-summer madness and neither project nor performance need be interpreted by a comparison with the Commedia dell'arte.

There is no evidence that English players were any more ambitious in improvisation than Incle, Belch, and Galt, who, with Post-haste as their poet bind themselves into a company in Marston's *Histriomastix*.[2] They intend to rely on their poet to write out the play, and when they ask him how he proceeds in the new plot of the Prodigall Childe, he informs them, 'Thers two sheets done in folio, will cost two shillings in rhyme'. Later they accept his offer of an extempore Prologue which consists of rollicking couplets upon this theme,

> Your Poetts and your Pottes
> Are knit in true-love knots.

Sly in *The Malcontent* was left to make a Prologue extempore and produced a bare five lines.

Meres' praise of the 'extemporall witte' of Tarleton and Wilson, which is echoed so often in Elizabethan literature, refers to their talent for composing rhymes upon given themes—suggested sometimes by the audience at the end of a play. Anecdotes in jest-books, however apocryphal they may be, give some idea of how they dealt with the riddles and questions with which the groundlings delighted to heckle them.

If it were not for his preliminary distinction between the comedians of Ravenna who would play extempore and the English comedians who are 'tide to a written device', Whet-stone's use of the word 'Theame' might be misleading in this connexion; but it is clear from the full context that the 'theame' is here the subject-matter suggested by the defini-tions of the Virtues and Vices that Signior Philoxenus pro-pounds. To a theme the Italians were expected to fit a plot, the Englishmen a rhyme.

A secondary meaning of the word 'extempore' as it was used in reference to Elizabethan acting is explained by Letoy the Phantasticke Lorde in Brome's *Antipodes* who keeps a private company of players. He discusses their

---

[1] 1 *Henry IV*, II. iv.
[2] Printed in 1610, but acted in 1598   and made over from an old play. See R. A. Small, *The Stage Quarrel* (1899).

talents with the Doctor who is arranging for a play to cure
Peregrine of his mania for travel:

> I thinke all perfect,
> But one, that never will be perfect in a thing
> He studies; yet he makes such shifts extempore,
> (Knowing his purpose what he is to speake to)
> That he moves mirth in me 'bove all the rest.

A little later, after a rehearsal, this player is reproved by
Quaylpipe the curate:

> My Lord, we are corrected . . .
> But you Sir, are incorrigible, and
> Take licence to your selfe, to add unto
> Your parts, your owne free fancy; & sometimes
> To alter, or diminish what the writer
> With care & skill compos'd: & when you are
> To speake to your coactors in the Scene,
> You hold interloquutions with the audients.

In answer to this By-Play argues,

> That is a way my lord has bin allow'd
> On elder stages to move mirth & laughter.

This Letoy admits, grudgingly,

> Yes in the dayes of Tarlton & Kempe,
> Before the stage was purg'd from barbarisme,
> And brought to the perfection it now shines with.
> Then fooles & jesters spent their wits, because
> The Poets were wise enough to save ther owne
> For profitabler uses.[1]

From this it appears that 'to speak extempore' was to gag,
keeping to the general drift of the plot but taking licence to
address topical comments to the audience.

Kempe, like Snug, announced that he was 'somewhat
hard of study'; while he played the clown this would hardly
be a disadvantage. His inability to learn a part would only be
another excuse for fostering his talent for gagging. Brinsley
Nicholson worked out an ingenious theory that Tarlton
was the jester whom Hamlet laments as Yorick and that
Kempe was the clown whose stale jests are pilloried in

[1] *Antipodes*, 1638, pr. 1640. Sigs. D 2 v, D 3 v.

the first Quarto.[1] In the earliest version of this speech the
reprimand of the clown who speaks more than is set down
for him, is remarkably personal:

> O t'is vile, & shewes
> A pittifull ambition in the foole that useth it.
> And then you have some agen, that keepes one sute
> Of jests, as a man is known by one sute
> Of Apparrell, & Gentlemen quotes his ieasts downe
> In their tables, before they come to the play, as thus:
> Cannot you stay till I eate my porrige? &, you owe me
> A quarters wages: & my coate wants a cullison:
> And, your beere is sowre: &, blabbering with his lips
> And thus keeping in his cinkapase of ieasts,
> When, God knows, the warme Clowne cannot make a iest
> Unlesse by chance, as the blinde man catcheth a hare:
> Maisters tell him of it.[2]

Reckoning that the Quarto of 1603 represents a performance of 1599–1600 Nicholson points to a curious
coincidence of dates. According to the First Quarto, Yorick's
skull 'hath been here this dozen year': Tarlton died in 1588.
But in the third Quarto of 1608 'it hath lain i' the earth
three & twenty years': the 'whoreson mad fellow' is no
longer intended to represent Tarlton. In this Quarto the
list of jests is omitted. Nicholson explains these alterations
by supposing that when Kempe left the Chamberlain's
Company in 1599 he was not on the best terms with Shakespeare, but that when he returned to England in 1601 after
his wanderings in Germany and Italy the disagreement was
patched up and the odious comparison with Tarleton and the
recognizable jests of the reproof removed. It is not known
precisely when Kempe came back to the Chamberlain's
Company, but in the third part of the *Pilgrimage to Parnassus*
which belongs to January 1602 he is amicably associated
with Shakespeare and Burbage. We do not know what effect
Hamlet's advice may have had; Kempe probably continued
with his 'pitiful ambition' to the end of his days, but no
amount of licence to rhyme and gag brings the impromptu
element in English drama into line with the Italian practice
of improvisation. If no dramatist had troubled to write for

---

[1] *New Shakespeare Society Transactions* (1880).   [2] Facsimile f. 2 and 2v.

the clown, if no clown had learned his lines, there would still be lacking the discipline of co-operation which was the secret of the improvising comedians.

In considering the appearance of the genuine Italian masks it is difficult to decide how literally we may take a curious passage in an Italian pamphlet, recently discovered by Miss Winifred Smith in the Archivio di Stato in Mantua. The writer professes to report an account received from Catholic fugitives of a most amazing spectacle which was represented in the City of London a little time before the death of the Queen (of Scots), and to be precise, on 24 April 1586.

One of the foremost gentlemen of that city, where comedies are produced with particular excellence and expense, arranged for a comedy to be performed in the great hall of his mansion in mockery of the Catholic Faith. The setting was to be marvellous and superb, and many of the chief persons of the city were invited. Among the other interludes was to be one presenting a Magnifico dressed as a priest, and a Zanni as a cleric[1] who were to pretend to celebrate Mass at an altar, and at the elevation of the Host one dressed as a devil was to spring out furiously and seize the Host from the Priest's hands. The comedy proceeded as arranged until the moment when the supposed devil appeared, but as soon as he laid hands on the Host many real and horrible fiends were seen plainly issuing from the dark profundity of Hell, and making their way through the murky air with great wrath they bore off the Priest-Magnifico, the clerk, the supposed devil and many of the performers with shouts and shrieks, and they were never seen again. Of those who were left many died of horror and shock, but the Queen, like another Pharaoh, hardened her heart and refused to tolerate the Catholic Faith.[2]

---

[1] 'un chierico vestito da Zani Sacerdo'. This I take to be an error for 'sacerdote'.

[2] The pamphlet is cast in the form of a letter from Paolo Lardi in Calais to Gioseppe Rosaccio in Venice and is headed: 'Copia / de una lettera / Venuta novamente / Dalla Fortezza di Cales Magn. / Città di Venetia.' . . . It was printed in Milan by Gio. Battista Colonia. My attention was first drawn to this account by a quotation in F. Marriotti's manuscript history of the Italian Theatre (MS. Magliabech, II. iii, p. 454–6) from G. A. Summonte's

Historia della città e Regno di Napoli (1765), part IV, lib. x, p. 307. I have not been able to trace this edition, but in the issue of 1748 the passage occurs in Book XI, ch. iii, pp. 48, 49. The colophon to part II of the first edition is dated 1599; part IV, in which this record is to be found, is dated 1643; Summonte's source was evidently the pamphlet which Miss Smith has since discovered in the Mantuan Archives (Arch. di Stato. E. XII. No. 2. 1586) and reprinted in *Modern Philology*, Nov. 1930, xxviii, No. 2, p. 208.

The precision of time and place reassure us that the report refers to an actual and not a typical performance, but it has not been possible to find any corroborating fact nearer than the letter of the Venetian ambassador in Spain for 20 January 1586, who says that Philip resented the 'masquerades and comedies which the Queen of England ordered to be acted at his expense. His Majesty has received a summary of one of these, as it was lately represented, in which all sorts of evil is spoken of the Pope, the Catholic religion and the King, who is accused of spending his time in the Escurial with the monks of S. Jerome, attending only to his buildings, and a hundred other insolences which I refrain from sending to your Serenity'.[1] Granted a fact from which the miracle might swell out, what is its significance? Even if, straining at the devils, we swallow the Magnifico and Zanni, we are still at a loss to know whether the masks concealed English or foreign actors and so indicate the influence of the Commedia dell'arte on the Elizabethan stage or another visit of the Italian players, or whether, after all, the pamphleteer may not have been using the familiar Italian terms for figures who to an English audience would merely represent an old man and his servant and not specifically Pantalone and Zanni.

ITALIAN MASKS IN ENGLISH DRAMA

The masks appear in three plays, in one or two masques and in two of the extant jigs. The earliest and best-known example is the Pantalone in the plot of the *Deadman's Fortune*, who may have prompted Collier's comparison between the stage 'platts' and the Italian scenari, though, oddly enough, as Dr. Greg has pointed out to me, he neglected to mention this unmistakable trace of the Commedia dell'arte when he advanced his theory in the *History of Dramatic Poetry*.[2] This Pantalone appears in what seems to be the farcical sub-plot of a tragi-comedy. On his second entry

---

[1] *Cal. State Papers, Venetian*, viii. 182. For mention of the spasmodic prohibition of plays deriding the Pope and the King of Spain see Ibid., Nos. 18, 58, 62, 69. Feb.–April and May 1559, and *Cal. State Papers* relating to Rome, Doc. 17, p. 9. See also *Eliz. Stage*, i,

p. 128, for a description of the burlesque Mass play which was intended as an afterpiece to *Ajax Flagellifer* in 1564; see i, pp. 243, 328 for similar performances in 1559 and 1614.

[2] 1831, iii, p. 398.

he is accompanied by his man who is surely to be identified with Pesscode who is in attendance on all other occasions. Creizenach takes it for granted that Asspida is Pantalone's wife. She has a lover Validore. Validore's man was played by b(oy) Samme. The maid who comes to Asspida as she is 'cutting of ruffes' is probably Rose who later helps the lovers to disguise. The plot entails several disguises, at the end of the second act Pantaloun enters

> whiles he speakes
> validore passeth ore the stage disguisde
> then Enter pesscode to them asspida to
> them the maide wth pesscodds apparell.

Perhaps the spectacles which are provided for the end of the third act enabled the jealous husband to thwart their first intrigue. The direction reads,

Enter pateloun & pesscode=enter asspida to hir validore & his man & b. samme to them the panteloun & pescode wth spectakles.

In Act IV the lovers are arranging for a more elaborate disguising:

> Enter asspida & [valydore] pescodde to hir
> Enters rose
> _____
> Enter panteloun & pescodde
> _____
> Enter aspida & validore disguisd like rose wth
> a flasket of clothes to them rose wth a
> nother flasket of clothes to them the pan
> teloun to them [to them] pescodde.

The plot seems to end with the discovery of some kind of substitution. It is impossible to say exactly how the lovers were united and the Pantalone hoaxed, but the last direction

> Ente the panteloun & causeth the
> cheste or truncke to be broughte forth

shows that this was an excellent specimen of an Italian farce.[1]

Our next Pantalone appears among the antic followers of Silenus in the *Maske of Flowers*.[2] His partner is a curtizan

---

[1] MS. Add. 10,449.

[2] *Maske of Flowers*. Presented by the Gentlemen of Graies-Inne, at the Courte of White-hall, in the Banquetting House, upon Twelfe Night, 1613. London. Printed by N. O. for Robert Wilson, & are to be sold at his shop at Graies-Inne. New Gate. 1614.

and the corresponding pair on Kawashae's side are Fretelyne
and a Bawde. Whoever designed the dance probably had in
mind a performance of P. M. Cecchini, better known by his
stage-name of *Fritellino*.

In *Blurt, Master Constable* at the end of a masked ball
'Zanies with Coaches enter sudainly';[1] and as an episode in
Dekker's *If this ben't a Good Play, the Divel's in't*, 'Shackle-
Soule enters leading in an Italian Zany, five or six Curtizans,
evry one holding a Jewell', and after a general dance 'the
Zany sings a sensual song in English'. The latter play was
printed in 1612, and Mr. W. J. Lawrence conjectures that
at its production at the Red Bull, Dekker was parodying the
Italians whom he supposes to have been in England in 1610.[2]

In the jig of *Amantes Amentes*, 1609, Rollenhagen presents
Gratiano, Doctor Juris, who is rejected by Lucretia in favour
of a student. The characters in the German version *Pickel-
herrings Dill Dill Dill* are a rich pantaloon, a braggart, a
jealous husband Zani, his wife Margretha, and a wooer
Dominus Johannes, or Pan Jan. There is no trace of the jig
in England, but Bolte believes that it was performed by
English actors in Dantzic early enough to influence
Waimer's *Elisa* in 1591.[3]

STAGE TYPES

In theory as in practice Elizabethan dramatists worked up
the characterization of the individual through the portrayal
of types. In Richard Edwardes's opinion,

the greatest Skyll is this, rightly to touche
All thynges to the quicke: & eke to frame eche person so,
That by his common talke, you may his nature rightly knowe:
A Royster ought not preache, that were to straunge to heare,
But as from vertue he doth swerve, so ought his woordes appeare:
The olde man is sober, the young man rashe, the Lover triumphyng in
      ioyes,
The Matron grave, the Harlot wilde & full of wanton toyes.[4]

Edwardes valued the stage types because they ensured
the moral function of comedy. The audience was not left

---

[1] 1602. Sig. D 2.

[2] *The Times Literary Supplement*, 11
Nov. 1920.

[3] See Baskervill, *The Elizabethan*

Jig, pp. 262, 331.

[4] *Damon and Pithias* (1571), Prologue.

for a moment in doubt of the dramatist's intention. The dangers of ambiguity are minimized when a character is labelled for immediate recognition and may be manipulated like a puppet. The possibilities of the gradual development and the delicate variety which gave the rich individual characterization of the later Elizabethan drama were as yet unforeseen. In spite of this advance the use of stage types persisted beyond the sixteenth century for the sake of convenience. Players and hack dramatists continued to make use of a formula of accepted characteristics for lack of time or skill to conceive of new and living characters. There is literary evidence of the recurrence of popular characters in the family resemblance between Ophelia and the pathetic heroines of Beaumont and Fletcher; in the villain heroes and villain accomplices of revenge drama. In comedy the recurrence of the pedant, the captain, the pandar, the astute and clownish servants serve to remind us that the practical dramatist recognized the value of having types ready-made by the Renaissance tradition, tried and popularized by the professional comedians.

The possibilities of classifying the characters of a particular play might almost be taken as a test of the proportion of literary or stage interests that go to its making. In the mind of the poet the personages become personalities; he aims at the creation of individuals. In the practice of the actor the character is often reduced to a type modified only by the personality of the actor himself. At the moment of production the latter may be the more effective process, but it has no chance of survival and looks ill against the permanence given by literary quality. Sir Topas is the Miles Gloriosus at one, Bobadil at two, and Falstaff at three removes. Undoubtedly an Elizabethan would recognize in each the underlying type of the braggart soldier, but for us the creatures of Lyly, Jonson, and Shakespeare are, in their several degrees, so excellently individualized that we gain little by comparing them with the lay figure.

The Italian masks are extreme instances of Renaissance tradition, and the professional comedians are responsible for popularizing types due ultimately to Latin comedy and its neoclassical modification, which were to develop along parallel lines in the drama of Italy, France, and England. In considering the English examples something must always be allowed for common origin and native development. In a few cases, however, these do not suffice to account for the noticeably Italianate quality, and in some cruder examples of character types we may suspect the influence of the Commedia dell'arte.

From Lucentio's description of Gremio as 'the old Pantaloon' it is clear that the behaviour of an old man in love was enough to suggest the Italian mask. In the *Apology for Actors* the other characteristics are stressed: 'Sometimes they discourse of Pantaloones, usurers that have unthrifty sonnes.'

But that almost every Pantalone was tormented by his love affairs, by his children, and his money, does not mean that all the amorous old men and the avaricious fathers of English drama were framed to the Italian model. There were several other sources of suggestion. In his monograph on the usurer in Elizabethan drama Mr. Stonex traces the contributions to the stage type of the morality figures of Avarice and Lucre, of the Jews in the plays of Marlowe and Shakespeare, and of the money-lenders whose tricks were so often exposed by the pamphleteers.[1] Again we must allow for intermediary English models. The fact that Shylock himself plays the part of the father in an Italianate love-intrigue is not evidence of the direct influence of Pantalone, but might well be derived from a study of Barrabas of Malta as a prototype of the jealous father or from the story by Massaccio di Salerno suggested by Dunlop as a literary source for the Jessica plot.[2] The behaviour and preoccupation of Gripe in *Wily Beguild* would suggest the influence of the Italian mask were it not that other echoes of Shakespeare in this play convince us that Shylock was the more likely prototype.

With Mammon, Pisaro, and possibly with Hog, the usurers of three plays for which no literary sources have been discovered, we are freer to consider the claims of a Commedia dell'arte original. As the resemblance of each of these old men to Pantalone depends chiefly upon his

[1] A. B. Stonex, *Mod. Lang. Ass. of America*, 1916, xxxi.
[2] *Merchant of Venice*, Furness Variorum, p. 319.

relationship to the other personages in the play as father, usurer, and wooer, it will be better to reserve the discussion of their characterization until we deal with the other Italianate features of the comedies in which they appear. It will then be seen that the lack of literary sources for the play as a whole and the coalescence of jealous, amorous, and avaricious tendencies in these characters in particular make the comparison with Italian masks irresistible.

THE PEDANT.

It is a matter of taste whether we prefer to see in Holofernes a caricature of Florio the pedant about Elizabeth's court, of Richard Mulcaster, of Thomas Hunt, Shakespeare's own schoolmaster, or an imitation of Rhombus in *The Lady of May*,[1] or of Paedantius of the Cambridge Comedy in 1581,[2] or a character imitated from Onofrio, a typical pedant of the Commedia erudita,[3] or Doctor Gratiano sometime pedant in the Commedia dell'arte.[4] While it seems impossible to decide which Shakespeare may have had in mind, the accumulation of possibilities contributes to our appreciation of his creature.

Other pedants in Elizabethan drama are more easily accounted for. The Commedia erudita is mainly responsible for the latinized jargon of Sir Boniface in *The Wise Woman of Hogsden*. The attraction of the chief figure in the Cambridge comedy of *Paedantius* was undoubtedly its satire of Gabriel Harvey. Parson Evans and Master Correction in Marston's *What You Will* are nearer to the schoolmasters of everyday life than to any stage type. From either of these sources of suggestion Sidney may have taken the idea of Rhombus for the entertainment of *The Lady of May*. But the only English pedant who appears to have been modelled on the Italian is Aminadab the schoolmaster in *How a Man may Chuse a*

---

[1] See the Variorum edition, pp. 352 and 355. For a full discussion of the Florio-Holofernes theory see Longworth-Chambrun, *Giovanni Florio, un apôtre de la Renaissance en Angleterre à l'époque de Shakespeare* (1921), pp. 163–79.

[2] Keller, *Sh. Jahrbuch*, xxxiv, pp. 275–8, quoted by W. Bond in his *Early*

Plays from the Italian, p. xxx.

[3] A. Fraunce, *Victoria*: translated from *Il Fedele* by Pasqualigo with an expansion of the part of the pedant. Ed. G. C. Moore Smith. See Boas, *University Drama in the Tudor Age*.

[4] O. J. Campbell, *Studies in Shakespeare, Milton and Donne*.

good Wife from a bad. His incompetence in dealing with cheeky schoolboys recalls the scene in *Li Due Trappolini* where Francese collects his pupils for a lesson 'al fresco'. He makes one repeat his lesson and another con his Latin, thrashing some and smacking others until the scholars beat him with their books, chase him into the house, and make off down the street. The schoolmaster in the English comedy is twice shamed in this way. His most provoking scholar is Pipkin the errand-boy of young Master Arthur's household, who behaves like the servant of Fulvio in *Il Finto Servo*, Locatelli's popular version of *Li Suppositi.* Zanni has changed clothes with his master and crosses the stage on his way to school, blurting out enormities of Latin grammar; and complaining that though he has eaten a whole book not a single letter has remained in his head: he implores Fulvio to let him have his own dear cheesy garments back before he ruins his uncomfortable gentlemanly clothes. Pipkin is just such a mischievous booby. He confides in the audience:

Let me see what age am I, some foure & twentie, & how have I profited. I was five yeare learning to crish Crosse from great A & five yeare longer comming to F. I there I stucke some three yeare before I could come to q. & so in processe of time I came to e perce e, & comperce, & tittle, then I got to a.e.i.o.u. after to our Father, & in the sixteenth yeare of my age, & the fifteenth of my going to schoole, I am in good time gotten to a Nowne, by the same token there my hose went downe: then I got to a Verbe, there I began first to have a beard: then I came to *Iste, ista, istud,* there my M. whipt me till he fetcht the blood, & so foorth' (E 2 verso).[1]

Pipkin arrives late for the grammar lesson and Aminadab threatens to flog him, but the booby edges away with the excuse that he had been sent on an errand. Aminadab promises to let him off if he will construe his lesson. Pipkin begins,

Conster it M. I wil, *Dicas* they say, *Propria* the proper man, *que maribus,* that loves mary-bones, *mascula,* miscald me.

Aminidab. A pretty queint & new construction.

Pipkin. I warrant you, M., if there be mary-bones in my lesson, I am an old dog at them. How conster you this M. *Rostra disertus amat?*

Aminidab. Disertus a disert, *amat* doth love, *rostra,* rost meat.[2]

This display of ignorance demoralizes the other scholars who vanish with impudent quips and gestures. Finding the pedant alone young Master Arthur inquires about Mrs. Mary the Courtesan; Aminadab conceals his own interest but is disturbed at the thought of a rival. He arms himself with a bill and headpiece and takes up his stand before her door muttering in doggerel,

> The wench I here watch with my bill,
> Amo, amas, amavi still,
> Qui audet let him come that dare,
> Death, hell & Limbo be his share.

The next moment the bravo enters looking round for 'the starveling schoole-maister,—That Rat, that shrimp, that spindleshanck, that Wren, that sheep-biter, that leane Envy . . .', threatening to

> hang him up
> Like a dried Sawsedge, in the Chimnies top:

Aminadab manages to hide, but the fright dissolves his courage and he determines

> *Per fidem*, I will end my life
> Either by poyson, sword or knife.

Instead of the requested rat-poison the apothecary provides the usual anaesthetic and Aminadab is content that

> This poyson shall by force expell,
> *Amorem* Love, *Infernum* hell.
> *Per hoc venenum ego* I,
> For my sweet lovely lasse will die . . .
> . . . And my sweet *Mary* not these drugges,
> Do send me to the Infernall bugges,
> But thy unkindnesse, so adieu
> Hob-goblins now I come to you.

Young Master Arthur, looking for a means of murdering his wife, prevents the suicide and steals the poison. Aminadab promises that

> Nay *Quintillian* said of yore,
> Ile strive to kill myselfe no more,

he accepts an invitation to dinner,

> In steed of poyson, I will eate
> Rabets, Capons & such meate:

and when the time comes his Grace is detailed and unctuous. The second grammar lesson delivered on the way through the churchyard is interrupted by the appearance of Mrs. Arthur in her graves-clothes. Master and scholars take her for a ghost and 'exeunt running', a means of clearing the stage which was found very convenient in the Commedia dell'arte.[1] Aminadab makes his final appearance when he is dragged before Justice Reason and accused of providing the husband with the poison: he is full of cowardly apprehensions but manages to shift the responsibility on to the apothecary.

The pedant's connexion with the main intrigue of *How a Man may choose a Good Wife* brings him into unusual prominence: his companions in the subplot are less fully developed, but they are also types common in the Commedia dell'arte. Mrs. Splay the Bawd lectures Mrs. Mary on the art of the courtesan, and helps her to play off the pedant, the bravo, and young Master Arthur one against the other in the style familiar on the popular Italian stage. There are many courtesans in Elizabethan drama whose trade reminds us broadly of the more plebian types in Italian comedies but the majority are English in their manners. The distinctively Italianate tricks of the courtesan in Barry's *Ram Alley* who makes a dropped handkerchief an excuse for going down into the street and hides Sir Oliver under the farthingale, are exceptional. The real Ram Alley was nearer than Italy and the dramatists were probably ready enough to find their models in the women of the London stews.

BRAVOS.

In spite of a blustering speech in which he compares the courtesan to Venus and himself to Mars, the part of Bravo the Swaggerer in *How a Man may Chouse* is too slight to stand a detailed comparison with the Italian braggarts. His

---

[1] See Scala, vii, xiv, xv, xxii, xxiv, xxx, xliv. Magliabechian MS. No. 1. Locatelli, i. 3, 8, 23; ii. 20, 25. Corsini, ii. 14. Venice, 33, 41, 45. Naples, i. 4, 37, 43, 52, 60, 66; ii. 16.

status is that of the hired 'bravo': Mrs. Mary sets him on to scare the pedant, to turn poor Pipkin out of her house, and to procure young Master Arthur's arrest.

The style of a semi-dramatic braggart is introduced into the *Ortho-Epia Gallica* as the most advanced exercise in the use of the French tongue. John Eliot draws attention in the preface to the 'martiall Rhetoricke of the Seignior Cocodrill', and when his bragger opens his mouth, his 'puffing' is so palpably an imitation of the Italian Captain's that the conclusion that Eliot had enjoyed the performance of Fabritio Fornaris's *Capitano Cocodrillo* during his wanderings on the Continent, possibly in Paris, or had had access to a copy of that actor's *Angelica* (1584), is irresistible.[1] The tell-tale name is here given in its French form as Seignior Cocodrill, later Crocodill, and for an English audience the bravo was often represented as a Frenchman. His broken English gave a comic effect equivalent to the use of the Spanish, Dalmatian, or Neapolitan dialects adopted by the ruffians of the Commedia dell'arte.

M. John So-de-King in *Jack Drum's Entertainment* may owe something to Greene's comic assassin. The scene in *James IV* when Jacques is persuaded to spare Dorothea is even further burlesqued in Marston's play when John meets the victim and hints what a bribe might do:

Bon iour Metre Pasquill, sance iest, me am hired to kill you, Mounsieur Mamon, Messieur; iouncke give me money to stab you, but me know there is a God that hate bloud, derfore, me no kil, me know dere is a vench, that love Crowne, derfore me keepe de money.

The title 'Basilisco' bestowed on him by Drum in the third act advertises the likeness to the Italian stage braggart sometimes known as the Basilisco di Bernagasso, and as we shall see Greene's play offers no parallel for the part taken by Marston's bravo in the farcical love intrigues, which might be lifted bodily from the Commedia dell'arte.

The swaggering Captain in *Ram Alley*, who is called Face

[1] 'Ortho-Epia Gallica / Eliots Fruits / for the French: Enterlaced with a double new Invention, which tea/cheth to speake truely, speedily and volubly / the French tongue . . . John Wolfe. 1593. Dedicated in an Italian letter to Robert Dudley. Professor Allardyce Nicoll to whom I am indebted for this reference quotes an apt parallel to Cocodrill's swagger from the *Angelica* in 'Masks, Mimes and Miracles', pp. 250–1. See also an article by F. Yates, 'The Importance of Ortho-epia Gallica', *Rev. of Eng. Studies*, vii.

in the list of dramatis personae and Puff at intervals during
the play, has more in common with Captain Spavento del
Vall'Inferno than with Pyrgopolinices or Bobadill who may
be regarded as the respective prototypes of the majority of
the old-fashioned and the modern braggarts of the Elizabethan drama. Face strolls to and fro hoping to be spied by
some great lady who might bestow on him £5,000, and tries
his fortune with 'the widow yclipped Taffeta'. His threat to
stuff tennis balls with Sir Oliver Smallshanks's beard drives
the knight to take refuge under the widow's farthingale as
the Captain is heard raging on the stairs. Taffeta gives Face
the reputation of swearing like 'a very Termagant', and we
recognize Andreini's habit of invoking the Hercules and the
Gods of Greek mythology. William Smallshanks has him
up on the tavern table as a performing baboon and the
Captain can only splutter,

> by Dis, by Pluto, & great Prosperpine,
> My fatal blade once drawn, falls but with death.
> Yet if you'll let me go, I vow by Jove,
> No widow, maid, wife, punk, or cockatrice
> Shall make me haunt your ghosts.

Shakespeare's braggarts Armado and Parolles, like Holofernes his pedant, are indeterminate types. Moth's conversation with Armado when he tries to encourage him by citing
instances of great men who have suffered from the pangs of
love remind us of the dialogues that Andreini wrote up in
the *Bravure*. The practical jokes played upon Parolles are
of the same type as the 'burle' devised by the professional
comedians, but these superficial resemblances account for
but a small part of Shakespeare's creations. The type of
the braggart Captain has been crossed with the fantastic
courtier: the simple outline has been so delicately filled in by
the shading of whimsical satire that in emphasizing the
origin of either we risk upsetting the balance of values.

CLOWNS AND ZANNI.

It is peculiarly difficult to decide how far the mask of the
Zanni influenced Elizabethan drama because the issue is
confused by the partial coincidence of the rôles of the clown
and the servant. According to the circumstances of the plot

a Zanni might play the astute slave, the stupid servant, the peasant, the small tradesman or official, or the free-lance buffoon. Though all six types appeared on the English stage it would be absurd to suppose a wholesale imitation of the Italian mask. It may help to make a preliminary distinction between the characters who remind us of Zanni by function as they are used as servants in an Italianate plot, and the characters for whom the resemblance is due to a common stock of 'lazzi'. The astute servant who acts as a play-agent is almost indispensable in a love-intrigue. We might trace his origin to the slaves of classical comedy. Jonson's Brainworm and his fellows the knaves in the bourgeois comedy of Middleton and Chapman are not specifically Italianate. Properly speaking their parts do not belong to the clown at all. It was through the economy of the Italian professionals who allowed the pair of Zanni to share the parts of the astute and stupid servants that the types became merged, so that the clown might inherit a share of his cunning. In English drama there are a few of these intermediate types who remind us more of the Zanni than of their classical prototypes. In *The Two Maids of Moreclack* Tutch manipulates the intrigue but he is noted in the dramatis personae as a clown. In *Englishmen for my Money* the plotter *par excellence* is Antony, but much depends upon Frisco, Pisaro's servant, who, although he is essentially a fool, has flashes of wit that keep the plot going.

It appears to have been the practice of Elizabethan dramatists to introduce a sub-plot or subordinate episodes involving characters or *motifs* common in the Commedia dell'arte into plays which are mainly founded upon some English chronicle or Italian 'novella'. Such shuffling of dramatic material is to be expected on any popular stage served by repertory companies and collaborating dramatists. The most decided traces of these borrowings are left by the clown's part in the farcical love-plots and incidental horse-play of tragi-comedies and romances might be accounted for as the semi-improvised antics of any professional buffoon, but it is precisely in connexion with these antics that we suspect the influence of the contemporary Zanni. When Strumbo the cobbler in the subplot of *Locrine* 'dites an

aliquant love pistle' to Dorothy, so that 'hearing the grand
verbositie of his scripture' she may love him for ever, he
outdoes Gratiano in mistaking the word, and Pulcinella in
the clumsiness of his 'amorous passions'. Like other elderly
lovers he coaxes Trompart to be his messenger reminding
him like the Italian lovers of the benefits he has received:
'how I have cherished thee alwaies, as if you had beene the
fruit of my loines, flesh of my flesh, & bone of my bone'.
When he meets Dorothy he rises to doggerel, as Pantalone
was wont to break into song. On the battle-field he makes use
of the old trick of pretending to be dead. Trompart laments
over him as absurdly as Flute over Bottom, but at the word
'theeves' the corpse springs up crying,

> Where be they? Cox me tunny, bobekin!
> Let me be rising. Be gone; we shall be robde by & by.

Lachi, writing in the tradition of the Commedia dell'arte,
contrives just such a dramatic effect in *L'Inimicizia tra i due
Vecchi con il Finto Indovino*. When the officers bend over
Pandolfo, who is pretending to be dead, he endures their
remarks until some one suspecting poison remarks, 'Take
this knife, George, and open him up'.

In Act IV Strumbo takes the audience into his confidence
with a lewd soliloquy and sits down to eat on the stage, he is
interrupted by the entrance of Humber who is famished and
reeling. He catches sight of the clown who tries to hide his
provisions and imagines that Jupiter has sent Mercury 'In
clownish shape to minister some foode'. He bullies Strumbo
to give him the victuals, but the ghost of Albanact intervenes
and the clown escapes. Remembering how often Zanni
would impersonate Mercury by adjusting the feathers in his
hat or by fitting his shoes as wings, Humber's illusion seems
to have a double point.

Mouse the clown in *Mucedorus* serves Segasto as faithfully
and as foolishly as the peasant Zanni who is taken on as a
servant in tragi-comedy and pastoral. The Italian dialogue
is lost for ever, but from the fragments that survive in the
expanded scenari it was apparently of much the same standard as the English repartee. Segasto asks his man,

> Dost know captaine Tremelioes chamber?

and the clown quibbles,

> I verie well; it hath a doore.
> *Segasto.* I thinke so, for so hath every chamber.
> But dost thou know the man?
> *Clo.* I, forsooth, he hath a nose on his face.
> *Se.* Why so hath everyon(e).
> *Clo.* That 's more then I know.

He makes further delays by mistaking the name 'Tremelio' for 'the meale man' and assures Segasto

> O maister, if there be no bodie within, I will leave word with his dog.
> *Se.* Why can his dog speake?
> *Clo.* I cannot tell; where fore doth he keep his chamber els?

Mouse, like Zanni, is always looking for a meal: as soon as Segasto sends him about his business he is 'straight to the kitchen dresser, to Iohn the cooke, & get me a good piece of beefe & brewis & then to the buttery hatch to Thomas the butler for a iacke of beare, & therefore an houre ile belabour myselfe'. On another occasion he comes on to the stage with a pot of ale which he breaks over the head of the old woman to whom it belongs. Again, like Zanni he is delighted with the office of executioner extraordinary, and deprived of his victim, the shepherd, begs his master to be hanged instead, pleading that

> It is but halfe an houres exercise.[1]

When he is sent through the woods to look out for 'a shepherd and a stray king's daughter', we are reminded of a situation in *Li Ritratti*, when Pantalone and Burattino are sent out to search Arcadia for Emilia, the daughter of the King of Scotland, who is wandering about as a shepherd in search of her lover Leander, the son of the King of Macedonia, who has taken the disguise of a shepherdess.

Trotter, the miller's man in *Fair Em*, is in much the same position as Burattino in *Le Grandezze di Zanni*. Early in each play the master offers his daughter as a reward for faithful service, so that in future the boor takes full licence of comic familiarity.

---

[1] Cp. *Il Creduto Principe, Serpe Fatale,* and *Cometa.*

In *The Birth of Merlin*, the situation of the clown accompanying his sister Joan in her search for the unknown father of the unborn Merlin affords an opportunity for gross comedy not unlike that in the scenes between the shipwrecked strangers and the peasantry before and after the birth of Pantalone and Zannolino.[1] The young magician grows up as quickly as the Italian prodigies, and when Joan presents him to his uncle the clown asks:

'What, this Hartichoke? A childe born with a beard on his face?' 'Yes,' Merlin replies, '& strong legs to go, & teeth to eat.' 'You can nurse yourself then,' says the clown. 'There 's some charges sav'd for soap & caudle.'

The English phenomenon survives longer than the Italian counterparts. To tease his uncle he conjures up an antic spirit who picks his pocket. Later Merlin touches the clown's tongue and puts him through the familiar comedy of pretending to be dumb.[2]

The farcical *motif* of the clown at Court, which we have already traced through the miscellanies, is variously exploited on the English stage when Shadow in *Fortunatus*, the shepherd's son in *A Winter's Tale*, Babulo in *Patient Grissel*, Clem in *A Fair Maid of the West*, Surdo in *Poor Man's Comfort*, and Juniper in *The Case is Altered*, are taken out of their station. Anything that Greene may seem to owe to the Commedia dell'arte for his performance as the clown turned gentleman in *Tu Quoque* probably belongs rather to the tradition of comedy in which master and servant change places.

The prologue for *Two Merry Milkemaids* makes a satiric thrust at the taste of the popular audience,

'Tis a fine play,
For we have in't a conjuror, a Divill,
And a clowne too; but I feare the evill,
In which perhaps unwisely we may faile,
Of wanting squibs & Crackers at their taile.

Many traces survive in the printed plays of the popularity of the horse-play between the clown, the devil, the conjuror,

---

[1] *Il Pantaloncino* in five acts. Loc. ii. 50. Cors. ii. 16. See App. G.
[2] Cp. *Li Duo Fidi Notari, La Man-* cata Fede, *Il Servo Ritornato, Il Falso Indovino, Il Fate Voi, Il Serpe Fatale, La Cometa, Magior Gloria.*

and the magician. Between the acts of *Doctor Faustus* the devils let off their squibs. In *A looking Glasse for London* the clown struts on after his encounter with the fiend, looking forward to a reputation as the only 'Kill-Devil in the Parish'. Miles, Friar Bacon's man, is terrified by the voice that he rouses from the Brazen Head as he fiddles with his master's books. The farce of mock magic was exploited in the Commedia dell'arte by the devil scares with which Pulcinella and Coviello end the acts, and is amply illustrated in the pastoral scenari. In the comedy of *La Magica di Pantalone*, Pantalone opens a gulf and disturbs a mountain in order to find his treasure and recover the wits of Zanni and Trappolino.

The invisibility game was played on both stages, Boccaccio's story of how the urchins pelted Calandrino when he was persuaded that by virtue of a magic stone he could go about unseen[1] was borrowed by Locatelli for the scenario of *Trappolino Invisibile*, by Verucci for *Pantalone Innamorato* (1619), and by Adriano for *Pietra Incantata*.

In *Two Merry Milkemaids* a magic ring enables Frederick, the student-conjuror, and Smirke, the clown, to tease the courtiers. Smirke's account of how he explored the possibilities of the charm reveals his Zanni nature: with 'hunger tumbling like a Porpin in my Maw, & doing the Somerset in my Guts, I smelt a surloine of Beefe hot from the spit, followed the traine close, set in my foote, drew my knife, slic'd me off a collop, clapt it upon a penny loafe, went me to a side Table, consumed it without anybody saying much good do you, or the Divell choake you'.

The slightly different effect on the English stage, where for a time at least the clown is master of the situation, is probably due to the imitation of the scenes in *Doctor Faustus* where the magician and his man interrupt the Papal banquet.

With much of this horse-play it is no more than the central ideas that suggest a comparison with the Commedia dell'arte, the details were left to the inspiration of the particular clowns, and probably varied slightly with each performance. It is hardly to be expected that for the common interludes of the clown and the sharper the English comedians would

[1] *Decameron,* Giorn. viii.

borrow cheating tricks from the Italian stage when there was such a tempting variety exposed in the streets and the coney-catching pamphlets.

As the clown was regarded as fair game for the cheat, so the foreigner was the clown's prey. The lisp of the excitable Frenchman would be equally amusing to English and Italian audiences. If the local dialects, particularly of Wales and Somerset, were more occasional on the English stage they were used to the same effect as the staple medley of Bergo-mask, Venetian, Bolognese, and Neapolitan in the Commedia dell'arte.

It is necessarily chiefly from their actions that we are able to judge the resemblance between English and Italian clowns, but on a few occasions we can trace a likeness in their tricks of speech. Zanni's idea of a sumptuous meal was a calf half boiled and half roast, two sucking pigs, and four cheeses.[1] Heywood's clown in *The Maidenhead Well Lost* gloats over the prospect of a wedding feast for which he was ordering

a gammon of Bacon roasted, & stufft with oysters; & sixe Black Puddings to bee served up in Sorrell-sops . . . Cherry-Tart cut into rashers & broyles; a Custard Carbonado'd.

Peter's attempt to decipher the list of guests is probably to be compared with the 'lazzo della lista'.[2]

The absurd mistakes of the clown in *Fortune by Land and Sea* as he repeats the proclamation against pirates are on a level with the 'spropositi' of Gratiano misreading the dowry list in Verrucci's *Pantalone Innamorato* (1619).[3]

To fill out the empty fifth act in the *Two Merry Milke-maids* Ranoff challenges any courtier to talk longer and louder than he. The clown wins and offers to take on any man in the composition of a love-letter. Smirke enters for these competitions, to parody the efforts of the Euphuistic courtiers, his love-letter and the verses praising small women in terms of cookery are the counterparts of the burlesques collected in the miscellanies for the use of Zanni and Pulcinella.

---

[1] *Grandezze di Zanni.* Cf. Bian-colleli, *Il Finto Principe.*

[2] See Petraccone, op. cit., p. 268.

[3] Act III, sc. iv. See *supra*, p. 31.

It is impossible to isolate 'lazzi'; one can only remark the tricks common to English and Italian clowns leaving the actual terms of the debt undecided. Cut off from all contact with the Continental stage, it is quite conceivable that Kempe and his associates should have discovered for themselves the effect of the delayed entrance, of bursting into tears, of weeping over an onion, of bringing food or animals on to the stage, of the direct address to the audience, of the use of dialect, mistaken words and parody, and that they should have taught themselves how to exploit the comedy of greed, sleepiness, stupidity, feigned death, and mock wooings, but the belief that any or all of these devices were within the scope of their invention does not damage the supposition that, given the chance, they would avail themselves of the short cut of imitation. Singly these 'lazzi' are not remarkable, but collectively, as part of the clownish repertory, they make a case for the Italian influence which should not be neglected. Academically we are apt to consider that one source is better than two, and feel bound to give the benefit of the doubt to the clown's originality, but practically it is unwise to reject the subsidiary sources of suggestion. It is upon this psychological principle that our belief in the influence of the Commedia dell'arte upon the craft of the English clowns must depend. Native invention and literary models take precedence but do not eliminate the possibility of the influence of the foreign professional who exploited the Renaissance types.[1]

With the exception of Grumio, who is imported into the *Taming of the Shrew* from the plot of the *Supposes*, the sources of other Shakespearian comedies hardly suffice to account for the likeness between the Zanni and the group of Italianate clowns, the Dromios, the Gobbos, Launce and Speed, Stephano and Trinculo. As the contact with the Commedia dell'arte may have taken place at some pre-Shakespearian stage, and have come to him either through the repertory of the clowns for whom the parts were designed, or through old plays influenced by an Italian tradition, it will be more convenient to postpone the discussion of Shakespeare's use

[1] For juggling and conjuring tricks and dancing in Elizabethan drama, see   L. B. Wright in *Mod. Phil.*, 1927, xxiv, and *Eng. Studien*, 1928, lxiii.

of the Commedia dell'arte until the connexions between the plays and the scenari are examined.

Cohn regards it as a sign of English influence that the clown is not left to improvise. It is therefore assumed that for the part given to the clown in the plays of Henry Julius of Wolfenbüttel, Jacob Ayrer, and in the miscellaneous collection of 1620 which represents the repertory of English comedians in Germany, we may supplement what we know from plays printed in England of the stock-in-trade of English buffoonery. But as this evidence is both delayed and indirect it is not satisfactory to draw on it for details in comparing the characteristics of English and Italian clowns. It is impossible to be sure how much of the comic business which the Anglo-German clown has in common with Zanni and Pulcinella was distinctively English, how much is German, and how much may be due to contact with Italian players at some earlier date in England or on the Continent. It is just as feasible that the Italian professionals may owe something to the English touring companies as that the English borrowed from the Italians.

The show of the 'Forces of Hercules' might be taken as an example of the difficulties of deciding which way the debt should be read. Part of the performance on St. George's Day given by the English comedians who accompanied the Earl of Leicester into the Netherlands in 1586 consisted of 'dauncing, vauting & tumbling, with the forces of Hercules, which gave great delight to the strangers, for they had not seene it before'.[1] Since Stow remarks that it was a novelty to the Dutch audience in 1586, we might be tempted to claim this form of entertainment as an English invention, but the 'Forze d'Ercole' is mentioned as part of the repertory of travelling comedians applying for a licence in Geneva in 1546.[2] Among the payments from the Privy Purse of Pope Paul III is one to the 'attegiatori che fecero la moresca et le forze di Hercole'.[3] On 15 November 1549 five Venetian comedians gave a show of 'histori vom hercules' in Nürnberg;

[1] Stow, Annales, 1592, p. 1215.
[2] Chambers, op. cit., i. 246.
[3] A. Bertolotti, Spesiere segrete e pubbliche di Papa Paulo III. Atti e memorie delle R. R. Deput. di Storia Patria per le provincie dell'Emilia, vol. iii, pte. i, p. 199.

and Johannes Romano and his companions presented 'die
labores Herculis' in Strassburg in June 1572.[1] A still earlier
mention of the 'Forze d'Ercole' as a *momaria* given in Venice
on Maundy Thursday 1528 may refer to a spectacular
entertainment: after Neptune, Mars, Mercury, and the other
deities had gone by on sea-horses, Hercules entered with
lion-skin, 'che faceva le sue forze con vari balletti et sacrifizii
e morte de Cacho, Zerbero ed altri'.[2] The performances of
travelling comedians were evidently acrobatic, but it is doubtful if they could have presented anything as elaborate as the
show referred to in Venice or to the staging for the feats of
Hercules recalled by Heywood in the *Apology for Actors*:

> . . . to see as I have seene, *Hercules* in his owne shape hunting the
> Boare, knocking downe the Bull, taming the Hart, fighting with
> the Hydra, murdering *Gerion*, slaughtering *Diomed*, wounding the
> *Stimphalides*, killing the Centaurs, pashing the Lion, squeezing the
> Dragon, dragging *Cerberus* in chaynes, & lastly on his high Pyramides
> writing *nil ultro*, oh, these were sights to make an *Alexander*.

It is more likely that Heywood had in his memory a
performance of his own version of the Hercules myth in the
Brazen Age. It may be mere chance that the earliest extant
mention of the 'Forces of Hercules' was by Italian and not
by English actors. The comparative dates do not finally
exclude the possibilities of English originality. We cannot
be quite sure who was the borrower, for after all this may
well be a case of a parallel development from a common
origin in the acrobatic feats of medieval strollers. Sir E. K.
Chambers quotes a record of a performance of 'entremetz
mouvans' of 'Labores Herculis' for the year 1468.[3]

JIGS

Our knowledge of the dramatic jigs, in which we might
expect to find some traces of the contact with the Commedia
dell'arte and the English clowns, suffers from the uncer-
tainty of date and origin of German versions. The two jigs

---

[1] Trautmann, op. cit. Oddly enough
it was precisely in this month that Sir
Thomas Smith in Paris noted the
Italian performance of 'carying of men
one upon another wᶜʰ som men call
labores Herculis'. As an amateur he

refrained from further description. See
supra, p. 348. Ottonelli (op. cit., p. 439)
regards this show as distinctively part
of the repertory of the charlatan.

[2] Molmenti, *Storia di Venezia*, p. 316.

[3] Op. cit., i. 152.

attributed to English players in which the Italian masks occur have already been described. Although the names are English in *Singing Simpkin*, the situations of the clown taking refuge in a chest to escape the blustering lover, the wife defending the clown, when his hiding-place is discovered, by assuring her old husband that this is only an innocent young man whom she has rescued from the bully, and the final beating when the old man has heard the clown and his wife gloating over their hoax, might be derived from any Italian farce, if one should wish to find a source for tricks so current in the cuckoldy anecdotes of the jest books.

Mr. Baskervill's study of the Elizabethan Jig could hardly be expected to include a description of the corresponding Italian farcical *intermezzi* since the earliest extant examples belong to the beginning of the eighteenth century, but the only difference between the interlude jigs and the Intermezzi for Pulcinella that are to be found in the Vatican manuscript and the miscellany of D. Placido Adriano is that in the Italian manuscript there is not always indication of a musical accompaniment. The *intermezzi* in this Perugian miscellany may be the literary outcome of a form of entertainment evolved and practised by the improvising comedians of the preceding century, but as we have no earlier or more popular examples we can only point to what may have been a parallel development.

PLOTS: MATERIAL AND STRUCTURE

It is not enough that from the consideration of the influence of the Commedia dell'arte we should exclude the particular plays for which sources in Italian literature can be identified: something further must be allowed for the way in which the urge for production among the English playwrights would propagate the themes, situations, and devices introduced by these translated and adapted plays.

DISGUISE.

The device of disguise is at least as old as the Graeco-Roman comedy of Plautus and Terence: with the dramatists of the Renaissance it became almost an obsession. The theatrical possibilities are so obvious that it would be useless pedantry to try to determine the precise sources of each

occurrence on the English stage. Given the lead in fiction
and printed drama, the situations of the girl-page, the young
lover as a servant, a physician or a woman, the old lover as
a tradesman, the servant as his master, as a stranger or a
necromancer, were multiplied and modified *ad nauseam*. Even
for the more remarkable situations of the boy-bride or the
girl-page redisguised as a girl, common to the English and
Italian popular stages, there are examples in the Commedia
erudita. The only variations which appear to be of English
invention are the spying disguise adopted by a husband, a
father, or a duke, and the multi-disguise plays which seem to
have been arranged to exploit the talents of a particular
actor.[1]

Offshoots of the drama of disguise are the devices of
substitution and concealment by which the lovers borrow
each other's clothes, and so, unwittingly, sort themselves
into the appropriate couples or manage to evade their parents
by being carried from house to house in coffins or chests or
washing-baskets. These more farcical effects, together with
the sensational scenes of supposed death and feigned or
temporary insanity, are particularly common in the commedia dell'arte, but they occur also in fiction and academic
comedy.

On the rare occasions when they evolved new dramatic
traditions, such as the popular shipwreck-pastorals, and the
comedies of the Clown-Prince, the influence of the improvising comedians is unmistakable; there is, I believe, little
doubt of the contact between the Commedia dell'arte and
the *Tempest*, and none in the case of Sir Aston Cokayne's
Trappolin supposed a Prince and the scenari of the *Finto
Principe*.[2]

If we were only concerned in trying to isolate plots or
situations in the scenario-collections as the sources of particular English plays, the rapid inter-development would be
a serious difficulty while we are still so uncertain of the
acting dates of Elizabethan drama. But there is no need to
confine ourselves to the problem of the individual playwright's acquaintance with Italian drama when it is more

---

[1] See V. O. Freeburg, *Disguise Plots in Elizabethan Drama* (1915). W. J. Lawrence, *Pre-Restoration Stage Studies*.

[2] See *Mod. Lang Rev.*, xxiii.

profitable for us to be able to understand the reaction which an Elizabethan dramatist might expect from his audience towards certain popular Italian themes.

It has already been shown in another connexion how little of the plot material of the Commedia dell'arte was invented by the professional comedians: their function was to popularize and propagate. Certain themes and plots becoming common property were accepted as dramatic conventions so that situations that seem to us grotesque, extravagant, or romantically attractive probably excited less interest and criticism from an Elizabethan spectator who would accept the lover-servant, the girl-page, the sleeping draught, and the problem of love and friendship for play-book material, as naturally as audiences of the twentieth century accept the recurrent devices of the film, the thriller, and musical comedy. Each audience is interested more in the variety of the solution than in the strangeness of the initial situation. If we lose our appreciation of the originality of Elizabethan drama as we realize the triteness of the material, by way of compensation we gain in understanding of the contemporary attitude, and so achieve a more just critical position.

When we have put aside the plays for which the sources are already known a few still remain to present a puzzling mixture of English and Italian elements for which critics hitherto have been unable to account satisfactorily. Here, in general theme, in the disposition of the dramatis personae, by the function of the characters, and at the turning points of the action we are continually reminded of the staple material of the Italian repertories. Placed beside purely native comedy we become conscious of the foreign strain; whereas alongside the Italian we are aware of the English treatment. The borrowing has evidently taken place in an earlier draft and the foreign material has been absorbed in the reworking as the play has been expanded and adapted from time to time. There is some evidence remaining in support of the two general suppositions of revision and collaboration upon which this explanation depends. Henslowe's diary and the survival of plays at two stages of adaptation provide us with examples of the process of revision. Bird and Rowley were paid £4 'for ther adicyones in doctor fostes';[1] Jonson re-cast *Everyman in his Humour*; Shakespeare rearranged chronicle plays, altered *Hamlet*, reconceived 'King Leir'.

Munday's reputation as 'our best plotter',[2] Nashe's admission that Greene surpassed him in 'plotting plaies',[3] Henslowe's payment to Jonson for a plot in 1597,[4] show that at least by one method of collaboration one man provided the complete plot in the form of a scenario which was then divided out either by themes or by acts to the assistant authors.[5]

It is hardly to be expected that we should find the precise original of any English play among the miscellanies of the Commedia dell'arte. Putting aside the probabilities that scenari have been lost, and that many Italian plays never attained the permanence of a written record, it is the nature of the material that it should be flexible. Themes and situations were continually reshuffled. If Italian professionals had little feeling for the integrity of a scenario, English dramatists in search of plot materials might be expected to have less. This seems to have been the case, and it is by now impossible to tell whether they worked from memory of Italian plays in England, from accounts of some performance in France or Italy, or from written scenari. We know too little of the intercourse between the contemporary stages to be able to choose between these three possibilities in the case of individual plays. The versions which are extant may be the result of several revisions. The authorship and chronology of Elizabethan drama is too uncertain for us to be able to trace borrowings to the taste of any particular period, company, or dramatist. Although the conclusions as to the influence of the Commedia dell'arte can only be tentative, the comparison is worth making for the sake of tracing the unmistakable but elusive Italianate flavour which prevails in spite of the English details of manners and setting. As the plays are examined severally it will be seen that the impression

---

[1] Henslowe, *Diary*, f. 108 v; Greg, i, p. 172. 22 Nov. 1602.

[2] Jonson, *The Case is Altered*, Act I, sc. i.

[3] Nashe, ed. McKerrow, iii. 132. 'While he liv'd . . . hee subscribing to

me in anything but plotting Plaies, wherein he was his crafts master.'

[4] Greg, ed. cit., ii. 188.

[5] See C. J. Sisson, 'Keep the Widow Waiting,' 1927.

can sometimes be traced to a common theme or situation, sometimes to a familiar arrangement of typical personages, or to the function of a particular character as a plot agent. Singly the points of resemblance might pass unnoticed: taken out of their context they might be dismissed as chance variations of common devices. But it is the accumulation of Italian characteristics in these plays that rouses the suspicion of contact with the mass of material in the collections of scenari. That English actors and dramatists could easily have invented the situation is a negative, defensive argument. We need not be jealous for their independence for there is little virtue in the invention of such plots: it remains a matter of taste whether we prefer to believe in their originality or their powers of adaptation.

So far no source has been discovered in English or Italian fiction or drama for *The Wit of a Woman*, *Englishmen for My Money*, *Jack Drum's Entertainment*, *Ram Alley*, Greene's *Tu Quoque*, and *The Hog hath lost his Pearl*. The grouping of the characters, the crudeness of the *motifs* continue to suggest the influence of the Commedia dell'arte, and what little we know of the authorship and circumstances of production does not contradict the impression. Each might be described in Gosson's admirable phrase as composed of 'a cast of Italian devices'.

The similarity between the dramatis personae of the scenari shows the tendency of the Commedia dell'arte towards a symmetrical arrangement which almost amounts to a pattern. The characters group themselves automatically into households consisting each of a father, a servant, a son, and a daughter, often one member of the family is lost or disguised at the beginning of the play, but by the third act the four lovers are sorted out and neatly arranged for the double marriage. When there is a mother living the caste generally includes a courtesan as her counterpart. Although there are rarely less than two Zanni there may be only one maidservant: occasionally a fantastic captain or a grotesque doctor is left without a mate. In the simpler farces numerical balance is substituted for interest in individuality. The plot is made by the repetition of a situation or the crossing of parallel themes. The lovers are whisked forward like couples in a dance, executing the same figures turn and turn about, exchanging partners momentarily.[1]

THE WIT OF A WOMAN

The symmetry of the cast for the anonymous comedy *Wherein is merily shewen; The Wit of a Woman*, with its four families, reminds us at once of the Italian method. The play is plotted like a catch. With four old men, Bario a merchant, Nemo a physician, Ferio a lawyer, and Dorio a captain who each have a son and a daughter, with two common disguise tricks a comedy is contrived by quadruple repetition:

'O, but Mrs. Balia, heere hath been double dealing,' says one of the deceived fathers in the last act.

'Marry, I thinke heere hath been treble dealing,' the Doctor retorts. 'What say you, Mr. Ferio?'

Ferio. Marry I thinke it hath been a song of four parts: What say you Maister Bario?
Bario. I say I know not what to say, but we sing all one tune.

The function of the minor characters is explained by the significance of their Italian names. Balia is the schoolmistress who acts as the nurse and messenger for the young women. The stupid servant is Goffo, the ruffian Bragardo, and his pert attendant Bizardo. Giro is the vintner's boy who reels on to the stage half drunk. The proper names Misa, Bilia, Dano or Dives, and Sir Lawrence for the old woman, the maid, the rich citizen, and the priest are generally discarded in the course of the dialogue. In the Quarto of 1604 the names and relationship of the four families are in a hopeless tangle, but the chief positions of the plot are clear.

The young women take hands not to disagree 'upon husbands' but 'if there come any to our mindes, let us have a-bout with our wittes, to fit our wils to the full'. The young men make a corresponding pact 'Wee foure wagges to foure mad wenches, our crosse sisters, let us to our wits, to laye them abroad for their loves, and though some of our parents

[1] *Li tre Becchi, Le tre Gravide, Li tre Matti, Li tre Orbi, Li quattro Pazzi, Li quattro Pollicinelli Simili, Quattro medici, 4 astrologi, e 3 vammene* [sic]. Scenari in which groups of lovers repeat the same tricks and plots: *Zanni Beccho, Il Servo Ritornato, Il Falso Indovino* (as parody), *Li Consigli di Pantalone, Costanza di Flaminia, Zanni finto morto.*

seeme not to favour us in such courses, let us doe them as little offence, and in our lives as much good as we can.'

The disguises they adopt served many Italian lovers. Fileno is to attend the ladies as a Doctor of Physic, Veronte will teach them how to read and write, Gerillo is to go wooing as a dancing master, Rinaldo as an itinerant painter. The writing master and the painter set up their signs, the dancing master gives a display, and while Fileno is engaged with his mistress in the house, Goffo, now called Foggo, with the usual lewd equivocations of the quack's attendant, interviews the neat maiden, the old woman, and the rich citizens who come as patients.

Meanwhile the fathers discuss the natures and upbringing of their children, and the Captain (now miscalled Giro), left alone, reveals that though he is 'old, foollish & froward', he is in love with his neighbour's daughter Giannetta. He hopes his wealth may win over the Balia.

The old physician is also suffering from 'this disease called love'. He remarks that Erinta Bario's daughter seems to suffer from the green sickness and visits her professionally. Bario leaves him for the State house 'about a little commonwealthes businesse' and the soliloquy in which the Doctor reveals his passion shows his addiction to Latin tags.

Bario and the doctor commission Rinaldo and Veronte to attend their daughters, and in the tenth scene the Balia leaves her charges to entertain the young men who take their chance of discovering their intentions in dialogues full of facetious equivocation. The scene ends with a dance: the lovers agree to go home to quiet the suspicions of their parents. On the way they meet with Bragardo preening himself before Bizardo on a visit to the ladies. None of the young men can resist the chance of a practical joke. Rinaldo sells him some black soap as a box of complexion, the dancing master trips him up in a Lavolta, Neofilo pretends to sweeten his breath with a foul pill, and the love character written out for him by Veronte contains nothing but a fool's cap and a coxcomb. The episodes with Bragardo could hardly be called a subplot; in the jargon of the scenari they would be 'burle'. The swaggerer makes one more attempt to board the wenches in face of the gallants and hopes he may meet with the cheaters to be revenged. This time he gets past the insolent servants

and is welcomed by the Balia who takes him into the house
with a false show of cordiality. In a few minutes he reappears
without hair and beard and explains to Bizardo that 'Mistris
Balia hath betrayed me, there was a wedding: & the dogges
that the tother day misused me were there, & fell upon mee,
& used me as you see, & but that I bestirred me with my
curtilax, I had never come away alive, but I will be revenged
on this house'. His thrusts are cut short by the maid who
sweeps him from the doorstep with her broom, 'What
Captain Swappes is it you? Ile be with you by & by' (just
as D. Diego di Mendoza is tumbled out by the servant in
Troiano's plot). The theme of the old men's wooing is
introduced by the Balia who speaks to Isabella for Bario.
Isabella confides in Giannetta who is equally averse to the
idea of being 'married to the Coughe, the Rewme, the Stone,
the Strangurie, the Gowte & the Dropsie', and they enlist
the wits of their 'sisters' to hoax the old suitors. Bario is so
eager for a young wife that he submits to the condition that
as part of the marriage settlement he shall endow his daughter
with £5,000 and his son with £20,000. Lodovica entraps
Ferio into promising to impersonate the old Doctor so that
he may satisfy the priest that the marriage between Gerillo
and Giannetta has parental sanction. This bargain is repeated
off the stage so that each couple is provided with an assumed
father and a handsome endowment, and each old man thinks
he is sure of his neighbour's daughter. When the Balia leads
them into the feast and discovers the quadruple hoax there is
nothing for it but to put a good face on the matter and to join
hands and promise that lovers shall inherit their lands and
goods, like the foiled fathers at the end of the improvised
farces. There is no need to ransack Italian fiction for the
source of this comedy which gives us the clearest instance
of the influence of the Commedia dell'arte. Properly speaking it has no story, but is constructed from the simple
materials of the theme of a double love-interest and a couple
of disguise manœuvres.

ENGLISHMEN FOR MY MONEY

The fact that in Haughton's *Englishmen for my Money*
comedy is made at the expense of the aliens in London

entirely from the English point of view does not dispense
with the impression that at some stage the play has been in
contact with the Italian scenari. The construction allows
for a triple repetition of the chief situations. Each of the
three daughters of Pisaro, a Portuguese merchant, has an
English and a foreign suitor. The Englishmen have mort-
gaged their estates to Pisaro but hope to recover their
fortunes by marrying his daughters, but the usurer who is
cunning enough to see through their designs favours the
foreigners. In spite of his instructions the daughters ob-
stinately encourage the Englishmen and are abetted by
Antony their tutor who plays the part of the astute servant in
contrast to Pisaro's clownish man Frisco. Pisaro is suspicious
of the tutor, and overhears him delivering love-messages and
tokens under cover of a lesson in moral philosophy. Antony
is dismissed and Frisco is instructed how to inquire for a
tutor skilled in music and languages to prepare the girls for
the foreign suitors.

Locatelli would have summarized as 'parole et azzi' the
quibbles and blunders that the stupid servant raises as Pisaro
tries to explain how he is to recognize the Frenchman who
will say, 'Awee', the Dutchman who speaks with his mouth
full, and the Italian with the 'Divell in his countenance'.

Antony warns the English suitors and leaves them to
direct Frisco to 'Paul's' where the old tutor is to be found in
a new beard. Frisco is only too pleased to end his search and
engages Antony as M. la Mouche.

Meanwhile Pisaro, half crazed with anxiety at bad news
of pirates which he hears in the Exchange, has invited the
Englishmen to dinner as well as the foreigners. When both
sets of lovers meet at his house we are reminded of the scenes
in which the daughter of Pantalone or Gratiano entertains
the rich foreigner whom her parents regard as a desirable
suitor. As Doralice teases the stranger Horatio[1] so Pisaro's
daughters leave the Dutchman, the Frenchman, and the
Italian stammering and bowing to the delight of the Englishmen.

Another familiar situation presents itself when Frisco
returns with the new tutor. The daughters and the English-

[1] *Oratio Burlato.*

men who are in the secret recognize Antony and stand by in trepidation as he is put through his paces in the three languages by his introduction to the genuine foreigners. The imposter carries it off, thanks to the kindly intervention of the women whose impertinence exasperates Pisaro.

The blundering Frisco gives the second turn to the intrigue. As he runs after the lovers with a message from the daughters that they will expect them at ten o'clock when their father is in bed, he meets his master with the merchants and, like any booby Zanni, explains his errand. Pisaro at once contrives a counter move: the foreigners are to come one by one disguised as the Englishmen. This is reckoning without the gleam of wit in Frisco, who promises himself the 'gallantest sport' in this night's work and promptly confides in Antony who warns the women.

The night-scenes in which Frisco and the Englishmen lead the strangers a dance about the city are written for audiences expert in the topography of London. While the details are entirely English they exploit a device common on the Italian stage by which women and servants cheat the rival lovers by rushing them to and fro in the darkness.[1] Only the Dutchman is allowed to realize that he has reached his destination; Laurentia engages him in conversation while her sisters fetch a rope and a basket and persuade him to be hoisted up to their window. They leave him swinging half way and mock him for a parrot, and offer him a cushion. An episode in a story by Pietro Fortini has been suggested as the source of Laurentia's trick.[2] If we are seeking parallels we might find the hint in Aristophanes, or the story of St. Paul's escape from Damascus. Regarding the incident from the theatrical point of view as a practical effect it is worth while considering two occurrences on the Italian stage of which record has survived. One is in Calmo's *La Spagnolas* where the bravo is hoisted up, the other in the scenario of *Li Vecchi Scherniti* in the Florentine miscellany. It was

---

[1] *Li due Trappolini, Li Finti Amici, Nozze degli Ebrei, Volubiltà di Flaminia, Fido Amico.*

[2] Compare P. Fortini (died 1562), Novella V. 'Un pedante credendosi andare a giacere con una gentildonna, si lega nel mezzo perchè ella lo tiri su per una finestra; resta appiccato a mezza via: di poi messolo in terra, con sassi e randelli li fu data la corsa', quoted by A. C. Baugh's edition of this play, p. 34, n. 2.

probably a favourite device when the stage conditions were suitable. As soon as Vandalle has restrained his outcries for fear lest the wenches will cut the rope as they have threatened, Pisaro enters below, remarking as before on the darkness of the scene, and gloating over the thought of the foreigner's success. As he lurks in the doorway he overhears the Englishmen arranging with his daughters to meet at the church, boasting that they will cancel their debts by the marriage. Pisaro calls to the tutor for his musket and hustles the girls within doors. Antony remains to advise the lovers; he has a plan ready for each but will only give a hint—like the Zanni who whispers his second schemes to the lovers—then, aware of Pisaro's eavesdropping on the balcony he raises his voice and pretends to reprove the young men for their ingratitude to his master. Pisaro, like Pantalone on another occasion,[1] is deceived into a favourable impression of the tutor's loyalty and prepares for the wedding feast. The intrigue takes on a new lease of life as when the plotters of the scenari, after the failure of the second 'burla', change their tactics for a last attempt. Antony comforts the women and gives them their instructions. Laurentia is to borrow his clothes, and 'for the other two some other drift devised must bee'.

Walgrave, Mathea's lover, is smuggled into the house disguised as Susan, a neighbour's daughter to whom Pisaro had promised a night's lodging during her mother's illness. Her appearance arouses the unpleasant trait in Pisaro which completes his resemblance to the stage-father of the Magnifico type. He complains of his lonely widowhood and makes love to the disguised Walgrave, but finding no response sends him in to be Mathea's bed-fellow.

The plan for Harvie, Marina's suitor, is the old ruse of feigned illness. Cozened by the rumour that Harvie is dying, Pisaro is greedy enough to sanction his nominal marriage with his daughter with the bargain that at his death she shall inherit his lands. No sooner is the deed signed than the dying man rises from his chair in lusty good health.

Laurentia's disguise is equally successful; passing as the tutor she is sent with a message to Heigham and returns with him as her husband. Mathea comes down wedded to

---

[1] *Servo Ritornato.*

the supposed Susan, and the enraged Pisaro has no course but to submit like all the duped parents of the Commedia dell'arte.

An interesting suggestion has been made by Mr. W. J. Lawrence that there may be some connexion between Haughton's comedy and the play of the *Three Sisters of Mantua*, which was acted at Court in 1578 and required as stage-properties a basket and pulley.[1] The supposition agrees nicely with the internal evidence. It would help to account for the Italianate features of the plot if we could imagine the earlier play as being intermediary between some foreign dramatic original such as a scenario or performance of the Commedia dell'arte, and the play as it was entered in the Stationers' Register in February 1598 and printed in 1616. We are left with this mere conjecture as to whence the Italian element came into a play so English in setting and sentiment; but when, or howsoever it was introduced, it is unmistakable to any one familiar with the contemporary Italian stage.

JACK DRUM'S ENTERTAINMENT

The alternative titles of *Jack Drum's Entertainment, or the comedie of Pasquill and Katherine* give a hint of the way in which the play may have come into being. It can be dated with some certainty as written for the Children of Paul's in 1600. In the Quarto of 1601 it is anonymous, but no one has doubted that Marston had at least a share in its composition. Hitherto the play has chiefly been studied in connexion with the War of the Theatres, and critics have been concerned to detect Marston's handiwork and to follow up traces of personal satire in the plot of the cuckolding of Brabant Senior, which is said to be based upon a story that Jonson once told to Drummond. In Brabant, Fleay is inclined to see Jonson himself: in Brabant Junior, Marston; in Mammon, Henslowe.[2] Sir Edmund Chambers will not go so far, but agrees that Sir Edward Fortune probably represents Edward Alleyn.[3] Absorbed by interest in the

---

[1] See *Review of English Studies*, April 1925, p. 216.
[2] Fleay, *Biographical Chronicle of the* *English Stage* (1891), ii. 74.
[3] *Eliz. Stage*, iv. 71.

controversial element and topical allusions it is easy to set aside the substance of the play which consists of a couple of crude plots, one tragi-comic and the other farcical, both blatantly Italianate in the characters and theme. The types of the spiteful, miserly, amorous, old man, the light, witty maidservant, the cowardly braggart and his booby companion, the good-natured clown, and the pair of sentimental and the pair of scheming lovers, might have stepped out of the Commedia dell'arte and brought with them the *motifs* of madness, feigned death, vituperation and the time-honoured ruse of the lover in the sack.

Sir Edward Fortune has two daughters, Camilia, whose love is 'just like a whiffe of Tobacco, no sooner in the mouth but out at the nose', and Katherine, the constant lover of Pasquill. The banter between the young men, spiced with satire of English manners and topical allusions, helps to make Camilia's part of the plot less obviously Italianate than the scenes that are devoted to Katherine and Pasquill, but considered in outline the former involves the familiar theme of the punishment of fickleness in a lover with scenes of jealousy, misunderstanding, pleading, and disdain, and the common situations of a lover who makes secret advances by means of the waiting maid and apparently plays false to his friend by forestalling him with his mistress, and so provokes the friend to an attempted suicide. Camilia cannot choose between the admiration of Brabant Senior, a married man, the open suits of his brother Brabant Junior, and the rich booby John Ellis, and what she takes to be the secret advances of Planet the younger Brabant's friend. She is swayed by the opinions of her maid Winifred who is in league with Planet. When Camilia fondles Ellis she rouses the younger Brabant's jealousy and provokes him into beating the booby; but when Winifred chooses to praise Planet she immediately professes herself 'Planet-struck', and formally refuses Ellis. To punish her fickleness Planet pretends to scorn her advances. He does not explain his tactics to Brabant 'least nice jealousie mistakes a friendly part', but the sight of Winifred delivering Camilia's scarf to Planet is sufficient to convince Brabant that his friend has supplanted him with his mistress. He determines to murder Planet, and sends his page to 'shoote him quite through and through' and to bring back his cloak and hat for a token. Dressed in his friend's clothes he goes to Camilia, who is deceived by the disguise and beseeches him as Planet to soften his disdain. Brabant is horrified to realize how much he has wronged his friend and tries to stab himself, but he delays so long, calling on Planet to accept 'the smoake of reeking blood' to expiate the murder, that Sir Edward Fortune has time to intervene; Planet walks in and asks calmly for his clothes, and the page explains the fraud.

The plot of Katherine and Pasquill is not broached until the second act which opens with two successive serenading scenes. Katherine is saluted with a song first from Puffe, the absurd courtier, and then from Mammon, the 'yeallow toothed, sunck-eyde, gowtie shankt usurer'. She shuts the window on this disgusting old man as he woos her with the promise of his wealth in the song,

> Chunck, chunck, chunck, chunck, his bags doe ring,
> A merrie note with chuncks to sing.

He looks in the corner to witness a love-scene between Katherine and Pasquill, who indulge in speeches full of euphuistic conceits and end by capping each other's pro-testations in a passage of rhyming stichomythia in the style approved for the dialogues of reciprocal love between the *innamorati* in the miscellanies.

Pasquill. When I turne fickle, vertue shall be vice.
Katherine. When I prove false, Hell shall be Paradise.
Pasquill. My life shall be maintain'd by thy kinde breath.
Katherine. Thy love shall be my life, thy hate my death.
Pasquill. Oh, when I die let me imbrace thy waste!
Katherine. In death let me be constant, true & chaste!
Pasquill. Heavens graunt, being dead, my soule may live nie thee.
Katherine. One kisse shall give thee mine eternally.
Pasquill. In faire exchange vouchsafe my heart to take.
Katherine. With all my mind. Weare this, Ned, for my sake.

Mammon hires John So-de-King to murder his rival, but Pasquill has no difficulty in persuading the bravo, who is a comical coward, to take a bribe. He sends him to call Mammon, 'that he vainely triumph in my bloud', warning us that 'I have some painting which I found by chaunce in loose Camilia's chamber, with that Ile staine my breast'. John makes off, 'Hee, by Gor, I smell a rat, me flee'. With Brabant and Planet as witnesses Mammon mourns the death of the 'vertuous youth', pretending that his last words had been, 'Katherine . . . hold M. Mammon dear'; but when he is left alone gloating and singing the corpse rises and strikes him. Mammon rushes out thinking he has met with the ghost of his victim. At the rumour of Pasquill's death Katherine loses her wits and passes over the stage raving and tearing her hair. No sooner has she gone out than Pasquill appears to reassure Sir Edward, and hearing of her frenzy rushes in pursuit. Later in Act III, Katherine, now in only a petticoat, searching wildly for her lover, meets the live Pasquill just in time for him to save her from stabbing herself. Again they embrace extravagantly and she is restored to serenity. But as her lover goes out to fetch her a gown Mammon spies her through his spectacles; and filing his tongue to smooth lines taken from Lyly's *Woman in the Moone* makes up to her promising, 'To furnish' her 'with brave abiliaments'. When she resists him he resorts to a trick stolen from Sidney's *Arcadia* and dashes her face with the venomous oil of toads. As Pasquill returns Katherine rushes out trying to hide her disfigurement. The shock sends Pasquill mad, and he immediately begins to rave in Latin and snatches at Mammon's bonds and indentures, tearing them as though they were almanacks. The usurer's rage is brought to the pitch of desperation when he is informed that his ships have foundered and his house is burnt; he stumbles out yelling, 'Roome for Mammon, roome for usurie'.

The dramatist makes the most of the lover's madness, and in Act IV gives Pasquill a scene to himself in which he breaks a basket of eggs and raves in scraps of mythology. Meanwhile Katherine's disfigurement has been cured by a beldame's herbs: Pasquill is restored to his senses by gazing at her under the influence of music.

John So-de-King serves in a triple capacity. As a Frenchman he is the butt of Brabant and Planet; as a bravo, the instrument of Mammon; as an amorous braggart, the catspaw of two sub-plots. In the third act, when Planet has confessed to Winifred that his affection for her was only feigned as a means of approaching his mistress, the maid is left free to occupy herself completely with her other suitors, John Drum the free-lance clown and John So-de-King. She plays off one lover against the other by the sack-trick, a device which was only less common on the English stage than in the Commedia dell'arte. She promises the Frenchman that she will wait for him in a sack in two hours' time, and meanwhile sends a message to John Drum that she will be his if he will tie himself up in the sack which Timothy Tweedle will provide. The first lover comes in carrying the sack which he supposes contains his mistress and drops it with a disgusted, 'He Jack Drum, Jesu vat made you dere?', as its real occupant puts out his head. The Frenchman is never allowed the revenge that he promises himself: he is merely a puppet character with no claim to poetic justice, when next we hear of him he is being used in the conspiracy to make Brabant Senior a cuckold.

Three plays which all came to the printer's hands between 1611–14 show signs of the influence of the Commedia dell' arte, but from what we know of the acting dates it does not seem likely that this group represents a revival of the taste for popular Italian plots. The first edition of *Ram Alley* belongs to 1611: the earliest notice is the entry in the Stationers' Register 1610, but Mr. Lawrence, who has identified the author as a young Irish nobleman, Lording Barrey, suggests 1607/8 as the probable date of composition.[1] *Greene's 'Tu Quoque'* was acted at least two years before it was printed in 1614.[2] For *The Hog hath lost his Pearl* there is a more definite date. A letter from Sir Henry Wotton written 1612/13 refers to the circumstances of production:

On *Sunday* last at night, and no longer, some sixteen Apprentices (of what sort you shall guess by the rest of the Story) having secretly learnt a new Play without Book, intituled *The Hog hath lost his Pearl*; took up the *White-Fryers* for their Theater: and having invited thither (as it should seem) rather their Mistresses than their Masters; who were all to enter *per buletini* for a note of distinction from ordinary Comedians. Towards the end of the Play, the Sheriffs (who by chance had heard of it) came in (as they say) and carried some six or

---

[1] *Studies in Philology*, 1917, xiv.   [2] *Eliz. Stage*, iii. 269.

seven of them to perform the last Act at Bridewel; the rest are fled. Now it is strange to hear how sharp-witted the City is, for they will needs have *Sir John Swinerton*, the Lord *Major*, be meant by the *Hog*, & the late Lord Treasurer by the *Pearl*.[1]

There is nothing in what we know of the stage history of this second group of plays to explain the anglicizing process through which the Italian material may have passed. We do not know whether Barrey, Taylor, and Cooke worked over old plays or whether they borrowed themes, devices, and situations separately and promiscuously to serve as plot scaffolding. The traces of the Commedia dell'arte that come up so clearly under the X-ray of criticism are of little artistic value in comparison with the presentation of English city life with which the details of the play are concerned.

RAM ALLEY

The titles of Barrey's play, *Ram Alley or Merry Tricks*, indicate its form and subject matter. Ram Alley was notorious for its stews and the play was no doubt intended to attract by the realism of the lewd wit of the dialogue and the discovery of the sharp practice of the knavish Lawyer Throat and the bawds and courtesans. All that was needed by way of plot to display this side of London life was a rough framework of disguise tricks. The faithful lady as a page and the courtesan as an heiress served. Constantia, the daughter of Lady Somerfield, dressed as a boy attends Boutcher, her fickle lover, on his visits to Taffeta and saves him from suicide when he finds that he has been forestalled by the decrepit rival Sir Oliver Smallshanks. She offers to console him with the real Constantia and appears at the dénouement in her woman's dress apologizing to her mother for her adventure and converting her lover. This theme had been naturalized so long that it could hardly be regarded as a sign of the influence of the Commedia dell'arte if it were not for other familiar Italian material.

A scene in the second plot reproduces one of the most effective situations of the popular Italian comedies. Will Smallshanks' plan to dupe his father by passing off Frances, a common courtesan, as an heiress is the counterpart of a

---

[1] *Reliquiae Wottonianae* (1685), p. 402.

scene in the *Epidicus*, one of the commonest of Plautus's plots
to be reworked. It was reproduced for the Commedia erudita
in Cieco d'Hadria's *Emilia*, which was then drafted for improvisation and variously entitled *Le due Schiave* (Loc. i. 28),
La Schiava (Cors. i. 2), and in the Neapolitan miscellany
Emilia. Of these three extant scenari Locatelli's is the most
circumstantial. Pantalone's son leaves word with Zanni the
servant that before his return he is to procure for him Cintia,
a slave with whom he is in love. Pantalone confides to
Zanni that he is expecting the arrival of Clarice his daughter
whom he has not seen for nearly twenty years. Zanni seizes
his chance and after acquainting Cintia with as much of
Clarice's history as he can remember he presents her to
Pantalone as his daughter. When he first sees her Pantalone
'gazes at her with delight, and then turns away saying, "I am
not a bit happy, somehow I don't feel it in my blood that she
is my child" '. Zanni says this is because it is so long since
he saw her, how could he feel an affection for her when he
had only seen her once? 'True, true,' says Pantalone. After
this he asks her name, and Zanni, pretending to sing, moves
to and fro saying, 'Clarice'. Pantalone turns on him saying, 'Be
quiet, you brute: don't talk to yourself'. One by one he puts
her through the questions for which she has been prepared,
and all the time Zanni prompts her by the singing trick.
Pantalone gets furious and at last asks her the name of the
old woman whom she had left with her mother, saying, 'if
she can tell me that I will be sure that she is really my
daughter'. Zanni is in despair because he does not know the
name: no more does Cintia, but turning to Pantalone she
says that since she has been able to answer so many questions
to his satisfaction it is now her turn to assure herself that he
is really Pantalone, and that if he can tell her what the old
woman is called she will be certain that he is her father.
Then Pantalone praising Cintia says, 'She's a fine girl, and
she's quite right, now to convince her that I am her father,
I will tell her that the old woman's name is Filippa'. 'Filippa,
Filippa', cry Cintia and Zanni delightedly, and with by-play
over 'Filippa' (*azzi di filippa*) they go into the house. So in
the English play Sir Oliver kisses the girl and inquires after
her father, and William saves the situation by interrupting to

answer the unexpected question himself. The subsequent intrigue in which Throat the Lawyer marries the girl by fraud only to discover that she is nothing but a poor witty adventuress, is not remarkably Italianate.

In the farcical sub-plot, however, we encounter a group of characters who might have stepped out of the Commedia dell'arte. The behaviour of Captain Puffe as the braggart and of Adriana and Taffeta as the typical bawd and courtesan has already been described.[1] Sir Oliver Smallshanks, who has been duped like a Pantalone-father over the supposed heiress, now takes heart as a Pantalone-lover and woos Taffeta. While he is engaged with the courtesan the Captain is heard storming on the stairs. Sir Oliver in a panic inquires if she has not an inner room and Tutchin suggests a trunk or a chest as a hiding-place. Adriana's idea of pushing him under his mistress's farthingale may have been original, but it is also Zanni's trick to escape his rival the French servant Jacobillo and Coviello the Neapolitan doctor in *Il Pantalone Impazzito* by Fr. Righello, a comedy entirely in the popular tradition published in 1613. As Puffe advances defying all the constables and halberdiers with whom he is threatened he kicks at the farthingale and discovers the Knight. Before it can be proved who is the greatest coward, the Captain, the Knight, or his companion Justice Tutchin, a servant separates them and the Captain retires. Even this fright does not cure Sir Oliver; as in the Commedia dell'arte his misfortunes become comic by repetition, and at his second visit to the widow he is driven behind the hangings to avoid his son who treats the listener to some sharp home-truths.

The resemblance between Tutchin and Gratiano does not go far: he is only a reluctant wooer and is loath to visit Lady Somerfield when Sir Oliver wants to be rid of him: Barrey uses him chiefly as a confidant and may be adapting Kempe's caricature of the foolish justice rather than borrowing from the Italian mask of the Doctor.[2]

GREENE'S 'TU QUOQUE'

A summary of the action of *The City Gallant* shows Cooke making use of a few common Italian situations as the

---

[1] *Supra*, pp. 396–7.   [2] *Parnassus*, Act IV, sc. iii.

scaffolding for a play which by its presentation of London
life in the taverns, stews and prisons strikes the reader as
peculiarly English. The performance of Thomas Greene as
Bubble the good-natured Clown which gave the play its
alternative title of *Greene's 'Tu Quoque'* might be taken as a
measure of the relationship between the English and the
Italian elements. Bubble, the servant of a knavish gallant
Staines, is suddenly enriched by the death of a usurer uncle.
He changes places with his master and is accepted by Sir
Lionel Rash as a desirable suitor for his daughter. The
mainspring of the comic situation corresponds to Zanni's
trick in *Il Finto Servo*, a brisk popular version of *Li Suppositi*;
the introduction of the rich booby to the young who openly
flouts him has its counterpart in the scenes in Locatelli's
Oratio Burlato; and the trick by which Staines, disguised as
an Italian makes off with Bubble's cloak, provides the hue
and cry exit for which the Italian coneycatching 'lazzi' were
contrived. But the details of the clown's part are purely
English and the play owes more to the personality of the
actor, to his gesture, and the intonation of his catchword,
'Et tu quoque', than to the comic ideas which the dramatist
seems to have borrowed from the Commedia dell'arte.

Other parts of the play are Italianate in structure. As
Bubble is a good-natured booby of the type of a 'Pulcinella
sciocco', so his counterpart Will Rash is the correspondingly
astute servant. As the son of Sir Lionel he is above the
Coviello type in rank, but his talent for organizing an
intrigue and his lack of all sentimental interest in the final
marriages fit him for the part of the Coviello plot-agent. He
manipulates the love affairs of his sisters Gertrude and Joyce
with young Geraldine, a neighbour's son, and Staines the
penniless gallant who is disguised as a man-servant.

These lovers are remembered as types rather than as
persons. Geraldine and Gertrude are shy and sentimental
and will not acknowledge their love for each other: Joyce
and Staines are bold, railing, and scornful. Their speeches
for all the matter that they contain, collapse into the formulae
of the miscellanies and might be summarized as soliloquies
of a diffident lover, of lover unrequited, and dialogues of
wooing and disdain.

The most obvious Italian traces appear in the scene in which Joyce and Will Rash bring matters to a head between Gertrude and Geraldine by the device of feigned death. The young man is persuaded to lie flat on the stage with a veil sprinkled with blood over his face. Gertrude is called from the window and rushing down she overwhelms him with kisses and lamentations. Reassured by this demonstration of her real feelings he rises. Gertrude is angry to think of the foolish figure she has cut, but does not go back on her word to Geraldine. For the rest of the play this pair of lovers is occupied in revenging themselves upon Joyce and Staines by putting them into an equally embarrassing position. Their efforts culminate in a night scene in which three couples of eloping lovers (for Spendall and the widow are also taking advantage of the dark) pass to and fro over the stage terrified at the thought of meeting Sir Lionel and scared by Will Rash who prowls round the house with a lantern to spy on these 'little children of Cupid that walk two by two'. This typical scene leads up to an equally common dénouement which emphasizes the likeness between the English and Italian fathers. On the morning appointed for the marriages of Gertrude and Joyce with the two rich blockheads Bubble and Scattergood, Sir Lionel and old Geraldine come to wake up their daughters and discover that they have been at church an hour ago with the lovers of their choice. Bubble and Scattergood came in rubbing their eyes, cheated of their brides, and the fathers can only assent weakly to the marriages which have been consummated before their consent was asked.

THE HOG HATH LOST HIS PEARL

Taylor may have had the tale of Carracus, Albert and Maria, the afflicted lovers of *The Hog hath lost his Pearl*, from some chapbook romance, but his source does not appear to be extant. It is therefore worth pointing out the correspondence between his dramatic material and the stock-in-trade of the tragi-comedies of the Commedia dell'arte. Carracus, the lover of Maria, the daughter of Old Lord Wealthy, is superseded by his friend Albert. After debating the rival claims of love and friendship, the deceiver mounts the ladder and is received as Carracus, who arrives later and waits below depending upon his friend's good faith. As he retires to see that the horses are in readiness for the elopement, Albert descends and now that his pleasure is over is immediately stricken with shame. He repents loudly in a soliloquy but does not confess to Carracus who goes off safely with Maria. Albert retires into the woods to wear out his life as a hermit and relieve his conscience by carving his story on the trees. Maria's explanation of how she came by Albert's ring rouses Carracus to suspicion, not of his friend's faith, but of his wife's honesty. At his accusation she swoons and is carried into the house. Carracus, imagining she is dead, begins to rave and compares himself to Orpheus seeking his Eurydice. He is too crazed to take in the Nurse's announcement that his wife had recovered and has taken a vow of voluntary banishment.

Disguised as a boy Maria wanders into the woods until she comes to one of the trees upon which Albert has engraved the story of his repentance. Although she is faint with hunger she has strength left to decipher his twenty-three lines, and to announce her pardon in time for the hermit to overhear. As she is about to faint with exhaustion he takes her into his cave, promising that she shall be entertained by the melancholy stories of Albert and his repentance.

Carracus, meanwhile, after a mad scene in which he enacts the monarch and refers to Maria as sleeping, wanders into the same woods dancing fantastically and raving against women. Albert overhears him, and helped by the Echo manages to make sense of his random answers. He offers to cure his distraction at an enchanted well and returns him to Maria with his senses restored. The lovers are reunited; Albert is pardoned and, returning to the city, they are forgiven and accepted by Old Lord Wealthy.

Madness and supposed death as the consequence of the treachery of a friend and the accusation of an innocent lady follow the expected sequence of the tragi-comedies of the popular Italian stage which proceeds in the normal course to a happy ending contrived by a scene in which the lover's frenzy is miraculously cured and the villain makes a handsome apology. The change of scene from the outside of a house with a balcony to a wood with the entrance to a cave is the favourite double setting of Italian plays of this type.

The rest of the play is concerned with the elopement of Rebecca, the daughter of Hog the usurer, with Haddit, a prodigal gallant whom Hog has ruined. The usurer tries to press the suit of Young Lord Wealthy, and the perversity of the daughter drives the lover to bribe Peter the serving man to help him. Rebecca agrees to rob Hog and run away, she steals her father's keys and connives with her lover and Lightfoot his cousin and a hired player in a plan to cheat the usurer with a scene of faked conjuring. Lightfoot, disguised as the spirit of Croesus, persuades Hog that he can change his silver into gold, and his gold into pearls. While Hog stands gloating over the prospect the imposter hands over the money, the jewels, and the mortgage paper to his accomplices who are dressed as the spirits Ascarion and Bazan. It is not until Peter and Young Lord Wealthy, who have been intoxicated by the conspirators, stumble out of the cellar that Hog realizes that he is doubly ruined, for the heir refuses to think of marrying Rebecca now that she has no dowry to bring. A little later the married couple steal back separately, Rebecca with a tale that she has been chased through the streets by robbers, Haddit pretending to condole with the usurer and offering to take his daughter without a dowry if he will destroy the mortgage on his lands. Hog agrees and promises publicly to forswear all usurious practices.

It was suspected on the occasion of the first production that Hog was meant to represent the Lord Mayor of London. Certain characteristics may have had an English original but functionally the usurer is a typical Pantalone-father. The correspondence between the English usurer and the miserly Venetian is borne in upon us by the familiar scenes of the forced betrothal, the conjuring hoax which succeeds thanks to his greedy credulity, and the promise of wholesale amendment provoked by the failure of his schemes, which is the tradition of the dénouement of 'Pantalone Avaro'.

TRACES OF THE COMMEDIA DELL'ARTE IN SHAKESPEARIAN DRAMA

The discussion of the influence of the Commedia dell'arte on Shakespearian drama must be restricted to those plays for which hitherto there has been no satisfactory explanation of the Italianate elements. In *Twelfth Night*, *The Merchant of Venice*, *The Taming of the Shrew*, *Romeo and Juliet*, *Measure for Measure*, and *All's Well that Ends Well*, the sources in 'novelle' and literary drama have the stronger claim. The production of the corresponding plots in the collections of scenari is interesting for contrast rather than for comparison, in order to show the different appeal made by the poetic and theatrical treatment of common themes. As we lose sympathy with the Italian actress who follows her lover as a page when the pathos of the situation has staled into sentimentality and her enterprise leaves her hard and pert, it is delightful to find that the old stock can still put out new shoots in Julia and Viola whose appeal is by virtue of their personalities and has little to do with their romantic circumstances. The means of Jessica's elopement is a commonplace on the Italian stage, but dipped in poetry the freshness of the story is timelessly preserved in the starlight scene in Portia's garden. Such comparisons may be valuable from the point of view of aesthetic criticism, but they cannot be supported by any historical connexions. If the dramatist made no deliberate use of the Commedia dell'arte he is not to be praised or blamed for the change of values.

In one instance, however, it will perhaps be as well to give a more detailed notice of a dramatic parallel in the Commedia dell'arte. It is generally taken that Shakespeare owed something to Italian fiction for the main intrigue of the *Merry Wives of Windsor*. Among the anecdotes of cuckoldry there are many versions of the story of the husband who receives the lover's confidences and directs him how to proceed in his intrigue with his wife, and many devices by which the lover might be conveyed away. Variants appear in the *Fishwife's Tale of Brainford*, in the story of Lucius and Camillus in the seventeenth-century collections *Westward for Smelts*, 1620, and *The Fortunate, the Deceived, and the Unfortunate Lovers*, 1625. The nicest correspondence of detail is divided between three Italian stories, two in Straparola's *Tredici Piacevoli Notti*, 1569, and one in *Il Pecorone* of Ser Giovanni Fiorentino. In the story of Fileno several lovers and ladies communicate to each other the addresses of the same gallant; in *Nerisio of Portugal*, the lover hides in a heap of clothes and afterwards recounts his adventures to the husband. According to Straparola the lover escapes under a pile of dirty clothes. The fact that these stories were apparently not available in anything but the original Italian until long after the performance of the *Merry Wives* does not convince us that Shakespeare could not have made use of them. He might have had the substance for the asking from friends who had more Italian than he; or, since his use of the story was not literary, the hint of a tavern anecdote would have been sufficient. But since the tales can only be regarded as analogues the claims of certain stage parallels may also be considered.

The scenario of *Li Tre Becchi* in the Corsini and Magliabechi manuscripts is a gross farce of the substitution and discovery of three lovers who obtain their ends by the connivance of the husbands whom they are out to cuckold. The student Leandro is in love with Cintia the wife of Coviello. Coviello amuses himself with Flaminia the wife of Pantalone. Pantalone courts Franceschina, the wife of Zanni who stands for the third cuckold, but has not time to retaliate with any clandestine love-affair. Leandro's appointed disguise of a dumb beggar is so effective that Zanni does not recognize him and waylays him to carry in to Flaminia the chest of lemons in which Coviello is concealed. Reproaching Flaminia for the way in which she is deceiving her husband, Zanni congratulates himself on the honesty of his own Franceschina, quite unaware that she is at this moment entertaining Pantalone. She coaxes him by the tart trick ('lazzo della torta'), to let her cover his head with a cask so that the grinning Pantalone may slip away behind. Pantalone then becomes the victim of a similar trick as Flaminia persuades him to shut his eyes while Coviello escapes to Cintia, who deceives him in his turn by dismissing Leandro the supposed beggar with a plate of soup. The first crop of confusions are summed up when Leandro, who is at length detected by Zanni, confides all that has happened in Coviello's house. Zanni passes this on as a good story to Pantalone, who returns the compliment by explaining the trick of the tart and the cask, and is rewarded by Zanni's account of the lover in the chest of lemons. At this point Coviello reappears and is informed that the beggar was actually Cintia's lover. The act ends with a triple shouting of 'Cuckold'.

To continue the intrigue Franceschina borrows Cintia's wash-tub, into which she packs Pantalone and covers him with clothes. Zanni is persuaded to carry in the tub, and after some alarming remarks about throwing the washing straight into the boiler, he deposits it in the house and tells Franceschina that he is going away into the country. Returning on the sly he hears the lovers caressing and knocks furiously at the door, threatening to set fire to the house. But before any damage is done Pantalone is bundled out with the washing and lost in the alarm, which brings out the other guilty couples who have meanwhile repeated their visits. Leandro gives a general explanation and hands over each guilty wife to make peace as best she can.

The old jests of the lover confiding his amorous adventures to the husband of his mistress, with its consequent episodes in which both the lover and the husband are hoaxed, is worked up in another pair of scenari, *Il Mastro di Terentio* in the Correr collection and its variant *La Scuola di Terentio* in the Neapolitan miscellany.

The tradition that the *Merry Wives* was composed within fourteen days to satisfy Elizabeth's whim to see Falstaff in love suggests that Shakespeare may have eased the practical difficulty by taking some old play as a foundation. Such a common and obvious means of working against time has already been suggested by the editors of the New Cambridge Shakespeare to explain what they regard as survivals of an old play in which the hero was 'a lackadaisical sentimental swain, Euphuistic in address'.[1] Without agreeing to the somewhat over-nice criticism of lines and speeches which are produced as evidence of this imperfect refashioning, it is undeniable that there are traces of Italianate material still only half absorbed by the English setting. In explaining this the analogues in translated stories have the older but not necessarily the stronger claim.

[1] Ed. cit., p. xxiv.

The textual problems of the first Quarto suggest that some intermediary version was available for the actor-pirate,[1] this play may have been in closer contact with the Continental stage traditions. On a popular stage titles are rarely good clues to the substance of a plot, but it is perhaps worth mentioning that the lost play by Dekker called *Treplisitie Cuckowlles*[2] gives a neat translation of the title *Li Tre Becchi*, and that *The Jealous Comedy* was acted as a new play on 5 January 1592.[3] Possibly it was through one of these plays that the Italian material was passed on to Shakespeare.

In two other plays, the *Comedy of Errors* and the *Tempest*, certain resemblances to the Commedia dell'arte may be accounted for as direct borrowings taking place most probably at a pre-Shakespearian stage of development. No single scenario has come to light which could be regarded as a source for either of these plays, but the more we know of the nature of the Commedia dell'arte the less we expect the evidence of the contact between the two dramas to take this form: the scenari should not be studied singly but as they group themselves into the stage traditions of the farces of mistaken identity and the comic pastorals or shipwreck plays. The development of these traditions has been described in outline in Chapter III; the details of the variation may be studied in the representative scenari reproduced in the Appendix.

To recognize the relationship between the scenari and Shakespearian drama it is necessary to visualize the English and Italian plays from the same angle. If we were to insert a summary of the action of the *Tempest* and of the *Comedy of Errors* among the scenari of Locatelli's miscellany the resemblance would be remarkable. We are to look to the broad outlines of the action, not to the details of poetic conception, and are to keep in mind the possibilities of old plays which may have been at Shakespeare's disposal.

The coincidence of the action of the *Comedy of Errors* with all the chief features of the plays of mistaken doubles in the Commedia dell'arte is almost complete, but something must

---

[1] *First Quarto of the Merry Wives,* ed. W. W. Greg, 1910.
[2] Henslowe's Diary, 1 March 1598,

f. 44 v I. See Greg, ii. 191.
[3] Ibid., i. 15, ii. 156.

be allowed for a common inheritance from the *Menaechmi* of Plautus. The setting of Ephesus, the use of the terms 'Erotes' and 'Sereptus', corruptions of the Latin *erraticus* and *surreptus*, to distinguish the two Antipholi, show that the *Menaechmi* was unquestionably the basis of the *Comedy of Errors*. What is Plautine in the play Shakespeare could easily have taken for himself from the original, perhaps with the help of some friend who had more than his 'small Latin', or by means of 'W. W.'s' translation which appears to have been circulated in manuscripts some years before it was printed in 1595, or, as is still more probable, he may have taken it over with an old play. The scene in which the courtesan lures Antipholus of Syracuse in spite of Dromio's warning, Pinch's dealings with the madman, Dromio of Ephesus announcing his freedom, are nearer to the Latin than to any modifications which survive in Italian. The Commedia dell'arte specialized in knocking scenes, but the retorts of Dromio of Syracuse to the battering of Antipholus and Dromio of Ephesus is more likely to have been an adaptation of the scene between Mercury and Sosia in the *Amphitruo* (IV. ii).

But when we come to consider the amplifications of the *Menaechmi* theme it is obvious that while the classical comedy was Shakespeare's ultimate it was not his immediate model. These amplifications fall into three groups: the framework concerning the Duke, Aegeon, and the Abbess; the introduction of Luciana as a confidante for Adriana and a wife for Antipholus of Syracuse; and the addition of twin slaves which brings about the extra complications of the cooling dinner, the lost purse, and the disputes over the rope-end and the unpaid-for chain. Before considering the sources and dramatic value of these additions the problem of authorship must be faced. Topical allusions in Act III, scene ii, of the text as we have it in the Folio limit the period of composition to 1589–92, but the editors of the New Cambridge edition find traces of a pre-Shakespearian version in the doggerel of III. i. The scene has been taken over and the first ten and the last thirty-nine lines which are in blank verse have been revised. Mr. Dover Wilson points out that it is only in this scene that Balthazar appears, and that when

the kitchen-maid is mentioned again she is not Luce but
Nell: evidently these are 'ghost' characters belonging to an
earlier play. This editor accounts for the confusion by supposing that when the copy was prepared, presumably from
players' parts, the stage-directions were touched up by some
one who did not trouble to read the dialogue carefully but
relied on his memory of an older draft of the play in which
the names were slightly different. Thus the Luciana of the
dialogue of Act ii appears as Juliana in the stage direction
and first speech heading of Act iii, scene ii. Antipholus of
Ephesus is sometimes distinguished by the Plautine adjective
surreptus, although it is not strictly appropriate to the story
in Shakespeare's play, for he was not stolen but lost at sea.
These internal and stylistic evidences of a pre-Shakespearian
version are supported by the mention of two plays in the
Revels Accounts. One is the *History of Error*, acted on
7 January 1577 at Hampton Court by the Children of Paul's;
and the other the *History of Ferrar* at Windsor 1583 on
'Twelf daie at night', which title is generally explained as a
slip, by oral confusion, for 'History of Error'. One, or both
of these, if indeed they are not identical, may have been the
old play that Shakespeare chose to rewrite.

By studying the corruptions of the Folio text alongside the
amplifications of the *Menaechmi* material it is possible to
arrive at some idea of what this old play was like. From the
doggerel scene we gather that it made use of the farce of
twin slaves as well as twin masters. It evidently contained
in Juliana an extra woman corresponding to Shakespeare's
Luciana, and a kitchen wench called Luce who made an
effective appearance. In explanation of the fact that the
proper name Aegeon occurs only in the dialogue while in
the stage directions and speech headings the clumsy sub-
stitutes 'Mer of Siracusa'; 'Merchant', or 'Mar. Fat[her]' are
used, the editors of the New Cambridge edition suggest that
'Shakespeare was revising an old play and could not be
bothered to remember the name Aegeon except when it
cropped up in the dialogue upon which he was working. In
the same way, though the speech-heading "Ang." is employed
for Angelo in ii. i and ii, he becomes "Gold." (Goldsmith) for
the rest of the play'. This is hardly sufficient to help us to

decide whether the story of Aegeon and Aemilia was part of
a play or whether it was Shakespeare's invention. Mr. Alison
Gaw, who endeavours to minimize Shakespeare's responsibility for this early comedy, finds such stylistic differences
between the blank verse of the first and last scenes and the
intervening acts that he contends that the speeches of the
Duke are more in the style of Kyd.[1] In order to explain
the discrepancy between the names Juliana and Luciana,
Luce and Nell, avoiding the theory of a Hand B who was
responsible for the stage directions, Mr. Gaw prefers to
suppose that Luciana is Shakespeare's unique contribution
to the dramatis personae. He suggests that the name was
chosen for the sake of euphony before the possible confusion
with 'Luce' was noticed, and that Shakespeare altered it
momentarily to Juliana and then on second thoughts preferred
to change 'Luce' into 'Nell' and keep the form 'Luciana'.

While it seems impossible to solve these nice problems of
authorship it is plain that in the Folio text are traces of three
stages of the play's development. These three strata are:
first, an anglicized version of the *Menaechmi*; secondly, the
expansion of such a play by the incorporation of extra
characters and twin slaves; thirdly, Shakespeare's revision of
this old comedy with the possible addition of the setting and
the excision of some scenes between the minor characters and
the clowns. This imaginary division needs some qualifica-
tion. The first and second stages may never have existed as
separate productions, but may merely represent the development of the material in the mind of the dramatist. There
may also have been a fourth stage at which the original
Shakespearian version was cut to fit it for a provincial tour.
The editors of the New Cambridge edition 'feel pretty sure
that Shakespeare's version was longer than the text which
has come down to us, perhaps by as much as three or four
hundred lines'. For the slight treatment of the courtesan
and the kitchen wench there is an ingenious explanation:
'such scenes would require the use of the inner-stage, and
one of the outstanding features of the received text is that the
inner-stage is never employed'. Of the eight difficult passages in which obscurities and broken lines are explained as

---

[1] *Publications of the Mod. Lang. Assoc. of America,* xli. 3.

the result of theatrical cuts only the final instance in Act v, scene i, ll. 346–51, is very convincing.

Putting aside this last hypothetical revision for the moment we may return to inquire into the sources of the amplifications of the second stage. Whoever was elaborating the *Menaechmi* theme in order to provide a farce for the English players seems to have been acquainted with the ways in which the comedy of mistaken identity was exploited on the Italian stage. The details of the variations played upon the confusion of twin lovers, masters, fathers, and servants may be studied in detail in the representative scenari printed in the Appendix. It has been shown that although the scenari which made use of the double confusion of twin masters and twin servants belong to the seventeenth century there is every reason to believe that they represent an acting tradition of an earlier period. It is not hard to believe that the dramatist of the *Comedy of Errors* took his choice of the Italian methods and materials to fill out his farce. To have seen the see-saw action of a 'doubles' play with its denials, beatings, jeerings, defiances, jealousies, and apologies and to have caught up the mere suggestion of doubling those doubles would be enough for this diviner of the springs of laughter.

By status the Dromios of Shakespeare's play are the slaves of Latin comedy, but in behaviour and misfortunes they are the servants of the Commedia dell'arte. They are beaten as regularly as any Zanni and for the same reasons. The excuses that provoke misunderstandings are ordinary enough, the misdelivery of any message or trinket will serve. In *Li sei Simili* it is actually a ring and a chain that are mislaid. The scenes in *Li due Trappolini* which exploit the common confusion over lost money offer the closest parallels to the disputes between Antipholus of Syracuse and the two Dromios over the mislaid gold.

In summarizing this scenario we may for our convenience distinguish between the two Trappolini by calling the first, the servant and his twin brother, the stranger, though they are used for errands by the old men and the lovers indiscriminately.

In the first act of this play Francese the schoolmaster promises to send his servant Trappolino to Pantalone with a hundred *scudi* for the expenses of Clarice his future bride, Pantalone's daughter. When Trappolino the stranger arrives looking for his lost brother, Francese mistakes him for his own man and scolds him for dawdling; he gives him the 100 *scudi* for Pantalone. Trappolino bestows the money safely but does not deliver it. He is amazed that every one in Frascati hails him by name and that one gives him money, another goods, and another a thrashing. Pantalone is assured that the money has been dispatched, but when he meets Francese's servant this Trappolino naturally denies all knowledge of it and tells Pantalone that he and Francese are liars. Pantalone informs Francese, who next meets Trappolino the stranger. He admits that he has had the money but has left it at a friend's house for fear of thieves; Francese orders him to deliver it at once. Meanwhile Pantalone continues to demand the money from the servant Trappolino who persists in his denial. Pantalone objects that he has already acknowledged that he has received it. Trappolino gives him the lie. At length Pantalone manages to arrest the servant while Francese and the officers capture the stranger. The brothers are brought face to face and identified as the lost twins.

But the charge upon which Trappolino the stranger is arrested depends upon another confusion, for the twins are also harnessed to the love intrigue. Francese's son Fabritio courts Isabella the daughter of Pantalone. Clarice, Francese's daughter, is attracted by Lelio a young stranger, the lost son of Pantalone, who prefers Isabella without realizing that she is his sister. Isabella, however, is faithful to Fabritio and promises to help Clarice with Lelio. They spy Trappolino the stranger passing under the window and mistaking him for Trappolino the servant order him to deliver a letter to his young master. Trappolino says he does not know Lelio, and will not act as their pander; they give him a ring and he agrees to do whatever they ask if they will allow him to keep it. He goes off wondering how he may find Lelio and on the way makes an assignation with Franceschina the serving woman to come to her after dark. The first young man whom he meets happens to be Fabritio, who seizes the letter and in a fit of jealous suspicion dismisses the bearer with a beating. As soon as Fabritio has read the letter which contains an appointment with his rival Lelio, the other Trappolino appears. The disappointed lover turns on him. Trappolino says he knows nothing of the plan but suggests that Fabritio should go at the trysting hour disguised as Lelio.

When Isabella asks the servant Trappolino if Lelio has had the note, he takes it that she is drunk and to satisfy her pretends that he has delivered it, and that her lover has promised to come. She gives him a letter for Fabritio and Franceschina repeats her invitation to come to her at night, not realizing that she is speaking to another Trappolino. The servant informs Lelio that Isabella has sent word to Fabritio to come to her and suggests that Lelio should go as Fabritio. That night Lelio, dressed as a woman according to the disguise appointed for Fabritio, meets Fabritio, also as a woman, calling himself Lelio; each embraces the other for his mistress. The women make the same mistake. Pantalone, returning late and none too sober, bears off Franceschina; and the two Trappolini finish the scene arm in arm each thinking he has hold of the waiting-maid. At the beginning of the third Act the lovers sort themselves out and after discovering that Lelio is the lost son of Pantalone obtain their parents' consent to the suitable marriages. The Trappolini are more alarmed at their mistake and terrified that they are seeing ghosts rush out in opposite directions without waiting for an explanation. The discovery of their relationship is saved for the last scene. With such a general training the Trappolini would have made admirable Dromios.

Here and there from among the 'doubles' scenari even closer parallels for episodes in the *Comedy of Errors* might be produced. When the Goldsmith arrests Antipholus of Ephesus to make him pay for the chain, Dromio of Syracuse is sent to Adriana to fetch the purse which is to be found inside his desk, and the wife gives the money to the stranger servant who brings it to his real master. Antipholus of Ephesus is left waiting until his own Dromio offers him, instead of the money, the rope's-end which he had procured for Antipholus of Syracuse. In *Il Tradito* (Loc. i. 22) the Zanni contrives a similar misunderstanding to revenge himself on Horatio the lover disguised as a servant whose airs of superiority have roused Zanni's jealousy. A thief is hired to

bring Horatio a message that his master Pantalone has been
arrested for a security of 100 *scudi*: Horatio is to come to him
at once to the Libreria delle Nave with the casket of jewels
which he will find in his closet (*studiolo*). Zanni then warns
Pantalone that the jewels are missing and that they will be
found on Horatio. They lie in wait for him as he returns
from his wild goose chase, and beat him and strip him. His
protests of honesty are useless: Pantalone finds the jewels in
his wallet and is convinced of his dishonesty until the general
explanations and pardons at the dénouement.

Zanni would perjure himself for a plate of macaroni, the
Captain's attendant is continually reminding his master that
it is time for dinner: 'methinks your maw, like mine, should
be your clock', says Dromio of Ephesus trying to hurry the
stranger Antipholus home to the burnt capon.

Perhaps it is hardly worth remarking so obvious a subject
for a clown's conversation as his hunger, but the adventures
with the kitchen wench are more distinctively Italianate.
Roman slaves had no time for women, but the Zanni were
always ready to carry on an intrigue or exchange an impertinence with the waiting-maid. Dromio of Syracuse did
not appreciate the attentions of fat Nell (iii. 2), and his
experience has some correspondence with that of the brother
of the 'unbelieving Zanni' in the Correr scenario, who arrives
to look for lodgings in the city: 'Argentina calls to him; he
is surprised. She caresses him and he says he does not know
her. She says she is with child by him; he gives her the lie;
she strikes him and goes in weeping.'

The scenes between Nell and Dromio take place behind
the scenes, and the editors of the New Cambridge edition
suspect that they have been cut for a travelling performance,
for Nell 'is a character which the young Shakespeare must
surely have felt an irresistible temptation to make something
more of than has come down to us'. The use of narrative
instead of presentation might be accounted for in another
way. It is possible that here we come upon a Shakespearian
reaction to the type of amusement catered for by the horse-
play of the Commedia dell'arte. He seems to have had little
taste for this mixed clowning. For his many fools there are
but two country wenches, Audrey and Jaquenetta. If we

suppose that the Italianate material was incorporated by his predecessor fresh from the performance of the Italian players, it is just possible that Shakespeare made this rearrangement himself for artistic reasons. The sympathetic treatment of the women gives some support to the theory that as Shakespeare revised he refined. Plautus made Menaechmus' wife a mere scold: Flavia in Locatelli's version is almost equally wronged by Silvio and she rebounds; but Adriana yields and seeks to know her fault. In the Commedia dell'arte the neglected lady who suspects that her husband has found some fresh attraction, flames up with jealous anger. Suspecting Antipholus with the courtesan, Adriana finds herself in the same position but fundamentally she is of a gentler disposition; she is more grieved than angry and admits, 'My heart praies for him, though my tongue doe curse'. Functionally Luciana might be compared to the second lady of a Commedia improvisa who is used as the confidante to the *prima donna* and the consolation prize for the deserving stranger. But Shakespeare treats her kindly; she is not merely useful. The slight poetic touches raise her above the type and give her individuality.

There are no parents in the *Menaechmi* but their appearance in the English play provides for the closing scene of the family reunion which is almost *de rigueur* in the Commedia dell'arte. This may have been the object of whoever first thought of adding the character of Aegeon and Aemilia, but in the final version the likeness to the Commedia dell'arte is less noticeable. Whether it was invented or adopted, Shakespeare used the story of the condemned merchant to give an air of pathos and gravity. Such an alteration in the temper of the play has led to the criticism that at this first attempt to reconcile farce and romance Shakespeare fell between two stools.[1] With such imperfect evidence it would be unwise to lay more stress on the direction of Shakespeare's genius; we can only suspect that already he was working away from the farcical Italian material with which the *Comedy of Errors* at some stage of its development had come into contact.

If, as we suppose, it was Shakespeare's tendency as a poet to

[1] Ed. cit., p. xxii.

work away from the Commedia dell'arte, while as a dramatist he made use of its material even in this early play, it may surprise us less to find ourselves at the other extreme of his career recognizing the *Tempest* as the second play in which there are unmistakable traces of the use of the dramatic traditions of the Italian popular stage.

Research into the sources of the *Tempest* has discovered in Thomas's *Historie of Italye*, 1561, an account of how Prospero Adorni, Lieutenant of the Duke of Milan, rose to be Governor of that city by the help of Ferdinando King of Naples, and how he was later ousted by his brother Antony.[1] This, together with a few analogues of the story of Ferdinando and Miranda and a handful of literary borrowings from Golding, Florio, Sir William Alexander and the accounts of voyages,[2] gives us some idea of the miscellaneous character of the raw material with which Shakespeare worked on this occasion.

But the central situation of the shipwreck of two groups of strangers on to an enchanted island where a magician, himself also a stranger, rules the inhabitants by magic and fear; the dramatic possibilities afforded by supposing a relationship between the strangers and the magician which allows him to revenge an old wrong through the trial of lovers and the torments of spiriting; and the peculiarities of structure which preserves the unity of time by causing the magician to foresee the end of his dominion over the spirit world and after putting forth all his powers to justify and save himself and voluntarily to renounce his art, are left unexplained. It is generally assumed that for once Shakespeare troubled to invent his own plot.

It may be remembered that these were precisely the dramatic materials of the pastoral tradition of the Commedia dell'arte described in Chapter III. If we could see filmed first the *Tempest* and then one of the Italian scenari, so far as the action and essential stage effects are concerned, there would be little to choose between them.

In a pamphlet published in 1913 Professor Ferdinando Neri first drew attention to the scenari of the Arcadian plays

---

[1] Variorum, p. 343.

[2] Cf. v. i. 33. Golding, *Metamorphoses*, II. i. 154–63; *Essays of Montaigne*, i. 30, trans. Florio, 1603, IV. i. 148–58; cf. W. Alexander, *Tragedie of Darius* (1603).

as possible prototypes of the *Tempest*.[1] Working from the
five which were printed as an appendix to this study in the
development of the comic-pastoral tradition, H. D. Gray
made a more detailed comparison from the English side in
Studies in Philology, 1921, and used the scenari parallels in
an attempt to reconstruct an earlier draft of the play before
it was revised for the Court performance in 1611. So far the
matter has hardly received the consideration that it deserves
from English critics who are waiting presumably until the
scenari be made more accessible and the methods of the
Commedia dell'arte more generally understood.[2]

With the exception of *L'Albore Incantata* in Scala's *Teatro*,
and Neri's five reprints, the scenari are still in manuscript in
Rome and Naples, written in the professional jargon which
presents few obscurities but does not make easy reading.
Editions of the seven extant plays which make further use
of the popular tradition are rare in this country. In Appendix
G there will be found a full account of these documents with
a collation of the variants in the different miscellanies.
Scenari for which the Italian text is already accessible in
Professor Neri's pamphlet are translated for the convenience
of English readers: of other scenari on the outskirts of the
tradition the irrelevant parts have been summarized in
Chapter III.

The nature of the Commedia dell'arte makes it impossible
to present the case less awkwardly, but with the details
accessible for reference it is justifiable for the purposes of
direct comparison to use the norm drawn up from the chief
variants. It will be remembered that the favourite setting is
either the coast of Arcadia or a lost island; the dramatis
personae consists of a magician who has a somewhat malicious
interest in the love-affairs of a group of nymphs and shepherds among whom one may be his daughter and another the
lost son of the Magnifico or the Doctor who are shipwrecked
on to this coast with the Zanni. The magician's attendants
are satyrs, demons, or rustics of the cruder sort. A climax is
artificially contrived by supposing that in the arrival of the

---

[1] *Scenari delle Maschere in Arcadia,*   of the *Tempest'*, *Rev. of English Studies*,
Città di Castello, 1913.   i, p. 129.
[2] See Sir E. K. Chambers, 'Integrity

strangers the magician foresees the overthrow of his dominion, and so exerts himself to thwart the marriages of the Arcadians and the plots in which strangers and inhabitants combine against him. At the dénouement the magician discovers the relationship between himself, the lovers, and the strangers, ends the play by renouncing his magic and sometimes agrees to leave the island and return to civic life.

Here, surely, is the structural model of the *Tempest* which is built out from a central dramatic situation and not, as in the *Winter's Tale*, along the line of a narrative romance. It may be suspected therefore that Shakespeare observed the unity of time in the *Tempest* not so much because of any dissatisfaction with the technique of his other romance as because of the accidental difference in the form of his source. With the story of the *Winter's Tale* already expanded into the form of a novel in Greene's *Pandosto* a dramatist would naturally avoid all unnecessary effort in reorganizing his material. The bias in favour of presentation as opposed to narration on the Elizabethan stage had eradicated any prejudice against the violation of the unity of time. On the other hand, if the idea of the *Tempest* was derived from the Commedia dell'arte it would naturally take shape as a dramatic situation not as a story, and there would be little temptation to present Prospero in Milan before his banishment. The most effective treatment would be to let Prospero discover the past to Miranda, even at the risk of making his audience restless by so unusually long a narrative.

Without denying that he could have invented such a plot, or forgetting that there were magicians in the English drama before Prospero, that there was nothing novel in the appearance of part of a ship on the Court stage, that there were many storms real and theatrical, it seems more reasonable to suppose that Shakespeare worked with the framework of a scenario, elaborating the parts by literary borrowings, than that, plotting independently of the Commedia dell'arte, he should have devised a play which in its main appeal and many of its subordinate effects coincides so remarkably with the contemporary Italian tradition.

Given the likeness between the general outline of the *Tempest* and the pastoral scenari we notice at once how the material has been reworked. The sea-change that it has suffered by the tides of poetic reconception needs no comment. But it is tempting to speculate a little over certain alterations.

The most remarkable difference is the simplicity of the love-plot. Here are no wilful petulant shepherds and nymphs; all our attention is concentrated upon Ferdinand and Miranda whose affections are ideally unvexed. Everything in the treatment of the lovers suggests that the play as we have it was designed to celebrate a betrothal. It was performed on 27 December 1612, the night when Elizabeth Stuart was formally promised to the Elector Palatine, and possibly the earlier performance in 1611 celebrated a similar festivity. Not the boy-player of Miranda but the Princess was to be the cynosure. Such an occasion would make a complex love-intrigue inappropriate, even supposing Shakespeare had wished to repeat the situations which he had used already in *A Midsummer Night's Dream*, where, so far as the behaviour of Helena, Hermia, Demetrius, and Lysander is concerned, we have the vicious circle of enchanted lovers of the Commedia dell'arte. Deprived of the rival lovers to provide difficulties and delays Shakespeare made use of some version of the fairy story of a Prince who is put to log-bearing before he can win his Princess, to prove Ferdinand's worth and Miranda's independence. The scenes in Ayrer's play of *Die Schöne Sidea*, in which Engelbrecht, the Prince who is lost while hunting, woos Sidea, the daughter of Ludolf, a defeated noble who has taken refuge in the woods and practises magic, present the closest parallel yet discovered to this part of the *Tempest*. It is impossible to tell whether the idea of dramatizing this old fairy story originated in England or in Germany. Ayrer makes no claim to originality, his 'Thirty Inimitable, beautiful Comedies and Tragedies of all kinds of Memorable ancient Roman histories and other Political stories and poems, Also six and thirty other beautiful, merry and entertaining Shroventide plays or Farces' are 'Gathered from manifold old poets and writers, with special assiduity, for his own pastime and amusement, and composed in German rhymes for the stage', and it is therefore assumed that in cases of coincidence between his plays and Elizabethan drama the German is working from notes or memories of the performance of the English travelling comedians. But in this instance, the facts that Ayrer died in 1605 and that we have no evidence of the existence of the *Tempest* before 1611, makes it difficult to decide whether Ayrer was indebted to the repertory of the English players or whether the English players conveyed the story of the *Schöne Sidea* to England and so passed it on to Shakespeare. There are always the possibilities of an earlier Shakespearian version or of a pre-Shakespearian play, but in the case of the *Tempest* Cohn prefers the theory of an old German original. Remarking Ayrer's habit of retaining the names of the principal personages of the play from which he is borrowing, Cohn considers that an English original for *Die Schöne Sidea* with its distinctively German nomenclature is unlikely.[1]

If Ferdinand is to represent the bridegroom elect he can hardly be the son of a Pantalone: better that his parent should be a guilty king who may be made to repent, than the best-intentioned of the Magnifichi. The occasion would be an ample reason for changing the status of the shipwrecked strangers from merchants, captains, and doctors, to courtiers, without urging Shakespeare's marked predilection for rank.

With Alonzo instead of Pantalone, and Gonzalo instead of Gratiano, the episodes and topics of the scenes in which we become acquainted with the strangers must be altered. The Italian Doctor used to drive his companions off the stage with one of his tirades, and continue to harangue the audience on his idea of a library: Antonio and Sebastian watch Gonzalo winding the watch of his wit, and jeer at his favourite topic, the Government of an ideal Commonwealth. There were no nymphs with whom the courtiers might console themselves, and hunger, the inexhaustible subject of comedy, was the prerogative of their servants. It was therefore impossible for them to amuse themselves as the Italian comedians were wont to do by embracing each other by mistake, by stealing food, and recounting absurd dreams. Instead, during the familiar scene of sleeping on the stage Antonio and Sebastian reveal their mean natures by the conspiracy

[1] *Tempest*, Variorum, p. 341.

against Alonzo and Gonzalo who are saved by what they take
to be the warning of a dream. The conspirators are protected
by their rank from the indignity of being turned into dogs,
asses, swine, or frogs, but such strange shapes, presumably
making use of antic heads, appear in the course of the play.
There is no actual metamorphosis on the stage, but Prospero
reminds Ariel of his imprisonment in a cloven pine and
threatens,

> If thou more murmur'st, I will rend an Oake
> And peg-thee in his knotty entrailes, till
> Thou hast howl'd away twelve winters.

Ariel's transformations are finer apparitions than the appearance of the nymph from a tree or a flower.

Instead of the sight of the shepherdess at the mercy of the
satyr, the attempt on Miranda by Caliban is referred to as
an old crime and Stephano's intention as a projected one.[1]
The familiar echo scene is transmuted into Ariel's song to
remind Ferdinand of his drowned father. The device of the
flying banquet is used more for its spectacular than for its
comic effect.

Trinculo and Stephano are left to exploit the appeal of low
comedy which the Italian servants shared with their masters.
Their offices and liveries as butler and jester do not conceal
the resemblance to the Zanni. Except that they prefer drink-
ing to wenching they inherit all the unpleasant characteristics,
even to the sound of their names they are 'two Neapolitans
'scaped'. Farmer first observed that since the composition
of the *Merchant of Venice* Shakespeare had acquired the
Italian pronunciation of 'Stephano', and suggested that he
had learnt it from Jonson's correct use in *Everyman in his
Humour*.[2] In 'Trinculo' Croce hears an echo of Neapolitan
slang. In place of Elze's derivation from an imaginary loan-
word *trincare, trincone*, introduced into Italian by German
landsknechts, it is suggested that etymologically it is more
likely to come from *Trincole*, which occurs in street cries and
popular Neapolitan songs of the sixteenth century. This
word is recognized by Andreoli and glossed as 'con fronzoli,
ninnoli, cianfrusaglie, gingilli'. Croce ventures that the

[1] I. ii. 349. III. ii. 117.   [2] See *Tempest*, Variorum, p. 5.

form may have been carried beyond Naples as one of the fantastic Zanni names.[1] While for Warburton's clumsy explanation of Stephano's cry, 'O touch me not, I am not *Stephano*, but a Cramp' (v. i. 339), which he supposes may be a quibble upon 'stephano' and 'staffilato, lashed or flayed', Croce has to offer another Neapolitan word, *stefano*, slang for 'stomach'. There are many ways by which a popular song might find its way on to the stage or into the streets of London and suggest the form 'Trinculo' to Shakespeare, or to Tompkis who uses it in *Albumazar* (1614).

The behaviour of the buffoons gives more substantial proof of their origins. When Trinculo is dragged from under 'the siege of this mooncalf' the effect is equivalent to the sensational appearance of Burattino from the mouth of the whale and Zanni from the boulder. According to the *Arcadia Incantata* the Zanni recognize each other with 'lazzi of touching and fear'. So Stephano implores his companions, ' 'Pre thee doe not turne me about, my stomacke is not constant' (II. ii. 117), Zanni is always homesick and looks forward to his return to the taverns of Bologna. Trinculo wishes himself in a travelling show in England with Caliban that 'strange fish': Stephano would tame the monster and get to Naples with him. There is no need for them to dress up as the gods to cozen the islanders into bringing them offerings of food; the taste of Stephano's liquor is enough to make Caliban hail him as divine and promise that

> I with my long nayles will digge thee pig-nuts; show thee a Iayes nest, and instruct thee how to snare the nimble Marmazet: I'le bring thee to clustering Philbirts, and sometimes I'le get thee young Scamels from the Rocke. (II. ii. 173–7.)

In appearance Caliban resembles the satyr attendant but in function he is to be compared with the rustics who have a grudge against the magician and make their attack supported by the strangers. His plan to kill Prospero, to burn

---

[1] *Nouve Curiosità Storciñe*, 1922, p. 117 seq. Elze, *Jahrbuch der d. Sh. Gesellschaft*, xv. 253. If Stefano had been the jester and Trinculo the butler Elze's derivation might have been supported by quoting the catchword 'Trinca' of the drunken German in *La Gratiana* (see *supra*, p. 209), a play which certainly belongs to the tradition of the popular pastorals: but Shakespeare has given Stephano charge of the bottle.

his book and hand over Miranda to Stephano, naturally leads
up to the buffoonery of mishandled magic. On the Italian
stage when Pantalone and Pulcinella get hold of the En-
chanter's book time is allowed them for many antics before
they are finally borne off into the cave or confronted by the
magician himself. At the moment when we might expect
such scenes in the *Tempest* the Masque of Juno and Ceres is
summoned, and then just as they reach their height the revels
are rudely interrupted by Prospero, who dismisses the dancers
and prepares to defend himself against a conspiracy of which
he has full cognizance through the warning of Ariel. If it
were not that every time we read the play we are spell-bound
by the loveliness of his apology we might resent the intrusion
of a revenge which now seems beneath his dignity. In
accounting for this awkwardness of construction it is necessary to find some theory which will allow for the fact that
while some of the speeches are dramatically clumsy, poetically
they are superb. If there was a revision Shakespeare was
evidently his own reviser. But it is more likely that he
found himself forced to cut to make room for the additions
appropriate to a special performance, than that he worked
over the play with any desire to refashion it for his own satisfaction.

The editors of the New Cambridge edition present the case
for revision and abridgement. As bibliographical evidence
of revision they remark thirty-three broken lines, the incor-
rect division of verses, and the printing of verse as prose: as
stylistic, the mingling of verse and prose in I, II. i. 2, III. ii,
IV. i, and the continual verbal echoes (I. ii. 140, note p. 91).
The inconsequence of detail in Prospero's account of Sycorax
(I. ii. 261), the digression by which Caliban's name is introduced into the dialogue just before his entry at l. 322, the
inconsistency of Ariel's theatrical appearance after Prospero's
injunction,

> be subject
> To no sight but thine, and mine: invisible
> To every eye-ball else:

and the unique instance at the beginning of Act v of the
immediate re-entry of characters who have concluded the
previous scene are accounted for as cuts and patchwork.

Without agreeing with every detail as to the extent of the revision it seems very probable that the play as we have it has been adapted for a special performance, and that the disturbance was chiefly occasioned by the incorporation of the masque. Mr. Gray[1] tries to account for the clumsy interruptions in Act IV by supposing that in the original design the sub-plot was further developed along the lines of an Italian comedy.

The proportions of the play hardly bear out his theory that the cuts necessitated by the interpolation of the masque entailed another scene dealing with the Caliban conspiracy. Although the bulk of the horse-play takes place off, the description that Ariel gives of the misadventure of the clowns as they followed him 'Calfe-like' through 'tooth'd briars, sharp firzes, pricking gosse, & thorns' until they stepped into the 'filthy mantled poole' and were left 'dancing up to th' chins', does not read like a summary of scenes that might have been presented. The entry of 'Caliban, Stephano, and Trinculo, all wet' a moment later is a more practicable and equally effective appearance. In the following scene the buffoons have their fair share of the action. We would hardly expect Shakespeare to allow his clowns the gross freedom of the Zanni.

For reasons of style, therefore, one would prefer Mr. Gray's alternatives that the scenes cut concerned the courtiers and either presented the second attempt on Alonzo's life referred to by Antonio and Sebastian in III. iii. 11–13 or introduced the Duke of Milan's 'brave son' whom we hear of but never see (I. ii. 442).

It might be offered as a third theory modifying and combining these suggestions that at one stage of the play's evolution it was by the comic punishment inflicted upon Caliban and his companions that the lovers were entertained. It is usually taken that Prospero refers to the spirits who are to appear as nymphs and reapers when he bids Ariel,

> goe bring the rabble
> (Ore whom I give thee powre) here, to this place:
> Incite them to quicke motion, for I must

[1] *Studies in Philology* (1921).

> Bestow upon the eyes of this yong couple
> Some vanity of mine Art: it is my promise,

and Ariel replies:

> Before you can say come, and goe,
> And breathe twice; and cry, so, so:
> Each one tripping on his Toe,
> Will be here with mop, & mowe. (IV. i. 37–47.)

But if it were not for the dances that follow in the Folio
version it would be more natural to take 'rabble' to mean
Trinculo, Stephano, and Caliban, particularly as Prospero,
after commending Ariel for his performance as a harpy
which left the Courtiers distracted with terror, their swords
useless in their hands, tells him he is now to be used 'in such
another trick'. The phrases, 'Incite them to quicke motion',
and Ariel's 'each one tripping on his Toe', certainly suggest
dancing, but the 'mop and mowe' would be more appropriate
if it were to be of a grotesque character. It would be foolish,
however, to lean on so fragile a rhyme. The dances may or
may not go with the masque.

Actually the nymphs and shepherds are no more an
integral part of the play than the more elaborate personages
who precede them. Their appearance would be particularly
delightful at Court but might have been an unnecessary
expense in the city theatre. Supposing that at one stage there
had been no dances, the scene in which the buffoons dress up
in the glistering apparel and are hunted off by 'spirits in the
shape of Dogs and Hounds . . . Prospero and Ariel setting
them on' might pass as the show of the 'vanity of mine Art'
which Prospero conjured up for the lovers. Then, if the
dances were incorporated at the same time as the masque the
old direction might be allowed to stand in its convenient ambiguity: a more attractive spectacle was presented to the
noble lovers but somewhat hurriedly, for the sake of punish-
ing the conspirators in a scene which Prospero and Ariel
enjoy alone.

There is little to tell us how Shakespeare may have come
by the *Tempest* tradition. The editors of the New Cambridge
edition present as fossils four rhymed couplets and two lines
of doggerel and suggest that when he took up the play later

in his career 'he had an old manuscript to go upon, possibly an early play of his own, which may have been related to the original of *Die schöne Sidea*'. As three of these rhymes are internal, and the doggerel belongs to Trinculo they are not very convincing as survivals.[1] The editors consider that three separate speeches are a sign that at one stage of its evolution the *Tempest* was a loosely constructed drama like *The Winter's Tale* or *Pericles*.[2] But the dramatic refashioning which would have been entailed becomes unnecessary if once we admit the possibility of a scenario model. If Shakespeare had an old play to work from it is more likely to have been one which transmitted the Commedia dell'arte tradition as it had been picked up from some performance of the travelling comedians. We know that the Italian players gave a pastoral during the Progress of 1574. Some enterprising playwright may have preserved in a crude form the idea which was destined to be transformed into something so rich and strange.

GENERAL ESTIMATE

Judged by a study of particular plays it appears that the contact between the English stage and the Commedia dell'arte was considerable but that the Italian influence was mainly sporadic and superficial. Artistically it is almost negligible. It can hardly have been with any illusion as to their artistic quality that English playwrights drew on the scenari. It is of small importance that the plots of fourth-rate plays

---

[1] III. i. 24–5.   'If you'l sit downe
              Ile beare your Logges the *while*: pray give me that,
              Ile carry it to the *pile*.
    29–30.   It would become me
              As well as it do's you; and I should *do it*
              With much more ease: for my good will is *to it*,
              And yours it is against.
III. ii. 77–8.   I did not give the lie: out o' your wittes, and hearing too?
              A pox o' your bottle, this can Sacke and drinking *doo*.
III. iii. 32.   Who though they are of monstrous shape, yet note
              Their manners are more *gentle, kinde*, then of
              Our humaine generation you shall *finde*
              Many, nay almost any.
III. iii. 49.   I will stand to & feede,
              Although my *last*, no matter, since I feele
              The best is *past*.
[2] Ed. cit., p. 80.

such as *Jack Drum's Entertainment* in all probability were borrowed from an equally crude tradition of Italian farce. Haste or poverty would press the dramatist to use this seasoned timber as a convenient scaffolding for the support of the younger growth of poetry and satire while the English comedy of manners was still immature. Whereas, at the other extreme, in plays like the *Tempest*, the Italian material, if we may change the figure, is so transmuted by Shakespeare's heavenly alchemy that we need to imagine an earlier version to point out traces of that alloy that 'maketh the metal work the better'.

The value of this study of the relationship of the contemporary stages comes into view as we leave behind the particular instances for a general survey and consider what it meant that the improvising comedians kept in circulation a stock of dramatic material richer and in a more convenient form than anything to be found in the collections of 'novelle' or the anecdotes of the tavern, and *causes célèbres*.

From the point of view of the dramatist this common stock often deserves consideration as a secondary and sometimes as an alternative source of suggestion; and from this follows a line of criticism which as it is more elusive is aesthetically more valuable. The collection of analogues becomes almost as important as the detection of sources in estimating the relation between a dramatist and his audience. It is a considerable help in our efforts to understand a play to be able to discard some of the prejudices and preconceptions that the lapse of years has brought about and by assuming the attitude of the original audience to come a degree nearer to the purpose and experience of the dramatist.

Reconstruction of the physical conditions of the Elizabethan playhouse, resuscitation of the sense of the tradition of the Revenge plays have helped in this process of reorientation. It is hoped that this exposition of some of the conventions of farce and romance may contribute a background for other types of Elizabethan drama.

The Commedia dell'arte does not yield its secret easily although it is an open secret. As we speculate over its origin by tracing analogies with the Atellan farce, or over the possibilities of a revival by observing experiments on the post-war Russian stage, the suspicion grows into a conviction that improvised comedy is an art which cannot come by work alone but which cannot exist without it. There have been many transplantations and several partial revivals, both direct, as in the case of Gozzi's *Fiabe*, in the performances at Prague and at East London College, and indirect, as with Maurice Sand and other amateurs who have developed their own systems of improvisation for special groups of actors; but the Commedia dell'arte, as we understand it to have existed in the sixteenth, seventeenth, and early eighteenth centuries never has been, and probably never will be, restored.

The difficulty of finding an equivalent for the phrase 'dell'arte', acknowledged in the introduction, accidentally strikes out from a familiar expression a significant double meaning. The rendering, 'of the profession', which has been taken as the general implication, is not an exact translation. The distinction drawn between 'art' and 'craft' by the use of separate words 'artist' and 'artizan' is blurred by the Italian use of the word 'arte' in both connexions. In this case the fusion has a meaning, for the craft or profession preserves the tradition from which the art is to emerge, and in return, the artistic production gives a dignity to the profession. To regard the Commedia dell'arte merely as a professional experiment is to miss its finest possibilities: the very elusiveness of its charm suggests that sometimes it transcends craft and becomes art. Like the masque, it leaves no concrete example, but depends upon contemporary testimony and upon our imaginative reconstructions to interpret the broken pieces that remain.

APPENDICES

A. BURLESQUE VERSES CONNECTED WITH THE ZANNI

B. LISTS OF PLAYS CONNECTED WITH THE COMMEDIA DELL'ARTE

C. NOTICES OF THE PERFORMANCES OF *CHEREA, ZAN POLO, CIMADOR* AND OTHER VENETIAN BUFFOONS DRAWN FROM THE DIARIES OF MARIN SANUDO

D. ITALIAN ACTORS IN BAVARIA IN THE SIXTEENTH CENTURY

E. LISTS OF PLAYERS AND MASKS

F. HANDLIST OF SCENARI

G. SPECIMEN SCENARI
    1. TRAGI-COMEDIES; COMEDIES; FARCES
    2. PASTORALS

BURLESQUE VERSES CONNECTED WITH THE ZANNI

See CHAPTER II, p. 58.

(*a*) *From Collections of pamphlets in the British Museum*

Esordio che fa il patrone al suo servitore Zanni, esortandolo che vogli andar con lui alla guerra. Con la risposta del detto Zanni, fatta al suo patrone. . . . Con un pasto in lingua Bergamasca. [Bergamo? 1580?] Press mark 1071 c. 51.

Viaggio di Zan Padella. Con una Herculanea nova sopra il far sicurtà. Press mark 1071 c. 63 (20).

Il piacevole Viaggio di Cuccagna. 1588. Capitolo di Cuccagna. Press mark 1071 c. 63 (5).

Descrittione delle dilettevoli usanze Del Ricco e bel paese di Cuccagna. Dove chi piu dorme piu guadagna. Press mark 1071 c. 63 (54).

Il Sontuoso pasto fatto dal Zanni in lingua Bergamasca nel qual si interpone sedici linguaggi delle piu famose città de Italia. Press mark 1071 g. 12.

Vanto del Zanni. Dove lui narra molte segnalate prove, che lui ha fatto nel magnar, cosa dilettevole e bella. [Naples? 1530?] Press mark 11431 a. 43 and 11429 aaa. 17.

Testamento del Zan alla Bergamasca Nuovamente composto. In Brescia. Per Francesco Comincini 1619. The initials G. C. C. written in ink on the title-page hint that this was the work of G. C. Croce. See *infra*. Press mark 1071 g. 7 (58).

Canzone in sdrucciolo di duoi pastori, e altre bizarie ridiculose, cose non più viste e nuovamente poste in luce, opera di Zan Panza di vaccha da Cremona. In Bologna, Appresso Vittorio Benacci. Press mark 1071 g. 7 (31).

Saonetto de suprication, Zanne Menato Fraccaore da Tencaruola al Segnor Dottori da Pava. Published in Lovarini's *Testi di Letteratura Pavana*, App. 2, 1894.

Disgratie del Zane. Narrate in un sonetto di diciasete linguazi, come giungendo ad una hosteria, certi banditi il volsero amazar. . . . Poi fatoli dar da cena fa contrasto con l'hosto cosa bela e ridichulosa. [Siena? 1580?] Press mark 1071 c. 52.

Capitolo in lingua Bergamasca. Qual narra un insonio dellettevole, e come il povero Zanni dormendo li pareva esser Alin Ferno, e narra tutti gl'Artigiani che ci sono, Corun [*sic*] lamento

belissimo Composta novamente per Zan Fritella de Val
Luganega. Press mark 1071 c. 63 (29).

(b) *P. A. Tosi*, 'Maccheronee di Cinque Poeti Italiani del Sec. XV,
con un appendice di 2 sonnetti in dialetto Bergomasco,' 1864,
transcribes from the Collezione di Fr. Cherubini in the Biblioteca
Ambrosiana the following titles of Bergomask rhymes:

Stancie Amorose in lingua bergamasca del Zanul de Val Brembana ala
so bela Nina. Venetia, 1579.

Viaggio di Zan Fritada opera nuova e ridiculosa. xviith c.

Barzeletta nova in lingua bergamasca. Cantada da Zan Fritada alla
sua Sabadina. xviith c.

Due Canzonette nuove di un Amte [*sic*] con la risposta dell'Amata in
lingua Venetiana, Con un capitolo in lingua Bergamasca in
disperata, et due Napolitane bellissime: et nuove. xviith c.

Vita e costum de messir Zan Tripo om liberal e om che cercava li
comoditag. In Milano.

(c) The following are extracted from the bibliography of the work of
Giulio Cesare Croce made by O. Guerrini in 1879. The numbers
refer to the items in this catalogue.

15. Alfabeto bergamasco per il formaggio.

72. Il Pulice Canzone ridiculosa et bella sopra una vecchia et una
giovane che si spuliga vano una sera. Nuovamente data in luce
da Zan Salcizza da Bussetto. 1602. This is a reprint of the
Canzone delle Pulci.

89. Contrasto tra Pantalone e Zanni per amore della Franceschina.

98. Disgratie del Zani narate in un sonetto di 16 linguaggi.

99. Disputa fra Cola et Arlechino E l'Incauto con il Tempo operetta
piacevole di G. C. C. 1628.

129. Il Maridazzo della bella brunettina contains a Barcelletta alla
Bergamasca. 1585.

156. La Gran vittoria di Pedrolino contra il dottor Gratiano Scatolone
per amore della bella Franceschina. 1617.

170. Le nozze del Zane in lingua bergamasca nella quale si vedono
sedici linguaggi diferenti di G. C. C. 1626.

244. Sogno del Zani in lingua Bergamascha descritto in un sonetto di
molti linguaggi. 1631.

256. Testamento del Zani.

263. Vanto del Zanni.

266. Viaggio del Zanni.

(d) 'La Nobilissima anzi Asinissima Compagnia delli Briganti della
Bastina', by *Camillo Scaligero della Fratta*, Vicenza, 1597, contains
a Bergomask parody:

Fachinissimo Messer Durindel Rastellent della Vallada Bergamina, and a Contrasto between a Gratiano and a Bergomask.

(e) *Bocchini.*

Della Corona Macheronica Di Zan Muzzina. In 2 parts.

Maccheronica Corona di Canzonette dedicata al Potentiss[e]. Gran Zagno Re, e Monarca delle universe Vallarde Zagnesche Opera di Zan Muzzina Zagno della Valle Retirada. Parte Prima, Bologna 1634.

Il Trionfo di Scapino, Parte Prima. Di Bartolomeo Bocchini detto Zan Muzzina. Di Nuovo ristampato, e con nuova aggiunta adornato. Modano. Per Bart. Soliani. 1655.

Miscuglio delle rime zannesche. Di Zan Muzzina al Trionfo di Scappino. 2 parts.

LIST OF PLAYS CONNECTED WITH THE COMMEDIA DELL'ARTE

(1) PLAYS PUBLISHED BY THE PROFESSIONAL ACTORS AND ACTRESSES

Italics have been used to distinguish those plays which belong to the Commedia dell'arte tradition.

ANDREINI, F. L'Ingannata Proserpina. 1611 | see F. Bartoli.
L'Alterezza di Narciso. 1611 | see F. Bartoli.

ANDREINI, ISABELLA. La Mirtilla. 1588.

ANDREINI, G. B. See *supra*, Chap. V, pp. 320–8, and compare Bevilacqua in *Giornale Storico*, xxiii and xxiv.

BARBIERI, N. *L'Incauto, ovvero L'Inavvertito.* 1629.

The corresponding scenarii are: 'L'Incauto', Mag. no. 7; 'Oratio Inavertito', Ven. no. 46; 'L'Amante Inavertito', Nap. ii. 26.

La Clotilde, Comedia. Dedicated to Silvio Passerini Arciprete della Cattedrale di Cortona. Perugia 1649. Moland, op. cit., mentions also *L'Oristilla* and *Il Principe Eleuriendo di Persia;* of thése I have not seen any examples.

BARTOLO, S. detto *Mario* (d. 1709). La Costanza premiata nel Trionfo di Porsenna Re de' Toscana.

BIANCHI, B. detta *Aurelia.* L'Inganno fortunato o, L'Amata aboritta. 1659.

BIANCOLELLI, N. Il Nerone.

La Regina Statista d'Inghilterra, et il Conte di Esex. 1689.

Reduced to a scenario in MS. Cas. 4186, no. 38.

Il Principe tra gl'infortunj fortunato. In Bologna between 1664 and 1668. Rasi, i. 446.

BIANCOLELLI, O., detta *Eularia.* La Bella Brutta. 1663. From the Spanish. Rasi knows of no edition before that of 1666.

CALDERONI, F. Translated from the Spanish, 'Gl'Impegni per disgrazia', 1687, and in 1699 published Boccabadati's 'Quando sta peggio sta meglio ovvero la Dama innocente creduta colpevole' with additions. See Rasi, i. 544.

CECCHINI, P. M. *L'Amico Tradito.* 1633.

Reduced to a scenario in Ven. no. 2: 'Amico Infido'.

CALMO, A. See *supra*, Chap. IV, pp. 207, 239–45.

COTTA, P., detto *Celio* accademico Costante. Il Romolo. 1679.

Le Peripezie di Aleramo e di Adelasia ovvero La Discendenza degli Eroi del Monferrato. 1697.

FIORILLO, S., detto *Mattamoros*. L'Amor Giusto. 1605.
    La Ghirlanda. 1609.
    Tre Capitani Vanagloriosi. 1621.
    La Cortesia di Leone e di Ruggero con la Morte di Rodomonte.
       1614.
    L'Ariodante Tradito, e morte di Polinesso da Rinaldo Paladino.
       1629.
    La Lucilla Costante con le ridicolose disfide e prodezze di Policinella.
       1632.
LOMBARDI, B. L'Alchemista. 1583.
FORNARIS, F. *L'Angelica.* 1584.
    Corresponding to 'Il Finto Schiavo', Loc. i. 30.
GABRIELLI, GIOVANNI, detto *Sivello. Il Studio.* 1602.
LOCATELLI, DOMENICO, detto *Trivellino. Argomento* in French of
    Rosaura Imperatrice di Costantinopoli, 1648. Rasi, ii. 27.
NAPOLIONI, MARCO, detto *Flaminio.* Twenty-two plays from the
    Spanish. See Rasi, ii. 174.
D'ORSO, ANGIOLA. Di bene in Meglio, 1656. From the Spanish, 'Il
    Finto Medico', 1669. 'In questa comedia mi sono valuta di
    alcuni tratti comici, che nel ridicolo noi chiamiamo lazzi.'
    Reprinted as 'Il Ruffiano in Venetia e Medico in Napoli'.
    Roma, 1672.
To this edition is appended a list of the Spanish comedies already
translated and published by Angela d'Orso. They are:
    L'Industria contro la forza, e l'onore contro il potere.
    Il più improprio carnefice, per la più giusta vendetta.
    La Ruffiana di se stessa.
    Come possono stare in un sol cuore e lealtà di servo, e se
    d'Amore.
    Gli eccessi del Principe Carlo di Spagna.
    Il Male in peggio, convertito in bene.
    A chi l'Onor li offende e gran Pazzia se sente le punture di
    gelosia.
    Difendere l'Inimico.
    Gelosia, Onore e Prudenza.
    Con chi vengo, vengo. 1671. From the Spanish.
PARRINO, D. A. Amare e fingere. Undated. Allacci, 1675.
ROSSI, B., detto *Oratio. La Fiammella.* 1584.
SACCO, G. La Commedia smascherata, ovvero li Comici esaminati.
    1699. Rasi, ii. 457.
SCALA, F. *Il Finto Marito.* 1619.
    Compare 'Teatro delle Favole', no. 9; Loc. i. 32 and Nap. ii. 65.
SCARAMUCCIA, A. Rosalba. 1638.
VALERINI, A. Afrodite. 1578.

ZANOTTI-CAVAZZONI. L'Eraclio Imperatore d'Oriente. 1691.
Honore contro Amore. 1691.
Both translated from Corneille.

ANONYMOUS. *Truffaldino medico volante*, published by G. Morelli,
Milan, 1673.

> *The corresponding scenari are 'Medico Volante', Mag. and Nap. i. 59. See
> A. Neri, 'Giorn. Stor.' i. 75.*
> *See also 'Le disgratie di Policinella', Nap. i. 23, and 'Le Metamorfosi di
> Pulcinella', Per. no. 5, in Appendix B (3), p. 24, for the corresponding, but
> later plays.*

(2) PLAYS IN THE TRADITION OF THE COMMEDIA
COMPOSED BY DILETTANTI

AMBROSI, DON CARLO. *Il Finto Principe*. (*a*) Longhi, Bologna, no
date.
  (*b*) Lovisa, Venezia, 1729, in 12mo. Allacci.
For a discussion of the relation of this play to the scenari see *Mod.
Lang. Rev.* xxiii. 48.

BALBI, DOMENICO. *Il Primo Zanne Disgraziato Mezano da Matri-
monij*. Venetia, 1677.
  Il Secondo Zanne detto Bagattino Favorito da Amore. Venetia,
1678, 1696.
  El Pantalon Burlao. (*a*) Lovisa, Venetia, no date but licensed
on 1. 4. 1673.
  (*b*) The fourth edition was issued with the title of *Il Lippa*.

BENETTI, A. See *Lassari*.

BOMBARDIERI, ALESSANDRO. *Il Cieco Finto overo Raguetto Viandante*.
Roma, 1658, in 12mo.

BOSSI DA CHORI (*or* CORA), MELCHIOR. *La Gnaccara*. 1636 (Allacci).
  I have only found an edition for 1665. It was reissued as
La Pedrina in 1675 with Arlecchino in place of the servant
Gnaccara, but in Act I, sc. i, 'Gnac' is found in error for 'Arl.'

BRICCI, GIOVANNI, detto il *Circonspetto nella Congrega de' Taciturni*
(1581–1646). *I Difettosi*. (*a*) Viterbo, 1605; (*b*) Venetia, 1606.
  La Zingara Ladra, Mascherata in forma di Commedia. 1610.
See Mazzucchelli, *Scrittori d'Italia*, ii. 2085.
  La Dispettosa Moglie. (*a*) Venezia per G. Alberti, 1606
(Allacci and Mazzucchelli).
    (*b*) Venezia per D. Imberti, 1612. Licence dated
11. 10. 1611.
    (*c*), (*d*), (*e*) reissued in 1616 (Allacci); in 1621 and 1625
(Mazzucchelli and Quadrio).
    (*f*) Venezia, 1629.
    (*g*) 1667 (Allacci).

(*h*) 1672 per A. Zatta (Mazzucchelli).
(*i*) 1672 Roma per B. Lupardi (Mazzucchelli and Allacci).

La Tartarea. (*a*) Viterbo, Discepolo, 1614. Dedicated to Sig.
Girolamo Signorelli, Abbate di San Pietro in Valle Rasina.
19 Dec. 1613. With illustrations, a copy in the British
Museum.

(*b*) Viterbo, 1620 (Allacci and Mazzucchelli). Quadrio
remarks this edition and one in Venezia 1621 mistitled *Zingara Sdegnosa*; of neither of these have I been able to find any
trace.

(*c*) Pavia, 1622   ⎱ (Allacci and Mazzucchelli).
(*d*) Venezia, 1624   ⎰
(*e*) Venezia, Combi, 1629 (Mazzucchelli).
(*f*) Venezia, Salvadori, 1636 (Mazzucchelli and Allacci).
(*g*) Milano, F. Ghilosi, 1639 (Quadrio and Mazzucchelli).
(*h*) Bologna, 1674. Illustrated.
(*i*) Bologna, 1677 (Allacci).
(*j*) Roma, Fr. Tizzoni, 1677 (Mazzucchelli).

Pantalon Imbertonao. (*a*) 1617. Letter dated Roma 29 Nov.
1616. Illustrated.

(*b*) Viterbo, Discepolo, 1619, as *Pantalon Innamorao*. Di
nuovo ristampata, e corretta.

(*c*) Venezia, P. Farri, 1620. This is the same play.

(*d*) As *P. Imbertonao*. Venetia, Ussi, 1626.

(*e*) As *P. Innamorao*. Viterbo, Discepolo, 1629. This
is on the authority of Allacci, Quadrio and Mazzucchelli;
possibly this represents a repeated error of 1629 for 1619,
which is the only edition with the 'Innamorao' title quoted by
Allacci.

(*f*) As *P. Imbertonao*. Trevigi, Righettini, 1647. In the
copy in the British Museum (11715 a. 13) the play that follows
this title is the *Dottor Baccheton* by Gioanelli. This play is not
recorded by Allacci, but I have found a copy of an undated
edition sold by Lovisa of Venice preserved in the Bib. Vittorio
Emanuele in Rome, q.v. *infra*.

(*g*), (*h*) *P. Imbertonao*. Trevigi, Righettini, and in Pistoia,
Pier'Antonio Fortunati, 1648.

La Ventura di Zanne e Pascariello, comedia in Egloga. Viterbo,
1619.

Zingara Sdegnosa.

(*a*) Viterbo, Discepolo, 1620 ⎱ (Mazzucchelli).
(*b*) Venezia, Salvadori, 1621 ⎰
(*c*)   „   „   1634.

La Bella Negromantessa. (*a*) Viterbo, Discepolo, 1621.

    (*b*) Viterbo, 1628 (Allacci and Quadrio).

    (*c*), (*d*) Venezia, Salvadori, 1629 and 1634 (Allacci).

Li Strapazzati. Roma. G. Facciolti [*sic*], 1627. Mazzucchelli and *Apes Urbanae* (Allacci) quote the title as *Gli Strapazzi*; Commedia in Frottola (in versi). Roma, G. Facciotti, 1627 and 1672.

Pelliccia, Servo Sciocco, overo la Rosmira. Roma, Tizzoni, 1676. Catalogued by Allacci as 'Rosminda', 1676. Possibly to be identified with *Lo Scaramuccia* noted by Quadrio as one of the six comedies left in manuscript.

La Tartaruca. Roma, 1677. Left in manuscript (see *Apes Urbanae*, 1633): Gl'Incantati; Lo Scaramuccia; La Polissena; L'Osteria; Il Desviato; La Sidera; Li Bruti Silvestri; La Finta Peste; Giosofat.

    For non-dramatic works see J. N. Erythraeus, *Pinacotheca*, III. xxxvii, 1692; Mandosio, *Bibliotheca Romana*, pp. 306–11, 1682. Mazzucchelli, op. cit., II. iv. 2084; Quadrio, iii, pt. 2, p. 229; Allacci, *Apes Urbanae*, 1633. Several pamphlets are in the British Museum.

COMI, V. *La Zitella Cortegiana.* 1653.

CAPRICIOSO. *L'Amante Fedele, Pantalone Omicida et il Dottore Disonorato honoratamente.* Bologna, undated.

COTTA, L. A. *La Pirlonea.* Bologna, Longhi, undated. Allacci notes an edition in Milan, 1666, remarking 'ma veramente Lodovico Maria Cotta di Ameno'. In Melzi-Tosi, *Dict. di opere anonime e pseudonime*, I. 263, an edition is recorded for Milan, 1566. The style suggests that this is a slip.

DATTOMO, ANTONIO. *La Maga, con Frittellino Mago a caso.* Venetia, D. Lovisa, undated. The scene between Pantalone and the Doctor in Act I is slightly amplified but in many respects reproduced verbatim in *Paggio fortunato* by D. Lassi, 1690.

GABRIELI, GABRIELLO. ROMANO. *L'Innocente Fanciulla.* (*a*), (*b*) Venezia, Combi, 1601 and 1603 (Allacci).

    (*c*) 1605 in 8vo.

    (*d*) 1623 in 12mo ⎫ (Allacci).
    (*e*) 1629 in 12mo ⎭

GALLESI, F. See NANNI.

GATTICI, F. *La Bizzaria di Pantalone.* (*a*) Venezia, 1624 (Allacci).

    (*b*) Venetia, 1626. License dated 22 June 1619.

    (*c*) Pavia, 1627 ⎫ (Quadrio).
    (*d*) Milan, 1671 ⎭

Le Disgratie di Burattino. (*a*) Venezia, 1614 (Allacci).

    (*b*) Milan, Ferrioli, 1623 (Quadrio).

(c) Venetia, 1626. Licence dated 25 May 1619.

(d) Roma, 1628 (Allacci).

(e) Milan, Marelli, 1671 (Quadrio).

(f) Venezia, L. Pittoni 'senza anno ma è 1690' (Allacci).

(g) Bologna, Sarti, undated (Allacci). This is the same play as Le Disgrazie di Trufaldino. Venetia, 1690, L. Pittoni.

La Zitella Combattuta, overo le Disgratie di Biscottino. In the copy in Bib. Casanatense (Misc. 277) the initials F. G. are expanded to Fr. Gattici. Viterbo, 1673. Dedicated to Ill. and Ecc. Sig. D. Roberto Dudlei Conte di Warwich, by Fr. Leone.

GIOANELLI, B. *Arlechino finto bassa d'Algieri Vittoria il Cane del l'Ortolano, e Fichetto. Bullo per Amore.* Venetia, Lovisa, undated.

Il Dottor Baccheton. Venetia, undated. See *supra* under *Pantalone Imbertonao* and in list of scenari.

Pantalone Bullo overo *La Pusillanimità Coperta.* (a) Venezia, Lovisa, undated.

(b) Venetia, 1693 and 1710 (Allacci).

La Prodigalità D'Arlecchino mercante Opulentissimo, Perseguitato dal Basilisco Dal Bernagasso d'Etiopa. Venetia, undated, but with a dedicatory letter from Lovisa, 1693.
See *Basilisco di Bernagasso* in list of scenari (App. F).

GUGLIELMI, FR. ACCADEMICO INCOGNITO. *Intrighi d'Amore.* Orvieto, 1666. Allacci records as *Amorosi Intrighi*, 1636.

GUIDOZZO, GIACOMO. DOTTOR, E CAVALIER DA CASTEL FRANCO. *Il Capriccio.* Favola Boscareccia. (a) Allacci records issues in 1608 and 1610.

(b) Venetia, 1621, published by Lodovico Riccato da Castel Franco.

LACHI, FR. DAL BORGO ALLA COLLINA IN CASATINO. *L'Inimicitia tra i due Vecchi con il finto Indovino.* (a) Quadrio, Bologna, G. Monti, 1667.

(b) Bologna, 1684.
See *L'Inimicizia*, Loc. i. 49.

La Finta Spiritata. (a) Bologna, undated.

(b) Bologna, Longhi, 1670 (Quadrio and Allacci).

LASSARI, B., alias AL. BENETTI (Allacci). *Gl'Amori Disturbati.* 1660 and 1672. Copy examined 1687.

LIVIO, LUCIO. *Il Finto Negromante.* Venetia, Salvadori, 1629.

LUSAI. See SALVI.

M. S. G. M., i.e. GIO. SIM. MARTINI, according to a manuscript note in Allacci's 'Drammaturgia . . . accresciuta'. 1755. Brit. Mus. 839 i. 31. *Bragatto.* Vinegia, 1596. Allacci records editions for 1585, 1597, 1607 for Vinegia and from Trevigi 1614, 1633, 1675.

MERCURIJ, MICHEL'ANGELO. *Academico Desideroso de Ronciglione. Il Terremoto.* 1623.

MINACCI, P. FR., FIORENTINO. *La Finta Serva.* (*a*) Rome, undated.
(*b*) Bologna, 1683 (Allacci).

MONASENI, NICOLETTO. *Truffaldino finto Paagallo per amore Filsofo nell'Assemblea dei Matti.* Venezia, Lovisa, undated.

MONDINI. See TOMADONI.

MOSCHINO, SIG. N. N. detto *l'Accademico. La Pazzia de due Vecchi Amanti.* (*a*) Roma, 1676.
(*b*) Bologna, 1683 (Allacci).

NANNI, F., i.e. F. GALLESI. *Il Matrimonio in Mascara.* Bologna, Longhi, undated.

ORANZI, G. *Rosina.* Roma, 1652.

RICHELLI, FR. *La Serva Astuta.* Macerata, 1632. Recorded by Allacci as by Righelli, Foligno, 1611.
And see RIGHELLO, FR. MANTOVANO. *Il Pantalone Impazzito.*
(*a*) Viterbo, Discepolo, 1613.
(*b*) Viterbo, 1609 and 1621 (Allacci).

REVIGLIO LUSAI, i.e. VIRGILIO SALVI. *Capitano Schernito.* Macerata, 1653.

SERAFINI, GIULIO. *Il Maritaggio dell'Alchimia.* Rome, 1624. Allacci quotes as 'dell'Alchemista'.

SILVESTRIS, FLORIDO DE. *Academico Disunito detto l'Incapace.* The name is supplied in MS. on the title-page of the copy in the Bib. Casanatense Misc. 229 (4). *La Fuge dell'Hermana.* Bracciano, 1638. The dedicatory letter mentions two other plays which the author hopes to publish shortly: *La Combattuta Vedova*; *Li Duo Fratelli discordi.*

SINIBALDI DA MORO, GIO. *Gl'Otto Assortiti.* (*a*) Ancona, 1586, and Venetia, 1613 (Allacci).
(*b*) Venetia, 1606.

TIBERI, CARLO, ROMANO. *Il Disprezzato Accademico Nascosto. Escharistumerotos, overo I Contenti d'amore.* Landini, 1639.
Li Tre Amanti Burlati. Terni, 1637 and 1683.
Hoggi, corre quest'usanza. (*a*) Ronciglione, 1641.
(*b*) 1665 (Allacci).

TODESCHINI, BERNARDINO, DA VIGNANELLO. *La Fide Perregrina.*
(*a*) Bracciano, 1629.
(*b*) Venezia, 1598 (Allacci).

TOMADONI, SIMON, i.e. TOMMASO MONDINI. *Gl'Amori Sfortunati di Pantalone.* Venetia, Lovisa, undated.

Pantalone Mercante fallito. (*a*) 1693.

   (*b*) 1699 (Allacci).

VERALDO, P. *Le Tre Mascarate de i tre amanti Scherniti.* 1621. *L'Anima dell'Intrico.* (*a*) 1621.

   (*b*) Venezia, 1623 and 1629 (Allacci).

VERUCCI, VIRGILIO. *Li Diversi Linguaggi.* (*a*) Vinegia, 1609. Licence dated 3 Jan. 1608. It is curious in view of the licence date of that in Act II, sc. 5, Silvio, Pantalone's servant, is said to have entered his service on 25 March 1608.

   (*b*) Venezia, Spineda, 1627 (Allacci).

La Portia. (*a*) Viterbo, Discepolo, 1609 (Allacci). Licence dated 20 June 1609.

   (*b*) Viterbo, Discepolo, 1611 (Allacci).

   (*c*) Venetia, A. Turini, 1611. Letter to L. Cherubini dated 20 June 1609.

   (*d*) Venezia, A. Turini, 1615 (Allacci).

   (*e*) Ancona, Cesare Saccioppe, 1620 (Allacci).

   (*f*) Venezia, G. Imberti, 1621.

   (*g*) Viterbo, Discepolo, 1622 (Quadrio).

   (*h*) Venezia, Pietro Usso, 1628 (Allacci).

   (*i*) Allacci in *Apes Urbanae* refers to an undated edition.

This play was published as *Le Matrimonie per accidente.* Bologna, C. A. Peri, 1666.

Il Servo Astuto. (*a*) Vinegia, 1610. Licence dated 25 June 1609. In the copy in the Bib. Vittorio Emanuele, Rome, there is written 'Julio Butio Ana/gnino'. Possibly the owner was some relation of the Vincenzo Buzzi who possessed the originals of Locatelli's *Scena* in 1654.

   (*b*) Venezia, Vecchi, 1612 (Quadrio).

   (*c*) Venezia, Salvatori, 1630 (Quadrio).

Li Stroppiate. (*a*) Venezia, A. Vecchi, 1610. Letter dated 25 June 1610.

   (*b*) 1612 (Allacci, *Apes Urbanae*).

Ersilia. (*a*) Venezia, A. Turini, 1611. Letter 25 Aug. 1610.

   (*b*) 1622 (Allacci, *Apes Urbanae*).

   (*c*) Venetia, D. and P. Usci [*sic*], 1625.

Il Dispettoso Marito. (*a*) Venetia, A. Vecchi, 1612. In the British Museum there are two copies, 637 a. 23 (3) and 1071 l. 8 (6). The second omits from the title-page, 'si vendono in Roma su la piazza della Chiesa nuova al magazeno della Venetia'. In the copy in the Bib. Vittorio Emanuele, Rome, there is a letter from Il Dispettoso, Accademico Imperfetto to T. A. saying that his friend Verucci has made him a present of this comedy. A sonnet by Pietro Paolo Benvenuto is included.

(*b*) Rome, G. Sanese, 1612 (Allacci).

(*c*) Venezia, G. Imberti, 1621 (Allacci).

(*d*) 1626 (*Apes Urbanae*), and quoted as for Salvatori of Venice, 1626, by Quadrio.

(*e*) Pavia, G. B. de' Rossi, 1627 (Quadrio).

(*f*) Venezia, Ussi, 1627 (Allacci).

(*g*) Venezia, Salvadori, 1637 (Allacci).

For corresponding scenari see *La Innocente Rivenduta* (App. F).

Il Pantalone Innamorato.

(*a*) Viterbo, Discepolo, 1619 ⎤ (Quadrio).
(*b*) Rome, Dragoncelli, 1660 ⎦

(*c*) Bologna, Monti, 1663.

This play was issued as *Il Vecchio Innamorato* in Viterbo, 1619.

La Spada Fatale. (*a*), (*b*), and (*c*) Viterbo, Discepolo, 1618, 1620, 1627 (Allacci).

(*d*) Venezia, A. Salvadori, 1636. This play is here referred to as the author's eighth 'operetta comica'. To make this fit it is necessary to suppose an edition earlier than 1619 for *Pantalone Innamorato* or to reject Allacci's edition for *La Spada Fatale*.

For corresponding scenari see *La Cometa* (App. F).

La Moglie Superba. (*a*) 1621 and 1630 (Allacci).

(*b*) 1678 (Ronciglione).

For corresponding scenari see *Li Porci* (App. F).

La Vendetta Amorosa. (*a*) Viterbo, Discepolo, 1624 (Allacci and Quadrio).

(*b*) Viterbo, 1625. The dedicatory letter dated Roma, 13 June 1624, refers to this play as Verucci's tenth comedy, and hopes it may have as good success as the others which have been published eight and ten times in the various cities of Italy. The copy in the Bib. Vittorio Emanuele belonged to G. B. Rosati in 1681.

Pulcinella, amante di Colombina. Ronciglione, undated, published as *La Colombina* in Foligno, A. Alterij, 1628. Croce (*Pulcinella*, 1899, p. 34, n. 3) compares these editions, both of which are to be found in the Bib. Casanatense, and notes that in the second the prologue by Pulcinello is omitted, Fritellino is substituted for Tombolino, Burattino for Buffetto. M. Scherillo's error in attributing both plays to Giovanni Briccio is thus corrected by Croce. Bologna, G. Longhi, 1683 (Allacci).

For corresponding scenari see *La Fantasma* (App. F).

Le Schiave. (*a*) Foligno, 1629 (Quadrio). Cited in the *Apes Urbanae* as *La Schiava,* 1629.

    (*b*) Venezia, 1630 (Quadrio).

    (*c*) Venezia, 1668 (Allacci).

    (*d*) Bologna, 1683 (Quadrio).

    (*e*) Ronciglione, undated.

    For corresponding scenari see *Emilia* (App. F).

VOLPELLI, C. *I Veri Amanti.* (*a*) Viterbo, 1621.

    (*b*) Orvieto, 1534 [*sic*] (Allacci).

(3) ANONYMOUS PULCINELLA PLAYS COLLECTED IN THE BRITISH MUSEUM 11715 aaa. 41, PUBLISHED IN NAPLES IN 1824

Le Metamorfesi [*sic*] di Pulcinella Finto Astrologo, Statua, Ragazzo, e Mummia. Napoli, 1824.

L'Abitante della Guadalupo con Pulcinella Furbo Imbasciator Amoroso.

La Dama Giardiniera con Pulcinella Spaventato da Cerbaro Gane [*sic*].

La Giornata Critica di Pulcinella o siano Le Disgrazie.

Le Cento Disgrazie con Pulcinella persequitato da donne nutrice.

La Scommessa o sia le Gare tra Servi con Pulcinella Maestro di Cappella, e Senator Romano.

L'Avvocato de' Poveri o sia chi trova un Amico trova un Tesoro con Pulcinella VVVocato [*sic*] spropositato.

    See the scenario *Chi trova un amico.*

La Conversazione al Bujo con Pulcinella Confuso nel bujo per non trovare l'amante.

La Morta che sposa il vivo con Pulcinella Ladro di Sepoltura.

Flaminio pazzo per amore con Pulcinella studente spropositato.

Il Principe Valerio con Pulcinella nato da un ovo per suo soccorso.

Ernestina e Blifil o sia Dopo la Tempesta la Calma con Pulcinella tormentato dalla gelosia per la moglie.

La caduta di Tisaferno con Pulcinella creduto suo figlio.

(4) PLAYS IN WHICH THERE ARE TRACES OF THE COMMEDIA DELL'ARTE MATERIAL IN THE SUB-PLOT

'ACCADEMICO INFIAMMATO'. *Gratiano,* Favola Boscareccia, 1609. 1588, 1599, 1621 (Allacci).

BARTOLOMMEI. *Il Finto Marchese.* 1676.

BENNETTI, ALESSANDRO. *Scherno di Giove.* 1636.

BOSO (BOSSO) DA CORA, B. *L'Insolenza di Pascarello Citrolo.* 1635. *La Zingara Fattacchara, mascarata.* 1654. Cp. *La Z. F. d'Incerto.* 1654 (Allacci).

BRIGNOSALE. *Li Due Simili,* 1671, licensed 1664. 1669 (Allacci).

BUDRIO, CESARE DA. *Amore e sdegno di Dottore Gratiano, o il Gratiano Infuriato, Fuggi l'ozio.* 1679.
L'Invidia in Corte. Undated.
Cellio, M. *Florinda Regina di Patusa.* 1629.
CIMILOTTI, E. ACCADEMICO ESTUANTE. *I Falsi Dei.* 1599, 1614, 1619, 1620 (Allacci).
CITTADONIO, FR. (E. TAZZA). *Forza dell'Honore.* 1654.
FIAMMA, C. CONFUSO ACCADEMICO ORDITO. *Diana Vinta.* 1624.
GATTICI, F. *Le Pazzie Giovenili.* 1621 (Allacci); 1624, 1629, (Quadrio).
Gli Pensieri Fallaci. 1626. 1621 (Allacci).
MIEDEL(CHINI). ACCADEMICO RITIRATO. *Amanti Schiavi.* 1631. Composed *c.* 1623.
La Nascita d'Himeno. (1623.)
NANNI, F. *Fortuna de' Pazzi.* Undated.
RICCATO, LODOVICO. *I Pazzi amanti.* 1613, 1621 (Allacci). Copy examined 1638.
SORIO, O. *I Forestieri.* 1612.
ANONYMOUS. *Scola di Pulcinella.* Masquerade. 1676.

(5) PLAYS CONTAINING STRAY MASKS FROM THE COMMEDIA DELL'ARTE

ANGELONI, F. *Gl'Irragionevoli Amori.* 1616; Allacci, 1611. **Zuan Chiribino.**
BRIGNOSALE (LUSINO). *Comici Schiavi.* 1666. **Gratiano and Mezzetino.**
CASTELLETTI, C. *Stravaganze d'amore.* 1597; Allacci, 1584, 1587, 1605, 1613. **Gratiano.**
CENATI, B. *Silvia.* 1608; Allacci, 1605. **Tonello Bergomask and Zanetto.**
CICOGNINI. *Amorose furie di Orlando.* 1663. **Scappino; Pasquella; Riccolina.**
FRUSCADINI. *Amore vince lo sdegno.* 1673. **Braccolino; Argentina; Cola; Capitano Frenamondo.**
MODERATI. *Giardiniera.* 1614. **Cola Aniello.**
NANNI, F. *Finta Verità.* 1703. **Cigalon Battochio; Trappolino; Finocchio; Lisetta.**
NEGRI, N. *Candida.* 1591. **Pedroli Bergomask.**
D'ORSO, A. *Di bene in meglio.* 1656. **Zaccagnino.**
Il Finto Medico. 1672? **Colombina; Arlecchino.**
PANETTI. *Disonesto Amante.* 1642. **Pulcinella; Pantalone; Raguetto.**
PASQUALIGO. *Gl'Intricati.* 1581. **Graciano; Villano.**
ROTONDI DA SONNINO, F. *Vittoria.* 1650. **Batocchio; Cola; Pedante.**

SGAMBETTI. *Finta Zingara.* 1664. Allacci, 1651.

SILVESTRIS ACCADEMICO INCAPACE. *Est Locanda.* 1648. No masks but a plot of the popular type.

SOLINCORTE, C. *Lucinda.* 1633. Horribilibombardone (Captain); Zanbarile; Coglietto Francese.

TODINI. *Violenze Lacrimevole.* 1654. Pulcinella; Giangurgolo; Zanni.

VITTORI, L. *Zitelle Cantarine.* 1663. Trappolino, a page.

ZANE, QUINTO. *Impazziti Amanti.* 1629. Fritellino; Coviello; Colla.

NOTICES OF THE PERFORMANCES OF *RUZZANTE*, *CHEREA*, *ZAN POLO*, *TAIACALZE*, AND *CIMADOR*, AND SOME OTHER BUFFOONS IN VENICE, TAKEN FROM THE DIARIES OF *MARIN SANUDO*

Italics have been used to distinguish the performances of Cherea.

1504. Dec. 15. 'fo su la piaza un bel spectaculo, di uno cavalier, che *publice* cavò una piera a uno putin; et, per far rider, **Zuan Pollo** e **Domenego Taja Calze** fè uno soler *etiam* in piaza, et stravestidi fè belle cosse, *adeo* fo bello da veder.' VI. III.

1508. *Jan. 10. 'la sera a San Canzian in Biri fo fato la demonstration di la comedia di Plauto, dita Menechin. Fo bellissima. La fa Francesco Cherea; si che più avanti in questa terra è stà fato tal demonstration, cha questo anno, per ditto Francesco; vadagna e tien in festa la terra. Fece a una festa la Asinaria e poi egloge pastoral.'* VII. 243.

1508. Jan. 26. After a marriage feast, the 'Eterni' raided the house of Grimani, and **Stefano** and **Domenego Taiacalza** carried off two silver basins. 'E in Rialto fu fato per dilli bufoni una cria, atento erano stà mal tratadi ozi, e senza done, che haveano tolto questi bazili per cenar ben a so spexe.' VII. 256.

1508. *Dec. 31. Sanuto records the order for the prohibition of tragedies, comedies, and eclogues, made on 29 December, and comments: 'È da saper, l'autor di questo era uno Cherea, luchese, qual tramava di aver la loza di Rialto da li provedadori dil sal e cai di X per recitar dite comedie'.* VII. 701; and cp. Venturi, L. N. Arch. Ven. xvi, pt. 2, p. 220.

1512. *June 14. 'poi balato la sera, fu recitato per Cherea, e fatole demonstration di una tragedia et egloga pastoral assa' bella'.* XIV. 325.

1513. *Feb. 6. 'e la sera poi, a caxa dove sta el Signor Frachasso a la Zueca, fu fato certa demonstrazione di comedia di pastori per il suo Cherea', etc.* XV. 531.

1513. April 27. '**Zuan Polo** bufon' led a procession of the 'Eterni'. XVI. 187.

1513. May 2. 'Un bufon, **Zuan Polo,** fato il ballo di le donne fu fatto salti forti per do servitore, poi fato cantar a 4 villani da villa. Poi Zuan Polo disse alcune piasevoleze, e zugato di man sopra un schagno.' XVI. 207.

1514. Feb. 9. **Zuan Polo** entertained the Orator of Ali bei drago-
man, 'qual fe' assa' cosse di piacer in vari abiti et l'orator tra
gran piacer, et li doni ducati uno al zorno perch'el vada ogni
dì da lui a far bufonarie; et era altri che balava e atizava'.
xxiii. 583.

1515. Feb. 19. As the intermezzi for a performance of the 'Miles
Gloriosus', **'Zan Polo** feva *etiam* lui una altra comedia nova,
fenzando esser negromante et stato a l'inferno e fe' venir uno
inferno con fuogi e diavoli; fense poi farsi Dio d'amor, e fo
portà a l'inferno, trovò **Domenego Taiacalze** cazava castroni,
el qual con li castroni vene fuora, fè' un ballo essi castroni; poi
vene una musica di nymphe in uno caro triunfal quali cantavano una canzon, batendo martelli cadauna sopra una incudine
a tempo e fenzando batter un cuor', etc. xix. 443.

1517. Feb. 12. **Zuan Polo** jousts and is lamed. xxiii. 583.

1520. Feb. 13 and 14. Adelphi and Aulularia prepared. xxviii. 256.

1521. Jan. 9. 'Una bela e nova comedia per **Ruzante** et **Menato**
padoani.' xxix. 536.

1521. Aug. Sept. **Ruzzante** recited the 'Prima Oratione' at a banquet given by A. Cornaro. See Mortier, i. 88.

1522. Feb. 2. A tragedy given by **Cherea.** '*Poi recità la comedia di
padoani a la villana, e uno cognominato Ruzante e uno menato
feze ben da villani.*' xxxii. 439.

1522. Feb. 9. **Cherea** *newly come from Rome provides a comedy 'over
cosa di amore di Philarete inamorato di Charitea,* [sic] *et uno
Caliandro lo conseglia, et per via di uno orbo fu ajutato et ebbe
l'amata'.*
After Cherea '**Zuan Polo** con suo fiol, che ave dil bon'.
xxxii. 445–6.

1522. Feb. 12. 'Festa in chá Malpiero . . . di compagni Triumphanti.
. . . Et fo bufoni **Zan Polo** et altri.' xxxii. 450.

1522. Feb. 13. '*a li Crosechieri fo recitata una altra comedia in prosa,
per* **Cherea** *luchese e compagni, di uno certo vechio dotor fiorentino
che havea una moglie, non poter far fioli, etc.* Vi fu assaissima
zente con intermedii di **Zuan Polo** e altri bufoni, e la scena
era sì piena di zente, che non fu fato il quinto atto perchè non
si potè farlo, tanto era il gran numero di le persone.' xxxii.
458.
This unfinished comedy 'La Mandragora', plainly Macchia-
velli's 'Mandragola' was given in full on 16 February. Ibid.
466.

1522. Mar. 3. 'Fu fata certa Comedia a la vilanescha, per **Ruzante**
et **Menato** di Padoa.' xxxiii. 9.

1523. Jan. 5. '*a Crosechieri fu recitata una comedia nova in versi per* **Cherea** *lucchese et altri compagni.*' xxxiii. 564.

1523. Jan. 16. At the Crosechieri a comedy, 'cosa nova et molta piacevole'. xxxiii. 581.

1523. Mar. 5. '**Zuan Polo** incolpando di morte di homo, fu posto per li avogadori relasarlo *pro nunc.* Et fu presa.' xxxiv. 20.

1523. May 5. **Ruzante** at the 'noze Grimani' gave a 'Comedia ... qual questo inverno fu fatta ai Crosechieri, cossa molto discoreta da far la Signoria'. xxxiv. 124.

1523. May 17. 'A S. Trovazo fu recità in chiesia certa istoria in modo di comedia, autor **Cherea***.*' xxxiv. 148.

1523. June 31. 'Ozi al pasto dil Doxe, **Zuan Polo** buffon stravestito vene con do altri, et cantò una canzon in laude dil Doxe fata per lui, la qual comenza cussi come è notà qui sotto, e sempre ritornava ditti versi, ditto una stanzia: Dio mantegna Signori, nostro Doxe da cha' Gritti, et ve viega povereti, provede a la charestia.' xxxiv. 235.

1524. Feb. 4. In a masquerade by the 'Ortolani', 'prima buffoni **Zuan Polo** et altri, item **Ruzante** padoan, altri vestiti a la vilanesca che saltavano e ballavano benissimo; et sei vestiti da vilani putati [*sic*] che cantavano villote, et cadaun haver cosse rustical varie in man, come zape, badili etc., pale, vange, rastelli', etc. xxxv. 393.

1524. April 25. At a banquet there were '**Zuan Polo** con uno altro bufon, et uno che attizava . . .'. xxxvi. 256.

1524. May 5. 'Da poi pranzo e compito la comedia di alcuni inamorati, fe' far il Serenissimo in palazo, qual fo molto longa, ma alcuni recitavano ben, fata per **Cherea***,*' etc. xxxvi. 306.

1525. Jan. 2. '*una comedia per Francesco* **Cherea** *chiamata la Comedia orba, che fu bella.*' xxxvii. 396.

1525. Jan. 25. After the feast came 'bufoni, **Zuan Polo** et altre virtù.' xxxvii. 474.

1525. Feb. 1. At the feast of the 'Triumphanti', 'Fo 9 intermedii, et tre Comedie per una fiata in prosa per Zuan Manenti, detta Philargio et Trebia et Fidel. Poi **Ruzzante** et **Menat** padoani da Vilan feno una comedia vilanesca et tutta lasciva, et parole molto sporche, *adeo* da tutti fo biasemata, et si li dava stridor. Quasi erano da done 60 con caper sol soler, et scufie le zovene, che se agrizavano a quello era ditto per so' nome. Tutta la conclusion era de ficarie, et far beco i so' mariti. Ma **Zuan Polo** si portò benissimo, et li intermedii fonno molto belli, de tutte le virtù de soni e canti ch'è possibil haver, vestiti in vari habiti da mori, da todeschi, da griegi, da hongari, da pelegrini et altri assà habiti senza però volti, e **Zuan Polo** con l'habito prima di tutti si messe nome **Nicoletto Cantinella**. E in fine venino 8 da mate con roche, qual fe' un bel ballo in piva.' xxxvii. 560.

1525. Feb. 13. Instead of the offensive comedy there was 'quella di Ruzante a la villota', 'Et **Zuan Polo** si portò benissimo, et fo belissimi et assà intermedii'. xxxvii. 572.

1525. Feb. 20. 'una comedia bellissima per Cherea'. xxxvii. 621.

1525. Feb. 23. At the bullfight 'Fu fato un caro per Cherea con uno armato a l'antiga sora'. xxxvii. 639.

1525. May 25. 'comedia amorosa per Cherea'. xxxviii. 347.

1525. July 2. 'certa comedieta per Cherea . . .'. xxxix. 158.

1526. Feb. 5. 'Fo etiam fato una comedia a Sant'Aponal in chà Morexini per Zuan Francesco Beneti dacier e alcuni soi compagni in la qual se intrava per bolletini: era loco picolo, la fece Cherea, et fo una di Plauto di dò fratelli, non molto bella, la qual compite a hore 4 di notte.' xl. 785.

1526. Feb. 7. 'In questa sera, a hore 3 di notte, vene in corte di palazo una bellissima mumaria, . . . con **Zuan Polo** vestito di miedego di scarlato.' xl. 789.

1526. Feb. 7. 'in chà Trivixan, fo fatto uno bellissimo banchetto et recitate tre comedie, una per Cherea, l'altra per Ruzzante e Menato a la vilanescha, l'altra per el Cimador et fiol di Zan Pollo, bufona.' xl. 789. See *supra*, Chap. IV, p. 5.

1526. April 25. 'Una comedieta fatta per Cherea penzando esser stà preso da corsari, con alcuni altri puti e pute e poi liberati, e per festa comenzono a far baletti e balla la lodesana, demum dè ad atizar benissimo.' xli. 219.

1527. Feb. 17. 'una Comedia per Cherea, sichè steteno su gran piacer.' xliv. 120.

1527. Feb. Cherea's provision for the Festa at a fee of 50 ducats was judged a failure. xliv. 171–2.

1527. Aug. 30. The Orator of Hungary is lodged in Cherea's quarters 'in chà Duodo, per mezo il palazzo'. xlv. 686.

1527. Oct. 31. The Orator sends news by Cherea. xlvi. 257.

1528. May 17. 'Da Verona . . . a Francesco Cherea, vidi lettere.' xlvii. 478.

1529. June 6. After a feast in the Campo di San Polo . . . 'tornati fo recità certa comedia per **Zan Polo**. l. 439.

1529. Nov. 14. Letters to Fr. de' Nobili (i.e. Cherea) as the agent for Conte di Caiazo in Venice. lii. 281–293–369.

1529. Nov. 29. Mention of a son of Zan Polo who had been with Sier Polo Trun in a skirmish. lii. 313.

1530. Jan. 6. The French ambassador is lodged in Cherea's quarters. LII. 463.

1530. Feb. 3. 'Comedia a la bergamasca' 'Fu autor ... Andrea Razer et Zuan Maria ... la qual fo di Volpin Bonhomo, Machalosso, la Michiela, bravo sporcho, et altre cose.' LII. 553.

1531. Jan. 15. The Orator of Hungary occupies Cherea's quarters while Cherea is in Hungary. LV. 338.

Cp. A letter to Fr. de' Nobili detto Cherea from Roderico detto Sirmimiense from Buda, 25 Jan. 1531. LIV. 306.

1531. Sept. 9. Pietro Pereny lodged in Cherea's house. LIV. 576.

1532. April 21. Mention of Cherea's visit to Hungary. LVI. 77.

1532. May 20. Lunardo Dolfin writes to L. A. Dandolo from Trevixo describing two banquets: at the first 'havessemo trombe e piffari e quelli de le viole, **Zuan Polo** et 4 altri buffoni che ne deva spasso grandissimo'. At the second, 'Zan Polo *con la sua compagnia* di buffoni, con diverse sue fantasie, poi vene uno che saltava et fece cose grande, poi queste tre cortesane che ballavano ...'. LVI. 264–5.

1533. July 9. 'Da poi venuto zoso et Conseio, havendo **Zuan Polo** piacevole buffon preparado un soler apresso el Relogio, vestito da poeta con zoia di lauro in testa, suo fiol et uno altro travestidi, fè un sermon a tuti et dete fuora l'opera composta per lui a stampa di Rado Stizoso qual messe a soldi ... l'una.' LVIII. 542. See *supra*, Chap. IV, p. 43.

ITALIAN ACTORS IN BAVARIA 1549–90

The following notices of Italian actors in Austria and Bavaria during the sixteenth century, extracted chiefly from Trautmann's study 'Italienische Schauspieler am bayrischen Hofe', in *Jahrbuch für Münchener Geschichte*, 1887, vol. i, have been regrouped according to the native cities of the players in order to show the proportion of Venetians travelling in this profession.

Italics have been used for the names of the actors together with any indication of the cities with which they were associated.

From Venetia.

NÖRDLINGEN. 1559. *Bartholome von Venedig*, sampt 5 seinen mitgesellen *auch von Venedig*, als statt: oder hoffpfeiffern.
pp. 225–6.

STRASSBURG. 20 Aug. 1567. *Sperindi von Venedig* und Alexander von Polonia 'Ire kunststuck alhie mitt springen und comediis vier tag exercieren und üben'. p. 226.

LINZ. 12 Dec. 1568, 1571, and 1574. *Juan Thabarino Comediante*, noted by Rasi as a Venetian.

AUGSBURG. 20 Jan. 1569. Den vier Comedianten, dem *Jacob de Venetia* sambt seiner gesellschafft. p. 222.

VIENNA. 1570. *Juan Venetiano*, together with Horatio Florentino, Silvester Trevisano, and Jann Maria Romano. p. 230.

8 April 1570. *Julio comediante.* Trautmann suggests that he may be identified with *Giulio Pasquati of Padua*, the Magnifico of the 'Gelosi' who was with the Emperor in Prague in 1576.
p. 230, and Rasi, ii. 231.

Possibly the *Venturino* who was at Landshut in 1573 may be identified with the *Venturino Casparino Venetiano* who was at the Imperial Court in 1584. p. 249.

Comedians from other Italian Cities.

NURNBERG. 1560. *Johann von Mantua* sambt vier seinen mitgesellen.
p. 226.

VIENNA. 1562. Springer von *Maillant*. p. 292.

1565. *Collomaria des Herzogs von Ferrar.* Ibid.

1570. *Antonio Soldino florentino.* Ibid.

1570. *Horatio Florentino, Silvester Trevisano*, and *Jann Maria Romano.* See *supra* with Juan Venetiano.

STRASSBURG. 28 June 1572. *Johannes Romanus* und *Julius Parmensis* mit ettlichen Personen. . . . p. 290.

1576. *Alfonzo Neapolitano* ein Gaukler. p. 291.

1586. *Tammeny A. von Bononien* unnd Martin Thoman, springer und gauckler. p. 226.

1588. *Johanni Francisco Romano* . . . gaukler. See Schnorr, *Archiv für Litteraturgeschichte*, XIII. 62.

AT THE IMPERIAL COURT. 1590. *Jacob Brambila von Mailand*, Trautmann. p. 230.

Actors to whom no city is assigned.

IN VIENNA. 1567. *Andre Gallo*, Springer.

1569. *Flaminio*.

IN LINZ. 1568. *Francischo Ysabella*, Comediannte. p. 292.

IN VIENNA. 1573. *Juan Begera*, Springer.

1575. *Franceschina* and a company. Rasi, ii. 230.

1588. *Severo Laurini* and *Fortunato Bertholdo Paccio*.

Trautmann, pp. 292-3.

MASKS AND ACTORS

NOTE. Frequent references make it plain that the following lists have been drawn up mainly from L. Rasi's biographical dictionary *I Comici Italiani*. In the interest of economy I have aimed at the exclusion of all but the barest outlines of the careers of the players and appearances of the masks, giving only such details as were necessary to correct or supplement the mass of information in Rasi's compilation.

ACTORS TAKING THE PART OF THE *MAGNIFICO*

Albani, GIUSEPPE. In the company of the Duke of Modena 1650–1. Rasi, ii. 29.

Ardelio. In the company of the Duke of Parma 1664. Rasi, i. 854.

Arrighi, CIALACE. In an Italian troup under the protection of Cardinal Mazarin in 1645. Rasi, i. 212.

Benotti, LUIGI, of Vicenza. Sand is the only authority for the statement that Benotti was Pantalone for the FEDELI in 1630.

Braga, GIACOMO, of Ferrara. With Andriano Valerini in Milan in 1583 (GELOSI? or UNITI? See *supra*, Chap. V, p. 16). In 1614 with the UNITI; in 1619 with Martinelli in Paris. Referred to as dead in a letter from Cecchini 5 Dec. 1620.

(Calmo, Andrea. See Chap. IV, p. 30.)

(Cantinella. See Chap. IV, p. 45.)

Capellino. In Milan 1655 in the patronage of the Duke of Parma. Rasi, i. 585.

Carpiari. See list of Lovers.

Fortunati, TIBERIO, *c.* 1655. Rasi, i. 935.

Franchini, FRANCESCO, of Bologna. Mentioned by his son-in-law Carlo Cantù in 1647 (Rasi, i. 82) and probably to be identified with the 'FRANCESCO, bolognese', who played the Magnifico with G. M. Bachino's company in 1620. Rasi, i. 247.

Gaggi, GIOVANNI, *c.* 1660. Rasi, ii. 536.

Malossi, CARLO, of Parma, *c.* 1658. Rasi, ii. 67.

Pasquati, GIULIO, of Padua. Regularly associated with the GELOSI from 1574 and possibly with them earlier. Rasi, ii. 226.

Ricci, FEDERIGO. With the FEDELI in 1609, 12–14, 20.

Riccoboni, ANTONIO, of Venice. In the company of the Duke of Modena *c.* 1670–90. Played in London 1679. Rasi, ii. 346.

Romagnesi, MARC'ANTONIO, of Ferrara. Proposed by Cecchini in 1612 as a member of a prospective company for the French court. In 1616 with Scala's CONFIDENTI.

Rosa, RINALDO. In the patronage of the Duke of Modena at the end of the seventeenth century. Rasi, ii. 408.

Rosa, PIETRO. Pantalone in the eighteenth century. Ibid.

Scarpetta, GIUSEPPE. In 1613 described himself to the civil authorities of Bologna as 'già comico' and claimed 34 years' residence in their city. Rasi, ii. 521. An undated letter from the Comici COSTANTI mentions a 'Pantalone Scarpetta' who owed the company 30 zecchini for deserting them during Lent. It is probable, therefore, that the description 'Viniziano' given in the list for the special formation of the GELOSI in 1590 refers to his assumed dialect. In 1596 he was with the DESIOSI.

Turri, GIOVAN BATTISTA, of Modena. In Paris 1653. Rasi, ii. 605.

Ventura, BATTISTA, detto *il Beccaro*. Pantalone in the service of the Duke of Modena, *c.* 1655. Rasi, ii. 628.

DOUBTFUL CASES.

It was not unknown for the impersonators of other masks to play the Magnifico on special occasions. '*Lelio*' ANDREINI appears as a Pantalone in Rome in 1651 (Rasi, i. 929); '*Fritellino*' CECCHINI proposed himself for the part in 1620. 28 Dec. 1620. Letter in the Arch. Mantua. Serie Milan. E. xlix Busta. 1751.)

STEFANEL BOTTARGA. From the illustration on Plate xxxvi of the Recueil Fossard, this character might be claimed as a Zanni type. Other references suggest that it was a Pantalone part. The name occurs twice in Scala's 'Teatro', once as Stefanel (xxiii), and again with the distinctive surname of Bottarga (xxvii), and on both occasions it is used as an alternative for Pantalone. These indications are supported by the title of a burlesque quoted by F. Mariotti (MS. cit. cap. ii, p. 242), *Lamento di Giovanni Ganassa con M. Stefanello Bottarga suo padrone sopra la morte di un pidocchio.* The mention of an actor *ESTAFANEL BOTARGA* in Seville 1584, the use of the mask among the ACCESI who were in Paris in 1608, and the ambiguous line in which Grazzini refers to 'Zanni o Stefanello' as popular masks initiated by young Florentines, leave the matter undecided (*Madrigalese*, xxxiii; *Rime burlesche*, ed. C. Verzone, p. 296). Possibly it was an alternative part like those of Coviello and Tartaglia who might figure as masters or men to suit the occasion.

ACTORS TAKING THE PART OF THE *DOTTORE*

Agocchi, GIOVAN PAOLO, *Dottor Gratiano Scapazon,* writes to the Duke of Mantua 13.11.1593. He was to be found in Munich in 1603. Rasi, i. 11.

Andreazzo, *Gratiano* for the DESIOSI in 1590 and possibly to be identified with

Andrea Zenari, *Gratiano* for the UNITI in 1593, who may in his turn be related to the

Michel Zanardi of Ferrara, *Gratiano* for the UNITI in 1614. See Sanesi, p. 11.

Bagliani, PIETRO, *Gratiano Forbizone da Francolino.* Published *La Pazzia* in 1624. I have not been able to examine this play; it is presumably on the authority of its title-page that Rasi is able to assert that Bagliani played with the UNITI *c.* 1623. Bagliani did not invent the name *Forbizone* which occurs as early as 1583 in B. Lombardi's *Alchemista;* nor is he necessarily the original of the character in the burlesque *Indice Universale della Libraria o Studio del celebratiss. Arcidottore Gratiano Furbson da Franculin,* attributed to G. C. Croce. See Chap. II, p. 23, n. 52.

Bianchi, LODOVICO DE', da Bologna, *Dottor Gratiano Partesana da Francolino.* With the GELOSI at least from 1578. See Chap. II, p. 38 &c.

Dottore BOMBARDA, an actor owing money to Angelleli *c.* 1650. Recorded by 'Jarro', op. cit., p. 27, and among the masks in the *Testamento di Scapino.*

Bongiovanni, BORTOLOMIO [*sic*], of Piacenza, in 1609 with the FEDELI; in 1612–14 in the company led by T. Martinelli (FEDELI-ACCESI).

Bruni, DOMENICO, better known as *Fulvio,* among the GELOSI and Scala's CONFIDENTI, also played the parts of a *Romagnuolo* and a *Gratiano.* See the letters quoted by Saviotti in *Giorn. Stor.* xli, and 'Jarro', p. 28.

Burchiella, LUZ. *Dottor Gratiano delle Cottiche da Francolino.* With the GELOSI 1572 and 1578 (?). See Chap. II, p. 37.

Chiesa, GIROLAMO. *Gratiano de'Violoni.* With the AFFEZIONATI *c.* 1630. A *Dottor Violon* is mentioned in Fr. Gabrielli's *Testamento di Scapino,* 1638. The *Violone* referred to by Lodovico Bevilacqua in 1664 is probably Chiesa's successor. See Rasi, i. 655.

Francesco, *Gratiano Scattalone.* In the patronage of the Duke of Mantua in 1622. Rasi, ii. 525. Among the burlesques attributed to G. C. Croce is a 'Lassato over donativo che fa Maestro Martino a Caterinon nella partita sua di Bologna per Fiorenza, con la vera canzone di Caterinon fatta da Gratiano Scatolone da Bologna per far pace con la sua inamorata', 1621. See Chap. II, p. 23.

Lolli, G. ANTONIO, *Dottor Brentino,* 1661–92. Rasi, ii. 30.

Lolli, G. B. ANGELO AGOSTINO, *Dottor Baloardo* 1628–1702. Rasi, ii. 32. Rasi (i. 742) refers casually to Lombardi as *Lanternone* but I cannot discover his evidence. The name occurs again in Gioanelli's *La Prodigalità D'Arlecchino,* 1693. D'Ancona notices a *Dottor Lanterna* surviving in the Buffonata *Il Mercato* which precedes the Maggi. (See also *infra,* MILANTA.) Nor can I find upon what authority Sarti (*Teatro Bolognese,* p. 141) asserts that Bernardino Lombardi and his son Roderigo played for the CONFIDENTI in France in 1572 under the name of *Balanzoni. Ballanzone,* however, survives as one of the Doctor's nicknames on the puppet-stage. C. Ricci, *I Teatri di Bologna nei secoli XVII e XVIII,* derives it from a dialectal 'Balla, boasting'; but Sarti prefers the spelling with a single 'l', which makes possible the etymology of 'Balanza = bilancia, balance', satirizing the Doctor as a would-be arbitrator.

Materazzi, FRANCESCO, taking it by turns with

Muzio, ANGELO ANTONIO, as *Graziani* in the company of the Duke of Modena 1688. Rasi, ii. 112 and 589.

Milanta, GIUSEPPE, *Dottor Lanternone* in the company of the Duke of Parma 1655–87. Rasi, ii. 123. See also *supra,* A. G. B. A. Lolli.

Nannini, GIOVANNI, *c.* 1689. Rasi, ii. 174.

Nelli, HERCOLE, with the CONFIDENTI in Genoa, 17.7.1627. In 1650 he took the part of a *Zanni* in the company of the Duke of Modena, but in 1651 is mentioned again as Dottor Nelli.

Orlandi, GIUSEPPE, of Ferrara, in the company of the Duke of Modena 1675. Rasi, i. 200.

Paghetti, GIOVAN BATTISTA, in the company of the Duke of Modena 1686 and succeeded by

Savorini, GALEAZZO, *c.* 1689. Rasi, ii. 507.

Romagnesi, CINTIO, succeeded G. A. Lolli. Rasi, i. 433.

Soldano, ANIELLO. *Dottor Spacca Strummolo, Napolitano,* with the FEDELI in 1609. Published the *Fantastiche e Ridiculose etimologie* and *La Fondazione ed origine di Bologna,* 1610. Rasi, i. 164.

Zenari, ZANARDI, see *supra,* ANDREAZZO.

VARIANT NAMES FOR THE MASK OF THE *DOCTOR* FOUND IN PLAYS AND RHYMES BUT NOT YET IDENTIFIED WITH INDIVIDUAL ACTORS

Balestron. See *Testamento di Scappino,* 1638.

Graciano da BUDRI da Francolino, occurs in A. Pasqualigo's *Gl'In-*

tricati, 1581. The surname is common, see *Il Finto Principe* by C. Ambrosi (Allacci, 1729) for **Dottor Battocchio da Budri.** The Doctor in Andreini's *La Campanaccia* is **Gracian Campaz da Budri.** The name appears as **Dottor Campanazzius, de Budrio** in the title-page of *Scaramuzza memeo squaquera de civitate Partenopensi* quoted by Rasi, i. 890, and as **Campazzo da Budri** in the two comedies of D. Balbi, *Il Cacciatore*, undated, and *Il Secondo Zanni detto Bagattino favorito da Amore*, 1678.

Dottor *LUCERNA CANNELLACCIO*, is introduced by A. Scaramuccia into *Rosalba*, 1638.

Dottor *GRAS'DA MILAN dalle Foleghe, fiol de sopare nassad d'una donna, allevad a Bonarogna, della Terra de Francolin, dottorad in Ponte Molin*, is the absurd style assumed by the Doctor in *I Pazzi Amanti*, by L. Riccato da Castel Franco, 1638, Act IV, sc. 6.

Dottor *CARLETTO PIRLONE da Francolino* takes the title role in L. A. Cotta's *La Pirlonea*. For the dating of this play see Appendix B.

COVIELLO, Dottor Napolitano, occurs in Verucci's plays *La Portia*, 1609, and *Pantalone Imbertonao*, 1617. The name also was used for the parts of the servant, the old man, and the captain.

Dottor *CIGALON BATOCCHIO da Varegnara* is a late variation found in Nanni's comedy, *La finta verità nel medico per amore*, 1703, quoted by Sarti, *Teatro dialettale bolognese*, p. 99.

ACTORS TAKING THE PART OF THE *CAPITANO*

Ancatoni, DIEGO, Spaniard, *Capitano Sangue e Fuoco*, noted in Rome, 1658. Rasi, i. 39. One of the actors who owed money to Angelleli. 'Jarro', p. 27.

Andreini, FRANCESCO. *Capitano Spavento del Vall'Inferno*, with the GELOSI. See Chap. V, p. 17 seq.

In his *Bravure*, Rag, xvii, Andreini produces other fantastic names: *Capitano Ariararche, Diacatolicon, Leucopigo, Melampigo.*

Antonazzoni, FRANCESCO, gave up the more studious part of the 'amoroso' and took to the braggart soldier. Rasi, i. 964.

Beretta, FEDERIGO, *Capitano Spagnuolo, c.* 1675. Rasi, i. 354.

Bianchi, GIUSEPPE. *Capitano Spezzaferro*, in Paris 1645–80. Rasi, i. 417.

Boniti, NICOLA, *Capitano Spacca, Napolitano*. Rasi, i. 487.

Capitano CARDONE. With the GELOSI 1589 and the UNITI 1584 and 1593. Mentioned by Catrani in 1598. D'Ancona, ii. 525.

The mask is used by Scala and twice by Locatelli, i. 3 and 30, but the proper name of the actor is never revealed. See Chap. V, pp. 18, 19, and Chap. II, p. 54.

Fiala, GIUSEPPE ANTONIO, *Capitano Sbranaleone* in the company of the Duke of Modena, 1651. Rasi, i. 876.

Fiorillo, SILVIO, *Capitano Mattamoros*. In 1584 leader of a troupe in Naples; in 1600 in the service of the Duke of Mantua; in 1612 rejected from the company proposed for France as not being 'what he was six years ago'. Baschet, p. 225.

In 1614 Fiorillo belonged to the UNITI but still styled himself 'ACCESO' on the title-page of *La Cortesia di Leone*. In 1619 he was suggested, but evidently not adopted as a member of Scala's CONFIDENTI. In 1620–1 with the company of P. M. Cecchini, *Giorn. Stor.* xcii. 209.

Bartoli, A., p. cl, gives Fiorillo as the sole member of a company of Comici RISOLUTI which is otherwise unknown. In his play *Li Tre Capitani Vanagloriosi*, 1621, the companions of *Mattamoros* are *Don Corte Rincone* and *Tempesta*.

Fiorillo, TIBERIO *Scaramuccia,* for the UNITI in 1614 played a part which is an offshoot from that of the Spanish Captain: later he made his name as *Trapolino,* q.v.

Fornaris, FABRITIO DE, *Capitano Coccodrillo* with the CONFIDENTI 1571–84. Published *Angelica* in Paris, 1584.

Garavini, GIROLAMO, of Ferrara, *Capitano Rinoceronte* with the FEDELI until his death in 1624. Rasi, i. 986. The mask is used in Cotta's *La Pirlonea*.

Capitano D. Lopez is mentioned by Scala on 8 July 1615 as a member of the CONFIDENTI but his real name is not given.

Manzani, FRANCESCO, *Capitano Terremoto,* in 1661 translated *A gran danno gran rimedio* from the Spanish. Rasi, ii. 68.

Medoro possibly as Captain's part. See Cecchini's letter 22 July, 1620. Arch. Mant. Milano, xlix, Busta, 1751.

Tortoriti, GIUSEPPE, of Messina, played the Captain alternately with the masks of *Pascariello Tuono* and *Scaramuccia*. Rasi, ii. 591.

VARIANT NAMES FOR THE *CAPITANO* FOUND IN PLAYS AND RHYMES ETC. NOT YET ATTRIBUTABLE TO INDIVIDUAL ACTORS

CAPTAINS in plays belonging to the Commedia dell'arte tradition:
Bombarditamente in Verucci's *Dispettoso Marito*, 1612.
Dragonteo in Verucci's *Pantalone Innamorao*, 1619.
Fumovento in A. Bennetti's *Scherno di Giove, overo Li Dei Mascherati*, 1636.

Rompilancia⎱ in Briccio's *La Bella Negromantessa*, 1621.
Strappaferro⎰

Polimestre ⎱ in F. Gattici's *Le Pazzie Giovenili*, 1636.
Sferamondo⎰

Serpentone in Tiberii's *Li Tre Amanti Burlati*, 1683.

Sputasaette in D. Balbi's *Il Secondo Zanne*, 1678.

Scuotimondo in Lassari's *Gl'Amori Disturbati*, 1681.

Tagliavento in T. Lunardi's *Il Servo Fidele*, 1586.

CAPTAINS in rhymes and pamphlet literature:

Deluvio ⎱ 1613.
Spantega⎰

Spezzacapo⎱ 1606.
Sputasaette⎰

Belerofonte
Scarabombardone⎱ See Rasi, i, pp. 64, 73.
Smedola

ACROBATIC CAPTAINS from Callot's engravings:

Pasquarello, Meo Squaquara, Tagliacantoni, Bombardon, Cerimonia, Mam Gamba, Bella Vita, Zerbino, Babeo, Escgangarato, Grillo, Spessamonti.

CAPTAINS from Commedie Erudite:

Ascanio, Neapolitan. *Li Pensieri Fallacci*, 1626.

Bellerfonte⎱ *Prigioni d'amore.* Sforza degli Oddi, 1590.
Fagiuolo ⎰

Fiacavento, Sicilian. *La Vedova*, Cini, 1569.

Fracasso. *Emilia*, 1579, and *La Beffa*, 1584.

Frangimonte, known later as **Scarabombardone** in N. Biancolelli's *Regina Statista*, 1668.

Hannibale, in Parabosco's *Marinaio*, 1560.

Malagigi, in Piccolomini's *Alessandro*, 1562.

Spavento, in Parabosco's *Pellegrino*, 1552.

Taddeo, in Grazzini's *La Strega*, 1582.

Termodonte, in Della Rovere's *Lo Spedale*, 1646.

Tiberio, German, in Bulgarini's *Gli Scambi*, acted 1574.

Tinca, in Aretino's *La Talenta*, 1553. / a

Zeladelpho, in Gabiani's *I Gelosi*, 1606.

ACTORS TAKING THE PART OF THE *ZANNI*

Only those Zanni names which can be proved to have belonged to individual players are given in the first list; the fantastic coinages found in rhymes, plays, and scenari are relegated to the second. The difficulties of identification are increased by the habit of referring to actors by the name of their masks to the exclusion of their proper names, so that it has seemed more convenient in this case to allow the stage names to take precedence and determine the alphabetical order. This arrangement has the advantage of showing more clearly the inheritance of the masks from one generation of actors to another.

ARLECCHINO, played by TRISTANO MARTINELLI, DOMENICO BIANCOLELLI, EVARISTO GHERARDI. See Chaps. II and V.

BAGOLINO, a member of the CONFIDENTI in 1627 and 1638; an actor owing money to Angelleli ('Jarro', p. 27) and a member of the company proposed for the Duke of Parma in 1664, but hitherto not identified. Rasi, i. 854.

BERTOLINO. There was a Bertolino among the UNITI in 1584, but he could hardly have been the Nicolo ZECCA who played the part at least until 1670. In 1672 Ambrogia BROGLIA had assumed the mask. Rasi, i. 515.

BRIGHELLA. The name occurs as early as 1602 in G. Gabrielli's comedy *Il Studio,* and was used by a member of the CONFIDENTI in 1638.

D. BONONCINI and TOMMASO FORTUNATI adopted this mask at the end of the seventeenth century. Rasi, i. 488 and 937.

BUFFETTO, an actor in the company directed by Carpiani with whom Fidenzi wished to join up in 1638. Rasi, i. 881. Possibly this was the famous Carlo CANTÙ himself. (1609– c. 1676.) Rasi, i. 571.

BURATTINO. One of the actors with Ganassa in Spain, according to Ottonelli, *Della Cristiana Moderazione,* ii. 27. A member of the GELOSI in 1589, see Chap. V, p. 19. The mask is common in the plays and scenari, q.v.

CIAMBELLOTTO, stage name of an actor otherwise known only as GIOVAN PIETRO of PADUA, *fl.* 1546–9. See Chap. V, p. 256.

COLA, ANIELLO DI MAURO, with the ACCESI in 1605, and the FEDELI in 1609. See Chap. V, pp. 281, 286.

CORTELLACCIO, IPPOLITO MONTINI of the UNITI in 1614 and a member of the COSTANTI.

FARGNOCCOLA or FROGNOCOLA, a Zanni noted by Montaigne in 1581. See *Voyage en Italie,* ed. D'Ancona, 1895, p. 488. The alternative form is found among the rhymes of *Sivello* Gabrielli.

FARINA, when in August 1612 T. Martinelli describes an actor as *'ZAN FARINA overo SCAPINO,'* he can only be referring to FRANCESCO GABRIELLI, later *Scapino* of the CONFIDENTI.

The alternative names move from the general to the particular: Farina, with its allusion to the 'lazzo' of flouring the face, was the more common Zanni name and occurs as early as 1585 in G. S. Martini's *Bragatto* as **Gian Farina**.

FICHETO, on the authority of 'Jarro' and Sanesi, Lorenzo Nettuni played under this name with the CONFIDENTI in 1610 and in company with the Andreini in France in 1620. It was certainly the mask of Eustachio Lolli, *c.* 1650.

FINOCCHIO. Rasi refers to Silvio Gambi, an actor mentioned but once in 1595 as *Finocchio*. In 1620 Cecchini wrote that Paolo Zanotti had become as fine a Zanni as 'Scappino' and recommended him for the troupe proposed for France. From the list of the CONFIDENTI in 1627 it appears that Zanotti had taken the name of *Finocchio,* possibly punning upon the word either in its meaning of 'fennel' or in its idiomatic use, 'dare finocchio = to flatter'.

It was adopted successively by A. Cimadori (fl. *c.* 1675) G. B. Paruti (*c.* 1686); C. Zagnoli (*c.* 1689), and G. Bissoni (*c.* 1723).

FLAUTINO, Giovanni Gherardi, *c.* 1675. Rasi, i. 1006.

FRANCATRIPPE, Gabriele Panzanini da Bologna, with the GELOSI, the UNITI in 1593 and later with the COSTANTI. See Chap. II, p. 80, and V, pp. 262, 266.

FRITELLINO, Pier Maria Cecchini with the ACCESI, q.v. chap. V, 280 seq.

GALLOTTA, second Zanni for the FEDELI in 1619. See *Giorn. Stor.* xxiv. 103.

GANASSA, Alberto Naseli. See Chap. II, p. 81, and V, p. 259 seq.

GIANGURGOLO, an actor whose death is mentioned by E. Coris in 1658. Rasi, i. 700. See also *infra*, p. 158.

GONELLA, a Zanni suggested as a substitute for *Mezzettino* among Scala's CONFIDENTI in July 1627. See Arch. Med. Fa. 5176, c. 464.

GRADELLINO, C. Constantini acted under this name in 1687. Rasi, i. 708 and ii. 588. Garzoni and Bocchini record the mask of **GRADELLA,** a name suggesting a pun on the word for a 'grid'.

GUAZZETTO, Zanni for the AFFEZIONATI, *c.* 1634. In Verucci's *Pantalone Innamorato,* 1663, Guazzetto is a Perugian servant. Callot sketches him as a Zanni type, the name evidently puns upon the meaning of 'sauce or pottage'.

LUCCA, mask of Areliari in the company of the Duke of Modena, *c.* 1675.

MESCOLINO, the mask of Pietro di RE, *c.* 1625. Rasi, ii. 333. Probably meaning the 'meddler'.

MEZZETTINO, Ottavio ONORATI, Zanni for Scala's CONFIDENTI. Later used by Angelo COSTANTINI as a successor to Biancolelli's Arlequin. Rasi, i. 710.

PAGLIACCIO, according to Ottonelli (ii. 37) this mask belonged to an actor in the company of *Ganassa*: there is no further evidence.

PASQUINO, Giovan Battista TREZZI takes the place of Zanetti's *Truffaldino* in the company of the Duke of Modena. 1689.

PEDROLINO, Giovanni PELESINI DA REGGIO, see Chaps. II and V, for page references see Index.

POGGINO, Pier Francesco SCARLATTI, a pathetic appeal from this old actor, who at the age of 72 found himself almost completely blind and starving, survives in the Medici correspondence. Filza 1 Jan. 1620, 5141, *c.* 1137.

PULCINELLA. For a discussion of the development of this mask and its various impersonators see Chap. II, p. 88 seq. and Index.

RAVANEL, mentioned by Rossi in the list of comedians found by Bergamino in the underworld before 1584. See *La Fiammella*, 1584.

SCAPINO, Francesco GABRIELLI, faithful to Scala's CONFIDENTI. See Chap. V, p. 295 seq. Paolo ZANOTTI modelled himself on Gabrielli who had made a name for himself as a musical Zanni by his performance upon a variety of instruments. See *Testamento di Scapino,* and under Finocchio, *supra.* F. Bartoli records the performances of CHIARELLI and Antonio CAMERANI in the mask. Rasi, i. 652.

SIVELLO, Giovanni GABRIELLI, father of Francesco, a free-lance comedian giving mono-plays. Author of *Il Studio.* Rasi, i. 953.

STEFANEL BOTTARGA. See under 'Pantalone'.

STOPINO, an actor owing money to Angelleli. 'Jarro', p. 27. As a Zanni name Stopino occurs in the Florentine and Venetian miscellanies of scenari.

TARTAGLIA is often, but not exclusively a servant's part. He might appear as a parent, or older stranger, and is recognizable by his stammer. According to Rasi (i. 867), who gives no evidence and may only be quoting the untrustworthy Maurice Sand, the part was taken by Ottavio FERRARESE of whom Croce has found a trace in Naples in 1612. Though the mask seems to be more popular towards the end of the century and is commonly used in the Florentine, Venetian, and Neapolitan miscellanies, it certainly existed as early as 1613, when it is used by

Righello in *Il Pantalone Impazzito*. In the casting of the scenario of *Plauto alla Moderna* for the *Signori Convittori delle Camere piccole del Seminario Romano* in 1693 the part was allotted to S. Dom. Ricci.

TRAPPOLINO, though used as the surname was evidently the mask of a certain Giovan PAOLO. According to Quadrio, after a successful career as a Zanni he retired from the stage and ended his days towards 1630 in a hermitage near Venice. About this time Giovan BATTISTA, son of Silvio FIORILLO, assumed the mask. As a young man he had taken the part of Scaramuccia for the UNITI in 1614, but among the AFFEZIONATI in 1634, the CONFIDENTI in 1638, and later in the patronage of the Duke of Modena he is known as *Trappolino*.

TRASTULLO ('solace, pastime') is coupled with *Ganassa* by Lope de Vega in *Filomena*, Epistola IV. This suggests that it was a mask in the Italian company whose performances Lope relished in Madrid in 1588. See Perez Pastor, *Proceso de Lope de Vega por libelos contra unos cómicos*, 1901, p. 41. The name occurs also in F. Cittadonio's *Forza dell'Honore*, 1654, and in *Gratiano Infuriato*, 1679, by G. M. Cesarij da Budrio, and is one of the figures sketched by Callot.

TRIVELLINO was played by Andrea FRAJACOMI for the UNITI in 1614, but is better known as the mask of Domenico LOCATELLI (1613–71); in the second half of the seventeenth century the part was taken by Carlo SANGIORI. Rasi, ii. 502.

TRUFFALDINO (cp. Florio's gloss of 'truffarello' as 'a craftie, cheating, pilfering, cunnie-catching or crosse-biting knave') was among the few actors left with Cecchini in 1620 when the Andreini had swept off the pick of the company to France. See D'Ancona, *Lettere di comici*. Per Nozze Martini-Benzoni, 1893. See *supra*, Chap. V, p. 289. Later played by Francesco MOZZANA, *c.* 1650 (Rasi, ii. 168), and Marc Antonio ZANETTI, *c.* 1688. (Rasi, ii. 588 and 730.)

VOLPINO. G. Cesare BARBIERI was suggested as a second Zanni in the company of the Duke of Parma in 1664. Rasi, i. 854.

ZACCAGNINO, the mask of G. C. TORRI, *c.* 1650. In the illustration of the *Cucina per il pasto de Zantripuande* reproduced by Duchartre (p. 60), the Zanni playing with Mª. Bolzarina is labelled *Zan Zaccagni*.

ZANNI, SIMONE DA BOLOGNA for the GELOSI and G. B. VANNINI DA RIMINI for the CONFIDENTI seem to have been content with the simple original name. See also under H. NELLI, Dottore.

ZANNIN, the stage name of MAPHIO DEL RE of Padua, 1545.

ZANNI NAMES OCCURRING IN PLAYS, RHYMES, AND ILLUSTRA-
TIONS NOT YET IDENTIFIED WITH INDIVIDUAL ACTORS

See CHAPTER II, p. 99.

Baccalaro (cp. 'baccala, stockfish'). Bocchini, see Rasi, i. 458.

Badil (cp. 'badile, a spade'). See *supra*, App. A.

Baggatino, in Balbi's *Il Secondo Zanne detto Bagattino,* 1678.
The nickname, which is probably connected with 'bagati', a
Venetian coin worth less than a farthing, is found also in the
forms:

Bagot, see App. A.

Bagatellino in *La Fortuna* by C. Sicinio, 1610. The Bagattino of the
CONFIDENTI in 1627 was commended as a worthy successor to
Arlecchino.

Bagatto, see rhymes quoted by Stoppato, p. 26.

Battocchio (Florio glosses the word as 'a bell clapper . . . also a belly
clapper'). See *La Vittoria,* by F. Rotondi da Sonnino, 1650.
Bocchini prefixes it by Pitocco ('a crafty beggar', Florio).

Benoualla, see Callot's sketches.

Biscottino. In *La Finta Serva* Minacci advises the reader that the
part of *Biscottino,* the second Zanni, has been given in Tuscan,
so that those who are inexpert may play the fool each in his
own lingo, while those who can manage the Bergomask dialect
will be able to supply it for themselves.

Bizzarro ('fantastical') in Rhymes, see App. A.

Boccalino (cp. 'bocal, a bottle, sot') used by Bocchini. Rasi, i. 458.

Bragatto gives the title to G. S. Martini's comedy 1596 and is used by
Sorio in *I Forestieri,* 1611. Compare 'braghetta, a cod-piece'.

Broza (cp. 'brozze, scabs'). See App. A.

Candellotta (cp. 'candelotti, droppings of candles'). Bocchini.

Capella (cp. 'fare un capello ad uno, to give a check or rebuke'). Rasi,
i. 463.

Capocchia (cp. 'capocchio, a loggerhead'). Bocchini.

Chiappazza (cp. 'chiappare, to snatch' or 'Chiappa, haunch . . . clap').
Bocchini.

Cianfrone in Briccio's *Dispettosa Moglie,* 1629. Cianfrone is a
Neapolitan servant, but the gloss from Florio 1611 explains his
Zanni habits and origin: 'Cianfrone, Zanfrone, a lusty lad,
a swaggering gallant, a tosse-pot companion'.

Ciurlo, see Callot's sketches.

Coccolino ('the squatter') occurs once in A. Scarramuccia's *La Rosalba,*
1638.

Zan Corneto, see A. Beijer, plates xiv, xx, xxiv, xxxiv, xxxvii.

Cucorongna⎫
Cucubu ⎬ Callot's sketches.
Cucurucu ⎭

Culada (cp. 'culate, buttocks'). Rhymes, see App. A.

Descodo, see Modenese scenari.

Faloppa (the cod of a silk worm) occurs once in Verucci's *Ersilia,* 1625.

Filono, see Duchartre, p. 67.

Fracasso is a doubtful case; in Callot's sketch he is dressed as a Zanni, but in Secchi's *La Beffa* he takes the part of a Captain. The name with its meaning, 'hurly-burly', would be appropriate to both.

Fritada (cp. 'fritata, pancake'). See Garzoni and rhymes App. A.

Frognocola (cp. 'frignoccola, a phip or flurt with one's finger-ends', Florio, 1611). See Zerbini, op. cit., p. 59. Rasi, i. 956. Cp. *Farnoccola, supra,* App. A.

GABINETTO is a comic servant in Gioanelli's *Arlechino finto bassa d'Algieri* and Cicognini's *Moglie di quatro mariti.* In 1648 N. Zecca, *Bertolino,* enclosed a letter to *Gabinetto* who was in Florence. D'Ancona, *Lettere di Comici.* Per Nozze Martini-Benzoni, 1893. The name was used in the form of **Gabionetto** by an actor in 1687. Rasi, i. 878. (Cp. 'gabionetto, a large cage'.)

GIANGURGOLA. In N. Monaseni's *Truffaldino finto Paagallo,* he is the keeper of the madhouse. In *La Prodigalità d'Arlecchino* Gioanelli designates him Giangurgolo Patazzo Notaro. Bocchini spells the name **Zan Gurgolo.** Rasi connects the mask with the Calabrian Captains. Cp. Fracasso. See also *supra,* p. 52.

Lupino ('wolfish'). Bocchini.

Magagnia (cp. 'mafagnare, to corrupt'). Rasi, i. 956.

Mestolino (cp. Florio, 'a little mestolino, an idle gull, a loggerhead good for nothing but to handle a ladle'). See Callot.

Mortadella ('sausage') in Verucci's *Dispettoso Marito,* 1612.

Padella ('frying-pan'). See rhymes, App. A.

Pagnotta ('a bun', also, 'a squatting down') in Bricci's *Dispettosa Moglie,* 1629.

Pernoualla, see Callot's sketches.

Persutto (Bergomask, 'a ham') in Verucci's *Pantalone Innamorato,* 1663.

Pistone (Bergomask, 'pestle or arquebus') in Bricci's *La Tartaruca,* 1677.

Pocointesa ('little wit') in Lombardi's *Alchemista,* 1583.

Ratsa di Boio⎫
Razullo   ⎬ See Callot's sketches.

Rodelin ('rotella, a little wheel, or, rotellino, a goldsmith's tool') used by Bocchini and occurring in the scenari of the Venetian collection.

Scalogna ('a young onion'). Bocchini.

Scarsella ('a pouch'), see rhymes App. A.

Scartezza (possibly from 'scartassare', to rib-baste with a cudgell, also to raile at, Florio, 1611). Bocchini.

Scatolino ('a round flat box'). Bocchini.

Sonagio (possibly from 'sonacchiare', to be drowsy). Bocchini.

STENTERELLO, an eighteenth-century mask. See G. Cocchiara, 'St. e le Stenterellate' in *Giorn. Stor.* xcix, 1932.

Tombolino ('tumbler') in Verucci's *Pulcinella, amante di Colombina.*

Traccagnino in the *Infermità e Testamento . . . di Scappino.* See *supra,* p. 59.

Tramezzino ('meddler') in C. Tiberi's *Li Tre Amanti Burlati,* 1683.

Trippone (Florio glosses 'trippone' as a 'filthy, foule, fat greasie or gorbellied fellow'). Bocchini. Cp.

Zan Tripu of the rhymes and *Zan Tripuande* in the woodcut reproduced by Duchartre, p. 60. Nicoll, p. 358, corrects this as a misreading for the legend 'Cucina per il pasto de Zan Trippu quando prese moglie'.

Zan de la Vigna, mentioned by Garzoni.

ACTORS TAKING THE PART OF THE *INNAMORATO*

I return to the arrangement according to the proper names of the actors, using italics for the stage names when no other is recorded.

Allori, FRANCESCO, *Valerio,* flourished during the second half of the seventeenth century. Rasi, i. 29.

Andreini, G. B., *Lelio,* of the FEDELI. See Chap. V.

Angiolo, mentioned by N. Zecca in a letter to the Duke of Mantua, 8.12.1648, but not otherwise identifiable.

Antonazzoni, FRANCESCO, *Ortenzio* for Scala's CONFIDENTI. Chap. V. See also among the Captains.

AURELIO. That *Aurelio* might be taken either as a proper or an assumed name aggravates the difficulty of sorting out the actors referred to by this name alone. Rasi (i. 236) quotes a document published by Belgrano mentioning a certain *Aurelio,* apparently a professional, who directed a troupe of Genoese amateurs in 1610. There is nothing to help us to choose between Adriano VALERI *Aurelio* for the GELOSI, Marcello de' SECCHI *Aurelio* for the CONFIDENTI under Scala, and one of the two, and possibly three, other actors who used this name during the first half of the seventeenth century. In 1620 a young *Aurelio* took leave of absence from Cecchini and went home to Naples. Explaining his delay in returning to the company in 1621 he styled himself *Aurelio Fedeli,* presumably because he had formerly belonged to that company, since Silvio Fiorillo his travelling companion referred to him as *Aurelio a Porto.* The publication of this letter by Miss Winifred Smith in the *Giornale Storico* for 1928 (vol. xcii, p. 209) discredits Rasi's suggestion that this *Aurelio* was to be identified with the *Aurelio* TESTA who was killed in Naples in 1630. The connexion of *Aurelio* a PORTO with the FEDELI makes it unlikely, but not impossible, that he was the *Aurelio* described by Ottonelli—who met him in Florence in 1640—as the leader of the UNITI. Any one of these two or three might be the *Aurelio* described by F. Bartoli as a 'capo-comico' who flourished about 1630, the author of a lost pamphlet entitled *Della Cristiana Moderazione del teatro.*

Bachino, GIOVAN MARIA, *Fortunio,* mentioned by Cecchini in 1620. See Chap. V, p. 288.

Battista, VERONESE, mentioned by De Nores in the *Apologia contra l'autor del Veraldo* and assumed to be a contemporary of Pasquati and Orazio Nobili. Rasi, i. 307.

Bendinelli, GIACINTO, *Valerio* in the company of Eustachio Lolli *c.* 1650, died 1668. Rasi, i. 342.

Biancolelli, NICOLO, played the 'Inamorato' in the company of *Fabrizio c.* 1650. See App. B for a list of plays translated.

Botanelli, VINCENZO, ROMANO, *Curzio* played in an 'autò' in Toledo in 1579 for 50,000 maravedis and in 1581 was with *Ganassa's* company. See Cotarelo, *Revista de Archivos,* 1908, p. 52.

Bruni, DOMENICO, *Fulvio,* with the GELOSI in 1594 and the CONFIDENTI in 1615. See also among the *Doctors.*

Caccamesi, CESARE, an inamorato; died 1668. Rasi, i. 539.

Caccia, GAETANO, *Leandro* in the company of the Duke of Modena 1688–90. Rasi, ii. 588 and 694.

Caldironi, FRANCESCO, detto *Silvio,* commended by Riccoboni as one of the few fine comedians of the second half of the seventeenth century. Caldironi is found in Bergamo in 1664 and later was in particular request in Germany and Flanders. Rasi, i. 542.

Carpiari *or* **Carpioni,** MARC ANTONIO, *Orazio.* Rasi hesitates between the two forms of the surname and reproduces in facsimile a letter written to the Duke of Modena in 1641; later he identifies the actor mentioned in 1638 as 'il Carpiano', as Marc Antonio Carpiani detto *Orazio.* Fidenzi valued him as a

Pantalone, but this was evidently a temporary mask. Three years later he used *Orazio* instead of his Christian name. When the Andreini were stranded in 1626 they proposed to join up with Carpioni for the Carneval in Venice. *Giorn Stor.* xxiv. 125–6.

Castiglione, *Fulvio* with the CONFIDENTI in 1627. Possibly Castiglione was the 'Fulvio detto *Odoardo*' who yielded to *Aurelio* the Neapolitan during the friction between the ACCESI and FEDELI in Milan in 1620. See pp. 149, 303, 318.

Coppa, GIUSEPPE, *Virginio* in the company of the Duke of Modena, *c.* 1689. Rasi, i. 693. See under Bellisario and Ipsicratea (App. F).

Coris, BERNARDINO, *Silvio, fl. c.* 1643–58. Rasi, i. 701.

Costante, VIRGINIO, from the single notice of this actor at the head of the list of the Comici COSTANTI, quoted by Rasi, i. 743, it is not possible to determine whether *Virginio* was a stage or a proper name, or again, whether the company was known by his surname or he surnamed from the company. The letter is undated but evidently belongs to the first decades of the seventeenth century, for *Aurelio* de' Secchi, Virginio's fellow on this occasion, was dead before 1617.

Costantini, GIOVAN BATTISTA, detto *Cintio* in the company of the Duke of Modena during the last quarter of the seventeenth century.

Cotta, PIETRO, *Celio,* see list of plays published by actors and Rasi, i. 728.

Fabio, mentioned by B. Rossi in 1584 and by Garzoni in 1585.

Fabri, GIOVAN PAOLO, *Flaminio* with the UNITI in 1584, 1593, and 1614; with the GELOSI in 1603; and in 1612 suggested by T. Martinelli as a likely member for a troupe proposed for France; probably the *Flaminio* again recommended in 1619, but still with Bachino's company in 1620. See p. 288.

In 1608 Fabri published *Due Suppliche e due Ringraziamenti alla Bernesca, Quatro Sonetti Spirituali,* and *Rime Varie la maggior parte lugubri* in 1613. He contributed verses and prologues to three of G. B. Andreini's comedies.

Fabrizio, lover in the company of the Duke of Modena in 1664, and possibly to be identified with the *Fabrizio* who was leader of a company in Naples in 1650. Rasi, i. 854.

Favella, GIRONIMO, mentioned in 1631 as taking the part of the 'Disgraziatissimo innamorato'. Rasi, i. 863.

Fedele, see LUTIO.

Fidenzi, JACOPO ANTONIO, *Cintio* with the ACCESI in 1608 and 1613; with the FEDELI 1609 and 1617; with the CONFIDENTI in 1627; in the patronage of the Farnese in 1633 and 1650.

Rasi, i. 881. Fidenzi contributed verses to *Le Rime funebri* for *Delia* Rocca-Nobili in 1613; and published three sonnets and an ode as *Un Effetto di Divozione* in 1628; and *Poetici Capricci* in 1652. Rasi, i. 883.

FLAMINIO, an actor whose performance at Linz in 1569 is recorded by Trautmann.

Francesco Antonio, alias *Fabritio,* mentioned as acting in Sicily in 1621. He is probably the *Fabrizio* suggested by Martinelli for his company for France in 1620. See p. 289.

Grisanti, GIOVAN AGOSTINO, *Mario* a popular 'amoroso' at least between 1650 and 1664 in the patronage of the Dukes of Parma and Modena. Rasi, i. 1042.

HORATIO, described as a Florentine in the record of a payment for a performance at Linz in 1570. Trautmann, p. 292.

LAVINIO, with the AFFEZIONATI, *c.* 1632-4.

LEONARDO, in the company of the Duke of Modena in 1664. Rasi, i. 855.

LUTIO, with the UNITI in 1584, and possibly to be identified with the LUTIO FEDELE of the GELOSI as that company was specially constituted in 1593. See Chap. II, p. 36, and V, p. 267.

Maffei, BENEDETTO was brought up by *Flaminia* Cecchini. It is not certain whether his assumed name of *Il Furioso* was a stage name or merely a nom-de-plume for his *Discorsi da Commedia.* Rasi, ii. 51.

Mangini, ANDREA, *Adriano* with the UNITI in 1614.

Napoleone, MARCO, *Flaminio* in the patronage of the Dukes of Parma and of Modena in the middle of the seventeenth century. Napoleone translated 22 plays from the Spanish and was probably the author of the comedy of *Flaminio pazzo per amore* and the possessor of the miscellany of speeches for the hero of this play which is now in the possession of Senatore Croce. See *supra,* p. 106.

Narici, BERNARDO, of Genoa, *Orazio* in the patronage of the Duke of Modena during the last quarter of the seventeenth century.

Negri, DOMENICO DE, *Curzio* with the UNITI in 1614.

Nobili, ORAZIO, of the GELOSI. See *supra,* p. 263.

ODOARDO, in the company of the Duke of Modena in 1664. Rasi, i. 855.

OTTAVIO, with Vittoria Piissimi. See *supra,* p. 263.

Parrino, DOMENICO ANTONIO, *Florindo* from 1675 until his retirement in 1686, in the patronage of the Duke of Modena.

Petignoni, RINALDO, *Fortunio* with the GELOSI from 1574; with the UNITI in 1594.

Pilastri, FRANCESCO, *Leandro* with the UNITI in 1593–4, and possibly the *Leandro* of the CONFIDENTI in 1618.

Ranieri, BARTOLOMEO, *Aurelio* in the patronage of Ferdinando Carlo and popular in Modena, Mantua, and Paris during the last quarter of the seventeenth century.

Raparelli, GIOVANNI, of Viterbo, *Orazio* married *Angiola* and played in the company of the Duke of Modena for a few months. He was arrested in 1658 and no more is known of his movements. Rasi, ii. 324.

Rechiari, LUCA, *Mario* and later *Leandro,* a contemporary of Ranieri. Rasi, ii. 334.

Ricci, BENEDETTO, *Leandro* (1592–1620), nephew of Federigo Ricci Pantalone. Played the second lover for the FEDELI in 1609; with Martinelli in France 1613–14. Possibly Ricci was the *Leandro* who appeared with the CONFIDENTI only during 1618.

Rivani, GIOVANNI, probably one of the lovers in Martinelli's troop for France in 1620.

Romagnesi, in the company of Locatelli in Paris until his death in 1660. Rasi, ii. 394. He was probably the son of Marc Antonio *(Pantalone) Orazio.*

Rossi, BARTOLOMEO, *Orazio.* The publication of *La Fiammella* in Paris 1584 and the references which it contains to the CONFIDENTI of that period associate Rossi with the company.

Scala, FLAMINIO, *Flavio* with the UNITI in 1598; with the ACCESI in France in 1600–1; director of the second CONFIDENTI. See pp. 131–3, 293–5, and Index.

Schiavi, CARLO, *Cintio,* in the patronage of the Duke of Modena during the second half of the seventeenth century. Rasi, ii. 530.

Secchi, MARCELLO DE, *Aurelio,* played in the companies of the COSTANTI and, at least in 1615, with the CONFIDENTI. He died in 1617. See *supra,* under *Aurelio* and *Virginio Costante.*

Servillo, FRANCESCO, *Odoardo, fl. c.* 1660. Rasi, ii. 536.

Sondra, GIUSEPPE, *Flaminio,* in the patronage of the Dukes of Modena and Tuscany during the second half of the seventeenth century. Rasi, ii. 544.

Testa, *Aurelio,* killed in Naples in 1630. See *supra,* under *Aurelio.*

Tommaso, MARIO DI, of Siena, *Lepido* in Naples 1575. See B. Croce, *Teatri di Napoli,* p. 776.

Torri, ANTONIO, *Lelio,* mentioned casually by Rasi as possibly the father or brother of *Anna Maria Torri,* a singer in the patronage of the Duke of Modena. Rasi, ii. 589.

Turri, *Virginio,* in Paris in 1653, unsuccessful on the stage. Rasi, ii. 606.

Valerini, ADRIANO, of Verona, ***Aurelio,*** with the UNITI and GELOSI. See *supra,* p. 264.

Zanotti Cavazzoni, GIOVAN ANDREA, ***Ottavio*** (1632–95), in the service of the Duke of Modena at least from 1647. See list of actors' publications (App. B). Rasi, ii. 742.

Zuccato, VALERIO, possibly played the part of the lover, he is recorded by Sansovino as a comedian in Venice during the first half of the sixteenth century.

ACTRESSES TAKING THE PARTS OF THE *INNAMORATE*

Alberghini, ANGELICA. In 1583 this actress offered her services to the company of the Duke of Mantua. She was probably the ***Angelica*** celebrated by Corbelli after the performance of an amalgamated company of the GELOSI and UNITI in Bergamo *c.* 1580. In 1591 she belonged to the CONFIDENTI and Rasi suggests that she is to be identified with ***Angelica*** the wife of Drusiano Martinelli. Probably she was related to *Lodovico Albergina, Veneziano* recorded in the census of the Mantuan population in 1590, 1591, 1592.

Allori, FRANCESCA, detta ***Ortensia,*** wife of Francesco Allori, q.v. *supra.*

Amorevoli, VITTORIA, detta ***Isabella,*** with the UNITI in 1584 and later with the GELOSI. Rasi, i. 309 and 743.

Andreini, ISABELLA (1562–1604), with the exception of an appearance among the CONFIDENTI in Genova 1589 and among the UNITI in 1601, Isabella was the 'prima donna' of the GELOSI. See Chap. V, p. 265 seq. For poems by and to Isabella Andreini Professor Nicoll has drawn attention to the collection of Borgogni, *Le Muse Toscane,* 1594, pt. 2, pp. 27–30, and *Rime di Diversi Illustri Poeti,* 1599.

Andreini, VIRGINIA-RAMPONI, detta ***Florinda*** (1583–1628), wife of G. B. Andreini and the 'prima donna' of the FEDELE. See *supra,* p. 285 seq.

Andreini, *Lidia,* second wife of Giovan Battista Andreini. See under Virginia Rotari.

ANGELA, commended by Rogna for her performance in Mantua, July 1567. D'Ancona, ii. 449.

Antonazzoni, MARIA DOROTEA, detta ***Lavinia,*** with Scala's CONFIDENTI. See *supra,* p. 295 seq.

Arcagiati, ANNA, detta ***Rosaura,*** in the patronage of the Duke of Modena in 1690. Rasi, i. 694.

Armani, VINCENZA, detta ***Lidia,*** in pastorals ***Clori,*** was the favourite of Federigo Gonzago. Rogna in 1567 and De Preti in 1568 compare her productions in Mantua with those of *Flaminia*. In 1569 she was poisoned in Cremona, and Adriano Valerini, one of her most ardent admirers, provided an effusive funeral oration. Rasi, i. 202.

AURELIA, ROMANA, with the specially constituted GELOSI in 1590.

Austoni, VALERIA-ANTONAZZONI, wife of Battista Austoni and a member of Scala's CONFIDENTI. See *supra*, p. 296.

Bachino, *Silvia,* wife of Giovan Maria Bachino and praised by Cecchini in 1620 as an excellent comedienne.

Bagnacavallo, LIDIA DA, mentioned by B. Rossi as dead in 1584 and celebrated by Garzoni in 1585.

Bajardi, ANTONELLA, of Bologna, detta *Vittoria,* probably to be identified with the Cantella Bajardi who, according to F. Bartoli, took the title-role in *La Vittoria migliorata* in 1620.

Barbarizza, CONCORDIA, recorded in Mantua in 1590. Her precise part is not mentioned. Rasi, i. 265.

Bianchi, BRIGIDA, detta *Aurelia* (1613–1703), the wife of *Orazio* Romagnesi who acted chiefly in France between 1640 and 1683. She composed a comedy, *Inganno fortunato*. Rasi, i. 419.

Bianchi, ORSOLA, sister of Brigida, also a 'prima donna'.

Biancolelli, ORSOLA, *Eularia*. See under CORTESI.

Biancolelli, FRANCESCA-MARIA-APOLLINE, detta *Isabella* (1664–1747), made her début in 1683 but left the stage in 1695 on her marriage. Rasi, i. 437.

Bolico, GIULIA, was invited to join the CONFIDENTI in 1583. Since she refused, D'Ancona supposes that she is to be identified with the Giulia BROLO who appears among the UNITI in the following year. D'Ancona, ii. 485.

Caldironi, AGATA, detta *Flaminia,* wife of Francesco Caldironi.

Camia, GIULIA, of Piacenza, noted in Mantua in 1590.

Castiglione, *Leonora,* with the CONFIDENTI in 1627; in 1630 she begs the Duke to free her from the company of *Leandro* and *Brighella,* but in 1638 she is still associated with them under the leadership of Fidenzi.

Cecchini, ORSOLA, detta *Flaminia,* wife of Pier Maria Cecchini of the ACCESI.

Chiesa, *Isabella,* of the AFFEZIONATI, *c.* 1632–4.

Clarini, VIRGINIA, detta *Rotalinda, c.* 1665, took the parts of older women in serious plays. Rasi, i. 671.

Concevoli, *Florinda,* petitioned to hold a lottery in Milan in 1606 and was allowed to present comedies subject to the usual censorship in 1612.

Constantini, *Diana,* in the company of the Duke of Modena, *c.* 1681. Rasi, i. 723.

Coppa, *Aurelia,* wife of Giuseppe Coppa, q.v.

Coris, *Eularia,* is celebrated for her part in G. B. Andreini's *Maddalena lasciva e penitente.*

Coris, *Florinda,* the wife of Bernardino Coris mentioned in 1643. Whether the *Orsola Coris,* part of whose correspondence with the Duke of Mantua in 1658 is reprinted by Rasi, is to be identified with, or was related to either of these actresses is uncertain.

Cortesi, ORSOLA, detta *Eularia,* wife of Domenico *Biancolelli.* On the retirement of Brigida Bianchi, *Eularia,* who had taken the part of the 'seconda amorosa' for twenty-three years, became 'prima donna' in the Parisian company, until her own retirement in 1691. In 1666 her translation of the Spanish comedy, *La Bella Bruta,* was published in Paris. Rasi, i. 435.

D'Orso, *Angela,* in the patronage of the Prince of Parma during the third quarter of the seventeenth century. Rasi, i. 792.

EMILIA, with the UNITI in Milan in 1594.

Fanegotti, ISABELLA, detta *Vittoria.* In a letter which Rasi dates as about 1660 Isabella protests against acting as the 'serva' side by side with *Flaminia*; Rasi suggests that this was

Fiala, MARZIA, detta *Flaminia, née* NARICI, wife of G. A. Fiala, q.v. under Captains. Rasi, i. 861 and 878.

Fiorillo, BEATRICE, wife of Giovan Battista Fiorillo, first mentioned in 1639, but she may well have been one of the actresses in the company of the AFFEZIONATI who are known to us only by their stage-names. No doubt she was the 'Beatrice' whose performance in Paris in 1653 was commended by Loret. It is surely due to some scribal error that she should be connected with the mask of *Diamantina* which belonged to Patrizia Adami, her companion on this occasion. A *Beatrice* who is recorded by F. Bartoli as acting in Verona *c.* 1663, and another who was in the patronage of the Duke of Mantua in 1695, no doubt belong to a later generation.

Gabrieli, HIPPOLITA, in the patronage of the Duke of Modena in 1663. Rasi, i. 708 and 967.

Gabrielli, GIULIA, detta *Diana,* daughter of Francesco Gabrielli, q.v.

Garavini, MARGARITA, see LUCIANI.

Isola, ANTONIA, detta *Lavinia,* in the patronage of the Duke of Modena during the last half of the seventeenth century. The supposition that when *Lavinia* appears as Antonia Torri, her husband was Antonio Torri, detto *Lelio,* is inconsistent with the notice of *Lavinia,* as the wife of *Zaccagnino,* G. C. Torri, given by Orsola Coris, and confirmed by documents quoted later. Rasi, ii. 587–8.

Isola, ANGIOLA, detta *Leonora,* sister of Antonia.

Liberati, URANIA, detta *Bernetta,* played the part of 'seconda amorosa' for the FEDELI in 1619 and 1620.

Luciani, MARGARITA, detta *Flavia,* married Girolamo Garavini. Although her name only appears in the lists of the ACCESI in 1605 and 1606, she probably stayed with her husband in this company and followed him under the leadership of *Scapino* in 1627. *Supra,* pp. 293, 302.

LUCINIA, an actress recorded as a favourite in Florence by Fynes Moryson, not otherwise identifiable. See *supra,* p. 343. Could this be an error for 'Lavinia', Diana da Ponti?

LUCREZIA, of Siena, admitted as a member of a professional company in Rome in 1564. See *supra,* p. 256.

Maloni, LUCILLA
Maloni, VIRGINIA } Rasi quotes an undated letter in which these actresses ask leave to bring their company to Reggio: the former is probably the *Lucilla* who appeared among the UNITI in Milan in 1594, and the latter the 'Virginia Malloni' of the GELOSI in 1596. One or other must have been the mother of

Malone, Maria, who as *Celia* caused so much trouble in Scala's CONFIDENTI. See *supra,* p. 298 seq.

Marcucci, ANNA, detta *Angiola,* in the company of Fiala in 1686. Rasi suggests that this was Angiola, the daughter of Marzia Fiala. Rasi, ii. 502 and i. 879.

Martinelli, ANGELICA, wife of Drusiano Martinelli. See under ANGELICA ALBERGHINA and pp. 271, 274, 277, 357.

Millita, ANNA MARIA, detta *Cintia,* in the patronage of the Duke of Modena during the last quarter of the seventeenth century.

Minuti, BARBARA, detta *Florinda,* wife of Antonio Cortesi and mother of Orsola Biancolelli, q.v. Rasi, i. 435.

Nadasti, *Lucinda,* 'prima donna' in the company of the Duke of Modena in 1688, and probably the *Sucinda* [*sic*] who shared the part of the second lover with *Flaminia* under the leadership of *Fabrizio* in 1664. Rasi, i. 855 and ii. 173.

NORA, a Florentine actress with the GELOSI in 1590.

Pavoli, MARGARITA, of Mantua, appeals to the Duke of Mantua in 1589 to help her and 'nostro Pantalone': three years later she was favoured by his recommendation to the UNITI. D'Ancona, ii. 493.

Piissimi, VITTORIA, detta *Fioretta.* The consistent use of *'Vittoria'* rather than of *'Fioretta'* in reference to this actress suggests that she did not confine herself to the part of the serving-maid. For her appearance with the GELOSI, the CONFIDENTI, and the UNITI see Chap. V and Index.

Da Ponti, DIANA, detta *Lavinia,* with the CONFIDENTI in 1583, the UNITI in 1586, and the ACCESI in 1600–1, but best known as the leader of the DESIOSI, *supra,* p. 269 seq.

PRUDENZA, of Verona, played the 'seconda amorosa' for the GELOSI and is probably to be distinguished from

PRUDENZA, 'prima donna' of the AFFEZIONATI, *c.* 1632–4.

Rocca Nobili, CAMILLA, detta *Delia,* with the CONFIDENTI and famous for her versatility as 'lover, warrior, shepherdess, noble lady, maidservant and queen'. The foremost players of her day contributed to the 'funebre rime' which were published in her honour in 1613.

Rotari, VIRGINIA, detta *Lidia,* of the FEDELI. In 1620 Cecchini refers to this actress as *'baldina',* a nickname coined from the Christian name of her first husband, Baldo Rotari. She was accused of gross flirtation with G. B. Andreini, who protested that it would be a punishment indeed to find oneself enamoured of such a creature, but made her his second wife in 1628. See *supra,* pp. 287, 288, 292.

Sabolini, TERESA CORONA, detta *Diana,* in the company of the Duke of Modena in 1684. Rasi, i. 179. Married G. B. Costantini. Ibid. i. 723.

Sacchi, *Armellina,* in the company of the Duke of Modena in 1690. Rasi, i. 894.

Salamona, *Angela,* was one of the three married women who accompanied their husbands in the troupe of the CONFIDENTES ITALIANOS to whom special permission was granted in 1587. See Perèz Pastor, *Nuevos Datos,* pp. 19–23.

Servilli, ISABELLA, detta *Eularia,* in the patronage of the Duke of Mantua during the last quarter of the seventeenth century and the first of the eighteenth. Rasi, ii. 532.

Torri, ANTONIA, see ISOLA.

Trenta, LUCILLA, detta *Rosalba,* mentioned in connexion with the accusation of Niccolo Ala, her lover, in 1636. Rasi, ii. 602.

VIOLINA, suggested by D. Bruni in July 1616 as a possible substitute for *Valeria* Austoni in the CONFIDENTI. Her husband was characterless but she was a quick study. By September the Austoni were reconciled to the rest of the company and no more is heard of *Violina.*

VITTORIA, an actress commended in 1687. Probably in the company of the Duke of Modena with *Virginio* Coppa, her companion. See App. F under *Bellisario* and *Ipsicratea.*

Zuccato, POLONIA, wife of Valerio Zuccato, recorded in Paris in 1572 and dead before the publication of B. Rossi's *La Fiammella,* 1584.

ACTRESSES TAKING THE PART OF THE *FANTESCA*

Adami, PATRIZIA, detta *Diamantina* (1635–93). Her second husband was G. B. Lolli, *Dottor Baloardo,* with whom she acted in France until 1683. See also under BEATRICE FIORILLO.

Areliari, TEODORA, detta *Vittoria,* who played the maid to her husband's mask of *Lucca* in the company of the Duke of Modena in 1675. According to Rasi her daughter was also on the stage but no name is given (ii. 199).

BARZELLATA, wife of Francesco Bolognese, suggested by Cecchini to take the place of *Olivetta* in 1620.

Battista da Treviso⎫
Bernardini   ⎬ see *infra,* FRANCESQUINA.
                  ⎭

Biancolelli, CATERINA, detta *Columbina,* in Paris during the last quarter of the seventeenth century. See also under FRANCHINI.

Carletto, see *infra,* FRANCESQUINA.

Costantini, DOMENICA, detta *Corallina,* wife of Costantino Costantini, *Gradellino,* q.v.

Costantini, *Auretta,* daughter of Angiola D'Orso and wife of Angelo Costantini, *Mezzettino,* q.v.

D'Orso, MARIA TERESA, detta *Spinetta,* in the patronage of the Duke of Mantua during the last decade of the seventeenth century.

FIAMMETTA, with the AFFEZIONATI, *c.* 1632–4.

Fioretta, see *infra,* PIISSIMI.

FRANCESQUINA, an actress with the CONFIDENTI in Spain 1587 and with the UNITI in 1594. See also under S. RONCAGLI and L. ZECCA. The part was sometimes taken by a man and belonged to *Ottavio Bernardini, Battista da Treviso* and a certain '*Carletto*'. See D'Ancona, ii. 525.

Franchini, ISABELLA, detta *Colombina,* wife of Domenico Biancolelli, q.v.

Gabrielli, *Spinetta,* wife of Francesco, *Scapino* of Scala's CONFIDENTI, q.v.

Gardellini, GABRIELLA, detta *Argentina,* in the company of the Duke of Modena in 1688.

NICOLINA, with the FEDELI in 1612.

OLIVETTA, an unsatisfactory member of the ACCESI in 1620 and of the CONFIDENTI in 1627 (pp. 289, 302).

Paruti, MADDALENA FRANCESCA, detta *Pimpinella,* in the company of the Duke of Modena in 1686.

RICCIOLINA, a mask among the ACCESI in 1605 and the AFFEZIONATI *c.* 1632–4.

Roncagli, SILVIA, detta *Franceschina,* for the GELOSI.

de Secchi, *Nespola,* wife of Marcello de' Secchi in Scala's CONFIDENTI, q.v.

Toscana, ANGELICA, detta *Marinetta,* wife of Giuseppe Tortoriti, q.v.

Zecca, LIVIA, detta *Franceschina,* wife of Nicolò Zecca, q.v.

HANDLIST OF SCENARI

THE handlist of scenari has been prepared in support of the argument maintained in Chapter III. In addition to the alphabetical arrangement some attempt has been made to show, by cross references, the relationship between the miscellanies and the connexions between the manuscript plots and printed plays, illustrating the permutations and combinations of dramatic material.

The life of a plot is not fixed by its appearance in print or in a manuscript collection, but is rather to be determined by its relationship to an acting tradition. This can only be traced by suggesting the origins, grouping the variants and indicating the subsequent development of a given theme. It would be false policy to keep to the strict limits of the period proposed for this study. The use of the later material, however, has been eclectic. Notices of parodies and farces given by Italian comedians on the Parisian stage at the end of the seventeenth century,[1] and of the plays of Gherardi, Veronesi, Gandini, Goldoni, and the Riccoboni, whose careers lie outside the period, have been included only on account of connexions with earlier scenari or stage traditions such as the evolution of the masks of Arlecchino and Pulcinella.[2] It may be that there are still some titles which would be struck out were it possible to sample the contents, but lacking the original plots and critical extracts it has seemed wiser to err on the side of inclusiveness.

Wherever possible the earliest recorded date of performance has been given together with any indications of the age of the scenario, such as are offered by Parfaict and Gueulette. In the case of notices drawn from Riccoboni's lists where the arrangement is chronological, or from the *Dictionnaire des Théâtres* where it is alphabetical, page references have sometimes been omitted. Roman and italic type have been used to differentiate between the plots which are extant in the form of scenari or summaries (such as Gueulette's) and those for which only the titles and extracts (such as the *Dictionnaire des Théâtres de Paris*) have survived. The Italian titles have always been preferred, but in the case of scenari recorded by French authorities the alternative form has been included with a cross reference. Anonymous scenari are described under the heading 'scenario'. For the convenience of alpha-

---

[1] See *Les Parodies du Nouveau Théâtre Italien ou Recueil des parodies Représentées sur le Théâtre de l'Hôtel de Bourgogne*, par les Comédiens Italiens Ordinaires du Roy, 1738, in 7 vols.

Supplement in 3 vols., 1765.

[2] For the titles of other scenari played in the eighteenth century see A. Bartoli, op. cit., pp. xxxvii–xlvii.

betical arrangement the various spellings 'Pulcinella, Policinella, Pol-
cinella' and 'Arlechino, Arlecchino, Arlequin, Harlequin', &c., have
been reduced to the uniformity of 'Pulcinella' and 'Arlechino'. The
difference in form between the masculine and feminine, singular and
plural, has been disregarded, and 'finto, finta, finte, finti' have been
reckoned as a single form and the sequence has been determined by the
first letter of the following noun. French numerals have been made to
conform to the Italian, so that 'due and deux, tre and trois' need not
be separated. The following abbreviations have been adopted:

SCALA Il Teatro delle Favole rappresentative overo la Ricreatione
Comica, Boscareccia e Tragica, Divisa in cinquanta Giornate;
Composta da Flaminio Scala detto Flavio Comico. del Sereniss.
Sig. Duca di Mantova All' M. Sig. Conte Ferdinando Riario
Marchese di Castiglione di Val'Oreia et Senatore in Bologna.
In Venetia, apresso Gio. Battista Pulciani. 1611.

LOC. Della Scena de Soggetti Comici et Tragici di B(asilio) L(oc-
catello) R(omano) in two parts 1618 and 1622. MS. in the
Biblioteca Casanatense, Codices 1211, 1212.

CORS. for Raccolta di Scenari piu scelti D'Istrioni Divisi in Due
Volumi. MS. in the Biblioteca della R. Accademia dei Lincei
in the Palazzo Corsini, Rome. Codices 45 G. 5 and 6.

VEN. for a collection of 51 scenari in Venice, Museo Correr, Codex
1040.

4186 for a collection of 48 scenari in the Casanatense, Codex 4186.

MAG. for a collection of 22 scenari in Florence, Biblioteca Nazionale
Codex Magliabechiano II. i. 90.

BARB. LAT. for Selva di nuove comedie, Biblioteca Vaticana. Codex
Barb. Lat. 3895.

NAP. I for Gibaldone Comico di Varii Suggetti di Comedie, ed Opere
Bellissime Copiate da me Antonio Passanti detto Oratio il
Calabrese Per commando Dell'Ecc^me· Sig^r·· Conte di Casamar-
ciano 1700.

NAP. II for Gibaldone de Soggetti Da recitarsi all'impronto Alcuni
proprii, e gl'altri da diversi Raccolti di D. Anibale Sersale,
Conte di Casamarciano. Naples. Bib. Vittorio Emanuele.
Codices xi. A A. 40 and 41.

Per. Selva overo Zibaldone di concetti comici, raccolti Dal P. D.
Pl(acido) A(driano) Di Lucca. 1734. Perugia, Biblioteca Com-
munale, Codex A. 20.

Mod. Scenari catalogued under their titles in the Archivio di Stato in
Modena.

Gueulette. Traduction Du Scenario ou du recueil des scenes que
joseph dominique biancolelli jouoit en habit d'Arlequin, dans les

pièces Italiennes de son temps; rédigé, écrit de sa main; il mourut le 2 aoust 1688. Paris, Bibliothèque de l'Opéra. MS. 13736. Page reference is made to the more accessible transcript in the Bibliothèque Nationale, entitled, Traduction Du Scenario de Joseph Dominique Biancolelli; Dit Arlequin. Et l'histoire Du Théâtre Italien, Depuis l'année 1577, Jusqu'en 1750 ; Et les Années suivantes par M. G(ueulette). Fonds français. Collection de Soleinne 9388. As Professor Allardyce Nicoll points out, this 'so-called copy omits eight pieces'. I regret that I have not yet been able to consult the other MSS. containing matter relating to the late Italian comedy in France cited in *Masks, Mimes, and Miracles*, p. 379.

Dict. Dictionnaire des Théâtres de Paris, Contenant toutes les Pièces qui ont été representées jusqu'à présent sur les différens Théâtres François, & sur celui de l'Académie Royale de Musique: les Extraits de celles qui ont été jouées par les Comédiens Italiens, depuis leur rétablissement en 1716, ainsi que des Opéra Comiques, & principaux Spectacles des Foires Saint-Germain et Saint-Laurent. Des faits Anecdotes sur les Auteurs qui ont travaillé pour ces Théâtres, et sur les principaux Acteurs, Actrices, Danseurs, Danseuses, Compositeurs de Ballets, Dessinateurs, Peintres de ces Spectacles, etc., 7 vols. Paris, 1756.

Parf. C. and F. Parfaict. Histoire de l'ancien théâtre italien depuis son origine en France, jusqu'à sa suppression en l'année 1697, suivie des extraits ou canevas des meilleures pièces italiennes qui n'ont jamais été imprimées. Par les auteurs de l'histoire du théâtre françois. Paris, 1753 and 1767.

SP.F. C. and F. Parfaict. Mémoires pour servir à l'Histoire des Spectacles de la foire. 1743.

Ric. Nuovo Teatro Italiano, Che contiene le Comedie Stampate e recitate dal S. Luigi R. d°· Lelio. 3 vols. Paris, 1733. Containing a 'Catalogo Generale Delle Commedie Italiane rappresentate in Parigi doppo l'anno 1716'.

N. Th. It. Le Nouveau Théâtre Italien, ou Recueil Général des Comédies Représentées par les Comédiens Italiens Ordinaires du Roi. Enlarged edition 1753. The 'avertissement' explains that when the Italian comedians were recalled to France in 1716 they began to play in Italian and were persuaded to distribute 'Imprimés ou Argumens François, qui exposoient en abrégé le sujet de la Pièce, avec le nom des Acteurs, qui devoient y représenter'. Riccoboni improved on this and provided as well a detailed synopsis in Italian and French: after a run he published three plays in the expanded form. In 1728 these 'canevas' and

'Comédies Italiennes' were printed after the Arguments, but were withdrawn from the three-volume edition of 1733. In 1753 an enlarged edition was produced and brought up to date with an introductory memoir. The first volume contains an alphabetical catalogue and the remaining five volumes reprint the expanded plays in French with their Vaudeville music.

Hist. Anec. (J. A. J. Desboulmiers). Histoire anecdotique et Raisonnée du Théâtre Italien Depuis son établissement en France jusqu'à l'année 1769, contenant les analyses des principales pièces et un catalogue de toutes celles, tant italiennes que françaises, données sur ce théâtre avec les anecdotes les plus curieuses de la vie et des talents des acteurs et des actrices. Paris, 1769. 7 vols.

Loret and Robinet. La muze historique: ou, recueil des lettres en vers contenant les nouvelles du temps (1650–65), continued by Charles Robinet.

M. de F. Mercure de France; fondé en 1672.

M.G. Mercure Galant, 1672; as Nouveau Mercure Galant, 1678–9.

Moland. L. Moland, Molière et la Comédie Italienne. 1867.

Allacci. L. Allacci, Drammaturgia. Accresciuta e continuata fino all'anno. 1754.

Quadrio. F. S. Quadrio, Della Storia e Ragione d'ogni Poesia. 1739–52.

'Yorick.' (P. G. Ferrigni), La Storia dei Burattini.

Rasi. L. Rasi, I Comici Italiani. Biografia, bibliografia, iconografia. 1897–1905.

Bartoli. A. Bartoli, Scenari Inediti della Commedia dell'arte. 1880.

Neri. F. Neri, Scenari delle Maschere in Arcadia. 1913. Città di Castello, Lapi.

ABBATIMENTO D'ISABELLA. Cors. ii. 47.

ABBATIMENTO DI ZANNI. Loc. i. 11. Partly from N. Secchi's *L'Interesse.*

Accidenti del Vittorioso Goffredo. 1648. Described by Allacci as a scenario but not certainly belonging to the Commedia dell'arte.

LA ACCONCIA SERVA. (*a*) Loc. i. 16. (*b*) Cors. ii. 51. Reprinted by A. Valeri, Nuova Rassegna.

L'ACCORDIE E SCORDIE, OVERO GUERRA E PACE. Nap. ii. 63.

Adamira, o la statua dell'honore. Ric. 12.12.1717. Derived from Adamira o la statua del Honore, by G. A. Cicognini. N.T. It. i. xxxv. See also Riccoboni's expanded play with this title.

LI ADELFI DI TERENTIO. Cors. ii. 39. Based on Terence's *Adelphi.* Cp. *Il Fromento,* Loc. i. 39.

L'ADRASTO. Cors. i. 37. A tragedy in 5 acts.

L'ALBERGO NOBILE. Nap. ii. 87.

Al Fin medica il tempo ogni Pazzia. Scenario printed for a performance in 1695. Bib. Casanatense, Misc. Fol. 72.

*Alfonso. Ibid. Cp. Fonso.

L'Alvarado in the repertory of Diana Costantini, 1681. Brunelli, p. 109.

L'ALVIDA. Scala, 43. Reprinted by Petraccone, p. 332.

L'AMANTE ASTUTO. Codex Vat. Lat. 10244, sc. 8.

Les Amans brouillés par Arlequin Messager balourd. '3 acts: ancien'; anonymous, 9.7.1719. Extract in Dict. i. 62, with the alternative title *Li Sdegni.* Worked up into

Arlequin Balourd, Com. Italienne. 5 acts, prose by M. Procope Conteaux. Haymarket, London, 1719.

Les Amans Dupés. 5.7.1723. Dict. i. 65.

L'Amante difficile. Ric. 17.10.1716.

L'Amante fra le due obbligazioni. Bartoli, p. xlvii.

L'AMANTE GELOSA. Nap. ii. 7. Reprinted by Del Cerro, *Nel Regno delle Maschere,* p. 403.

L'AMANTE INAVERTITO. Nap. ii. 26. See *L'Incauto.*

Amanti Ingannati. Ric. 5.7.1723.

L'AMANTE INGRATO. (*a*) Loc. i. 23. (*b*) Nap. ii. 44. Cp.

LI AMANTI INGRATI. Cors. i. 22.

L'AMANTE INTERESSATO. Ven. 1.

AMANTI LICENZIATI. Nap. i. 88.

L'AMANTE LUNATICO. Nap. ii. 11. Possibly connected with

    (1) *Lo Smemoriato,* Arlequin compétiteur de Lelio, q.v.

    (2) *Il Lunatico.* (*Le Capricieux.*) Paris before 1668, Gueulette, *Hist. Anec.* i. 61.

L'Amante nascosto e la dama velata. (*El Escondido y la tapada* or *L'amant caché.*) Dict. 12.5.1706 and 3.11.1716. Taken from Calderon's *Casa con duos puertas.*

Gli Amanti che non s'intendono. 4.12.1718. Dict. Taken from Boccabadati's *Di amor non inteso.*

L'AMANTI SENZA VEDERSI. Nap. ii. 81.

L'AMANTE TRADITO. Ven. 50. See *Il Tradito.*

L'Amante Volubile. (*Lelio amant inconstant, et Arlequin Soldat insolent.*) Ric. 25.6.1716. Noted as 'ancien' in Dict. iii. 269. Possibly connected with

AMANTI VOLUBILI. (*a*) Nap. i. 2. (*b*) Codex Vat. Lat. 10244, sc. 7.

Gli AMICI INFIDI. 1632. Printed by Bartoli, lx.

Amare e fingere. Repertory of 'Eulalia' 1681. Brunelli, p. 1681. Modena title.

AMICO INFIDO. Ven. 2. Corresponding to P. M. Cecchini's *Amico Tradito*. Distinct from

L'AMICO TRADITO. Ven. 12. Corresponding to Scala's *Flavio Tradito*.

Amor nato nel fuoco. (*Le bonheur du hazard.*) 15.5.1717.

Gli Amori alla caccia. Dict. One act, 10.7.1716. Ric.; with French scenes, 10.7.1718. Dict. and Hist. Anec. i. 233.

AMOR COSTANTE. (*a*) Loc. ii. 24. (*b*) Cors. ii. 11, taken from Piccolomini's *Amor Costante*, played in Vicenza 1561 with scenes by Palladio. See *supra*, p. 176.

AMOR PER FAMA. Nap. i. 5.

AMORE ET HONORE DI RAMIDORO. Nap. ii. 89. Possibly derived from Lope de Vega's *Pobreza estimada*, or *Pobreza non es vileza*. The plot suggests a connexion with *Gentilhuomo campagnuolo*, q.v.

AMOR NON VUOL RIVALI. Gueulette, Dict. i. 268. Cp. *Non vuol rivali amor*. 1.10.1716. Ric. and Modena title.

L'AMORE SUPRA L'ODIO, E LA RAGGIONE. Barb. Lat. 3895, no. xiii. Possibly connected with Salvi's *Amor vince l'odio*, quoted by Allacci.

AMORE TRA NEMICI. Nap. ii. 8. Not connected with the eponymous play by Cicognini but possibly related to other plays by M. Stanchi, 1662, and G. B. Seriati, 1672, recorded by Allacci. See *Principe Sidonio* (S).

*Amore trionfante dell'odio. 1654. Casanatense. Printed scenario for a performance by the Collegio Inglese probably not belonging to the Commedia dell'arte.

AMOROSI INCANTI. Cors. i. 2. Cp. *Incanti Amorosi*. For *L'Amour extravagant*, see *Le figlie inamorate del Diavolo*.

Les Amours d'Arlequin. Dict. 11.5.1746.

L'AMPHITRIONI. Ven. 38, and

L'ANFITRIONI. Cors. ii. 19, with its correspondent *La Tramutazione*, q.v., are adapted from Plautus' *Amphytrion*.

Li Annelli Magici. 13.5.1717. Dict.

AQUIDOTTO. Nap. i. 4.

L'ARBORE INCANTATO. Scala, 49. Abstract given by W. Smith, op. cit.

ARCADIA INCANTATA. (*a*) Nap. i. 1. Reprinted by F. Neri and E. Petraccone. (*b*) With a variant in Per. No. 6. Caprin (*Rev. Teatrale Italiano*, 1905) suggests that this theme was brought to France by Michelangiolo Fracanzano in 1685. It appears in Paris 13.2.1717, with an extract in Dict. i. 157. Du Charni (*Trois lettres sur la Comédie*) says it has been given at the Foire as *Arlequin jouet des Fées*. The same theme is used in *Arlequin dans l'Isle Enchantée*, 4.2.1722, and in the *Naufraggio d'Arlequin* or *Arcadie Enchantée*. M. de F. 11.6.1740, and an extract in Dict. iii. 488. Distinct from

Arcadie enchantée. 13.7.1747. Dict. i. 159. See also *Sogno Avverato*. Dict. v. 20.

L'ARCADIA TRAVAGLIATA PER L'IRA DI DIANA CONTRA ENEA. 4186, no. 13.

Argentina, or the Sorceress. A Comedy. King's Theatre in the Haymarket. 1726 by the Company of Italian Comedians. Brit. Mus. 1344.1.13.

*Argomento dell'azzione Rappresentativa in ballo co' gesti L'Acquisto di Durindana. Scenario for the performance of a ballet in 1638. Bib. Casanatense. Misc. 658.

*Aristeo, by M. Cevoli, scenario printed for a performance in 1653. Bib. Casanatense Misc. 658.

Arlequin amant malgre lui (ou, *Le Jouet de la Fortune*). 30.8.1748. Dict.

Arlecchino amante per Compiacenza. 3 acts. 1.1.1740. Dict. ii. 155. Reduced to one act and played as

*Arlequin Barbier paralitique. 2.1.1740.

ARELQUIN BALOURD, see AMANS BROUILLÉS.

ARLEQUIN BARONE TEDESCO, see BARONE TEDESCO.

ARLEQUIN BERGER DE LEMNOS. Gueulette gives no Italian title but notes 'per Cinthio'. MS. cit., f. 345.

Arlecchino buffone di Corte. Ric. 20.5.1716. Played by A. Costantini 28.11.1739. Dict. ii. 155. Hist. Anec. i. 140. See Rasi, ii. 351. Cp. *La Maggior Gloria*.

Arlequin cabaretier, turc et Capitan espagnol. Paris, 1680. Moland, 30.6.1682.

Arlequin Cartouche. A. Riccoboni. 5 acts. 1721. Dict. iv. 473.

Arlecchino nel Castello incantato. 19.3.1740. Bartoli, xxxix.

Arlecchino cavaliere per accidente. Reprinted by Moland (p. 269) from a redaction given by Cailhava.

*Arlequin comédien aux champs élisées. French play. Bib. Française, iii. 123.

Arlecchino condannato a morte. Ric. 12.10.1716. See *Isole*.

Arlecchino Cortegiano. Ric. 22.8.1716.

Arlecchino corsaro affricano. Ric. 5.1.1718.

ARLECCHINO CREDUTO PRINCIPE. Gueulette, f. 173 for 1668. No doubt to be identified with *A. Roy per Hazard* for which on ff. 276 (*bis*) and 308 Gueulette gives 'additions', cp.

1. *Arlecchino creato Re per caso.* Nov. 1672. Moland.
2. *A. cru Prince, ajouté par Magie.* Dict. vii. 360.
3. *A. prince par hazard.* 14.9.1741. Dict.

4. *A. principe per accidente*, Rossi's repertory 1779. Rasi. 'Yorick' gives *A. finto Principe* as the title of a puppet play in the seventeenth century. See also *The Mask*, 1913, p. 13. See *infra*, *Il Creduto Principe*.

ARLEQUIN CRÛ LELIO, see IL CREDUTO MATTO.

Arlequin dans l'isle de Ceylan. 23.8.1717, and 25.8.1717. Ric. and Dict. Hist. Anec. i. 184.

ARLEQUIN DANS L'ISLE ENCHANTÉE, see ARCADIA INCANTATA.

Arlequin démarié par jalousie. 9.8.1717. Dict.

Arlecchino Demetrio. 1.8.1717. A tragicomedy adapted from a comedy by Boccabadati, taken from the *Histoire de Moscovie.* Dict. i. 226, and vii. 360.

Arlequin Dévaliseur de Maisons. Quoted by Riccoboni in the *Hist. du théâtre italien*, p. 67, for the 'lazzo' of the cherry-stones. Also given as

*Arlequin et Scapin dévaliseurs de Maison. Dict. vii. 362, and as

*Arlequin fourbe par necessité. Dict. vii. 363, referring it to *Pantalon Amant Malheureux.* 11.5.1740 and 26.5.1747.

Arlecchino disperato di non andare in prigione. Dict. i. 198 and vii. 359.

ARLEQUIN DOGUE D'ANGLETERRE ET MÉDECIN DU TEMS. Gueulette quotes from the Mercure Galant for Sept. 1679. Moland for 7.4.1682.

Arlequin Duelliste, 1 act. 21.11.1727. Dict. vii. 361. Possibly a revival of

*Arlequin dupe vengé. Moland, 274. See also *A. finto Gentilhuomo.*

ARLEQUIN ÉCOLIER IGNORANT, ETC., see DOTTOR BACCHETTONE.

ARLEQUIN ESPRIT FOLLET. Gueulette, 1670 'per Cintio', f. 280.

Arlecchino facchino fortunato. Ric. 11.12.1716. From a comedy by Boccabadati. Dict. i. 249.

Arlecchino falso bravo. 28.11.1721. From Boccabadati, revived by Gandini 16.9.1745 as *Scaramouche, le faux Brave.* Dict. vii. 412.

Arlequin feint Guéridon, Momie et Chat. 6.12.1716. Dict. vii. 362. See *Pantalone Speziale.*

Arlecchino finto Gentilhuomo, Duellista per forza. Ric. 28.5.1716. Dict. i. 247 and vii. 361. Possibly connected with

*Arlequin Gentil-homme par hazard. 3 acts. Dominique (Biancolelli). Feb. 1708, Spectacles des Foires, ii. 176. Played as

Arlequin Maître et Valet. 25.10.1717. Nouveau Théâtre Italien, i. xlv, and Dict. vi. 6. See also *Don Giovanni d'Alverado.*

Arlequin feint Magicien. Dict. vii. 749. Played with the alternative title *Les Tuteurs Trompés.* See also *Arlequin et Scarron juifs errants*, etc.

Arlecchino finto Mèrcante da canzoni, capitano, vaso di Naranci, Lanterna e comare. Ric. and Dict. 11.11.1716. See also *Harlekin Friseur.*

Arlecchino finto Pantalone e Capitano. (*A. cru Pantalon Scaramouche et Turc.*) 14.8.1716. Dict. iv. 103; vii. 6. 360. Given by Riccoboni as *Le Père Trompé.*

Arlecchino finto Satua [*sic*] *e Papagallo.* Ric. 20.8.1716. Probably connected with Monaseni's play quoted by Quadrio. Played also as *Arlequin Enfant Statue, et Perroquet,* Dict. vii. 361.

Arlecchino finto Scimmiotto. Bartoli, xlvii.

Arlecchino garzone geloso. 6.3.1747. Bartoli, xxxix.

Arlequin Gazetier d'Hollande. 29.4.1724. Dict. vii. 363.

Arlequin Génie. 12.8.1752. Ibid.

Arlequin heureux par hazard. 'D'un ancien auteur accommodé au Théâtre par A. Riccoboni. 1716.' Dict. iv. 471.

ARLEQUIN HOTTE ET MASSON. Gueulette, f. 461.

ARLEQUIN JOUET DES FÉES, see ARCADIA INCANTATA.

ARLEQUIN JOUET DE FORTUNE, see MONDO AL ROVESCIO.

Arlequin et Scarron juifs errants de Babilone. Gueulette, f. 390. See *Trompeurs Trompés.*

Arlequin juif, peintre et tailleur. Paris, 1680. Moland, 24.6.1682.

Arlecchino ladro. Ric. 20.10.1721. See *A. Cartouche.*

Arlequin ladron, prévot et juge. Gueulette, f. 193. Played in 1667. Cp. *Ladro, sbirro e giudice.* Ric. 2.6.1716, and *Pollicinella ladro, spia, giudice e Boia.* Nap. ii. 73. It was taken to the Foire by Dominique (Biancolelli) and is recorded as a puppet play in the seventeenth century by 'Yorick'.

Arlichino maestro di Scuola. 27.6.1716. See *Scuola di Terenzio.*

Arlequin maistre d'amour. Riccoboni, *Hist. du théâtre italien,* p. 45, notes this as an old Italian theme belonging possibly to the sixteenth century.

Arlechino marito senza moglie. (*Le Pot Pourri.*) 22.6.1744. Dict. i. 254 and vii. 668. See also *Insalata.*

Arlequin mari de la femme de son Maître, et Marchand d'Esclaves. Dict. vii. 377. See also *Cameriera.*

ARLEQUIN MÉDECIN D'EAU DOUCE. Gueulette, f. 284.

Arlequin Militaire. 1.9.1746. Mercure de France.

Arlecchino muto per forza. (*A. muet par crainte.*) 16.12.1717. Dict. i. 256 and iv. 472.

Arlechino nell'Isola Incantata. At the Tuilleries, 4.2.1722. Bartoli, xxxix. See *Arcadia Incantata.*

Arlequin notaire maltraité. (*Les Erreurs de l'Amour.*) 1716. Dict. iv. 471.

Arlequin et Pantalon cocus sans femme. 4.8.1721. Spectacles des Foires, ii. 177.

Arlequin Parvenu. M. Gurrini. 1.8.1755. Dict. vii. 750. Containing devices used in *Les Jumeaux,* q.v.

Arlequin peintre. 1 act. 1.10.1716 and 22.2.1744. Dict. i. 268 and vii. 378. See also *Non vuol rivali amore.*

Arlecchino perseguitato da' quattro elementi. Bartoli, xlviii. Given in the repertory of C. Rossi in 1779. Rasi.

Arlequin persécuté par la Dame Invisible. 25.5.1716. See also *La Dama creduta spirito folletto.*

ARLECCHINO POETA EPULINO (?). (A. POETE APALITENSANT (?)). Gueulette, f. 280 (quoted by Nicoll, as 'e putino', p. 381).

ARLECCHINO PORCO PER AMORE. Gueulette, f. 361.

Arlecchino Prencipe in Sogno, &c. (*Harlequin Prince in a Dream, German Baron, Flying Physician,* and *Pretty Marget.*) Haymarket, 1726, by the Italian Comedians. Brit. Mus. 1344.1.13 (2). See also *Barone Tedesco.*

ARLEQUIN ROY DE TRIPOLI, see LA PROPRETÉ.

Arlecchino Scanderberg. 1.2.1740. See *Le double dénouement.* Dict. ii. 156 and 338.

Arlecchino e Scapino ladri. 20.5.1741. Bartoli, xl, revived as

Arlequin et Scaramouche voleurs. 5.12.1747. Dict. vi. 260.

**Arlecchino e Scapino maghi per caso.* 15.7.1743. Bartoli, xxxix.

**Arlecchino e Scaramoccia rivali.* 25.5.1720. Bartoli, xl. Possibly revived as

Arlecchino e Scapino rivali per Corallini. 24.9.1744. Bartoli, xxxix.

Arlecchino Secretario publico. Ric. 17.5.1717.

Arlichino sempre Arlichino. (*Les Comédiens esclaves.*) Ric. 10.8.1726. Cp.

**Arlequin toujours Arlequin,* sujet italien en un acte. Mis en Comédie, et rédigé par Scènes, avec des changemens & des augmentations par Sieur Terodak Arlequin François de la Comédie Italienne de Paris. Représenté à la Haye . . . 1750. Brit. Mus. 163 d. 44.

Arlichino servo di duoi padroni. Ric. 31.7.1718. Hist. Anec. i. 236. (*A. valet de deux maîtres.*) See also *Servo di due patroni.*

Arlichino sfortunato nella Cocagna. Ric. 25.5.1718. (*A. malheureux dans la prospérité.*)

Arlichino smaritato per gelosia. (*A. demarié.*) Ric. 9.8.1717.

Arlecchino soldato e bagaglio. Moland for July 1673. Gueulette, f. 224, gives 'Additions à la comédie d'Arlequin soldat et bagage'.

Arlequin soldat déserteur. Paris, 1680. Bartoli, xxxviii.

ARLEQUIN SOURI. Gueulette, f. 284.

Arlequin tombé dans les puits. Paris, 1680. Bartoli, xxxviii.

ARLEQUIN TOURMENTÉ PAR LES FOURBERIES DE SCAPIN, see DISGRATIE D'AR-
LECCHINO.

Arlichino traditore di se medesimo. Ric. 3.5.1717.

ARLEQUIN VALET ENCHANTÉ, FINGO [*sic*] ET MARGOT LA PIE.
Gueulette, f. 284.

Arlequin Valet étourdi. Paris, 1680. Bartoli, xxxviii. Moland,
4. 1682 at S.-Germain-sur-Loire. Riccoboni (*Hist. du théâtre
italien*, p. 45) notes this as an old, possibly a sixteenth-century,
scenario. The theme was used by Rosimont with an alternative title, *Qui pro quo*, 1671. Dict. iv. 360 and vi. 5. See also
Servo Sciocco.

Arlequin vendageur. Paris, 1680. Bartoli, xxxviii.

Arme e Bagaglio. Bartoli, xlviii.

ARME MUTATE. Loc. i. 48; Cors. i. 23; Nap. i. 3.

Arte vinta dall'arte. Bartoli, xlvii.

*L'Aspetta Mora. A comedy by G. A. Cicognini played 'all'improviso' by his troop, *Gl'inconstanti*, 6.2.1623, in Florence.
Probably to be identified with his *Finta Mora*, licensed in
1623, printed 1625.

L'ASTROLOGO. Ven. 5. Derived from *L'Astrologo* by G. B. Della
Porta. See V. Rossi, *Rendiconti del R. Ist. Lombardo*, Ser. II,
vol. xxix, p. 883, 1896. Reprinted by E. Petraccone, op. cit.,
p. 383.

ASTUTE SEMPLICITÀ D'ANGIOLA. Nap. ii. 93. P. Toldo connects
this scenario with the tradition of *L'École des femmes*. See
also Sanesi, op. cit., p. 40.

*Astuzie di Bragato, played in Bologna, 1673. Possibly to be connected with

L'ASTUZIA DI MARIOLO. Nap. ii. 4.

*Astuzie di Truffaldino e Arlecchino. In Rossi's repertory in 1779.
Rasi. Probably reworked in

L'ASTUZIE DI ZANNI. Loc. ii. 23, and Cors. ii. 10.

L'ATEISTA FULMINATO. 4186, no. 4. Reprinted by F. de Simone
Broüwer, *Rendiconti della R. Acc. de' Lincei*, Ser. V, vol. 10,
p. 391, 1901, and by Petraccone, p. 374. A. Farinelli (*Giorn.
Stor.* xxvii. 15, 29) can find no exact Spanish original, but as
Miss Smith (*Mod. Phil.* xx. 301) points out, there is every sign
of Spanish influence in the thematic material.

*Athamante. Bib. Vaticana. It seems unlikely that this fragment of
a tragedy has any connexion with the Commedia dell'arte.
See F. Neri, *La Tragedia*, 1904, p. 160, n. 1.

L'AUBERGE D'ARLEQUIN JUGE, PARTIE, AVOCAT ET TÉMOIN. Gueulette, f. 492.

AUSA. Ven. 20.

AVARITIA. Nap. i. 79. See *Vecchio Avaro*.

AVOCATO CRIMINALE, CIOÈ IL ROSILDO. 4186, no. 47.

GLI AVVENIMENTI. Scala, 42. An abstract of this 'opera mista' is given by W. Smith.

BALDOINO E CARLOTTO. 4186, no. 16. Possibly derived from Lope de Vega's *Marqués de Mantua*.

LA BALIA GRANDE. Nap. i. 26. See *Li Scambi*.

Balorda. Ric. 23.11.1717. Dict. i. 372.

La Bambina nata di furto. By Principe Ercolani di Bologna. Bartoli, xlvii.

IL BANCHETTO. Loc. ii. 43.

LI BANDITI. Loc. ii. 33.

LA BARBARITÀ DEL DOTTORE (*Cruauté del Dottore*). Gueulette, f. 182.

BARLIARIO [*sic*] or BAILARDO. Nap. i. 85. Reprinted by Petraccone, p. 438.

IL BARONE DI FOENESTE. Gueulette gives no Italian title for this scenario which was recorded by Robinet as played in France in 1674. See Hist. Anec. 113.

BARONE TEDESCO. Ven. 48 and Nap. ii. 75. Cp. Ric. *Arlichino Barone Tedesco*, 16.8.1716, quoted with the alternative title *Les Deux Flaminia*, Dict. vii. 473. Cp. *Arlecchino Barone Svizzero*, 10.12.1742, Bartoli, xxxix. *Le Baron allemand*, Gueulette, ff. 64–85, is Biancolelli's version. Probably Gorini's *Barone Polacco*, 1730, is a derivative. 'Yorick' quotes it as a puppet play in the seventeenth century, and *Arlequin Baron Allemand ou le Triomphe de la Folie* was a play given in the Foire, 3.2.1712. Spectacles des Foires, ii. 173.

IL BASILISCO. Codex Vat. Lat. 10244, sc. 10, probably to be identified with

BASILISCO DI BARNAGASSO [*sic*]. (*a*) and (*b*) Nap. ii. 23 and 24. (*c*) Per. f. 19. (*d*) Gueulette, ff. 28–35 gives alternative titles. It was given by Biancolelli in Paris before 1668 as *B. di Berganasso* and played until 1716 as *Dragon de Moscovie* or *de Transilvanie*. (*e*) Cp. *Arlequin persécuté par le Basilisco del Berganasso*, 16.7.1716, Dict. i. 269 and vii. 379. (*f*) Among the Modenese scenari two corresponding titles are noted by E. Re, *Giorn. Stor.* lv, 1910. See also *Dom Basilisque de Bernagasse*, a French play in 6 acts. 1708. Bib. Fr. iii. 246. Toldo suggests that this scenario may have had some influence on *Tartuffe*. 'Yorick' quotes the title for a puppet play in the seventeenth century.

BASTARDA IMPERTINENTE. Nap. i. 43.

LA BATTAGLIA. (*a*) Loc. ii. 42. (*b*) Cors. i. 42.

Beist in der Liebe. Scenario in German and Italian played in 1688. MS. in the possession of Senatore Benedetto Croce.

Belfonte Inavvertito. Modenese title. See *L'Incauto.*

LA BELLE-MÈRE SUPPOSÉE, see LA FINTA MADRIGNA.

BELLISARIO, SCENARIO DELL'OPERA DI. (*a*) 4186, no. 29. (*b*) Nap. i. 72. Derived from *La Caduta del gran Capitan Belissario sotto la condanna di Giustiniano Imp^{re}.,* 1663, adapted by G. A. Cicognini from Lope de Vega's *Exemplo mayor de la Desdicha, y Capitano Bellisario.* Trautmann quotes from a letter from Chabo de St. Maurice to the Duke of Mantua, 31.5.1687, thanking him for the comedians Virginio and Vittoria who have given satisfaction in *Belisario,* op. cit., pp. 261 and 309. See App. E under *Coppa.*

LA BELLISSIMA, COMMEDIA IN TRE PERSONE. Mag. no. 3.

DON BERNARDO DI CABRERA. 4186, no. 39. Intrigue of Spanish type possibly connected with M. Napoleone's translation from Ivan de Vigliega's *La prospera fortuna de Don Bernardo de Cabrera.*

BERNARDO DEL CARPIO. Nap. i. 73. Probably derived from Lope de Vega's *Mocedades de Bernardo.*

LE BIZARRIE D'ARGENTINA CAVALIERE E GENTILDONNA. IPPOLITO E BOFFETTO CREDUTI TURCHI CON ZACCAGNINO AMANTE DISPERATO COMEDIA NUOVA. 1643. Modenese scenari was printed by Paglicci-Brozzi in *Rivista Teatrale Italiano,* anno viii, vol. 13, fasc. 2.

LES BOHÉMIENS, see ZINGARI.

LE BONHEUR DU HAZARD, see AMOR NATO NEL FUOCO.

La Buggia imbroglia il buggiardo. Ric. 15.5.1720. Quoted by Parfaict as *Les Menteurs Embarrassés.* Taken from the Spanish via Boccabadati, and used by Romagnesi for *La Feinte inutile.* 22.8.1735. Dict. iii. 394.

Bugia verità. In the repertory of Diana Constantini, 1681. Brunelli, p. 109.

BURLE DI FEDELE. Cors. i. 38.

BURLE DI FILANDRO. Loc. ii. 13.

BURLE D'ISABELLA. Scala, 4.

IL CABALISTA, O IL CAVALIER DEL INDUSTRIA. (*Chevalier de l'industrie.*) 1670. Gueulette, f. 280. Riccoboni gives an alternative French title, *Lelio fourbe intrigant.* 11.7.1716. Derived from the Spanish comedy which gave Corneille the plot for the *Galant doublé.* Dict. iii. 270.

Cabinet. 1.10.1742. Dict. ii. 1, quoting *Mercure de France* for Oct. 1742, p. 2281.

La Caccia. Scala, 37.

Il Calamaro Prigioniero. Modena. See *Giorn. Stor.* lv.

Il Calamaro ruffiano onorato. Ibid.

CAMERIERA. (*a*) Nap. i. 7. (*b*) Per. f. 208. (*c*) Included in the repertory of Diana Constantini, 1681. Rasi, i. 723. Cp. *Arlequin mari de la femme de son maître,* &c., revived as *La Cameriera.* 2.9.1739. Dict. vii. 423. Identified with *La Cameriera nobile.* Ric. 15.6.1716.

Il Cane del Ortolano. 6.7.1716. Ric. gives as an alternative title *La Dame amoureuse par envie.* Caprin, *Riv. Teat. It.,* 1905, suggests a connexion with Ameyden's play, but according to Dict. vii. 466 it is connected with G. A. Cicognini's *La Moglie di quatro mariti.* See also Hist. Anec. i. 148. In repertory of company of the Duke of Modena *c.* 1681. Brunelli, p. 109.

Canuto. In the repertory of 'Eulalia' in 1681. Brunelli, p. 109.

IL CAPITANO. Scala, 11.

IL CAPITANO BURLATO. Nap. i. 49. See *Oratio Burlato.*

LE CAPRICIEUX, see AMANTE LANATICO.

LI CARCERATI. Cors. i. 19.

Il Carcerier carcerato. Bartoli, xlvii.

CARNOVALE. Loc. ii. 38.

CASA CON DUE PORTE. Nap. i. 10. Repertory of 'Eulalia', 1681. Brunelli, p. 109. Played in Paris, 22.6.1716, as *Maison à deux portes difficile à garder, ou Arlequin amoureux par opinion.* Dict. vii. 568, and as *Contretemps.* See also Riccoboni, *Réflexions,* p. 74. Translations and adaptations of Calderon's *Casa con dos Puertas mala es de guardar* by Napoleone. D'Ouville and Corneille offer a variety of means by which this plot might come to the Italian players.

LE CASE SVALIGGIATE. (*a*) Nap. ii. 6. (*b*) Gueulette, f. 147. Probably to be identified with *La Casa svaligiata,* or *Pantalon amant malheureux ou Arlequin dévaliseur de maison.* 27.5.1716. Dict. iv. 67. Played in May 1740. Bartoli, xlv. Décharni, 'Première Lettre historique sur la nouvelle Comédie Italienne', finds a resemblance to Molière's *Les Fâcheux.* Moland notes that Molière borrows a trick from this comedy for *L'Avare.*

LA CASTA E COSTANTE IPSICRATEA, see IPSICRATEA.

IL CASTIGO DELLA DISONESTA MOGLIE. Ven. 15.

DONNA CATERINA D'ARAGONA. 4186, no. 22.

IL CATTIVO MARITO, see IL MARITO.

CAVADENTE. Scala 12. Cp.

CAVADENTI. Nap. ii. 94.

IL CAVALIER DISCRETO. Ven. 6.

CAVALIER ERRANTE. Nap. i. 41.
CAVALIER DEL INDUSTRIA, see CABALISTA.
CAVALIER INGRATO. Ven. 17.
CAVALIER INNORITO DAL SUO NEMICO OBLIGATO CON AGGRAVIO.
Nap. ii. 90.
IL CAVALIERE PAZZO O SIA IL GIUOCO DI FORTUNA. Codex Vat. Lat.
10244.
CAVALIER PERSEGUITATO. By N. N. MAG. Printed by Bartoli, no. 16.
IL CAVALIERO DA I TRE GIGLI D'ORO. 4186, no. 23.
†CELINDA. Untitled scenario in Barb. Lat. 3895, f. 26.
CHI LA FA, L'ASPETTI. Nap. ii. 28. Possibly connected with a comedy
of this title played in Bologna in 1667. Allacci quotes comedies
with the same title by Piterni, Panuzi, Polani and by an anony-
mous playwright, which I have not been able to find. In 1765
Pietro Rosa expanded from the scenario and printed *Chi la
fa l'aspetta, ossia I due fratelli Veneziani perseguitati dalla
calunnia e resi felici dalla magia*. Rasi, ii. 408.
CHI OPERA INGANNI SE STESSA OFFENDE. Nap. ii. 29.
Chi soffre speri. Printed scenario for an 'Opera musicale' from the *Decamerone*, v. 9. Cas. Misc. See Ademollo, *Teatri di Roma*, p. 25.
Chi trova un amico trova un tesoro, o sia il Dottore avvocato
de' poveri. F. Bartoli gives this title from the repertory of
R. Lombardi who died in 1795, but the sub-title suggests an
ancestry in the *Dottore Bacchettone* tradition, q.v. See also
under Pulcinella plays. App. B (3).
CHI VUOLE AMMOGLIARE RESTA AMMOGLIATO. Nap. ii. 32.
D. CHISCIOTTE DELLA MANCIA. Printed scenario for performances
in 1692 and 1731. Cas. Misc., f. 172. See *Un pazzo
guarisce l'altro*.
LA CIECA. Cors. ii. 1. Cp. *Zanni Beccho*.
CINTIO INFELICE E FLAMINIA COSTANTE. Ven. 33.
CINTIO GIUOCATORE. Codex Vat. Lat. 10244, sc. 6.
Cit [sic] de l'Espagne. Modena title, and in the repertory of Diana
Constantini, 1681. Brunelli, p. 109.
Il Ciro. Printed scenario for a tragedy given in Parma 1652 and in
Rome 1654. Cas. Misc. 658. 7. Probably not of the Com-
media dell'arte tradition.
CLARINDA PERSEGUITATA. 4186, no. 15.
CLAUDIONE MERCANTE FALLITO. Cors. i. 30. Cp. *Gratiano mercante
fallito*. Loc. ii. 25.
Colarara. Composed by Academicians of Rome. Ric. gives an alter-
native title, *Le Docteur et Pantalon amans invisibles*. 8.7.1716.
Dict. ii. 332. It was reconcerted as *Vecchi Inamorati*.
23.8.1747. Ibid. vi. 186.

Le Collier de perles. Gueulette gives no Italian title and produces only the printed programme referring to Robinet, f. 180. Moland records that it was by M. Girardin and played in July 1672. See also Hist. Anec. 101.

Colombina marito per compiacenza. 18.4.1719. Mercure de France. Dict. ii. 114 for extract and French scenes.

COLONELLO INDIANO. Nap. i. 16.

Le Combat à cheval. Paris, 1680. Bartoli, xxxviii.

LES COMÉDIENS ESCLAVES, see ARLICHINO SEMPRE ARLICHINO.

LES COMÉDIENS PAR HAZARD, see LES DEUX ARLEQUINES.

COMETA. Loc. ii. 40. The same plot is given in a pastoral setting in *Il Serpe Fatale,* Loc. ii. 39, and its correspondent *Il Serpe Incantato.* Cors. ii. 24. Scenari composed on the same theme are:

(a) *La Spada mortale.* Cors. ii. 46.

(b) *Figlio della morte, ovvero Cardellino cornuto voluntario.* Nap. i. 81.

(c) *La Spada Fatale.* Mag. Printed Bartoli.

Traces of the theme are found in *Le due fonti incantate, la Principessa muta, e Buffetto Governatore.* 4186, no. 44. This common plot appears to be derived from a tragicomedy by Virgilio Verucci, *La Spada Fatale,* 1618, 1620, 1627, 1636. It is possible on the other hand that Verucci was expanding a scenario current among professional comedians. See *supra,* pp. 215-19. Don Antonio Ceruto remarks the performance of a comedy entitled *La Spada dannata,* in Mantua, July 1567 which may belong to the tradition. D'Ancona, op. cit. ii. 452.

LA COMMEDIA IN COMMEDIA. (a) Loc. i. 43. (b) Cors. i. 34. Reprinted by Petraccone, p. 350, and E. del Cerro, *Nel Regno delle maschere* distinct from

LA COMMEDIA IN COMMEDIA. Nap. i. 39.

La Congiura de' Carbonari. Bartoli, xlvii.

LI CONSIGLI DI PANTALONE. Loc. i. 40.

IL CONTE DI SEX. (a) 4186, no. 48. Cp. *La Regina d'Inghilterra.* (b) Nap. i. 64 and Mag. Several suggestions have been made of plays from which these scenari might be derived. Parfaict refers to La Calprenède's *Le Comte d'Essex,* 1638; De Amicis and Caprin to Coello's *Dar la vida por su dama* of which the first extant edition was published in Barcelona in 1638. See W. Smith, Pub. of the Mod. Lang. Ass. of America, 1924. The scenario may well be older than any of these plays for in July 1692 a performance of *L'histoire Angloise contre la Roine d'Angleterre* was posted to be played in Paris. Winwood, *Memorials,* i. 425. If this dealt with the recent affair between Elizabeth and Essex it was a curious fulfilment of his observation on 12 May 1600, that 'shortly they will play me upon the stage'. *State Papers, Dom.* cclxxiv. 138. Bartoli refers to the tragedy, *Conte d'Essex*, by Boyer, 1678.

I Contratti Rotti et Arlequin savetier vindicatif. 10.6.1716. Noted as 'très ancien et sans origine', Dict. ii. 170. See C. Gozzi, *Opere*, iv. 35. Cp. *Le Savetier*, 20.5.1747, Dict. v. 55, where a connexion with Rosimont's *Avocat sans Étude* is suggested.

Convitato, Dona Isabella. In the repertory of 'Eulalia', 1681. Brunelli, p. 109.

CONTRETEMPS, see CASA CON DUE PORTE.

IL CONVITATO DI PIETRA. (*a*) 4186, no. 24. Printed by F. de S. Broüwer in *Rendiconti della R. Acc. de' Lincei*, Ser. V, vol. xix, 1901. (*b*) Nap. i. 47. Reprinted by Petraccone, p. 428. (*c*) Gueulette's record of Biancolelli's version is reprinted by Castile-Blaze, *Molière Musicien*, in illustration of his use of the Don Juan theme. See also *Agiunta al Convitato di Pietra.* Feb. 1673. Gueulette, f. 117. Ric. 17.1.1717, and with alterations on 4.5.1743. Dict. ii. 539, and Hist. Anec. i. 85. The scenario belongs to the tradition of the Don Juan plays which is discussed further by Bartoli, p. xxxvi, n. 10, and Moland, chap. xi. A synopsis is given by K. Mantzius, *Hist. of Theatrical Art*, trans. L. von Cossel, 1903, vol. ii, p. 233. 'Yorick' quotes the title for a puppet play in the seventeenth century.

†*Corallina.* A series of plays advertising this mask are recorded in the Dict. for the middle of the eighteenth century, ii. 173–93.

IL CORNUTO PER OPINIONE, see MARITO PIÙ ONORATO.

CORRIERO BALORDO. Nap. i. 42.

LA CORTEGIANA ONESTA. Ven. 34, and among the titles of Modenese scenari noted by E. Re in *Giorn. Stor.* lv. Possibly connected with *La Comédie des Comédiens, ou la Courtisane vertueuse.* Bib. Fr. iii. 436.

LA COSTANZIA DI FLAMINIA CON LE FURBERIE DI STOPPINO. Ven. 28.

COVIELLO BARBIERO, ROFFIANO, LADRO E FINTO DIAVOLO COL DOTTORE FURBO MAL PRATTICO. Nap. ii. 18.

COVELLO CORNUTO. Nap. ii. 51.

COVELLO TRADITOR DEL PADRONE. Nap. ii. 38.

COVELLO E POLLICINELLA AMANTI DELLE PROPRIE PADRONE. Nap. ii. 58.

Il creduto matto. Paris. 18.6.1716. As an alternative title, *Arlequin crû Lélio, ou Lélio jouet de la Fortune.* Dict. iii. 271. Derived from the Spanish.

LA CREDUTA MORTA. Scala, 7.

IL CREDUTO MORTO. Scala, 22.

Il Creduto Principe. (*a*) 4186, no. 20. The following scenari and plays present variants of the theme:

(*b*) *Nuovo Finto Principe.* Nap. i. 11.

(*c*) *Finto Principe.* Nap. ii. 48.

(*d*) *Il Finto Re.* Nap. ii. 49.

(*e*) *Il Finto Principe.* Mag. Printed by Bartoli.

(*f*) *Truffaldino finto Principe.* Acted by amateurs in Bologna, 1682. See Sarti, op. cit.

(*g*) *Arlecchino Creduto Principe.* Gueulette, q.v.

(*h*) *Trappolin, suppos'd a Prince,* adapted by Sir Aston Cokayne from an Italian scenario. 1651. See *Mod. Lang. Rev.* xxiii.

(*i*) *Il villano creduto principe, il principe creduto villano, il valore premiato, le dame concorrente. Opera mista.* Seventeenth century. Modena.

(*j*) *Il Girello,* a musical burlesque. 1668 and 1674.

Il Crispo. 4186, no. 6. There are in the Cas. Misc. f. 172, two copies of the printed scenario for the performance of D. Ansaldo Grimsaldi's *Crispo* in 1628 and 1653 but this does not offer a satisfactory model for the scenario in MS. 4186. Allacci records plays on this subject by Annibale Marchese (1715) and by G. F. Savaro del Pizzo (1662).

La Dame amoureuse par envie, see Cane del Ortolano.

La Dama Demonio, see Arlequin persecuté. Cp. La donna demonio.

La Dame amoureuse par envie, see Cane del Ortolano.

La Dama creduta Spirito folletto. Nap. ii. 68. Notices of other versions and performances of Calderon's popular play, *La Dama Duende* are:

(*a*) Ric. 25.5.1716, and again as *Spirito Folletto, ou Lutin amoureux,* 28.11.1722.

(*b*) *Spirito Folletto.* Title of a Modenese scenario 1675, 1682, 1683.

(*c*) *Esprit Follet,* commedy by d'Ouville. 1641. Parf. vol. ix, Table Chronologique, p. 25.

(*d*) Revived by Veronesi, 21.5.1744, as *Coralline Esprit follet,* and on 6.3.1755 as *Camille Esprit follet.* Dict. ii. 179 and vii. 424.

(*e*) Rasi quotes a sonnet by Alviani celebrating the appearance of Angiola Nelli in *Spirito Folletto.*

Demetrio. (*Arlequin Démétrius.*) Ric. 1.8.1717.

Demetrio Moscovito. Printed scenario for performance of a tragedy by G. Teodoli in 1653. Cas. Misc. 658.

Demonii sono le donne, o pure la Donna Sfarzosa chiarita. Nap. ii. 55. Taken from Lope de Vega's *Diablos son mujeres.*

Il Descienzo di Coviello. Per. no. 1.

La désolation des deux comédies. 9.10.1718. Hist. Anec. i. 250.

Le deuil de Scaramouche et d'Arlequin. Paris. 21.6.1680 and 21.6.1682. Moland and Bartoli, xxxviii. See *L'Ospedale de' Pazzi.*

Diana e Columbina finte dive. Title of a Modenese scenario.

DIARBECH. Two copies of the printed summary as performed in 1692 are in Cas. Misc. 979 and Misc. f. 172.

DIAVOLO PREDICATORE. Nap. i. 66. Taken from Lope de Vega's *Diavolo Predicatore.* See Caprin, *Riv. Teat. It.,* 1905.

Il Diavolo Zoppo. 16.3.1746.

Di amor non inteso. 4.12.1718. From Boccabadati. See *Gli amanti che non s'intendono.*

IL DISCENZO. Nap. ii. 43.

LE DISGRATIE D'ARLECHINO, viz. *Harlequin's Misfortunes; or, his marriage interrupted by Brighella's Cunning. With his comical circumcision.* Acted by the Italian Comedians at the Haymarket Theatre, 1726. Brit. Mus. 1344.1.13 (3). See also *A. tormenté par les fourberies de Scapin.*

DISGRAZIE DI COLAFRONIO. By N. N. Mag. Printed by Bartoli.

DISGRAZIE DI FLAVIO. Scala, 35.

LE DISGRAZIE E FORTUNE DI PANDOLFO. By N. N. Mag. Printed by Bartoli, no. 20. Reprinted by Del Cerro, *Nel Regno delle Maschere.*

DISGRATIE DI POLICINELLA. Nap. i. 23. The corresponding play *Le cento disgrazie con Pulcinella perseguitato da donne nutrice,* was printed in 1824. Compare *Les vingt-six infortunes d'Arlequin.* 3.9.1751. Dict. vi. 234. Cp. *I trenta-due disgrazie d'Arlecchino.* Goldoni, *Memorie,* i, chap. 41, and *I trenta-due disgrazie di Truffaldino.* Bartoli, xlvii.

†DAL DISORDINE IL BUON ORDINE NE NASCE. Untitled scenario in Bib. Corsini, codex 976.

LI DISPETTI. (*a*) Loc. i. 7. (*b*) Cors. ii. 36.

DISPREZZARE, CHI S'AMA. Nap. i. 22.

Il Dissoluto. Bartoli, xlvii.

Divorce d'Arlequin avant sa mariage. Played once on 12.10.1720, but noted as 'très ancien'. Dict. ii. 325. Cp. *Il Divorzio d'Arlichino.* Ric. 12.10.1720, and *Divorce d'Arlequin et d'Argentine.* 3 acts played first 13.5.1741, Dict. ii. 325, and revived 10.6.1744 as *Il Divorzio d'Arlecchino e Corallina.*

Le Docteur amoureux. 3 acts, played for the first time 22.6.1745. Dict. ii. 332.

Le Docteur Avocat pour et contre, ou, juge de son ennemi. 24.6.1755. Gurrini.

Le Docteur Médecin amoureux. 6.7.1717. See *Nozze in Sogno.* Dict. ii. 332.

DON GILE, SCHIAVO DEL DEMONIO, see under SCHIAVO.

DON GIOVANNI D'ALVERADO, see under GIOVANNI.

Donna Anna. Modena title and in the repertory of Diana Constantini in 1681. Brunelli, p. 109.

DONNA CATERINA, see under CATERINA.

La Donna custode d'un segreto. Bartoli, xlvii.

La Donna demonio. Vatican Cod. Lat. 10244. Reprinted by G. M. Monti in *Rivista abruzzese di scienze, lettere ed arti,* xxxiv. 1919.

DONNA ZANNI. Nap. i. 40.

LA DONZELLA DI LAVORO. Nap. ii. 71.

LE DOPPIE GELOSIE. Gueulette, ff. 1–6.

Doppio matrimonio d'Arlichino. Ric. 12.5.1721. Noted by the Dict. vii. 576 as anonymous and 'très ancien'. See also Hist. Anec. i. 453.

DORINA, SERVA NOBILE. Nap. ii. 76. Possibly connected with DORINA, LES DEUX RIVAUX DUPPÉS PAR ARLEQUIN. Ric. 12.1.1719.

LA DOT PER LA METEMSICOSA. Gueulette, f. 437.

IL DOTTORE BACCHETTONE. Nap. ii. 72. Mag. Bartoli, no. 22. Reprinted by E. Pettraccone, p. 396.

DOTTOR BURLATO. Nap. ii. 37.

IL DOTTOR DISPERATO. Scala, 13.

Il Dottore disgraziato in amore con Belfonte e Gramustino impazziti per accidenti. Title of a Modenese scenario recorded by Re in *Giorn. Stor.* lv.

Dottore Giudice Padre. By R. Lombardi, comico di Bologna. Bartoli, xlvii.

DOTTORE INNAMORATO, see GRAZIANO INNAMORATO.

IL DOTTORE E PANTALONE AMANTI INVISIBILI, see COLARARA.

Dottor pedante scrupuloso. (*Arlequin rival du Dottore.*) Ric. 29.7.1719. Cp. *L'Ipocrita,* 'scenario antico'. Paris. 23.1.1718. Given at the Foire S.-Germain et S.-Laurent as *Arlequin Écolier ignorant et Scaramouche Pédant Scrupuleux.* The corresponding play is Gioanelli's *Il Dottor Baccheton,* undated. The connexion with *Tartuffe* is discussed by A. Neri (*Giorn. Stor.* i) who suggests that the scenario goes back to Scala's *Il Pedante*; and by Del Cerro who suggests Aretino's *Ipocrito* as a prototype; there is, however, no close resemblance. See also *Chi trova un amico trova un tesoro.*

LE DOUBLE DÉNOUEMENT, see ARLECCHINO SCANDERBERG.

DRAGON DE MOSCOVIE, or DE TRANSILVANIE, see BASILISCO DI BARNAGASSO.

LI DUBBII. (*a*) Loc. ii. 34. (*b*) Cors. ii. 18.

La Duchessa di Sassonia. In the repertory of 'Eulalia', 1681. Brunelli, p. 109.

LI DUE AMANTI FURIOSI. Ven. 5. Reprinted in *Giorn. Stor.* xcvii, 1931. Derived from Della Porta's *La Furiosa.*

LI DUE ANELLI INCANTATI. Nap. ii. 74. Cp. *Li anelli Magici.* Ric.
13.5.1717.

I DUE ARLECCHINI. Gueulette, f. 126. Cp.

*Li due Arlecchini con scene francesi. Given for the first time 20.3.
1718. Dict. ii. 300.

Les deux Arlequines. Dict. i. 300, referring to *Les Comédiens par
hazard*, by Gueulette, 15.3.1718, which included Riccoboni's
one-act farce. See also *Les Jumeaux.*

LI DUE CAPITANI. Loc. ii. 7.

LI DUE CAPITANI SIMILI. Scala, 17.

LI DUE FIDI NOTARI. Scala, 20.

LI DUE FINTI PAZZI. Cors. ii. 42.

LI DUE FINTI ZINGARI. Scala, 32.

LES DEUX FLAMINIA, see BARONE TEDESCO.

LE DUE FLAMINIE SIMILE. Ven. 11.

I due folletti. Bartoli, xlvii.

LE DUE FONTI INCANTI, LA PRINCIPESSA MUTA, E BUFFETTO GOVER-
NATORE. 4186, no. 44. See also *La Cometa.*

LI DUE FRATELLI RIVALI. (*a*) Loc. ii. 10. (*b*) Cors. i. 15. Reprinted
in *Giorn. Stor.* xviii, 1891.

LI DUE FRATELLI AVELENATI. Ven. 43 corresponds to *I fratelli
avelenati.* Nap. i. 60.

LI DUE FRATELLI SIMILI CON LA PAZZIA D'AMORE. Loc. ii. 8.

I due gemelli Truffaldini. Bartoli, xlvii.

I due Lelio, e due Arlichini. New 15.7.1716. Dict. ii. 301. Revived
29.12.1740 as *Les Jumeaux* and noted as derived from
Secchi's *La Moglie.* Cp. *Les quatre semblables.* 1754. Dict.
vii. 473. See also *I quattro Simili.*

Li due Mezzetini, in the repertory of the *Confidenti* in November
1615.

I Due Orazi et le due Cinzie. Played 22.11.1622 in Florence. See
Solerti, *Musica, Ballo e Drammatica alla Corte de' Medici
1600–37.* 1905.

LI DUE PANTALONI. Cors. i. 5. Corresponding to

Li due Pantaloni et due Arlecchini con le scale. New 30.11.1716,
but noted with a French title by Parfaict as 'très ancien'.
Dict. ii. 303. Connected with *Escalades Nocturnes.* Dict. vii.
501.

LI DUE PULCINELLI SIMILI. Per. f. 197.

I DUE RIVALI INGANNATI, see LA DORINA.

LE DUE SCHIAVE. Cors. i. 16. See *Le Due Sorelle Schiave.*

LE DUE SCHIAVE. Loc. i. 28. See *Emilia.*

LI DUE SCOLARI. Cors. ii. 7. Distinct from

LI DUE SCOLARI. Ven. 25.

LI DUE SIMILI D'ANDREINI. Nap. i. 48. Corresponding to

DUE SIMILI CON LE LETTERE MUTATE. Ven. 29. I am indebted to
T. Beltrame for pointing out that these scenari correspond to
G. B. Andreini's comedy *I duo Lelii simili*, 1622.

I DUE SIMILI. Loc. (*a*) and (*b*) i. 24 and 25. A performance of a
scenario with this title is noted by Malherbe for Sept. 1613.
Baschet, p. 242.

DUI SIMILI. Per. no. 9. 1736.

Li due simili Belfonte e Gramustino. Modenese title.

DUO SIMILI CON LE LETTERE MUTATE. (*a*) Ven. 29. (*b*) Corresponding
most closely to Nap. i. 48.

LE DUE SORELLE RIVALE. Ven. 23. Derived from E. Lucchetti's *Due
Sorelle Rivale*. See also Dict. v. 187.

LE DUE SORELLE SCHIAVE. Loc. ii. 9. Corresponds to Cors. *Le Due
schiave.*

I due Tartaglia. Bartoli, xlvii.

LI DUE TRAPPOLINI. Loc. i. 13 and Cors. i. 32.

LI DUE VENEZIANI. Loc. ii. 6. See *Due Pantaloni.*

Educazione perduta. Ric. 4.10.1717.

Gl'Effetti della Lontananza. Ric. 5.10.1717.

ELISA ALI BASSA. Loc. ii. 38.

EMILIA. Nap. i. 15. Derived ultimately from the *Epidicus* of Plautus
by way of Groto's *Emilia*. There is a close connexion between
Locatelli's plot and *La Schiava* of Verucci, 1629. See *supra,*
Chap. III. Corresponding scenari are: *La Schiava,* Cors. i.
2, and *Le Due Schiave,* Loc. i. 28. See also *Le Furberie di
Scapino.*

Endimione, o L'amor vendicato. By A. Riccoboni and Biancolelli.
Tuilleries, 27.1.1721, and Hôtel de Bourgogne, 6.2.1721.
Dict. ii. 388.

ENFANT GÂTÉ, see MADRE COMPIACENTE.

Gli equivoci dell'amore. 1667 and played 10.9.1716. Taken from
Ante todos mi dama. Dict. ii. 430.

L'EQUIVOCI D'UNA NOTTE. Nap. ii. 61. Cp. *Equivoci* in the repertory
of Diana Constantini, 1681. Brunelli, *Teatri di Padova,*
p. 109.

Ercole. Ric. 19.12.1717.

L'ERMAFRODITO. Cors. i. 10. Distinct from

L'ERMAFRODITO. 4186, no. 35.

*Gli Errori dell'amore con Flaminia amante risoluta e disperata, o
La Rissoluta.* Ric. 23.5.1716. Given with the title in French
in Dict. ii. 440.

Errore del nome. Du Charni, op. cit. i. 35–6. Taken from Lope de Vega's *Verdad sospechosa.*

ESCALADES NOCTURNES, see LI DUE PANTALONI ET DUE ARLECCHINI CON LE SCALE.

Esclave perdue et Retrouvée. 24.6.1716. Hist. Anec. i. 145. See *La Schiava perduta e riperduta.*

EL ESCONDIDO Y LA TAPADA, see AMANTE NASCOSTO.

EULARIA BALORDA. Nap. i. 45. Possibly connected with **Eularia muette par amour.** Paris, 1680. Bartoli, xxxviii. Yorick quotes *E. muta per amore* for a puppet play in the seventeenth century.

LA FABRICA. (*a*) Loc. ii. 45. (*b*) Cors. ii. 21. Rearranged in LE FABRICHE. Nap. ii. 46.

IL FALSO INDOVINO. (*a*) Loc. ii. 37. (*b*) Cors. ii. 13.

IL FAMOSO TRIUMVIRATO CON LO SPARTIMENTO DEL MONDO FRA OTTAVIO, LEPIDO, E MARC' ANTONIO. 4186, no. 11.

LA FANTASMA. Loc. i. 19. Derived from Plautus' *Mostellaria.*

LA FANTESCA. Loc. i. 17. Derived from Della Porta's *La Fantesca.* Corresponding to *Il Furbo.* Cors. i. 8.

IL FATE VOI. Loc. ii. 27.

LA FEDE INFEDELTÀ. Ven. 10.

LA FEINTE INUTILE, see LA BUGGIA IMBROGLIA IL BUGGIARDO.

*****La Femme jalouse.** A. Riccoboni composed in verse 1704 and played in 1716. Dict. iv. 521. See *Moglie gelosa.*

FESTINO AMOROSO CON LE CINQUE LETTERE CAMBIATE. Nap. i. 8.

IL FIDO AMICO. (*a*) Scala, 29. (*b*) Ven. 22.

FIGLIA DISUBEDIENTE. (*a*) Nap. i. 19. (*b*) Gueulette, ff. 20, 28, played in 1667. Dict. ii. 579. Hist. Anec. i. 52. See also 13.8.1716.

La Fille Errante. 30.3.1753, but probably older. Dict. vii. 522.

La figlia fuggitiva. Bartoli, xlvi.

Le figlie inamorate del Diavolo. (*L'Amour extravagant.*) Ric. 13.6.1717. Dict. vii. 522.

FIGLIO DELLA MORTE, OVERO CARDELLINO CORNUTO VOLONTARIO. Nap. i. 81. See *La Cometa.*

FIGLIOL PRODIGO. Cors. ii. 29. See *Li Porci.*

Filli di Scio. 25.11.1618 in Florence. Probably derived from Della Rovere's *Filli di Sciro.*

FINTI AMICI. (*a*) Loc. i. 34. (*b*) Cors. ii. 31. See also *Il Ragazzo delle lettere.*

FINTO ASTROLOGO. Loc. ii. 22. See *Zingara.* Cors. i. 21. Distinct from

FINTO ASTROLOGO. Nap. i. 46. Taken from Calderon's *Fingido Astrologo.*

Finto Bravo. Nap. ii. 42.

Finta Celia. Ric. 23.8.1719.

Finto Cieco. (*a*) Scala 34. (*b*) Ven. 39. (*c*) Nap. i. 38.

Finto Gioannico. Nap. i. 27.

La Finta Madrigna. (*a*) Nap. ii. 54. (*b*) MS. Vat. Lat. 10244.
   sc. 3. Cp. Ric. *La Finta Madrigna,* 30.7.1716, and 30.6.1740.
   With French title, *La Belle-Mère Supposée,* i. 403.

†Li Finti Maestri. Untitled scenari in Barb. Lat. 3895, f. 31.

Il Finto Marito, see Il Marito.

Finti Mariti. Cors. ii. 27. Corresponding to

Li Finti Morti, Loc. i. 35, but distinct from

Finte Morte. Nap. i. 52. See also *Giostra Amorosa.*

Il Finto Negromante. Scala, 21. Possibly connected with a play
   of this title by L. Livio quoted by Allacci for 1629. 'Yorick'
   has this title for a puppet play in the seventeenth century.

La Finta Notte di Colafronio. Mag. Bartoli, no. 2.

La Finta Pazza. Scala, 8. Distinct from

La Finta pazza. Loc. ii. 3. Cp. *Li Tre Matti.* Possibly connected
   with *La Finta Pazza e Achille in Sciro,* by G. Strozzi, 1641.
   Moland, p. 173. Du Charni, ii. 16, 17, remarks a likeness to
   Regnard's *Folies amoureuses* and to Molière's *Amour Médecin.*
   To these Sanesi adds Sorel's *Palais d'Angelico.* Cp. *La Folle
   supposée.* Ric. 1.6.1716. Dict. ii. 607.

Li Finti Pazzi. Loc. i. 33.

La Finta Prigione. Loc. ii. 23.

Il Finto Principe. Nap. ii. 48. See *Creduto Principe.*

Il Finto Re. Nap. ii. 49. See *Creduto Principe.*

Il Finto Schiavo. Loc. i. 30. Derived from Della Porta's *Olimpia,*
   probably by way of F. Fornari's *L'Angelica,* 1584.

Li Finti Servi. Scala, 30.

Il Finto Servo. Loc. i. 36. Taken from *Gli Suppositi* of Ariosto.

Il Finto Servo del Cicognini. Ven. 26. Rossi can find no
   resemblance to any play of Cicognini's; possibly it was from
   a scenario of his composition.

I finti Sicari. By Principe Ercolani di Bologna. Bertoli, xlvii.

La Finta Sorella. Ven. 8. Corresponding to *La Sorella Picciola.*
   Nap. i. 9, q.v.

Li Finti Spiritati. Nap. ii. 3. Possibly connected with F. Lachi's
   Finta Spiritata. (Allacci), 1670.

Il Finto Tofano. Scala, 24.

Li Finti Turchi. (*a*) Loc. i. 31. (*b*) Cors. ii. 18. Corresponding
   mainly to

Li Finti Turchi. Nap. ii. 25. The title is found among the
   Modenese scenari. Cp. *Pantalon cherche trésor,* &c.

La finta volubilità. (*La feinte inconstance.*) Ric. 15.10.1716.

FLAGELLO DEL PADRONE. Nap. ii. 59. Cp. *Truffaldino ballordo, flagello alle fortune del suo padrone.* Dated 1680. Printed by E. Re, *Riv. Teat. It.,* 1910. Cp. *Il flagello del suo patrone, o, Pulcinella servo sciocco.* Printed 1803. Probably a variant was the *Servo Sciocco,* 8.6.1716, noted in Dict. i. 299.

FLAMINIA SCHIAVA. Played for the first time in 1610. Derived from Cecchini's play. Printed by Paglicci-Brozzi in *Gazz. Mus. di Milano,* 1891, No. 38.

FLAMINIA SOLDATA PER VENDETTA, see SOLDATO PER VENDETTA.

FLAMINIO DISPERATO. Bib. Vittorio Emanuele. Rome, 1641. Printed by Martucci in *Nuova Antologia,* vol. iii, 1885.

FLAVIO FINTO NEGROMANTE. Scala, 28.

FLAVIO TRADITO. Scala, 5. Summarized by W. Smith in *Mod. Phil.,* 1911. Cp. *Amico Tradito.*

LA FLORA. 4186, possibly taken from Andrea Salvadori's *Flora,* acted in Florence 1628. Solerti, op. cit., p. 189.

Les Folies de Coraline. 8.1.1746. Dict. ii. 598.

LA FOLLE SUPPOSÉE, see LA FINTA PAZZA.

Fonso. Bartoli, xlvii. See *Alfonso?*

LA FORESTIERA. Loc. ii. 17. Corresponding to *La Pellegrina.* Cors. i. 26. According to T. Beltrame (*Giorn. Stor.* xcvii) the scenario is derived from Bargagli's *Pellegrina;* but I do not find any resemblance sufficient to warrant the connexion of plots.

FORNARO GELOSO. Nap. i. 53. Cp.

Il Fornajo geloso. (*Arlequin jaloux vindicatif.*) Ric. 31.8.1718.

FORSENNATA PRINCIPESSA. Scala, 41. Summarized by W. Smith in *Mod. Phil.,* 1911. Reprinted by Petraccone, p. 341, and from him by I. A. Schwartz in *The Commedia dell'arte and its influence on French Comedy in the Seventeenth century,* 1933.

FORTUNA DI FLAVIO. Scala, 2. W. Smith, *Mod. Phil.,* 1911, and see *The Commedia dell'arte,* for a discussion of the possible influence of the mountebank scenes on Jonson's *Volpone.*

LA FORTUNA DI FORESTA PRINCIPESSA DI MUSCOVIA. Scala, 50.

LA FORTUNATA ISABELLA. Scala, 3. Summarized by Moland.

FORTUNA NON CONOSCIUTA. Nap. ii. 15.

FORZA DELL'AMICIZIA. Codex Vat. Lat. 10244, sc. 9. Probably to be identified with the play by A. Riccoboni. 6.2.1717. Dict. ii. 615. Revived by Veronesi, 5.2.1748. Dict. vi. 136, and vii. 530. In Rossi's repertory 1779. Rasi. Probably taken from G. A. Cicognini's *Forza dell'Amicizia.*

*FORZA D'AMORE. Prologue and summary of a comedy by S. Costanti di Napoli in Bib. Vaticana Codex Ott. Lat. 2418. The plot is not disposed in the usual form as was probably not intended for improvised recitation.

La forza dell'educazione. Ric. 26.12.1716.

La Forza del fato. In the repertory of 'Eulalia' in 1681. Brunelli, p. 109. Ric. 5.8.1719. Hist. Anec. i. 361, and Dict. ii. 619. Caprin, *Riv. Teat. It.*, 1905, connects it with a play by Cicognini.

LA FORZA L'ASTIMOSA [*sic*, i.e. LASTIMOSA]. 4186, no. 40. Derived from Lope de Vega's *Fuerza Lastimosa.*

FORZA DE LA MAGIA. Barb. Lat. 3895. Distinct from
FORZA DELLA MAGGIA. Nap. ii. 9.

La forza del naturale. Ric. 11.10.1717. According to Dict. vii. 530, 12.10.1717. Derived from Moreto's comedy. Dict. ii. 623.

La forza del sangue e dell'amicizia. 18.6.1740; again on 31.12.1745, Dict. ii. 624, and with the alternative title *Pantalon dupe* in 1755. Dict. vii. 531 and 636. Possibly derived from *Fuerza de la Sangre* by Guillem de Castro y Belvis.

A FOURBE, FOURBE ET DEMI per Cintio. Gueulette, f. 332. Played 18.10.1674. Hist. Anec. i. 127. See also Dict. i. 20.

I fragmenti italiani. Ric. 5.12.1718.

I FRATELLI AVELENATI. Nap. i. 60. See *Li Due F. Avelenati.*

FRATRICIDA CRUDELE, LE FINTE CACCIE CON BERTOLINO IMPICCATO. 4186, no. 32. See *Giustitia Catalana*, no. 17.

Les Fripiers. Paris, 1672. Biancolelli, see Nicoll, p. 384.

IL FORMENTO. Cors. ii. 14. Distinct from
IL FROMENTO. Loc. i. 39. See *Adelfi.*

I Funerali d'Arlecchino. 30.11.1744. Dict. ii. 655.

Les fourberies d'Arlequin. In the repertory of A. Constantini, 21.10.1739, and again in 1741. Dict. vii. 533. Cp. *Les Fourberies d'Arlequin*, one act. 3.2.1722. Dict. ii. 634 and Sp. F. ii. 218.

LE FURBARIE DI COVIELLO. Per. f. 327. Cp. *Trappolaria.*

Le furbarie di Scapino. Noted by Riccoboni, 25.1.1726 and (*Hist.*, p. 72) as old. According to Parfaict a revision by Romagnesi, 15.7.1741, of *Arlequin tourmenté par les fourberies de Scapin.* Dict. v. 85. Bartoli, p. lxi, refers back to Groto's *Emilia.*

LE FURBARIE PER VENDETTA, *or Brighella's Revenge contrariated by Argentina, with Harlequin's Transformations, viz. A physician, Master of Musick, Lady Pancake, Swaggerer, Giant, and Grand Bashaw. Together with his comical Agress and Regress to and from the Tower.* Played by the Italian Comedians at the Haymarket, 1726. Brit. Mus. 1344.1.13 (4).

IL FURBO. Cors. i. 8. See *La Fantesca.*

Li Furti. Loc. ii. 32. Derived from *Il Furto* by Fr. D'Ambra.

Il Gabinetto. 1.10.1742. Bartoli, xli.

La Gageure. Gueulette, f. 433.

*La Galatea. By A. Lolli. Probably this is an author's scenario and was not meant for improvising comedians. Printed in *Propugnatore di Bologna*, N.S., vol. iv, p. 199, 1891.

Gare della Gelosia. Nap. i. 13. Possibly connected with *Gare di sdegno, d'amore e di gelosia. Played in Bologna, 1674.

Le garre del matrimonio. (*Le mari dupé.*) A. Riccoboni. 8.10.1716. Dict. iii. 316. The plot is taken from *Armida* by Calderari.

D. Gastone di Moncada. In the repertory of Diana Constantini in 1681. Brunelli, p. 109. Ric. 2.11.1718. Caprin, *Riv. Teat. It.*, 1905, refers it to Cicognini's *D. Gastone de Moncada.*

La Gelosa Isabella. Scala, 25.

La Gelosia. Loc. i. 47. Corresponding to *Grotta di Mescolino.*

†Gelosia e Fedeltà di Rosalba. Untitled scenario of a tragicomedy in Barb. Lat. 3895.

Le Gelosie dei maritati. (*Les Malheurs des Mariés.*) Ric. 16.9.1717, and Dict. vii. 570.

Il Geloso non amante e l'amante non geloso. Nap. ii. 80.

La Gelosa Guerriera. Cors. i. 50.

I Gemelli. Ric. 4.11.1717. Taken from *Prigione d'amore*, by Sforza degli Oddi. Dict. iii. 242.

*Le Gemelle. Summary of a comedy in 5 acts found in Bib. Vaticana Codex Ott. Lat. 2418. Probably not intended for improvised recitation.

Le Gentilhomme campagnard, ou les débauches d'Arlequin per il docteur Lolli. Gueulette, f. 274. Cp.

Gentilhuomo Campagnuolo. 1670. Bartoli, xxxviii. See also *Amore e honore di Ramidoro*, and *Gli Stravizzi d'Arlecchino.*

La Gerla, see Zerla.

La Presa di Gerusalemme. 4186, no. 18.

Il Giardino. (*a*) Loc. ii. 46. (*b*) Cors. i. 29. Corresponding to Giardino Metaforico. Nap. i. 21.

La Giostra. Loc. ii. 41. Cp. *La Pazzia di Doralice.*

Giostra Amorosa. Nap. i. 37. See also *Finti Mariti.*

Don Giovanni d'Alverado. Nap. i. 14. Cp. *Il Servo Padrone.* Per. Probably connected with Scarron's translation of *Don Juan d'Alverado* as *Jodelet maître et valet*; and with *Il Finto Marchese overo le Gelose Cartelle*, by M. M. B. Accad. Assinato, 1676. See also *Arlecchino finto Gentilhuomo Duellista per forza.* Ric. 28.5.1716.

*Giovanna d'Arco. Bib. Arsenale. Paris, 6099, xviiith century. See Mazzatinti, iii. 153, and A. Valeri, op. cit.

Il Giuocatore. A. Riccoboni. 6.12.1718. Dict. iv. 472 and Hist. Anec. i. 260.

GIUOCO DELLA PRIMIERA. Loc. i. 1. Reprinted by E. del Cerro, *Nel Regno delle maschere.* Corresponding to *Sententia in favore.* Cors. ii. 9.

GIUCO DI FORTUNA, see IL CAVALIER PAZZO.

GIUDICII DEL CIELO. Nap. i. 69. Derived from *Lo que son juyzios del cielo,* by Perez de Montalvan.

I GIUDICI DEL DUCA D'OSSUNA, quoted by Gueulette with the French title and noted as 'per Cintio', f. 286.

Giudice Padre. By Principe Ercolani di Bologna. Bartoli, xlvii.

LA GIUSTITIA CATALANA. (*a*) 4186, no. 17. (*b*) Another version is given in no. 32 as *Il Fratricida crudele, le finte caccie con Bertolino impiccato.*

GIUSTO CASTIGO. Scala, 40.

IL GIUSTO PRINCIPE. (*a*) Loc. ii. 52. Reprinted by W. Smith, *Romanic Review,* xiii. 1922. Corresponding to (*b*) Cors. i. 24. For another version see *Principe Severo.* Loc. ii. 51. 'Yorick' quotes this title for a puppet play in the seventeenth century. Cp. *Rev. of English Studies,* vi, 1930. F. E. Budd, *Philanira,* and Whetstone's *Promos and Cassandra.*

IL GRANCHIO. (*a*) Loc. i. 46. (*b*) Cors. ii. 30. (*c*) Nap. i. 12. Derived from *Il Granchio,* by Salviati, 1561. See also *La Mula* where several *motifs* are repeated.

LE GRANDEZZE DI ZANNI. Loc. i. 10. Corresponding to *La Nobiltà di Bertolino.* Cors. ii. 5, and *La Nobiltà,* Cors. ii. 35. Possibly connected with Agresti's *Villano arricchito insopportabile* (Allacci), 1625.

IL GRAN MAGO. (*a*) Loc. ii. 214. (*b*) Cors. i. 5. See App. G.

GRATIANO MERCANTE FALLITO. Loc. ii. 25. Corresponding to *Claudione mercante fallito,* q.v. As there is no connexion between this scenario and Tomadoni's play of *Pantalone mercante fallito* (see App. B (2)), it is probable that Riccoboni's scenario of *Pantalone mercante fallito,* given 18.10.1716, belongs to another tradition.

GRAZIANO INNAMORATO. Cors. ii. 41. See *La Schiava.* Possibly to be identified with *Le Docteur amoureux.* 22.6.1745. Dict. ii. 332.

La Griselda. Ric. 23.8.1717.

LA GROTTA DI MESCOLINO. Nap. i. 25. Cp. *Gelosia.* Cp. *La Grotta di Finocchio,* 21.9.1716, with the French title *Grotta di Scapin,* and the note by Parfaict that Scapin played Finocchio in a mask as in Italy, but because in Paris he was usually seen with an uncovered face he removed the mask after the second scene. Dict. iii. 50.

La Grotta incantata. Bartoli, xlvii.

LA GROTTE NOUVELLE. Gueulette, f. 190.

LA GROTTA VECCHIA. Ibid., f. 187.

GUARDIA DI SE STESSO. Nap. i. 70. Taken from *El Alcayde de se mismo* by Calderon. Cp. *Roberto, o vero il carceriero di se stesso.* Played in Bologna, 1697.

Harlekin Friseur, oder die Zaubertrompete. Pantomime in 3 acts in German, 1778. Brit. Mus. 11745 ee. 22.

Der lustig-singende Harlequin oder Pickelhaerungs-hochzeit. Ibid.

L'HIPOCRITE. Gueulette, f. 289. Cp. *L'Ippocrita.* Ric. 23.1.1718, and *L'Ipocrita* in Rossi's repertory in 1770. See also *Dottor Bacchetone.*

HONORATÀ POVERTA DI RINALDO, see under RINALDO.

L'HUOMO DA BENE. Nap. ii. 79. Taken from *El huomo de bien* by Lope de Vega.

L'HUOMO POVERO TUTTO PENSIERI OVVERO CHI TUTTE VUOLE, TUTTO PERDE. Nap. ii. 1.

Gl'Ignoranti furbi per interesse. 13.10.1717. Dict. iii. 135.

GL'IMBROGLI DI COVIELLO. Per. no. 18.

L'IMBROGLITI INTRIGHI. Ven. 35.

L'Impatiente. Ric. 8.11.1717. Described as 'canevas italien sur un canevas François de M. Coypel'. Dict. iii. 136–7.

Gl'Impegni. In the repertory of 'Eulalia' in 1682. Brunelli, p. 109.

L'Impegno contro l'amico. Ric. 26.5.1717. 'Ancien', Dict. ii. 408.

L'IMPEGNO DEL CASO. (*Les engagemens da hazard.*) Gueulette, f. 198. Moland derives this play from '*Croire ce qu'on ne voit pas et ne pas croire ce qu'on voit*', from Calderon. See Bartoli, xxxvii, n. 2.

L'Impostore suo malgrado. A. Riccoboni. 4.7.1717. Dict. iii. 138. Hist. Anec. i. 181. From Moreto.

IMPROPRIO CARNEFICE. Repertory of Diana. 1681. Brunelli, p. 109.

L'INCAMISCIATA. Cors. ii. 6.

LI INCANTI AMOROSI. Loc. ii. 20. Corresponding to *Amorosi Incantati.* Cors. i. 12.

L'INCAUTO, OVERO L'INAVVERTITO. (1) Bartoli. Taken from Barbieri's *L'Incauto.* Variants of the theme are:

(a) *Oratio Inavertito.* Ven. 46.

(b) *L'Amante inavertito.* Nap. ii. 26.

(c) Probably *Belfonte inavvertito,* a Modenese title.

(d) *Lelio amante inavertito.* Ric. 17.6.1716.

See also *Truffaldino ballordo.*

L'INCORONATO CIECO. 4186, no. 3.

Gl'Influssi di Saturno. Bartoli, xlvii.

Gl'Inganni dell'Inimicizia con le multiplicate stravaganze de matrimoni. Title of a Modenese scenario.

INGANNI. Nap. i. 31.

INGANNI DI FLAMINIA. Ven. 40.

Inganno fortunato. (L'heureuse surprise.) 18.5.1716, with T. Vicentini as Arlequin. Parfaict notes that it contains scenes from a Spanish play. Dict. iii. 75, 76. This was probably *L'Inganno fortunato, overo L'Amata aborrita* translated from the Spanish by Brigida Bianchi, 1685.

INGIUSTO RETTORE. Nap. i. 58. See *Principe Severo.*

INIMICI DEI VECCHI. Ven. 41. Distinct from

Inimicizia. Loc. i. 49. Corresponding to Lachi's play, *L'Inimicizia tra i due Vecchi.* Printed 1684.

L'INNAMORATA SCALTRA, OVERO LA DAMA SCALTRA. Per. 1716.

L'INNOCENTE TRAVAGLIATA. Gueulette, f. 132. Paris, 4.2.1718, Dict. iii. 317, and Ric. 6.2.1718.

L'INNOCENTE INGANATA COI DUPLICATI SPONSALITII. Title of a Modenese scenario.

L'INNOCENTE PERSIANA. Scala, 45.

LA INNOCENTIA RIVENDUTA. (*a*) Cors. ii. 12. (*b*) Nap. ii. 3. Corresponding to

LA INNOCENTIA RIVENUTA [*sic*]. Loc. i. 4. See App. G. The theme of this tragicomedy is taken from *Il Decamerone, Giorn.* II. ix. It is worked up into a play *Il Dispettoso Marito* by Verucci. It was revived by Dominique Biancolelli as *La Femme fidèle ou les apparences trompeuses.* Lyons, 1710, printed 1712. Cp. *Innocente venduta e rivenduta,* or, *Adulterio Innocente,* or, *Arlecchino fléau des Turcs.* Dict. vii. 363, and 18.8.1716. Dict. i. 19. Played 4.1.1740 by the company of A. Constantini. Dict. ii. 156. 'Yorick' gives *Innocenza Riconosciuta,* as the title of a puppet play in the seventeenth century.

L'Innocenza Difesa. Opera musicale. Cas. Misc. 11. Probably connected with the play of this title quoted by Allacci for 1722 and derived from *Innocenza Giustificata,* 1699. It is included here because the theme is that of the *Principe Severo* tradition, q.v.

L'INNOCENZA INFELICE ET IL TRADIMENTO FORSENNATO. Nap. ii. 83. Compare a title quoted by Allacci, *L'Innocenza difesa nel Tradimento Occulto, ovvero, il Perdono è cosa da Grande.* L. Raimondi, 1685. Cp.

L'INSALATA. Nap. ii. 45, and Per. 1737. Possibly connected with *L'Insalata, o, Arlecchino marito senza moglie,* and with *Le Pot Pourri.* 10.1.1720. Ric.

L'Interesse, o la figlia creduta Maschio. Ric. 30.5.1716. Taken from Secchi's *L'Interesse* and augmented by Riccoboni ; said to have given Molière something towards the *Dépit amoureux.* Dict. ii. 579. MS. note.

INTRICHI AMOROSI. Cors. i. 49.

GL'INTRIGHI D'AMORE, OVVERO LA FINESTRA INCANTATA. Bartoli. Translated by K. Mantzius, op. cit., vol. ii, p. 350. Probably connected with

*Les Intrigues amoureuses. By Veronesi. 28.9.1733. Dict. vii. 558.

GL'INTRICHI DI COVIELLO PER LA MOGLIE. Nap. ii. 50.

INTRICHI DELLA NOTTE BEN RIUSCITI. Nap. ii. 17.

Les Intrigues de Scapin. 13.5.1755. Dict. vii. 558.

L'INTRONATI. (*a*) Loc. i. 50. (*b*) Cors. ii. 15. (*c*) Ven. 51. Derived from *Gl'Ingannati* of the Intronati of Siena, 1531.

INVENZIONE DI COVIELLO. Nap. ii. 12.

L'IPOCRITA, see IL DOTTOR BACCHETTONE.

LA CASTA E CONSTANTE IPSICRATEA CON I TRIONFI DI POMPEO NEL REGNO DI PONTO NELLA FARSAGLIA. 4186, no. 5. Among the mask names assigned in the margin are Virginio and Vittoria who are probably the couple distinguished by their performance in Vienna in *Belisario*, q.v.

ISABELLA ASTROLOGA. Scala, 36.

ISABELLA SOLDATO PER VENDETTA, see VEDOVA COSTANTE.

ISOLE. (*a*) Nap. i. 36. (*b*) Ven. 4. The only reason for the naming of this scenario seems to be that Isole was the actress's name. See Dict. i. 210. T. Beltrame (*Giorn. Stor.* xcvii) remarks a likeness to G. B. Andreini's *La Turca*, but to this I cannot agree. Cp. *Arlequin condamné à mort par conversation, ou, Scapin vindicatif.* Ric. 12.10.1716. Dict. i. 210, and *Arlequin pendu par conversation.* Dict. vii. 379.

L'Italiano infrancesato. Ric. 30.6.1717. Dict. iii. 223.

L'Italiano maritato a Parigi. A. Riccoboni. 25.6.1716. Dict. iii. 225. Hist. Anec. i. 154. Bartoli, xliv.

La Joûte d'Arlequin et de Scapin. 2 acts. 13.4.1744. Dict. iii. 199.

Juifs de Babylone. Moland. 1.7.1680.

Les Jumeaux. 4.11.1717. From *Prigione d'amore*, by Sforza degli Oddi. Dict. iii. 242. Cp. *Les Deux Arlequins Jumeaux* which was arranged so that one actor might take both parts. Dict. vii. 384. Probably distinct from (1) *Les Jumeaux ou Les Ménechmes*, 4.12.1705, and (2) *Les Jumeaux*, 1740, which is said to be derived from Secchi's *La Moglie.* See also *Les deux Lélios* and *Arlequin parvenu.*

I ladri alla fiera. Ric. 14.11.1717. See Du Charni, *Lettre* iv, p. 15. Dict. vi. 255. Hist. Anec. i. 191.

LADRO AMOROSO. Nap. ii. 88.

LADRO, SBIRRO E GIUDICE, see ARLEQUIN LADRO, etc., in the repertory of the company of the Duke of Modena, *c.* 1681. Brunelli, p. 109.

LE LADRONIE ACCIDENTALE. Nap. ii. 77.

Lealtà con Valore. Printed scenario for an opera drawn from Ariosto. Cas. Misc. 12.

LÉLIO AMANT INCONSTANT ET ARLEQUIN SOLDAT INSOLENT, see L'AMANTE VOLUBILE.

LÉLIO DÉLIRANT PAR AMOUR, see L'HOSPITALE DE' PAZZI (under O).

LÉLIO FOURBE INTRIGUANT, see CABALISTA.

Lelio inavertito. (*L'amant étourdi.*) 1.9.1717; May 1728, as *Contretemps.* Dict. iii. 269. See *L'Incauto.*

Lelio prodigo. 21.6.1716. Adapted by A. Riccoboni from Boccabadati. Given with the French title, *Lélio prodigue et Arlequin prisonnier par complaisance.* Dict. iii. 271.

Scenario del Leone. Two printed scenari for performances of a Latin tragedy in 1646 and 1652. Cas. Misc. 658 and Misc. f. 172. Probably not belonging to the Commedia dell'arte.

Le Liberal malgré lui. A. Riccoboni. 12.12.1716. Dict. iii. 273.

LE LIBERTIN, see MADRE COMPIACENTE.

LA LITE. Loc. ii. 48. Not connected with

La Lite, Loc. ii. 47, as Valeri supposed.

Lucilla Costante. Played by the *Accesi* in Milan, 1632. Cp. Fiorillo's *Lucilla Costante,* 1632.

LUCREZIA ROMANA. Nap. i. 71, and in the repertory of Diana Constantini in 1681. Brunelli, p. 109.

Il Lunatico. Gueulette. See Hist. Anec. i. 61. See *Amante Lunatico.*

Le Lutin Amoureux. Ric. 28.11.1722. Dict. iii. 282. 20.11.1722. Played with French scenes. Cp. *Spinetta Lutin amoureux.* Parfaict records the excellent performance of Flaminia in the scene of the Tirade which was taken from Regnard's *L'Homme à bonnes fortunes.*

La Madre compiacente. 28.11.1717. Riccoboni gives alternative titles: *Le Libertin, ou, L'enfant gâté.* Parfaict records M. Mario's excellent performance of *L'enfant gâté.* Dict. iii. 274.

Maestro di ballo. Ric. 15.11.1719. Dict. iii. 294. Probably derived from Calderon's *El Maestro de Danzar.*

LA MAGA. Cors. ii. 18.

LA MAGIA D'AMORE CON BERTOLINO CREDUTO GENTILHOMO DI CORTE SENZA LA PAZZIA. 4186, no. 7.

The Same, 'CON LA PAZZIA'. Ibid., no. 10. There are some slight alterations in Act III.

LA MAGICA DI PANTALONE. Cors. ii. 44.

La Magie naturelle, ou la magie sans magie. Dec. 1678. Moland.
See Bartoli, xxxviii. See also *Natural Magic.*

MAGIOR GLORIA. (*a*) Codex Vat. Lat. 10244, sc. 11. (*b*) Nap. i. 34.
Cp. *La Maggior Gloria d'un grande è vincere se stesso, con
Rastellino spia muta, buffone attaccato alla corda.* Modenese
title, and cp. Brunelli, p. 109, and *Magior Gloria, ou, Arlequin
Bouffon de Cour.* Ric. 20.5.1716. Dict. i. 204. The tradition
probably goes back to Lope de Vega's *La mayor virtud de un
Rey,* and extends to F. Gallesi's *Principe vincitor di se stesso,*
1723. See Sarti, op. cit.

IL MAGO. Cors. i. 13. See App. G.

Il Mago della barba verde. By Felice Sacchi, comico, detto 'Felicino
Sacchetto'. Bartoli, xlvii.

MAISON À DEUX PORTES DIFFICILE À GARDER, see CASA CON DUE PORTE.

MA MAÎTRESSE EN [?EST] PRÉFÉRABLE A TOUT OUTRE CHOSE. Gueulette,
f. 207, gives the Spanish title as *Aules che lodo mi damma.*

MALA LINGUA. Ven. 19. See *Tradito.*

LA MALADIE DE SCARAMOUCHE. Gueulette, f. 380.

La Maladie di Spezzafer. Paris, 1680. Moland, 1681.

MALIZIE DI COVELLO. Nap. ii. 36. Printed by C. Levi in *Riv. Teat.
It.,* anno xi, vol. 16.

LA MANCATA FEDE. Scala, 27.

IL MARESCIALE DI BIRON. 4186, no. 14. The relationship to *El
Mariscal de Biron* by Juan Perez de Montalvan is discussed
by W. Smith in *Mod. Phil.* xx. 3, 1922–3.

Il Maritarsi per vendetta. In the repertory of 'Eulalia' in 1681.
Brunelli, p. 109.

I Mariti senza moglie. 22.12.1742. Dict. iii. 317 and 333. Cp.
Pantalone e Arlichino becchi senza mogglie, 4.8.1721.

IL MARITO. Scala, 9. Reprinted by Petraccone, p. 302. This
scenario was later expanded by Scala into *Il Finto Marito,*
printed 1619. Cp.

IL FINTO MARITO. (*a*) Loc. i. 32. (*b*) Nap. ii. 65.

LE MARI DUPÉ, see LE GARE DEL MATRIMONIO.

LE MARI. Gueulette, f. 289. Possibly connected with

Il Marito, o Columbina mari per complaisance. 18.4.1719. Bartoli,
xli. 'Yorick' gives this title for a puppet play in the seventeenth
century. Cp. *Mari supposé.* 7.5.1745. Dict. iii. 316.

Il Cattivo marito. 5 acts. 13.6.1747. Dict. iii. 356. Possibly to be
identified with *La moglie virtuosa e il marito vizioso* (*La Femme
virtueuse*), or with *Pantalon debauché, ou Arlequin qui se trahit
lui-même.* A. Riccoboni. 29.6.1716. Dict. iv. 69.

IL MARITO PIÙ ONORATO CORNUTO IN SUA OPINIONE. Nap. ii. 86.
Printed by C. Levi in *Riv. Teat. It.,* anno xi, vol. 16, p. 257.

Cp. *Il Cornuto per opinione, ou Arlequin cocu imaginaire.* Ric.
10.11.1716. Cp. *Il Ritratto, overo Arlecchino cornuto in suo
opinione.* Moland refers to this scenario in connexion with
Molière's *Sganarelle, ou le Cocu imaginaire.*

MASCHERATA NOVA. Ven. 24. Reprinted in *Giorn. Stor.* xcvii, 1931.

IL MASTRO DI TERENTIO. Ven. 31. Corresponding to *La Scola di
Terenzio.* Nap. ii. 14.

Il Matrimonio egale. Commedia in soggetto, eighteenth century.
Modena.

MATRIMONIO PER FURTO. Nap. ii. 31. Possibly connected with
Matrimonio per Inganno by S. del Pizzo, 1662.

I Matrimoni tra i vivi e i morti. 26.1.1722. Dict. iii. 324.

LA MEDAGLIA. Nap. i. 8.

MEDICO DI SUO HONORE. 4186, no. 1, 1642. Derived from Calderon's *El Medico de su honra.*

MEDICO PANERALIO, PULCINELLA MEDICO PER FORZA. Per. no. 15.
The theme is used in *Pulcinella finto Dottore, ovvero le Nozze
Contrastate,* 1728.

MEDICO VOLANTE. (*a*) Bartoli, no. 8. (*b*) Nap. i. 59. Reprinted by
P. Toldo, *Atti della R. Acc. delle Scienza di Torino,* xlii, 1907.
(*c*) Gueulette, ff. 95–107. (*d*) In the repertory of Diana
Constantini, 1681. Brunelli, p. 109. Cp. *Arlecchino Medico
volante.* 14.6.1716 and 23.12.1739. Dict. ii. 155. Hist.
Anec. i. 76. Probably the source of Molière's *Médecin Volant.*
See Moland. Cp. *Gramustino medico volante.* Modenese title.
Plays on this theme are:

(*a*) *Le Médecin Volant.* 1662. Bib. Fr. iii. 63.

(*b*) *Le Médecin Volant.* By E. Boursault. One act. Dict. 486.

Truffaldino medico volante, comedia nova e ridicola, published by
G. Morelli al Segno della Fortuna, Milano, 1673. This was
apparently written up from the scenario. See A. Neri, *Giorn.
Stor.* i. 75. *Truffaldino medico alla moda, overo Medico Volante.*
Undated and anonymous, published by Lovisa, noted by Allacci.

LES MENTEURS EMBARRASSÉS, see LA BUGGIA IMBROGLIA IL BUGGIARDO.

La Mère contredisante. 3.2.1718. Dict. iii. 402.

Merope. Ric. 11.5.1717. Hist. Anec. i. 175.

LE METAMORFOSI D'ARLECCHINO. Gueulette, f. 254. A. Constantini played in a comedy of this title in 1739 but the piece
is described as new. Dict. ii. 155 and iii. 419.

LE METAMORFOSI DI PULCINELLA. Per. no. 5, 1730. Reprinted by
Petraccone, p. 445, and Del Cerro, p. 464. The play of *Li
metamorfesi di Pulcinella finto astrologo, statua, ragazzo e
mummia,* 1824, belongs to this tradition. Brit. Mus. 11815
aaa. 41. Distinct from

Les Métamorphoses de Polichinelle. 1740. Dict. iii. 420.

Les Métamorphoses de Scaramuccia. 23.9.1745. Dict. vi. 104.

La Metempsicose d'Arlequin. A. Riccoboni and Dominique (Biancolelli). 19.1.1718. Dict. i. 444 and iii. 423.

D. Micco è Lesbina. Ric. 17.8.1729.

†Mɪ ʙᴀʀɢɪᴀᴢᴢɪ. Untitled scenario in Barb. Lat. 3895, f. 28. Two versions are given. The title is suggested by the concluding words.

*La moglie gelosa. Ric. 7.6.1716. Dict. ii. 522. See *Femme jalouse.*

Mᴏɢʟɪᴇ ᴅɪ ꜱᴇᴛᴛᴇ ᴍᴀʀɪᴛɪ. Nap. i. 90. There is no connexion with Cicognini's play as Caprin supposes.

Mᴏɢʟɪᴇ ꜱᴜᴘᴇʀʙᴇ. (*a*) Loc. ii. 28. (*b*) Cor. i. 31.

Iʟ Mᴏɴᴅᴏ ᴀʟ ʀᴏᴠᴇꜱᴄɪᴏ ᴘᴇʀ Cɪɴᴛɪᴏ. Gueulette, f. 269, gives the French title as *Le monde renversé, ou Arlequin jouet de la fortune.* Played in July 1669. Moland.

Iʟ Mᴏɴɪʟᴇ. Ven. 32.

Mᴏɴᴛᴀɢɴᴇꜱᴇ. 4186, no. 43. Probably derived from Lope de Vega's *Famosa Montañesa.*

Lᴀ Mᴏʀᴛᴇ ᴅɪ Lᴇᴏɴᴇʟʟᴏ ᴇ Bʀɪꜱꜱᴇɪᴅᴀ. 4186, no. 26.

I Mᴏʀᴛɪ Vɪᴠɪ. Gueulette, ff. 6–17. Dict. iii. 461. Bartoli, xxxv, n. 5. The titles suggest that the following plays and scenari belong to the tradition:

(*a*) *Les Morts Vivans,* a farce played in Paris, 1573.

(*b*) *I Morti Vivi.* Sforza degli Oddi, 1576. Jacopo Pagnini, 1600.

(*c*) *Muertos Vivos.* Lope de Vega.

(*d*) *Les Morts vivans.* M. d'Ouville, 1645.

(*e*) *Arlecchino e Scapino morti vivi.* 20.2.1750. Bartoli, xxxix.

Il Moto perpetuo. Commedia all'improviso by the *Inconstanti* in Florence. 22.10.1621. Solerti, op. cit.

Lᴀ Mᴜʟᴀ. Loc. ii. 44. See also *Il Granchio.* Distinct from Lᴀ Mᴜʟᴀ Gʀᴀɴᴅᴇ. Cors. i. 20.

La Nascità del primogenito del Truffaldino. Bartoli, xlvii.

Natural Magic. A short play after the Italian manner. New Theatre Little Lincoln's Inn-fields, 1697, by Mr. Peter Motteux and other hands. See *La Magie naturelle.*

Nᴀᴜꜰʀᴀɢɢɪᴏ ᴅɪ ʟɪᴇᴛᴏ ꜰɪɴᴇ. Nap. 120.

Nᴀᴜꜰʀᴀɢᴇ ᴅ'AʀʟᴇQᴜɪɴ, see Aʀᴄᴀᴅɪᴀ Iɴᴄᴀɴᴛᴀᴛᴀ.

Lᴀ Nᴀᴠᴇ. (*a*) Loc. ii. 26. (*b*) Cors. i. 33. Reprinted by F. Neri and E. Petraccone, p. 360. See App. G.

Negligente. One-act scenario by A. Riccoboni. 24.4.1721. Dict. iii. 490.

Ne la Damma, ne la spada si fide al amico. Biancolelli, i. 44. See Nicoll, p. 385.

***Ne Meno amore si libera da Amore.** Printed scenario for perform-
ance in 1682. Cas. Misc. Connected with Calderon's *Psiques
y Cupido* and probably not intended for improvising comedians.

NERONE IMPERADORE. Nap. i. 68. Reprinted by Petraccone, p. 417,
and Del Cerro. In the repertory of Diana Constantini, 1681.
Brunelli, p. 109. Probably derived from Lope de Vega's
Neron Cruel directly or through the translation of N. Biancolelli, *Il Nerone*, 1666, or of C. Boccaccio, *Nerone*, 1679.

LA NINFA DEL CIELO TRADITA NEL HONORE, CON LA FORZA DEL
PENTIMENTO. 4186, no. 38. Possibly derived from *Contessa
Bandolera, ninfa del cielo*, by Tirso da Molina.

NOBILE PLEBEO. Nap. i. 50.

LA NOBILTÀ. Cors. ii. 35. A variant of

LA NOBILTÀ DI BERTOLINO. Cors. ii. 5. See *Grandezze di Zanni*.

NON AMANDO. Nap. i. 89.

NON PUÒ ESSERE. (*a*) Nap. i. 33. Reprinted by Petraccone, p. 469.
(*b*) Per. no. 3. Reprinted by del Cerro in *Rivista d'Italia*,
xiv, 1911. Cp. (*c*) *Argomento e scenario della commedia
intitolata Non può essere, overo custodire una donna e fatica senza
frutto*. Played at Carneval, 1682, in the Palazzo del l'ecc.
Sig. Marchese del Carpio ambassadore di S.M.C. Derived
from Lope de Vega's *Non puede ser* or from a re-arrangement
by Moreto. This theme is borrowed by English dramatists in
Crown's *Sir Courtly Nice*; *Tarugo's Wiles, or the Coffee House*,
1668; *Sir Thomas Callicoe or the Mock Nabob*, 1758; *The
Midnight Hour*, 1787.

NON VUOLE RIVALI AMORE. Gueulette, f. 116. 1.10.1716. Dict. i.
268. Hist. Anec. 94. Bartoli, xxxvi. Cp. *Arlequin Peintre*,
and *Amor non vuol rivali*. Possibly the title quoted by Brunelli
among 'Eulalia's' comedies, *Non vuol viver amore*, is an error
for the above.

***Argomento delle Nozze degli Dei.** Printed scenario for a spectacular
show presented in 1637 by G. C. Coppola. Cas. Misc.
658. See Solerti, op. cit., p. 201.

LE NOZZE DEGLI EBREI. Ven. 7.

Le Nozze in sogno. (*Docteur médecin amoureux.*) Ric. 6.7.1717.
'tres ancien'. Dict. ii. 332.

LE NOZZE INTERROTTE. Nap. ii. 85.

Le Nozze Sfortunate d'Arlecchino. Ric. 27.11.1718. According to
Parfaict this was a bad copy of *M. de Pourceaugnac* and was
only played once. Dict. iii. 176.

LA NUOVA PAZZIA. 4186, no. 12. A variant of *La Pazzia d'Aurelio*,
no. 41.

Nuovo Finto Principe, see Creduto Principe.

Obligo più che amore ovvero il Moro. Nap. ii. 92. Derived from Della Porta's *Il Moro*.

L'Oggeto odiato. Nap. ii. 27. Cp.

L'Oggetto odiato sempre avanti agli occhi. Modenese title. See F. Bartoli, ii. 240.

Ohimè il cuore. Gueulette, ff. 57–64 with French title *Le Cœur me fait mal*. In the repertory of Diana Constantini in 1681. Brunelli, 1681.

L'Omo povero tutto cabala. Ibid., and for 'Eulalia'.

L'Onorata fuga di Lucinda da P. C. Bartoli, no. 10.

Oratio Burlato. Loc. i. 21. See *Capitano Burlato*. The main plot is taken from della Porta's *Fantesca*.

Oratio Innavertito. Ven. 46. See *L'Incauto*.

Orlando Furioso. (*a*) Loc. ii. 1. (*b*) Cors. i. 1. Drawn from Ariosto. Flaminia Cecchini played Angelica, Bradamante, and Isabella in Mantua.

Ormondo del Pona. 4186, no. 34.

Orologio. Ven. 37.

L'Orseida in 3 parts. Scala, 46, 47, 48. See W. Smith, *Commedia dell'arte*, for an abstract.

L'Ortolano. (*Le Jardinier.*) Ric. 2.11.1716.

L'Ospedale de' Pazzi. Nap. ii. 53. Cp. *L'hôpital des foux ou le deuil d'Arlequin*. Gueulette, ff. 17–20. See also *Le deuil de Scaramouche et d'Arlequin*. Distinct from

L'Hospitale de' Pazzi, o Lélio délirant par amour. Ric. 24.9.1716. Cp. *Lélio délirant par amour et Arlequin Écolier ignorant*. Dict. iii. 269.

L'Ospite Amoroso. Cors. i. 35.

Oste Geloso. Nap. i. 83.

Padre Crudele. Bartoli, no. 6

Il Padre ingannato. Ric. 14.9.1719. Dict. iv. 90. As *Le Père de Bonne Foi*. Hist. Anec. i. 365. Distinct from

Padri Ingannati. Nap. i. 84.

Padri partiali. 29.5.1718. Dict. v. 94 and Hist. Anec. i. 229.

I padri rivali delle loro figlie. Ric. 19.8.1717. According to Parfaict by an anonymous French author. Dict. iv. 103.

*Il Pandolfo. Scenario for *Commedia per musica*, 1748. Modena.

Pantalon, Amant malheureux, see La Casa Svaligiata.

Pantalon dupé. Played only once. 2.3.1746. Dict. iv. 71. See *La forza del sangue*, &c.

Pantalone mercante failleta [sic]. (*Pantalon Banqueroutier Vénitien.*) 22.7 and 18.10.1716. Dict. iv. 68.

Pantalone et Arlichino mariti senza moglie. Dict. vii. 637.

Pantalon Patroncin. Goldoni, *Memorie*, i, chap. li.

Pantalone spetiale. (*Apoticaire ignorant.*) Ric. 6.12.1716. Parfaict gives an alternative title: *Arlequin feint Guéridon, Momie et Chat ou Apothicaire Ignorant.* Dict. vii. 362.

IL PANTALONCINO. (*a*) Loc. ii. 50, in 5 acts. Corresponding to (*b*) Cors. ii. 50 in 5 acts. (*c*) Cors. ii. 16 in 3 acts. See App. G.

PATRONE E SERVO. Nap. i. 18.

PAZZIA D'AURELIO. 4186, no. 41. See *Nuova Pazzia*.

PAZZIA DI CINTIO. Nap. ii. 16.

Pazzia di Delia. Played in Florence in Jan. 1610.

LA PAZZIA DI DORALICE. Loc. i. 9. Reprinted by Petraccone, p. 366. See also *La Giostra*.

Pazzia del Dottore. In the repertory of Diana Constantini, 1681. Brunelli, p. 109. Played in Bologna in 1687, by the Accademia del Porto. Ricci, *Figuri teatrali*. Possibly connected with *L'Invidia in Corte*.

LA PAZZIA DI DORINDO. Loc. ii. 5. A slight rearrangement of LA PAZZIA DI FILANDRO. Loc. ii. 4. Printed by F. Neri.

La Pazzia d'Eularia. Gueulette, f. 283.

Pazzia di Flaminia. Given by the *Accesi* in Florence, 1623.

LA PAZZIA DI FLAMINIO NEL PRESUPPOSTO TRADIMENTO DI CINTIA. 11.5.1680. Manuscript in the possession of B. Croce. See *supra*, p. 106.

LA PAZZIA D'ISABELLA. Scala, 38. Abstract given by W. Smith, op. cit., p. 112.

La Pazzia di Lavinia. Played by 'Lavinia' Antonazzoni of the *Confidenti* in Bologna, 1615. Rasi, i. 171.

La Pazzia di Lelio. Given by the *Uniti* in Florence, 1604.

UN PAZZO GUARISCE L'ALTRO. Printed from a Manuscript in Vienna by E. Maddalena, *Sitzungsberichte der K. Ak. der Wissenschaften*, vol. cxliii, Phil.-hist. Classe, 1900. See also *Don Chisciotte*.

IL PEDANTE. Scala, 31. For a discussion of this scenario in relation to *Tartuffe* see Moland; W. Smith, op. cit.; A. Neri, *Giorn. Stor.* i. 75; and P. Toldo, ibid. xxiii. 247.

Di peggio in peggio. Bartoli, xlvii.

*Pelagio. Printed scenario for a performance in 1652. Probably not belonging to the Commedia dell'arte. Cas. Misc. Fol. 172.

LA PELLEGRINA. (*a*) Cors. i. 26. (*b*) Nap. ii. 10. See *La Forestiera*, Loc. ii. 17.

PELLEGRINO FIDO AMANTE. Scala, 14.

CAVALIERO PIGNATTERO COL PRINCIPE DISSOLUTO, E BUFFETTO FORNACIERO DI PIGNATTE E BOCCALI. 4186, no. 43.

PENSIERI VANI. Ven. 36.

LE PÈRE TROMPÉ, see ARLECHINO FINTO PANTALONE.

LA PEREGRINA. Modena.

IL PEREGRINO AMANTE. Nap. ii. 62.

D. PERICCO SPAGNUOLO. Nap. ii. 47. Corresponding to *Pulicinella marchese di Chiochiava*. Per. no. 7.

LA PERNA. Cors. ii. 26.

PER OGNI SCAMPO MILLE INTOPPI. Nap. ii. 69.

PIETRA INCANTATA. Per. no. 13.

PITTOR FORTUNATO. Nap. i. 27.

LI PITTORI LADRI. Nap. ii. 64.

PLAUTO ALLA MODERNA. Printed scenario for a performance in 1693. Cas. Misc. Fol. 172.

POLLICINELLA BURLATO. Nap. ii. 56. Sanesi, op. cit., p. 40, connects this scenario with *Policinella pazzo per forza* as possible sources for *M. de Pourceaugnac*.

PULCINELLA DISAMMOGLIATO. Codex Vat. Lat. 10244, sc. 5.

POLLICINELLA FINTO REGENTE. Nap. ii. 19.

POLICINELLA INAMORATO. Nap. ii. 33.

POLLICINELLA LADRO, SPIA, GIUDICE E BOIA. Nap. ii. 73. See also *Arlecchino Ladro*, &c.

POLICINELLA DAMA GOLOSA. Nap. ii. 70.

PULCINELLA MARCHESE DI CHIOCHIAVA. Per. no. 7. See also *D. Pericco Spagnuolo*.

POLLICINELLA PAZZO PER FORZA. Nap. ii. 91. See also *P. Burlato*.

POLLICINELLA PITTORE. Nap. i. 32. See also *Arlequin juif, peintre et tailleur*. Bartoli, xxxviii.

POLLICINELLA SPOSO E SPOSA. Nap. i. 82.

*LE PONT NEUF. Gueulette, f. 253. 'Je ne crois pas aucune pièce de théâtre.'

LI PORCI, OVERO SPECCHIO DE GIOVANI. Loc. i. 42. Corresponding to

LI PORCI. Cors. ii. 34 and

FIGLIOL PRODIGO. Cors. ii. 29. These scenari seem to be derived from Verucci's *Le Moglie Superbe*, 1621. See *supra*, pp. 215–19. A French version appears in *Piphagne*, 1615. Bib. Fr. iii. 465. The 'lazzi' used by Locatelli persist in the repertory of the Areliari till the end of the seventeenth century. Rasi, i. 199. For the relationship to the theme of the prodigal son see F. Neri, *Le Parabole, Studi sul Teatro Italiano Antico*, 1915.

Le Port-à-l'Anglais ou, les Nouvelles Débarquées. 25.4.1718. Hist. Anec. i. 198.

IL PORTA-LETTERE. Scala, 23.

LE POT POURRI, see ARLECCHINO MARITO SENZA MOGLIE.

IL POZZO. (*a*) Loc. ii. 47. (*b*) Cors. i. 25.

POZZO INCANTATO. Nap. i. 17.

IL POZZO DEL PASQUATI. Ven. 27.

LI PRIGIONI DI PLAUTO. Loc. ii. 31. Based on the *Captivi*. Reprinted by Petraccone, p. 356.

PRIGIONIER VENDICATIVO. Nap. i. 6. See *Zanni Vendicativo*. Cp. LE PRISONNIER VENDICATIF. Gueulette, f. 197.

IL PRINCIPE D'ALTAVILLA. (*a*) Loc. i. 6. (*b*) Cors. ii. 32.

Il Principe Geloso. Ric. 30.5.1717. Caprin, *Riv. Teat. It.*, 1905, connects this play with G. A. Cicognini's *Principe Geloso.*

PRINCIPE POLLACCO. Nap. i. 44.

IL PRINCIPE SEVERO. (*a*) Loc. ii. 51. (*b*) Nap. i. 58. See *Il Giusto Principe*. Printed by W. Smith in *Romanic Review*, xiii, 1922.

LA PRENCIPESSA TIRANNA. Codex Vat. Lat. 10244, sc. 12.

LE PRODEZZE DI RODERIGO. 4186, no. 27.

La Propreté, ou Arlequin Roy de Tripoli. Gueulette, f. 413. Possibly to be identified with *La Propreté ridicule.* Paris, 1678. Bartoli, xxxviii.

IL PROTEO. (*a*) Loc. i. 41. (*b*) Cors. i. 45.

QUATTRO ARLECCHINI. Gueulette. Parfaict records a performance in which women took the parts of the Arlequins, 4.10.1716, and notes that it is 'très ancienne'. Dict. iv. 319. Cp. *I quattro Zanni* in which G. Fortunati played Arlecchino. F. Bartoli, and Hist. Anec. 66.

QUATTRO FINTI SPIRITATI. (*a*) Ven. 3. (*b*) Scala, 33.

QUATTRO MEDICI, QUATTRO ASTROLOGI E TRE UOMMENNE [*sic*]. Nap. i. 62.

LI QUATTRO PAZZI. (*a*) 4186, no. 37. (*b*) Bartoli, no. 15. Translated and reprinted in *The Mask*, vol. iv, p. 112.

I QUATTRO POLLICINELLI SIMILI. Nap. i. 61. See also *Zanni finto morto*. Ven. 45.

Les quatre Scaramouches. Paris, 1680. Bartoli, xxxviii.

LI QUATTRO SIMILI DI PLAUTO. Nap. ii. 67. Cp. *I Quattro simili*, Modenese title, and *Les quatre semblables, Comédie Française* in verse by Dominique (Biancolelli) played 5.3.1733. Dict. iv. 320. Connected with *Les deux Lélios et les deux Arlequins*. Possibly *I quattro simili* by P. Chiesa (died 1678), noted by Colagrosso, op. cit., p. 73, belongs to the tradition.

IL RAGAZZO DELLE LETTERE. Cors. ii. 38 and corresponding to IL RAGAZZO PER LE LETTERE. Nap. ii. 39. Printed by C. Levi in *Riv. Teat. It.*, anno xi, vol. 16, p. 237. See also *Li Finti Amici*.

I Quattro Zanni. Bartoli, xlviii.

QUI PRO QUO, see ARLEQUIN VALET ÉTOURDI.

*Ragguaglio del Costantino. Tragedia. Printed scenario of a performance in 1653. Cas. Misc. 658.

Il Re Dormendo. Bartoli, xlvii.

IL REGALO DELLE DONNE. Gueulette, f. 210. Played 2.5.1668. Moland.

LA REGINA D'INGHILTERRA. See *Conte di Sex.* In the repertory of Diana, 1681. Brunelli, p. 109.

*La Regina d'Italia. Tragicommedia da rapresentare nel Teatro di Lombardia, 1721. Museo Correr. Codex Cicogna 80, ff. 239v.–240v. The characters are allegorical. Pantalone Bullo represents Venice; Gratiano, Pontefice; Brighello, the Duke of Savoy; Arlecchino, the Duke of Mantua. Rossi considers it was never intended for stage presentation by improvising comedians. *Giorn. Stor.* ix, p. 296, n. 4.

LA REGINA STATISTA REGNANTE. 4186, no. 2. Played in 1658 by Raparelli who intended to kill in earnest. (Rasi.) In the repertories of Diana Constantini, Isabella Sevilli, and Teodora Ricci. Rasi and Gozzi Memoirs. For the derivation of the theme from Spanish drama see W. Smith, op. cit. p. 129.

Le Remède anglois ou Arlequin prince du quinquina. Biancolelli, i. 78, 1680. See Nicoll, p. 387.

IL REMEDIO A TUTTI I MALI. Gueulette, f. 243. Played in Sept. 1668. Hist. Anec. 95.

LA RICCA SUPERBA. Ven. 16.

RICCO EPULONE. Nap. i. 67. Printed by F. Neri in *Le Parabole*, 1915, p. 39. Corresponding to

IL RICCO CON LAZZARO POVERO. 4186, no. 33.

L'HONORATA POVERTÀ DI RINALDO CON I TRADIMENTI DI FLORANTE E CODARDIA DI GANO MAGANESE. 4186, no. 36. This plot which is ultimately derived from Ariosto may have come to the Comedians by way of Lope de Vega's *Las probeças de Reynaldos.* Cp.

LA PAUVRETÉ DE RENAUD DE MONTALBAN. Gueulette, f. 114, and *Rinaldo da Montalbano*, Ric. 6.4.1717, given as *Renaud de Montalban ou le sujet fidelle* [sic], *ou l'Honnorata pauvertà.* Dict. iv. 418.

RINEGATO PER AMORE. Nap. i. 28. See *Lo Specchio*, &c. Possibly connected with Lope de Vega's *Argel fingido y Renegado de amor.*

LA RISSOLUTA, see ERRORI DELL'AMORE.

LI RITRATTI. (*a*) Loc. i. 3. (*b*) As a piscatory, Loc. ii. 51. Corresponding to (*c*) Cors. i. 17.

IL RITRATTO. Scala, 39. Reprinted by Petraccone, p. 310, and from him by I. A. Schwartz, *The Commedia dell'arte and its influence on French comedy in the seventeenth century*, 1933. See Moland, p. 83, for a translation. W. Smith suggests that Vittoria, the comedienne in this plot, represents Vittoria Piissimi.

Il Ritratto, overo Arlecchino cornuto in suo opinione. See *Il Marito più onorato.*

RITRATTO AMOROSO. Gueulette, ff. 107–9, with the French title *Le portrait amoureux.*

Ritrosia per ritrosia. Ric. 23.6.1717. This scenario is described as 'très ancien' and was taken from Moreto. Dict. iv. 384.

LA RIVALTÀ FRA COVELLO E POLICINELLA. Nap. ii. 22.

ROSALBA BIZZARA. Nap. i. 78.

ROSALBA INCANTATRICE. Scala, 44. 'Yorick' gives this as a title of a puppet play in the seventeenth century.

Rosaura Imperatrice in Constantinopoli. Scenario composed in French by D. Loccatelli and played in 1658. Hist. Anec. i.44.

ROSILDO, see AVOCATO CRIMINALE.

RUBBERTO DEL DIAVOLO. Nap. i. 77.

RUBELLA PER AMORE. Nap. i. 73. Possibly connected with a play of the same title by Savarro del Pizzo. 1662.

LA RUFFIANA. Loc. ii. 18.

RUOTA DI FORTUNA. 4186, no. 31. Taken from *Rueda de la fortuna* by Mira de Mesçua, possibly through the translation by Belvedere. See Croce, *Teatri di Napoli*, p. 127.

SACCARIA. Nap. i. 55.

Il Salasso. Bartoli, xlvii.

SALERNITANA. Nap. i. 80.

*Il Sancio. Printed scenario for a musical performance in 1656. Cas. Misc. 658.

SANSONE. Nap. i. 86.

SAPERE APPORTA DANNO. Nap. i. 24. Probably from Lope de Vega's *El saber puede dañar.*

SARDINELLO INVISIBILE. Cors. i. 40. Corresponding to *Trappolino invisibile.* Loc. i. 14.

LE SAVETIER, see CONTRATTI ROTTI.

LI SCAMBI. Loc. ii. 30 and Cors. i. 7. The corresponding scenari are: *La Balia Grande* and *La Sorella*, a very free adaptation. Taken from Razzi's *Balia.*

LE GLORIE DI SCANDERBECH CON LA LIBERTÀ DELLA PATRIA SOTTO AMURAT IMPERATORE DI CONSTANTINAPOLI. 4186, no. 45. Possibly connected with Montalvan's *Escanderbech* or as Broüwer suggests with Salvi's melodrama, *Scanderbeg*, 1714. See W. Smith, who refers to G. W. Bacon, *Essay on J. Perez de Montalvan.*

PANÉGIRIQUE DE SCARAMOUCHE. Gueulette, f. 237.

SCARAMOUCHE, LE FAUX BRAVE, see ARLECCHINO FALSO BRAVO.

SCENARIO:

Scenario anepigrafo. In the Modenese Archivio, described by E. Re.

Scenario. Printed by Stoppato from Museo Correr Codex, già Cicogna 998, ff. 592–5.

Scenario. Printed by P. Toldo in *Giorn. Stor.* xlvi. 128, from Archivio di Stato di Parma.

Scenario for an Opera Regia in 3 acts with a prologue and intermezzi noted by E. Re in the Modenese archives. See also the scenario described by Massimo Troiano, chap. i. Scenario fragment in Codex Vat. Lat. 10206, pp. 91–2.

Scenario. Isabella Principessa di Egitto.

LA SCHIAVA. Reprinted by E. Re (*Giorn. Stor.* lv, 1910) from a Modenese manuscript.

LA SCHIAVA. Cors. i. 2. See *Emilia.* Also a Modenese title.

LA SCHIAVA. Loc. i. 27. Corresponding to *Graziano Innamorato.*

LA SCHIAVA DI MESSINA. Nap. ii. 5.

LE DUE SCHIAVE. Loc. i. 28. See *Emilia.*

LA SCHIAVA PADRONA. Nap. ii. 41.

*LA SCHIAVA. COMEDIA NUOVA E RIDICOLOSA. By G. B. Calderai di Vicenza, Cav. di Malta. Allacci quotes two editions, 1589 in 8vo, Vicenza per Ag. dalla Noce, and 1609, Venezia per Pietro Beltramo in 12mo. I have not been able to examine either of these, but from the synopsis of an edition for Pietro Bartoli, in Pavia 1602, described in *The Mask*, 1923, vol. ix, p. 13, it appears that this play belongs in every respect to the Commedia dell'arte tradition.

La Schiava perduta e riperduta. Ric. 24.6.1716. Taken from Plautus' *Mercator* and revived as *Coralline esclave perdue et retrouvée,* and again as *Événements de l'Esclave,* &c., and *Esclave retrouvée.* 25.5.1751. Dict. ii. 458.

LI DUE SCHIAVI RIVENDUTI. Bartoli, no. 4.

LA SCHIAVETTA. Cors. ii. 49. Corresponding to *Turchetta.*

Lo Schiavo felice. 25.1.1747. Dict. iii. 79.

LO SCHIAVO DEL DEMONIO. 4186, no. 28. Corresponding to *D. Gile, schiavo del Demonio.* Nap. i. 65. Derived from Mira de Mesçua, *Comedia famosa del esclavo del Demonio.*

SCIPIONE TRIONFANTE DI CARTAGINE CON GLI AMORI DI SIFACE, E MASSINISSA CON SOFONISBA. 4186, no. 19. Possibly connected with Boccabadati's *Scipione, ovvero, Le Gare Eroiche.* 1693.

SCUOLA DI TERENZIO, OVERO IL DOTTORE MAESTRO DI SCOLA. Nap. ii. 14. Cp. *Il Mastro di Terentio.* Ven. 31.

Arlecchino maestro di scuola o la scuola di Terenzio. 27.6.1716. Dict. i. 253.

La scuola delle Vedove. Museo Correr. Codex ii. 81. 1740. Imitated from *L'École des femmes.*

GLI SDEGNI AMOROSI, BURLETTA DI COMEDIA ALL'IMPROVVISO. By S. Frandaglia da Val di Sturla. 25.11.1615. First noted by Valeri, in the fondo Coquebert de Montbret di Rouen. See Mazzatinti, *Biblioteche di Francia,* iii. 179. Reprinted by P. Toldo in *Giorn. Stor.* lxiv, 1914. Not connected with LI SDEGNI AMOROSI. Nap. i. 39, and Ven. 42. Cp. *Les dédains, ou le dépit amoureux.* Gueulette, f. 123. Cp. *Li Sdegni.* Scenario antico. 19.7.1719. Ric. gives the alternative title, *Amans brouillés,* q.v.

SEGNO FATALE CON LI TRE FINTI CIECHI. 4186, no. 21.

LI SEI CONTENTI. (*a*) Loc. i. 2. (*b*) Cors. ii. 2.

LI SEI SIMILI. (*a*) Loc. ii. 11. (*b*) Cors. i. 47.

LA SEMIRAMIDE. 4186, no. 8. Possibly connected with plays of this title by Moniglia 1671 and Bonacossi, 1674, quoted by Allacci.

LA SENESE. (*a*) Loc. ii. 17. (*b*) Cors. ii. 3 in 5 acts.

SENSALE DI MATRIMONIO. Nap. i. 49.

SENTENTIA IN FAVORE. Cors. ii. 9. See *Giuoco di Primiera.*

LA SEPULTURA. (*a*) Loc. i. 20. (*b*) Cors. i. 14.

SERPE FATALE. Loc. ii. 39. See *Cometa.* Corresponding to SERPE INCANTATO. Cors. ii. 24.

Servo astuto. (*L'heureuse trahison.*) 27.1.1717. Based upon the *Epidicus* of Plautus. See also *Emilia.*

IL SERVO FEDELE. Cors. i. 47.

IL SERVO PADRONE. Per. no. 2. See *Don Giovanni d'Alverado.*

SERVO RITORNATO. Loc. i. 16. With a variant in SERVO SCACCIATO. Loc. i. 35. These scenari were expanded and printed posthumously as *Li Sei Ritrovati* by B. Loccatelli. See *supra,* p. 134.

IL SERVO SCIOCCO. In Codex Vat. Lat. 10244, sc. 4. Cp. *Il Servo Sciocco.* 8.6.1716. Dict. i. 300. Cp. *Le Capricieux* (*Lunatico*). Gueulette remarks 'c'est la comédie du valet étourdi'. See also *Arlequin Valet étourdi.*

SETTE INFANTE DEL'ARA. Nap. i. 57. In a letter dated February 1634, Leonora Castiglioni refers to 'I 7 Infanti dell'ara' with the machines needed for an allegorical prologue and epilogue. Rasi, i. 606. Several dramatists made use of this Spanish romance for the stage: the scenario seems to correspond most closely with the tragedy by Lope de Vega, *El Bastardo Mudarra*.

La sfida d'Arlecchino e di Scaramuccia. 19.4.1741. Dict. ii. 265.

PRINCIPE SIDONIO. By Urbano Giorgi, 1654. Barb. Lat. 3737. Corresponding to *Amore tra nemici*. See *supra*, p. 160.

Il Sincero a contratempo. Ric. 21.10.1717. Dict. iv. 472. Siviglia, in the repertory of 'Eulalia' in 1681. Brunelli, p. 109.

Lo Smemoriato, o Arlecchino compétiteur di Lélio. Ric. 6.6.1716. Parfaict gives the title as *Maître distrait, ou Lélio amant distrait*. Dict. i. 209. See also *Amante Lunatico*.

Il Sogno avverato. 13.10.1751. Dict. v. 200. See *Arcadia Incantata*.

SOLDATO PER VENDETTA. Nap. i. 56. See *Vedova Costante*. Cp.

SOLDATO PER VENDETTA O ARLECCHINO SOLDATO IN CANDIA. Gueulette gives also *Addition au Soldat en Candie*, f. 265. Cp. *Flaminia soldato per Vendetta*. 5.10.1716. Dict. ii. 584, and *Flaminia veuve fidelle* [*sic*]. Hist. Anec. i. 159.

LA SORELLA. Per. 10. See *Li Scambi*.

SORELLA PICCIOLA. Nap. i. 9. See a variant in Ven. 8, *La Finta Sorella*. T. Beltrame (*Giorn. Stor.* xcvii) remarks the use of 'motifs' from Della Porta's *Sorella* and Groto's *Emilia*.

Il Sospettoso. A. Riccoboni 29.1.1721. Dict. v. 223. Hist. Anec. i. 478.

LA SOVERCHIA BONTÀ DI VIRGINIO. Ven. 14.

LA SPADA FATALE. Bartoli.

LA SPADA MORTALE. Cors. ii. 46. See *Cometa*.

LO SPECCHIO. Scala, 16.

LO SPECCHIO CON LA TURCA CONSTANTE. 4186, no. 25. A variant is found in *La Forza d'Amore con la Turca costante*, no. 46. See also *Rinegato per amore*.

LI SPIRITI. (*a*) Loc. i. 18. (*b*) Cors. i. 6.

SPIRITO FOLLETTO, see LA DAMA CREDUTA SPIRITO FOLLETTO.

LA SPOSA. Scala, 10.

Lo Sposalizio della Signora Luna. By Andrea Nelvi. Bartoli, xlvii.

GLI STRACCIONI. By Annibal Caro. Per. no. 19.

Gli strattagemmi dell'amore. Ric. 26.11.1716. Taken from Moniglia's *Passa per forza*. Dict. iv. 471.

STRAVAGANZE D'AMORE. In 5 acts. Nap. ii. 52.

LI STROPPIATI. Cors. i. 27. Corresponding to *Travestita*. There is no connexion between this scenario and Verucci's comedy, *Li Stroppiati*, 1610.

Gli Stravizzi d'Arlecchino. Alternative title for *Gentiluomo campagnuolo*. Paris, 1670. Rasi, i. 34.

I SUPPOSITI. Ven. 30. The relationship between this and Ariosto's comedy is discussed by V. Rossi in *Rendiconti del R. Ist. Lombardo*, Ser. II, vol. xxix, 14, 1896. Reprinted 1895, *Per Nozze Flamini-Fanelli*. Bergamo. See also *Finto Servo*.

Il Supposto Marito. 7.5.1745. Cp. *Il Supposto Marito di Quattro spose*.

***La Svevia**. Printed scenario for the performance of a revenge tragedy in 1629. Casanatense Misc. in 4to 668.

La Tabernaria. Per. no. 8. Probably to be identified with *La Tavernaria*. Bartoli, xlvii. Caprin, *Riv. Teat. It.*, 1905, records that A. Fiorilli was still playing in the old scenario of *Tavenaria* in the company of Sacchi at the beginning of the eighteenth century.

Les Tapis, o, Les Tuteurs Trompés. Gueulette, f. 145. Slightly rearranged for performance on 14.9.1716. Dict. v. 585. Played with the alternative title *Arlequin feint magicien*. Ibid. vii. 749.

Li Tappetti Alessandrini. Scala, 26. Reprinted by Petraccone, p. 323. Distinct from

Tappetti Alessandrini. Nap. ii. 13, with its variant in

I Tappetti, ovvero Colafronio Geloso. By N. N. Bartoli.

Tartaglia istorico. Bartoli, xlvii.

Il Teatro senza commedie. (*Le théâtre sans comédie, et les comediens juges ciporties.*) Gueulette, f. 227. Played in July 1668. Moland.

Il Terzo del Tempo. Cors. ii. 50.

***Das Testament, oder der Kranke in der Einbildung**. Printed by von Weilen. See Sanesi, p. 35.

Le Teste Incantate. (*a*) Loc. i. 8. (*b*) Cors. ii. 48.

Il Thesoro. (*a*) Loc. ii. 49. (*b*) Cors. ii. 22. Derived from Groto's *Tesoro*.

Il Torneo. Cors. i. 43.

***Le Torri**. Bartoli, xlvii.

Il Tradito. (*a*) Loc. i. 22. (*b*) Cors. i. 3. (*c*) ii. 25 in 5 acts. (*d*) Reconcerted in Nap. ii. 21. (*e*) The theme is also adapted in *Mala Lingua*, Ven. 19, and in (*f*) *Amante Tradito*. Ven. 50. Printed by C. Levi in *Riv. Teat. It.*, anno x, vol. xv, p. 14.

Il Tradito. (*Lélio et Arlequin Rivaux.*) 13.6.1716. Taken in part from *Aulularia* and said to have given Molière a scene for *L'Avare*. Dict. iii. 270.

Il Traditor Fortunato. Nap. ii. 78. Cp.

Il Traditore. 13.6.1716. Possibly connected with

Il Traditore Fortunato. By P. Sucini. 1685. Cp. also *L'Heureuse*

Trahison, 'canevas ancien accommodé au Théâtre par A. Riccoboni'. 1717. Dict. iv. 471.

LI TRAGICI SUCCESSI. Scala, 18. See W. Smith in *Mod. Phil.*, 1909.

LA TRAMUTATIONE. Loc. ii. 36. See *L'Anfitrioni*. Cors. ii. 19. Only the main idea of physical transmutation of lovers is borrowed from Plautus' *Amphytrion*.

TRAPOLA AND TRAPOLE see

TRAPPOLARIA. (*a*) Loc. ii. 14. (*b*) Ven. 47. (*c*) Nap. ii. 60. Other variants are:

(*d*) TRAPOLE. Nap. ii. 20.

(*e*) TRAPOLA. Nap. ii. 34.

(*f*) LE FURBARIE DI COVIELLO. Per. no. 21 The plot is derived from Della Porta's *Trappolaria*, a comedy based on Plautus' *Pseudolus*. For a discussion of the relationship between the plays and scenari see M. Scherillo, op. cit., pp. 117–34. B. Croce, *I Teatri di Napoli*, p. 79, and *Giorn. Stor.* xxix, p. 24, and Caprin, *Riv. Teat. It.*, 1905. The scenario has been reprinted by A. Perrucci, op. cit., and by Bartoli, p. xxxi, as 'Trappoleria'. The English counterpart is found in Tomkins's *Ignoramus*. Distinct from

LA TRAPPOLARIA. Cors. i. 28. Reprinted by F. de Simone Broüwer in *Giorn. Stor.* xviii, 1891.

TRAPPOLINO INVISIBILE, see SARDINELLO INVISIBILE.

LI TRE CAPITANI. Ven. 44.

I TRE FIDI AMICI. Scala, 19.

LI TRE FINTI TURCHI. Gueulette, ff. 109–84. Played with the alternative title *Pantalone cherche Trésor et Arlequin crû Marchand*. 22.7.1716. Dict. iv. 68. See also Hist. Anec. i. 71. It is described as 'très ancienne', and mentioned in a letter 13.8.1664 from Calderoni at Bergamo. Sanesi, p. 29.

I Tre Gobbi. Played by the *Gelosi* in Mantua in 1582. Rasi, ii. 228. It was handed down in the repertory of Tabarrino and according to Sand (ii. 252) was played by Grattelard, *c.* 1620. The story, as it is told by Strapparola in his *Tredici Piacevoli Notti*, i. 3, is attributed to Zambu of Bergamo. See G. Rua, *Giorn. Stor.* xvi. 243–6, 1891.

LE TRE GRAVIDE. 'burla da Ricciolina'. Bartoli, no. 11. Reprinted by E. Petraccone, p. 390.

I TRE LADRI SCOPERTI. Gueulette, ff. 35–43. Played 12.8.1716. With French title, *Arlequin voleur*. See Hist. Anec. i. 58.

LI TRE MATTI. Loc. ii. 2. A variant described as by N. N. is printed by Bartoli, no. 18. See also *La Finta Pazza*.

TRE ORBI. Nap. i. 76.

LI TRE PRINCIPI DI SALERNO. (*a*) Nap. ii. 66. (*b*) Bartoli, no. 14.

Cp. *Le Prince de Salerne.* 24.9.1746. Dict. iv. 230. A translation is printed in *The Mask*, iv. 335.

Li Tre Satiri. (*a*) Loc. ii. 28. (*b*) Cors. i. 4. Printed by F. Neri. See App. G.

Li Tre schiavi. (*a*) Loc. i. 29. (*b*) Considerably rearranged in Cors. ii. 45.

I tre Veneziani Gemelli. By Cesare d'Arbes Comico. Bartoli, xlvii.

Triomvirat de l'amitié. Gueulette, ff. 43-5.

Il Trionfo della Medicina. Gueulette gives 'additions' and refers to Robinet for a performance in 1674.

Le Trompeur trompé, par Mr. S. auteur d'Arlequin e Scarron juifs &c. Gueulette, f. 371. Played 9.7.1745. Dict. v. 566.

Truffaldino, I trenta-due disgrazie di. Bartoli, xlvii. Cp. *I trenta-due disgrazie d'Arlecchino* (D).

Truffaldino ballordo, etc., see Flagello del suo padrone.

Truffaldino confuso fra il bene e il male. Bartoli, xlvii.

Truffaldino finto principe. Bologna, 1682. See Creduto Principe.

Il Truffaldino geloso. Bartoli, xlvii.

Truffaldino molinaro innocente. By Antonio Sacco. Bartoli, xlvii.

Il Truffaldino servitore di due padroni. Bartoli, xlvii.

Truffaldino ubriaco Ibid.

Il Turbante d'Asmodeo. By Felice Sacchi. Ibid.

La Turchetta. Loc. ii. 15. A variant of *Schiavetta.* Cors. ii. 49. T. Beltrame (*Giorn. Stor.* xcvii) points out that the theme corresponds to Dolce's *Fabrizia* which is in its turn derived from the *Negra.*

Il Tutore. Barb. Lat. 3895.

Le Tuteur. 7.1.1744. Dict. v. 577. Cp.

Il Tutore. In Rossi's repertory in 1779. Rasi. To be identified with *Tuteurs trompés,* see *Tappetti Alessandrini,* and *Arlequin feint Magicien.*

Il Tutore ingannato. 11.12.1733. As *Le Tuteur trompé,* and with new scenes. 7.1.1744. Dict. v. 577.

Il Vagabondo. Bartoli, xlvii.

Les valets d'operateur (nel servitor da palco) ou Les Levantins a la chévre de Calicut. Gueulette, f. 183.

I varii personaggi di Florindo. Bartoli, xlvii. Reprinted by R. Bonfanti. *Il Noto,* 1901.

Vecchio Avaro. Loc. i. 45. Cors. ii. 23. See also *Avaritia.* Nap. i. 79. Distinct from

Il Vecchio Avaro. Per. no. 20.

I Vecchi Burlati. Modenese title. Cp. a play with the same title by R. Ricciolo, 1606, quoted by Allacci.

Vecchio Geloso. Scala, 6.

IL VECCHIO INGANNATO. Nap. ii. 30.

I Vecchi innamorati. 23.8.1747. Dict. vi. 185. See *Colarara.*

I Vecchi scherniti per amore, ou les deux Arlequins et les deux Arlequines. 31.12.1733. Dict. vi. 195. See also F. Bartoli, ii. 284.

LA VEDOVA CON DUE MARITI. Nap. ii. 82.

LA VEDOVA COSTANTE, OVERO ISABELLA SOLDATO PER VENDETTA. Bartoli. See also *Soldato per Vendetta* for variants.

IL VELENO. (*a*) Loc. i. 5 (*Veneno*, [*sic*]). (*b*) Cors. ii. 40.

Vendetta Comica. Ric. 16.6.1718.

LA VENDETTA DEL MARITO. Bib. Corsini codex 976.

VENGAME, OVVERO IL FISCHIETTO. Nap. i. 75.

VENGEANCE DE SCARAMOUCHE, see PERSONAGGI DI S.

VESTE. Nap. i. 35.

IL VIAGGIO DI SCARAMOUCHE E D'ARLEQUIN ALL'INDE. Gueulette, f. 354.

Le Vicende amore e fortuna. In the repertory of 'Eulalia', 1681. Brunelli, p. 109.

Il Violatore deluso. 25.9.1716. From Boccabadati. With the alternative title *Lélio et Arlequin ravisseurs infortunés.* Dict. iii. 270, and vii. 563.

Vita è un sogno. Ric. 10.2.1717. See Caprin, *Riv. Teat. It.*, 1905, who derives it from Calderon through Cicognini. Repertory of 'Eulalia', 1681. Brunelli, p. 109.

VITTORIA CACCIATRICE, LO SCHERNO DELLI FAVOLOSI DEI ANTICHI CON LA METAMORFOSI E ZACCAGNINO CREDUTO. 4186, no. 9.

†IL VOLUBILE IN AMORE. Untitled scenario. Barb. Lat. 3895.

VOLUBILTA DI FLAMINIA. Ven. 9.

IL ZANNI ASTUTO. Cors. ii. 37.

ZANNI BARBIERO. Ven. 49.

ZANNI BECCHO. Loc. i. 12. A variant of *La Cieca.*

ZANNI FINTO MORTO. Ven. 45. See also *I Quattro Policinelli simili.*

ZANNI INCREDIBILE CON I QUATTRO SIMILI. Ven. 21.

La Zenobia. In the repertory of 'Eulalia' in 1681. Brunelli, p. 109.

LA ZERLA. Gueulette gives the alternative title *La Hotte*, f. 85.

LA ZINGHERA. Loc. ii. 10. Taken from *La Calandria* by B. Dovizi da Bibbiena. Distinct from

LA ZINGARA. Cors. i. 21. See also *Finto Astrologo.* Possibly one of these was the scenario played by Vittoria in Florence in 1589.

Gli Zingari. (*Les Bohémiens.*) 6.6.1748. Dict. vi. 397.

Part I. SPECIMEN SCENARI

TRAGICOMEDIES, COMEDIES, AND FARCES.

LI RITRATTI

TRAGICOMMEDIA PASTORALE

[*MS. Loc.* i. 3.]

1. Re di Scotia da Pelegrino.
2. Emilia figlia da Pastore.
3. Leandro figlio del Re di Macedonia da Ninfa.
4. Gratiano servo di Leandro, messo.
5. Pantalone.
6. Burattino servo.
7. Cardone Re di Granada.
8. Lelio Re di Portugallo.
9. Zanni Hortolano.
10. Nespia [*sic*, Nespola] sua moglie.
11. Cupido.
    Spiriti.
    Ombra.[1]
    La Scena si finge Arcadia.

Robbe.

Tutto bosco, una fonte, il tempio di Cupido,[2] robbe da mangiare, quattro ritratti piccoli, corone, habito da Pellegrino per il Re, una pala, fascie di legne.

ATTO PRIMO

Emilia, GRATIANO di A. in habito da pastore dice esserli stato mancato di parola di Leandro figlio del Re di Macedonia poiche tre anni sono s'innamorono l'uno dell'altro per fama e per lettere, che nessuno non lo sa et essersi mandati li ritratti l'uno dell'altro et che Emilia è figlia del Re di Scotia, et essersi partita del suo Regno et propria casa, et essersi vestita da Pastore per la parola datali di ritrovarsi in Arcadia,

[1] In the corresponding scenario in the Corsini collection there are the extra personages, Pastorella, Sacerdote, and Leone.

[2] The Corsini list has the more ex-planatory phrase, 'monte che apre con il tempio'. Bladders are also required. For other differences see the notes given to the translation.

che in questo tempo Leandro vi saria stato piglia il Ritratto di Leandro
facendosi sopra un lamento bagiando il Ritratto Gratiano la consola
in qo

Zanni, Nespola di B. vedendo Gratiano fanno azzi fuggendolo per
cognoscer chi sia Nespola si accosta ad Emilia credendolo un Pastore
discorreno assieme. Zan. entra in Gelosia alla fine si scoprono forestieri,
quali dicono esser venuti per vedere il Paese ameno, et delizioso. Grat.
gli dimanda da mangiare dandoli denari Zan. s'acquieta, et portono
fuori robbe da mangiare li ringrazia Grat. Emil. parteno per la strada
e Zan. Nesp. restano in qo.

Pantalone, Burattino di D. vedono Nespola s'inamora Zan. fa
azzi del vestito da Pant. volendole l'accostare grida intende esser
forestieri Zan. impaurito parte per la strada A. Nesp. dice voler seguir
Emilia cioè il pastore forestiere parte per la strada B. Pant. dice come
hanno perduto Leandro figlio del Re del Macedonia loro padrone, et
volerlo cercare per quelli boschi et anco veder di ritrovare Nespola
piacendoli la sua bellezza parteno per la strada E.

Leandro di B. in habito da Ninfa dice esser figlio del Re di Macedonia innamorato per fama di Emilia figlia del Re di Scotia et con
lettere dateli l'uno con l'altro parola di ritrovarsi in Arcadia dice non
trovarla, et haver perduto et smarrito li suoi servitori Pant. et Burat.
dice andar vestito da Ninfa per poterla cercare fra le Ninfe piglia il
Ritratto d[i] Emilia fa azzi discorre sopra le sue bellezze facendo
lamenti parte per la strada A.

Emilia, Nespola, Gratiano di C. Nespola prega Emil. scoprendoli
l'amor suo verso di lei. Emil. la discaccia non volendola udire parte per
la strada D. Grat. si mostra innamorato di Nespola facendo azzi lei
lo discaccia Grat. per trovar Emilia parte per la strada D. Nespola
resta in qo.

Pantalone, Burattino di A. non trovar Leandro vedeno Nespola
fanno azzi alla fine la mettono in mezzo la vogliono sforzare lei si
lamenta e grida in qo.

Leandro di D. recognosce Pant. et Burat. suoi servitori li brava
vedendo che vogliono sforzar Nespola di poi li ordina che vadino a
cercar si trovano Emilia. Pant. Burat. havendo fatto allegrezze per
haver trovato Leand. loro padrone parteno cercar Emilia per la strada
B. Leandro dimanda a Nespola ricetto nella sua capanna dice esser
Ninfa forestiera dicendoli haversi veduto una Ninfa forestiera. Nesp.
non haverla veduta et li fa carezze accettandola alla sua capanna in qo.

Zanni di E. con uno fascio di legne, dice venir dal bosco e della
paura che si ha messo Pant. vestito di Rosso vede Leandro parlar con
Nespola si crede che sia una Ninfa s'inamora di lui facendo azzi l'invita
con carezze tutti per andare alla capanna entrano per la strada C.

Cardone di B. armato di spada sola dice esser Re di Grenata et esser venuto cercando Emilia figlia del Re di Scotia sospira, et si lamenta per non poterla ritrovare in qo.

Lelio di A. s'abbocca con il Cardone al quale dice esser Re di Portugallo, et ambe dice si scognosce Re, et andar per il mondo cercando Emilia figlia del Re di Scotia, et esser venuti in Arcadia per haver saputo ch'era capitata ivi, dicono esser innamorati di lei per fama, et portar suo [seco] li Ritratti, et haverla addimandata al padre, il quale la concede per moglie a quel Cavaliere, che la trova vengheno fra di loro in contese delli meriti ciascuno reputandosi piu meritevoli dell'altro cacciano mano alle spade facendo costione in qo.

Zanni di C. con una pala si mette in mezzo li [?] spartisce pacefacendoli intende le loro controversie et contese Zan. dice haver lui appresso di se nella sua capanna quella che loro vanno cercando essi allegri fanno giudice Zan. della loro lite, et contesa che lui giudichi Zan. sententia che si debbe stare al detto di lei come si contenterà essi contenti Zan. mena fuori in qo.

Leandro di C. Cap°. [sic] et Lel[io] cacciono fuori li ritratti et guardano molto bene Leand. alla fine dicono non esser questa che essi vano cercando parteno per la strada D. Leandro intende da Zan. la controverzia et contesa delli cavalieri che vanno cercando Emilia Leandro havendo inteso il tutto si tramortisce nelle braccie di Zan. quale facendo azzi lo porta dentro per la strada C.

fine dell'atto P°.

ATTO SECONDO

Zanni, LEANDRO di C. vuol sforzar Leand. credendolo una Ninfa. Leand. lo scaccia minacciandoli dare[?] fanno azzi et gridano in qo.

Nespola di C. intende come Zan. vuol sforzare Leand. gli grida Zan. ostinato dice voler esser contentato da Leand. et volerla godere alla fine Leand. se li scopre per huomo et andar in quell' habito per trovar quella che cercavano quelli altri due Cavalieri. Nespola havendo inteso Leand. esser huomo s'inamora di lui, et vuol che la contenti, et godersi assieme in tutti li modi. Zan. entra in gelosia, et li grida Leand. li acquieta et dice che lei non temi per esser lui figliolo di Re, et li da denari promettandoli piu, et lo prega che vadi seco a cercar Emilia lui contento parteno assieme per la strada B. Nesp. resta discorre d'amore che porta ad Emilia credendola huomo cioè pastor forastiero, resta in qo.

Emilia di A. disperata per non trovar Leand. fa lamenti Nesp. la vede si crede che sia huomo essendosi di lei inamorata la abbraccia dicendo che vuol che la contenta. Emilia la scaccia et si fugge parte per strada B. Nesp. resta dolendosi della sua crudeltà in qo.

Cupido aprendosi il tempio apparisce à Nespola dicendoli il tutto Cupido entra riserrandosi il tempio Nesp. dice voler ritrovare Emilia per dirli quel tanto che li ha detto Cupido parte per la strada A.

Cardone di C. in collera contro Lelio suo rivale Capitonio [sic, i.e. Cardone] dice volerlo amazzare se non lascia l'amore di Emilia in qo.

Lelio di B. sdegnato contro il (Cap°). Cardone venghono a parole insieme prohibendo ciascuno lasciar l'amor di Emilia facciano mano alle spade per amazzarsi in qo.

Ombra s'intromette in mezzo alli Cavalieri essi restano di combattere per non si veder l'uno l'altro in qo.

Cupido aprendosi il tempio Cupido apparisce alli Cavalieri Ombra parte Cupido parla alli Cavalieri dicendoli il tutto essi havend udito Cupido bevono l'acqua del fonte per scordarsi di Emilia conforme li ha detto Cupido bevuta si senteno infiammati a combattere per l'acquisto delle donne di Cartagine Cupido entra dentro riserrandosi il tempio Cavalieri per la strada E.

Leandro, zanni di C. disperato di non poter ritrovar Emilia Zan. lo conforta et parte per la strada E. Leand. stanco per il lungo caminare et per la stanchezza va al fonte a dormire.

Emilia, nespola di A. intende da Nesp. tutto quello che li ha detto Cupido. Nesp. parte per la strada C. Emilia resta stracca per la stanchezza vuol dormire et sotto l'arbori si dorme.

Gratiano, Pantalone, Burattino di B. allegri che si sono ritrovati Grat. dice che Emilia va sotto habito di Pastore per non esser ricognosciuta, et esser sicura del suo honore Pant. dice che Leandro va sotto habito di Ninfa per poter andare fra le altre Ninfe cercandola discorrono per [?piu] dell'Arcadia, et del Paese, et tutti si scoprono innamorati di Nespola facendo azzi fra essi, alla fine stanchi si mettono lontani da Leand. et Emil. colgi à dormire et fingono dormire in qo.

Spiriti di strade se li colgono accanto abbraciandoli essi fanno azzi fingendo insogno godere Nespola alla fine svegliati s'accedano delli spiriti gridando tutti fuggono per strada.

fine dell'atto 2°.

ATTO TERZO

Leandro del fonte dice haver dormito et essersi insognato di ritrovar Emilia fa lamenti et piglia il ritratto mirandolo in qo.

Emilia svegliata da sonno con il ritratto di Leandro in mano rimirandolo, et alla fine guardando nelli ritratti Leand. dice che il suo ritratto si assomiglia tutto al Pastore et Emilia rimirando il suo ritratto dice che la Ninfa e simile al suo alla fine havendo fatti molti azzi insieme s'interrogano l'uno dell'altro, alla fine si scopreno per quelli che sono, et con allegrezza grande si abbracciano in qo.

Zanni, Nespola di C. intendeno che tutto di essersi ritrovati fanno allegrezze in qo.

Lelio, Cardone di A. intend[end]o che tutti di essersi ritrovata Emilia si contentano dicendo quel tanto che a loro ha detto Amore dicono voler menar seco Zan. et farlo riccho in qo.

Pantalone, Gratiano, Burattino di D. intendeno il tutto ciascuno ricognosce il suo padrone facendo allegrezze di essersi ritrovato Emilia, et Leandro in qo.

Re di Scotia in habito da pellegrino per non esser cognosciuto dice andar cercando Emilia sua figliola havendo hava [*sic*, hauta?] notitia ritrovarli nella Arcadia et esser venuto sotto quel habito alla fine Emilia ricognosce il Re suo padre al quale dimanda perdono lui li perdona sposandola con Leand. fanno allegrezze abbracciando il Genero. Piglia a star seco Zanni e Nespola et tutti allegri entrono a far le nozze, et d'accordo d'andare all'impresa di Cartagine per acquistar delle donne secondo li disce Cupido.

fine della commedia.

CUPIDO DICE À NESPOLA

Vana è sua spera pastorella cara
In van t'affanni, poi ch'in vano pensi
Quel che tu ami giovanetto sia
Ma come te, gl'è pur amante donna
Che sotto panni di huom nascosta starsi
e ricercando va suo amante fido
e perche già vi son due altri Heroi
Rivali nel suo amor à te comando
Che come verrà avanti à sua persona
Dirai che teco, alquanto si dimori
Che ben ritroverà il suo Leandro
Ch'in questa Vagha Arcadia lei ricerca
Ch'ai Vaghi Amanti io sarò scorta, e guida
Acciò si godesi con felice Amori
In nodo maritel con gioia, e pace
Hor qui ti lasso e tu il mio volere
À lei tosto farai palese, et chiaro.

CUPIDO DICE À LELIO ET À CARDONE

Cessi fra voi, valorosi Heroi,
d'amorosa contesa, e gran' disfida
Per amor dell'amata Emilia bella
Ch'à mio comando l'ombre tengon l'armi
Ai vostri [?foci] acciò niun perisca

e date orecchie à quel che far dovete
Emilia è dedicata al giovanetto
Leandro, ch'è d'etade a lei simile
Cosi nel concistor degl'alti Dei
È gia concluso col mio voto ancora
Ma à voi cari guerrieri è dato in sorte
Se pur in cio voi consentir Volete
Di fare di Cartagine l'impresa
Per acquistar queste due figlie belle
della Regina de si gran cittade
Per vostre care, et amorose moglie
Anzi alle fede della vostra legge
Saranno quelle obediente Ancelle
Pero convienvi battagliare in guerra
Coi mori à voi Rivali nell'amore
Ne punto dubitate che l'impresa
Voi vincerete, et con lor aspra morte
Eccovi mostro le bellezze rare
delle vaghe donzelle à voi promesse
che gia raccolte nel mio tempio io tengo.

LELIO À CUPIDO

Puoi [sic] felice, o nostra bona sorte
Eccoci pronti à far quanto comandi
Alato Dio, et nostro tonato duce.

CUPIDO À LELIO, ET À CARDONE

Bevete ad uno al fonte qui vicino
Acciò l'amor di Emilia vi scordiate
et a si alta Impresa i vostri petti
s'accendino per far novello acquisto.

CARDONE À CUPIDO

Siamo nel guerreggiar d'animo invitto
pronti all'impresa a far si grande acquisto
Donaci dunq'il tuo favor Divino.

NESPOLA À CUPIDO

Amor habbi pietate a miei tormenti
Soccorri alla mia pena al mio dolore
(acconta tue quadrelle al duro core)[1]
[?] l'alma poi ferirei il Core
Di quel crudel ch'è sordo ai miei lamenti.

[1] This line is erased and rewritten after line 4.

THE PORTRAITS

PASTORAL TRAGI-COMEDY

[Translated from Loc. i, and collated with the rearrangment as a Pescatory in Loc. ii. 51, and with the variant of the pastoral in Cors. i. 17.]

Dramatis Personae

Loc. i. 3.	Loc. ii. 51.	Cors. i. 17
1. The King of Scotland, as a pilgrim	*Omone*	
2. Emilia, his daughter, as a shepherdess	*Clitia*	
3. Leandro, son of the King of Macedonia, as a nymph	*Nicandro*	
4. Gratiano, servant of Leandro, messenger		Coviello
5. Pantalone		
6. Burattino, servant		Tartaglia
7. Cardone, King of Granada	*Don Sanceo, il Capitano*	
8. Lelio, King of Portugal	*Dorindo*	Lutio
9. Zanni, a gardener		Pasquarello
10. Nespola, his wife	*Licinia*	Flavia
11. Cupid Spirits Shade		

Noted as extra: Shepherdesses, Priest, Lion.

The Scene represents Arcadia

Properties.

Entirely a woodland scene: a fountain; Temple of Cupid; eatables; 4 little portraits; crowns; pilgrim's habit for the king; shovel; bundles of wood.

ACT I

Emilia, GRATIANO from A dressed as a shepherd narrates how Leandro, the son of the king of Macedonia, has broken his word to her; for three years they have been in love with one another by report and secret letters; they have exchanged portraits. Emilia, the daughter

---

1 In the piscatory arrangement the properties needed are nets, rods, and other fishing-tackle; two breast-plates and arms for the cavaliers; cooked fish on a covered plate for the joke; four similar portraits for the cavaliers; two portraits for Cupid's temple which is to be made so that it will open and shut.

of the king of Scotland, has left her home and is disguised as a shepherd in accordance with Leandro's promise to meet her in Arcadia; by now he should have arrived. She takes out the portrait and makes her lament over it, kissing his picture. Gratiano consoles her; at this:

Zanni, Nespola from B catch sight of Gratiano and have their antics of running away, not knowing who he may be. Nespola accosts Emilia, taking her for a shepherd; they have some conversation. Zanni grows jealous.[1] At last they reveal that they are strangers who have come to see this lovely and pleasant country. Then Gratiano asks for food, and offers to pay. Zanni is appeased and brings out food. Gratiano and Emilia thank them and go off by C.[2] Zanni and Nespola are left; at this:

Pantalone, Burattino from D see Nespola and fall in love with her. Zanni has his antics over Pantalone's clothes and shouts at their approach; learning that they are strangers he is scared and departs by A. Nespola announcing that she wishes to follow Emilia, that is the strange shepherd, goes out by B. Pantalone relates how they have lost Leandro, son of the king of Macedonia, their master; they will look for him in these woods and hope also to encounter Nespola whose beauty had pleased them; they go out by E.

Leandro from B dressed as a nymph says he is the son of the king of Macedonia and enamoured by report of the daughter of the king of Scotland, explaining how they have written to each other promising to meet in Arcadia. He has not found her yet and has lost his way and his attendants Pantalone and Burattino. He is disguised as a nymph so that he may search for Emilia among them. He takes out her picture and has his scene discoursing on her beauty; lamenting he goes out by A.

Emilia, Nespola, Gratiano from C. Nespola implores Emilia and discloses her passion for her.[3] Emilia is unwilling to listen to her, pushes her aside and goes out by D. Gratiano has his antics of wooing Nespola; she thrusts him aside. He goes out by D to find Emilia. Nespola remains; at this:

[1] In Loc. ii. 51 there is no mention of Zanni's jealousy, instead he draws the strangers into the Inn.

[2] The Corsini version has a slightly different scene. The shepherdess who has come in with Flavia (Nespola) falls in love with Emilia and asks Flavia to act as go-between. Flavia is jealous and reproves her. The shepherdess leaves them and they begin to eat again but the Wild Man interrupts with his trick of snatching the food from their mouths and scares them away. Pantalone and Tartaglia find the eatables and begin to make a meal. Pasquarello (Zanni), Gratiano, Emilia, and Flavia come out again; Gratiano and Emilia take their leave. Pantalone falls in love with Flavia and Pasquarello has his antics of jealousy apart; he goes out to fetch wood. Flavia follows Emilia being enamoured of her. Pantalone discusses the loss of Leandro with Zanni.

[3] In Loc. ii. 51 Coviello (Gratiano) enters later and promises to help Licinia (Nespola).

Pantalone, Burattino from A; they have not found Leandro. They spy Nespola and play their tricks; putting her between them they offer to molest her; she cries out for help, at this:

Leandro from D recognizes Pantalone and Burattino, his servants, and seeing that they are annoying Nespola, he chides them, ordering them off to make search for Emilia. They welcome their master with delight and go off by B to look for Emilia. Leandro begs Nespola to take him into her hut, saying that he is a stranger nymph, and inquiring if she has seen another foreign shepherdess. Nespola has not seen one; she caresses him and takes him to the hut; at this:

Zanni from E with a bundle of logs says that he has come from the wood and relates his scare at the sight of Pantalone dressed up in red.[1] He catches sight of Leandro talking to Nespola and supposes it is a strange nymph. He falls in love with her and with coaxing antics invites her into the hut. They go out by C.

Cardone[2] from B alone, carrying a sword. He announces himself as the king of Granada in search of Emilia, the daughter of the king of Scotland. He sighs and grieves that he has been unable to find her; at this:

Lelio from B salutes Cardone and announces that he is the king of Portugal. Both explain that they are princes travelling through the world in search of Emilia, the daughter of the king of Scotland, and that hearing she is in Arcadia they have followed her thither. Both are enamoured of her by report and carry her picture. Each has asked for her from her father, who has decreed that she shall be the wife of whoever can find her. They dispute each other's merits, each declaring himself to be the worthier. They draw their swords and set on.

Zanni from C with a shovel thrusts himself between the combatants, pacifies them and learns the cause of their dispute. He declares that he has in his hut the object of their search. They are delighted and appoint him judge of their controversy. He advises them to abide by the decision of the nymph herself. They agree. Zanni leads out

Leandro from C. The cavaliers produce their portraits and scan Leandro but decide in the end that this is not the lady of their search. They go off by D. Leandro learns from Zanni the dispute between the cavaliers who are in quest of Emilia; he swoons into the arms of Zanni, who has his antics of carrying him in by C.

ACT II

Zanni, Leandro from C. Zanni wants to force Leandro whom he takes for a nymph. Leandro beats him off. They have their scene together. Leandro shouts and at this:

---

[1] In Loc. ii. 51 Zanni's fear of Pantalone's red garments is not mentioned.

[2] Loc. ii. 51. The Captain says he will search the island.

Nespola from C hears that Zanni is trying to force Leandro: she shouts at him but Zanni is obstinate and swears he will be satisfied and wants to enjoy her. In the end Leandro reveals that he is a man going about in disguise in search of that nymph for whom the cavaliers are looking. When Nespola learns that Leandro is a man she falls in love with him and longs to be satisfied and for them to enjoy each other in every way. Zanni grows jealous and shouts at her. Leandro makes peace by telling him not to fear for he is a prince. He gives them money with a promise of more, begging him to go in search of Emilia. Zanni agrees and they go off together by B. Nespola is left discoursing on her love for Emilia, that is for the strange shepherd whom she supposes is a man; at this:[1]

Emilia comes from A in despair at not finding Leandro; she laments. Nespola takes her for a man and embraces her saying that she is willing to content him. Emilia pushes her away and runs off by B. Nespola is left complaining of her cruelty; at this:[2]

Cupid opens the temple and appears to Nespola to reveal everything. He re-enters, locking the door. Nespola wishes to find Emilia again to tell her all that Cupid has said. She goes off by A.

Cardone from C enraged pursues his rival Lelio, threatening to slay him if he will not cease from loving Emilia; at this:

Lelio from B vexed, chases Cardone. They quarrel, each insisting that the other should give up the love of Emilia, they draw swords; at this:

A Shadow[3] comes between the cavaliers; they stop fighting because they cannot see; at this:

Cupid[4] opens the temple and appears to the cavaliers. The Shadow disappears. Cupid addresses them and tells them all. When they have heard him they drink at the fountain in order to forget Emilia. Cupid's words are confirmed, and having drunk they feel enflamed with a desire to fight for the Carthaginian ladies. Cupid goes in locking the temple. They depart by E.

Leandro, ZANNI[5] from C, despairs that he cannot find Emilia.

[1] In the Corsini version there is an extra scene of recognition between Gratiano, Pantalone, and Tartaglia. They discover that they are rivals for the love of Flavia and suggest summoning her. They think better of this plan, and after some fooling, depart.

[2] In the Corsini version it is the shepherdess who tries to embrace Emilia, who goes out and leaves them arguing. Cupid emerges from the mountain.

[3] Instead of the shadow (*Ombra*), in the Corsini scenario the God Pan

reproves the cavaliers for wearying themselves to no purpose and promises that if they will pray at the temple of Cupid their petitions shall be heard. They make their oration and the temple opens. Cupid leads out two very beautiful women. The cavaliers are content and drink the water.

[4] In Loc. ii. 51 the second appearance of Cupid is not mentioned until the beginning of Act III. See note.

[5] In the Corsini version they enter separately.

Zanni consoles him and goes out by E. Leandro, worn out by his wanderings, for very weariness, goes to sleep by the fountain.

Emilia, NESPOLA[1] from A hears from Nespola all that Cupid has said. Nespola goes out by C. Emilia stays, and weak with fatigue wishes to sleep under the trees. She sleeps.

Gratiano, Pantalone, Burattino[2] from B rejoice that they have found Gratiano again. He tells them that Emilia is disguised as a shepherd in order to avoid recognition and to preserve her honour. Pantalone says that Leandro is disguised as a nymph so that he can make a search among the other nymphs.[3] They discuss Arcadia and the country-side. Each declares himself in love with Nespola. They have their scene together. At length, tired out, they lie down at some distance from Leandro and Emilia and pretend to sleep; at this:

Spirits enter and lie down beside them embracing them. They pretend to enjoy Nespola in their dreams, in dumb-show. When they wake up and see the spirits they all run away yelling.

ACT III[4]

Leandro by the fountain says that as he slept he dreamed that he had found Emilia. He makes his lament and produces the portrait and gazes at it; at this:

Emilia wakes up and admires her picture of Leandro. After a little Leandro declares that his picture exactly resembles the shepherd, and Emilia regarding hers sees the likeness to the nymph. In the end after many approaches [*azzi*] they question each other and at length discover themselves and embrace joyfully; at this:

Lelio, Cardone from A hear the whole story of the finding of Emilia. They are content and recount all that Cupid had said to them. They say that they want to make Zanni a rich man. At this:

---

[1] The shepherdess accompanies Flavia (Nespola).

[2] Tartaglia comes with Burattino in the Corsini version.

[3] In Loc. ii. 51 a new joke is provided. Pantalone and Burattino come in squabbling over a cooked fish. One says he hooked it, the other netted it; one cooked it, but who shall eat it? They decide that whoever shall be able to recount the more edifying dream shall have it. As they sleep Coviello comes in and eats the fish. When they wake they appoint him judge of the dreams. Pantalone says he has been to Heaven where his neighbour eat up the fish and he never tasted it. Burattino has been in Hell where some-

one devoured it under his very nose to spite him. Coviello makes them both keep quite still and then says that since neither was likely to return from these parts it seemed a pity to waste the fish, and he has eaten it. A similar 'burla' is suggested as an alternative in *Il Serpe Fatale*.

[4] In Loc. ii. 51 the third act opens with a renewal of the quarrel between the cavaliers. They are interrupted by Cupid who sends them on the quest of the Carthaginian ladies. Except for the inversion of an entrance or two the scenari are identical for the rest of the play.

Pantalone, Gratiano, Burattino from D are informed of all that has taken place. Each recognizes his master or mistress, and rejoices that they have been found; at this:

The King of Scotland disguised as a pilgrim announces that he has come in search of his daughter Emilia, hearing that she was to be found in Arcadia. He explains the reason for his disguise.[1] At this Emilia recognizes her father and begs his forgiveness. He pardons her and betrothes her to Leandro whom he embraces as his son-in-law. They are delighted. Zanni and Nespola are taken to be with Leandro, and with rejoicing they go in to make ready for the wedding and for the enterprise of Carthage to win the ladies according to Cupid's promise.

CUPID TO NESPOLA.

Vain is thy hope, fair shepherdess, in vain dost thou distress thyself, and fruitless are thy thoughts, for the youth whom thou courtest is a woman even as thyself and, going disguised as a man, she is in search of a faithful lover. And now that two other heroes are rivals for her love it is my command that whensoever ye meet thou shouldest tell the lady that she must stay with thee for a little while, and that she will certainly recover Leandro, and that in this lovely Arcadia she shall find that to fair lovers I am escort and guide that they may enjoy their happy loves in the tie of marriage with joy and peace. Now therefore I will leave thee, and do thou speedily and clearly make this known to her.

CUPID TO LELIO AND TO CARDONE.

Let there be an end of these amorous contests between ye, O valiant heroes, and cease the high challenge for the beloved and beautiful Emilia. At my command the Shade withheld your arms so that neither should perish. Give ear then and hearken what ye must do. Emilia is destined to marry the youth Leandro who is of a like age; thus was it agreed in the consistory of the Gods, and thus I gave my vote. But to you, noble warriors, if ye will but consent thereto, is allotted the capture of Carthage with the winning of the two lovely daughters of the Queen of that great city to be your dear and loving wives; faithful to your commands these shall be your obedient handmaidens. But it behoves you to battle with the Moors, your rivals in love; yet doubt not of the enterprise, ye shall be victorious, and at their bitter

[1] In the Corsini scenario there is an extra episode in which Pasquarello (Zanni) comes to the rescue of his wife Flavia who is being tormented by the buffoons. He beats them off with bladders. The noise brings out the Priest of Cupid who makes peace. He tells the King that he will present him with his daughter and summons all onto the stage.

death, behold I will show you the rare charms of these lovely damsels who are promised to you. Here in my temple I have them in safe keeping.

LELIO TO CUPID.

Happy are we in this our good fortune! Behold us ready to do thy will, O winged God, our thundering leader.

CUPID TO LELIO AND CARDONE.

Drink, each of you, at this fountain near at hand so that ye may forget Emilia and become inflamed for the new quest of so high an enterprise.

CARDONE TO CUPID.

Our warlike spirits are ready for the enterprise that offers so great a reward. Grant us therefore thy favour divine.

NESPOLA TO CUPID.

O Love, have pity upon my anguish, relieve my pain (fix your arrows in the hard heart), show to that cruel one who is deaf to my complaint the torment that I endure, and soften his heart.

LA INNOCENTIA RIVENUTA [sic]

TRAGICOMMEDIA

[*Loc.* i. 4, *compared with 'L'Innocente Rivenduta', Cors.* ii. 12.[1]]

Personaggi

1. Duca.
2. Corte del Duca.
3. Pantalone consigliere.
4. Horatio figlio.
5. Fabritio ⎱ fratelli.
6. Coviello ⎰
7. Doralice figlia.
8. Franceschina serva.
9. Zanni ⎱ Servi.
10. Burattino ⎰
11. Rais Turcho.
12. Furbo.
13. Oracolo.

La Scena si finge Messina

Robbe.

Una parte di bosco in scena; veste da Turcho, turbante, frezze, Archo, cassa grande; veste con manto per Doralice; habito da Gov^{re}; due anelli, collana d'oro, borsa con denari; oracolo, core, sangue, pugnale, corde.

ATTO PRIMO

Duca, PANTALONE, ZANNI, CORTE di Palazzo si dole dell'infermità della gotta della moglie, ritrovar remedio per guarirla dice voler parlare a l'oracolo si inginocchiono pregando in qo.

Oracolo di dentro risponde che una donna vedova donzella maritata la liberarà, tutti confusi non sanno intendere ne dechiarare fanno azzi nel explicare alla fine tutti parteno in palazzo. Pant. resta dice haver Fabrizio per suo figliolo addottivo che il duca l'ha fatto generale di due galere et voler per moglie Doralice voler parlarli per concludere il parentado batte in qo.

Doralice, FRANCESCHINA di casa intende come Fab. la vuol per

---

[1] For details of collation with this and other variants see the notes to the subsequent translation.

moglie Doralice ricusa se bene egli è accarezzato dal duca per haver promesso à Horat. otto anni fa se riscattava [Cov. cancelled] suo padre preso mentre andava in mercantia, et haverli dato la fede, ne saperne nuova alcuna, et per non dar sospetto di se non esser servatori ne homini in casa Doralice et Francª. in casa Pant. dice voler dire il tutto à Fab. parte per strada.

Horatio, BURATTINO di strada venir di viaggio dice otto anni fa haver pigliato per moglie Doral. et esser andato per il mondo per riscattare il padre di Doral. schiavo, ne haverlo mai potuto trovar dice haver dormito con Doral. ne haver la tocca [*sic*], haverli lasciato uno anello alla sua partita, et una veste, che non se la metti insino al suo ritorno, et Doralice haver dato uno anello a lui quale lo porta in dite ralegrandosi per haver inteso che lei non habbia preso altro marito, et conservato la sua castità et volerla sposare in qo.

Fabritio di strada che Pant. suo padre haverli detto che Doral. non volessi maritarsi per amor di Horat. si vedono insieme fanno compimenti. Fab. finge ralegrarsi del suo ritorno Horatio si loda di Doral. et della sua castità, et esser venuto per provarla Fab. dice esser restato da lui di goderla Horat. si meraviglia alla fine dice che potendola godere la godi, che portandoli li segnali la lasciarà et ritornerà in Spagna. Fab. il prometta fra due giorni di fare il tutto Horat. Burat. parteno per strada Fab. confuso della promessa ne sapere come si fare poter entrare da Doral. in qo.

Zanni di palazzo che cerca Pant. intende da Fab. voler dar 100 scudi se li basta l'animo di metterlo in casa di Doral. con patto di non farli dispiacere alcuno, ne meno scoprirsi. Zan. dice Francª. sua moglie sta con lei per serva, ma non praticava in casa perche Doral. non vuole che si vadino huomini, dice volerlo mettere dentro in una cassa che si serra di dentro, che lo introdurrà in casa con questa inventione Fab. loda l'inventione, et esser contento di fare il tutto Zan. porta fuori la cassa Fab. da una cathena d'oro à Zan. di 50 scudi et che di poi li darà il resto non havendo denari addosso entra nella cassa Zan. batte in qo.

Doralice, FRANCESCHINA di casa intende havere una cassa di certe robbe et volerli lasciare in serbo ma che Franª. non vorria che le tocassi. Doral. dice che la metti nella camera sua che sarà sicuro che niuno la toccherà Zan. porta dentro la cassa dicendo che quanto prima tornerà a pigliarla Doral. Franª. in casa Zan. resta vagheggia la collana donatali da Fab. dice volerla vendere se la mette al collo facendo azzi del gentilhuomo in qo.

Furbo di strada addocchia la collana di Zan. li fa la burla del grattece levandoli la collana parte per strada Zan. disperato essendosi accorto della burla lo corre dietro per strada.

fine dell'Atto. Pº.

ATTO SECONDO

Duca, PANTALONE, CORTE di palazzo torna di nuova a l'oracolo pregandolo non ricusa risposta della risposta [*sic*, rechiesto?] una volta fattali alla fine ordina esse bando che chi guarisce la moglie lo vuol far governatore assoluto del suo stato et mille scudi d'entrata tutti in palazzo.

Zanni di strada havendo fatto restituire la collana, et havere arrivato il furbo dice vuol Fabritio di casa di Doral. batte in qo.

Doralice, FRANCESCHINA di casa intende voler la sua cassa Doral. lo manda in casa à pigliarla Zan. entra, e porta fuori la cassa Doral. Franª. in casa, Zan. resta et apre la cassa, et esce fuori in qo.

Fabritio dalla cassa dà una borsa con 50 scudi à Zan. per il resto che li ha promesso, ne havendoli prima dato li denari per non ne restar senza. Zan. piglia li denari et porta via la cassa parte per strada Fab. resta dice che quando Doral. dormiva essere uscito fuori della cassa et haver scritto tutti li segnali della casa, et di lei havendo scoperto mentre dormiva et havendo preso un anello, che stava sopra un tavolino nella camera per piu contra segni mostrare à Horat. in qo.

Horatio, BURATTINO, di strada intende haver goduto Hort. [*sic*, i.e. Doralice] et per segnali li da li contra segni della casa, lei havere un neo sotto la tetta, poi li mostra l'anello quale dice haverglielo donato Doral. Horat. ricognosce l'anello si meraviglia della inconstanzia et dishonestà di Doral. et voler andarsene in Spagna Fab. parte per strada Horat. Burat. restano. Horat. dà l'anello quale li donò Doral. quando lui si parte simile à quello che Fabritio li ha, acciò lo mostri a Doral. dicendo che Horat. è amalato tre miglia fuori della Città, che debba venir subito, et nel bosco l'amazzi, et per segno li porti il core, e volerli donare 200 scudi Burat. fa azzi alla fine si risolve fare il tutto Horat. per strada Burat. resta havendosi fatto dare il pugnale da Horat. batte in qo.

Doralice di casa intende l'ambasciata da parte di Horat. suo marito ricognosce l'anello, dice volervi mettere la veste che li lasciò quando si parte mai piu haverla messa entra in casa, et esce fuori con la veste chiama in qo.

Franceschina di casa intende che habbi cura alla casa fino al suo ritorno. Doral. Burat. parteno per strada. Franª. resta in qo.

Fabritio di strada intende come Doral. è andata à trovar Horat. Franª. in casa Fab. resta addolerato dolendosi di Horat. in qo.

Pantalone di palazzo da parte del duca dice a Fab. che debbia andare con le sue galere contro una galeotta de Turchi, che fa gran danno Fab. dice non volerci andare parteno per strada.

Burattino, DORALICE del bosco per ammazzare Doral. fanno azzi alla fine Doral. lo prega dandoli le gioie, accio non l'ammazzi. Burat.

mosso à pietà la lascia e parte per strada Doral. resta addolorata in qo.

Raiis [*sic*] dal bosco turco dice esser fuggito dalla galeotta presa, et un'altra volta essendo stato schiavo in mano de Christiani dove poi fuggi havere imparato parlare Italiano prega Doral. che lo salvi donandoli un segreto buono per la gotta dentro una carafella Doral. esser buona per la duchessa, et cambiano l'habiti Doral. si veste da Turco, et Alij si vesti coli habiti di Doral. Alij parte per strada Doral. resta in qo.

Horatio di strada esser stata presa una galeotta de Turchi dalla galera fiorentina, et il Rais esser fuggito vede Doral. si crede il Rais della galeotta piglia Doral. teme non sia Horat. non ardisce dir nulla accio non l'ammazzi in qo.

Coviello di strada esser stato schiavo otto anni et libero per la galeotta presa haver molte gioie baratta con Horat. Doral. pensandolo il Rais della galeotta per una gioia dice voler andare à casa sua non ricognosendosi assieme per la lunghezza del tempo che non li sono visti Cov. Doral. parteno per strada Horat. resta in qo.

Burattino da strada dice haver ammazzato una pecora haverli cavato il core per mostrarlo ad Horat. dandoli et pretendere che sia di Doral. Horat. intende esser morta Doral. vede il core loda Buratt. volerlo pagare in qo.

Rais di strada da donna cole veste di Doral. Horat. vedendo la vesta si crede che sia Doral. lo ammazza, et voler ammazzar Burattino per non haverla ammazzata. Burat. si arricomanda non haverlo fatto per compassione (vogliono spogliarlo vedeno esser homo fanno meraviglie)[1] portando via il corpo parteno per strada.

ATTO TERZO

Pantalone, FABRITIO di strada li grida perche non sia voluto andare con le galere contra la galeotta quale haverla presa le galere fiorentine, et il duca essere in colera. Fab. si traviglia né sapere come entrare in gratia del Duca in qo.

Coviello, DORALICE di strada si pente havere comperato lo schiavo, ne conoscendola per Doral. figlia dice volendo vendere Pant. compra Doral. creduta turco per 50 scudi dicono volerlo donare al duca per entrarli in gratia entrano in palazzo. Cov. resta dice non saper la casa dove habiti Doral. sua figliola volerne dimandare in qo.

Burattino di strada intende andar cercando la casa di Doral. Buratt. l'insegna la casa, et dice haverla ammazzata Cov. vuole ammazzar lui. Buratt. fugge per strada. Cov. resta disperato per la figliola morta batte in qo.

---

[1] Cancelled.

Franceschina di casa ricognosce Cov. fa allegrezze di gioia fanno azzi della figliola Doral. facendo scopre essere andata da Horat. Cov. esser stata ammazzata, et voler querelare entrano in casa.

Pantalone, Fabritio di palazzo facendo allegrezze che il turco habbi guarito la duchessa dalla gotta et essendosi scoperto Christiano, il Duca haverlo fatto Governatore assoluto in qo.

Doralice, CORTE di palazzo si mette in sedia et voler dare audientia escendo in habito da Giudice tutti li fanno riverenza in qo.

Coviello di casa intende esser il giudice dà querela à un certo Burattino per haverli ammazzato sua figliola gridando giustizia in qo.

Horatio, BURATTINO di strada fanno far prigione Burat. per haver ammazzato Doral. Burat. dice non haverla ammazzata, ma haverla ammazzata Horat°. suo padrone e fatto prigione Horat°. Burat. è liberato ed [con ?] 100 scudi d'entrata per non haver fatto l'omicidio Horat°. confessa haverla ammazzata, perche havendoli data la fede di matrimonio, essersi goduta con Fabritio, Fab. confessa haverla goduta dando li contra segni et dell'anello Doral. fa meraviglie fa pigliar prigione Fab. quale lo condanna à morte come adultero, et Hor. ancora come omicida. Pant. mosso à compassione prega perdonarli due Fab. non essere altrimenti suo figliolo, ne chiamarsi Fabritio, ma Lutio, et haverli messo nome Fabritio per un suo figliolo quale andette [?] in Spagna. Horat. si scopre lui chiamarsi Fabri°. et essere andato in Spagna et essersi messo nome Horat. per alcune inimicitie Lutio esser fratello di Cov. menatoli via 19 anni fa Doral. si scopre non esser morta ne meno esser stata violata Fab. cioè Lutio scopre il tutto non havendo altrimente goduta ma il tutto haverlo fatto per guastar il parentado il morto dicene esser stato il Rais turcho, al quale diede la sua veste dichiarandosi ogni cosa si perdona à tutti Horat. sposa Doral. dicene volere avisare il duca del tutto facendo allegrezze tutti in palazzo.

fine della Commedia.

ORACOLA AL DUCA

Sono li prieghi tuoi al cielo ascesi
O della moglia pietoso marito
Et han li dei li tuoi desiri intesi
E di sua donna il lungo pianto udito,
Per il duol de suoi pie, che sono offesi
dal mal ch'a lei sarà grave, è infinito
se da donna non è quella sanata
che vedova, e virgin sia, e maritata.

INNOCENCE RESTORED

TRAGICOMEDY

[*MS. Loc.* i. 4, *collated with* '*L'Innocente Rivenduta*', *Cors.* ii. 12, *and* '*L'Innocente venduta e rivenduta*', *Nap.* ii. 3. *Compared with Verucci's* '*Dispettoso Marito*', 1612.]

Dramatis Personae

	Loc.	*Cors.*	*Nap.*
1.	Duke		
2.	His court		
3.	Pantalone, counsellor	*Magnifico*	Doctor
4.	Horatio, his son	*Fabritio*	General of the galleys
5.	Fabritio ⎫ brothers	*adopted son*	Cintio
6.	Coviello ⎭	*Captain*	
7.	Doralice, daughter of Coviello		Isabella, daughter
8.	Franceschina, her maid		Pimpinella
9.	Zanni ⎫ servants	*Trappolino, husband of*	Coviello
10.	Burattino ⎭	*Pettola*	Pollicinella
11.	Rais, a Turk		
12.	Thief		
13.	Oracle		Extra:
			Tartaglia, father of the General

Verucci in his play *Il Dispettoso Marito*, 1612, gives a more plebeian setting by making the gouty lady the wife of a certain Torbolonio di Palthanai of Venice. In his household acting as a confidential servant is Fabritio who explains that ten years ago he fled from Naples charged with homicide; later he is identified as the son of the merchant Colaniello. Horatio's part is taken by a Captain, Bombarditamente; Dalinda, whose parents do not appear, is his faithful wife.

The pair of comic servants is reduced to Mortadella from Bergamo; his wife is Erina. Allowing for this slightly smaller caste the intrigue presents the closest parallel to the scenario. (See also Chapter III, p. 217.)

The scene represents Messina

Properties.

The scene shows a part of a wood; Turkish clothes, turban, arrows, bow; big coffer; garment with a cloak for Doralice; habit for the

Governor; 2 rings; gold chain; purse of money; oracle; heart; blood; dagger and cords.[1]

ACT I

Duke, PANTALONE, ZANNI, COURT from the palace grieves over his wife's infirmity; he is seeking remedies for her gout and says that he will ask the Oracle how she may be cured. He kneels down praying; at this:

Oracle from within replies that a woman who is married, widowed, and yet a virgin shall free her. All are puzzled and unable to expound this riddle. At length they retire into the palace, leaving Pantalone[2] who says that the Duke has made Fabritio, his adopted son, the commander over two galleys, and that Fabritio wants Doralice for his wife. To speak with her and settle the matter Pantalone knocks; at this:

Doralice, FRANCESCHINA from the house learns that Fabritio wishes to marry her. Doralice refuses although he may be favoured of the Duke, because she has promised herself eight years ago[3] to Horatio should he be able to ransom her father who was captured while journeying as a merchant: she has given him her troth, and although she has had no news of him she will not allow any man, even as a servant, into the house in order to avoid suspicion. Doralice and Franceschina go in. Pantalone says that he must acquaint Fabritio with this and goes down the street.

Horatio, Burattino as travellers. Horatio relates how eight years ago he took Doralice for his wife and has since been journeying through the world to ransom her father from slavery but has never been able to find him. He says that he slept with Doralice but has not touched her; he left with her a ring and a garment which she is never to wear until his return. Doralice gave him in exchange the ring which he wears on his finger. He rejoices to think that she has not taken another husband and has preserved her chastity. Now he will espouse her, at this:

Fabritio comes up the street saying that his father Pantalone has told him that Doralice will not marry him because of her love for Horatio. They catch sight of one another and pay their respects. Fabritio pretends to be glad at the return of Horatio who praises the constancy of Doralice and announces that he has come to prove her.[4] Fabritio says that he could have enjoyed her. Horatio is astonished and

---

[1] In the Corsini scenario some extra details are supplied; the chain is to be prepared for the trick, a handkerchief, a throne, a beard for the Duke, a portal and a jewel are needed.

[2] In the Corsini version Pantalone does not enter until the court have gone into the palace.

[3] In Nap. ii. 3 the time was 7 years and 7 months and in Verucci 7 years.

[4] In the Neapolitan version Cintio has no intention of 'proving' Isabella, he is merely confused by the General's boast.

in the end says that if he can enjoy her, let him do so and bring proofs and he will go straight back to Spain. Fabritio promises to perform everything in two days' time. Horatio and Burattino depart, leaving Fabritio at his wits' end not knowing how to get admittance to Doralice; at this:

Zanni coming from the palace in search of Pantalone learns that Fabritio would give him 100 scudi if he had the nerve to introduce him into Doralice's house, promising that he will do no offence and not even disclose himself. Zanni says that his wife, Franceschina, is in Doralice's service[1] but that he is not acquainted with the house because Doralice will allow no men to enter. He offers to get him into the house in a coffer which locks from the inside.[2] Fabritio commends this idea and says that he is willing to try it. Zanni drags out the coffer: Fabritio gives him a gold chain worth 50 scudi with a promise for the remainder because he has no more money on him at the moment. He gets into the coffer. Zanni knocks; at this:

Doralice, FRANCESCHINA from the house is informed that he has a coffer containing his possessions which he wishes to leave in her charge but that Franceschina does not want to have anything to do with them. Doralice directs him to put it in her chamber for there certainly no one will touch it. Zanni carries in the coffer saying he will return for it as soon as possible. Doralice and Franceschina go in, leaving Zanni admiring the chain given him by Fabritio. He says that he wants to sell it. He tries it on mimicking the fine gentleman; at this:

Thief from the street eyes the chain and plays him the trick of rubbing up against him. He removes the chain and makes off down the street. Zanni discovering the trick runs after him in despair.

ACT II

Duke, PATALONE, COURT from the palace returns to the Oracle, imploring it to reply to the request previously made. The Duke at last orders a proclamation to be issued that whoever cures his wife shall be made absolute governor of his state and rewarded with a thousand scudi. They all go into the palace.[3]

Zanni comes up the street. He has overtaken the thief and recovered the chain. He announces that he will fetch Fabritio from Doralice's house; at this:

[1] Pimpinella, as Pollicinella's wife, does not belong to Isabella's household; Cintio has left Coviello in charge.

[2] In Nap. ii. 3 the General is conveyed in a sack borrowed from Pimpinella. The play loses seriousness by a scene when Isabella speculates as to whether it contains millet or flour; these antics finish the first act instead of the chain-stealing episode.

[3] This scene is not given in the Neapolitan scenario.

Doralice, FRANCESCHINA from the house hears that he wants his coffer. Doralice sends him into the house to fetch it. Zanni carries out the coffer. Doralice and Franceschina go in, leaving Zanni who opens the coffer and lets out

Fabritio coming from the coffer gives Zanni a purse with 50 scudi as the remainder of the money which he had not given him earlier for fear of being left without any. Zanni takes the money and carrying off the coffer goes down the street. Fabritio is left relating how as Doralice slept he had come out of the coffer and had written down all the noteworthy things in the house, how he discovered her sleeping and had taken a ring that lay on the table in her room as proofs to show Horatio; at this:

Horatio, Burattino come up the street and are told that he has enjoyed Doralice. As a proof Fabritio describes the house and reports that Doralice has a mole under her breast. He displays the ring saying that she had given it to him.[1] Horatio recognizes it and is amazed at the inconstancy and dishonesty of Doralice; he wants to return to Spain.

Fabritio goes out, leaving Horatio and Burattino. Horatio gives him the ring which was Doralice's parting-gift, the fellow to the one which Fabritio has had, and tells him to show it to Doralice with the tale that Horatio lies ill three miles out of the city and that she must go to him at once; then he is to murder her in the wood and bring her heart as a proof, and he will be rewarded with 200 scudi. Burattino has his antics but in the end agrees to all this. Horatio goes down the street, leaving Burattino with the dagger which he has made Horatio give him. He knocks; at this:

Doralice from the house is given the message from her husband Horatio. She recognizes the ring and saying that she will put on the garment which he left with her and which she has not worn since he left, she re-enters the house returning with the garment and calls for

Franceschina from the house. She is cautioned to take care of the house until her return. Doralice and Burattino go out leaving Franceschina; at this:

Fabritio from the street hears that Doralice has gone to find Horatio. Franceschina goes in; Fabritio is left aggrieved and lamenting about Horatio; at this:

Pantalone comes from the palace as from the Duke and tells Fabritio to set out with his galleys against a Turkish galley which is making great havoc. Fabritio says he does not want to go and they go off down the street.

Burattino, DORALICE comes through the wood to kill Doralice.

---

[1] In the Neapolitan version the General merely gives Cintio the ring.

They have their scene; at length Doralice implores him and bribes him with jewels[1] not to murder her. Burattino is moved to compassion and leaves her. Doralice remains overcome with grief; at this:

Rais the Turk comes through the wood saying that he is a fugitive from the captured Turkish galley. At one time he was a slave in the hands of the Christians from whom he escaped; by this means he had learned to speak Italian. He begs Doralice to save him, giving her a sovereign remedy for the gout in a phial. Doralice, thinking that it will cure the Duchess, changes clothes with him and dresses up as a Turk; Ali, disguised as Doralice, goes off: she remains; at this:

Horatio announces that the Turkish galley has been taken by the Florentine galleys and that Rais is a fugitive. Catching sight of Doralice he mistakes her for the Rais of the galley and lays hold of her. Doralice, fearing that it may not be Horatio, dares not speak for fear of being killed; at this:

Coviello comes in; he explains that he has been a slave for eight years and is now freed by the capture of the galley. He has many jewels and bargains with Horatio for Doralice, supposing that she is the Rais of the galleon. Coviello wishes to go to his home; they do not recognize each other after so long an absence. Coviello and Doralice depart leaving Horatio; at this:

Burattino comes in saying he has killed a sheep and taken its heart. He shows this to Horatio pretending that it is Doralice's.[2] Horatio is told that she is dead, and on seeing the heart he praises Burattino and wishes to pay him; at this:

Rais comes in dressed as Doralice. Seeing the garment Horatio supposes it to be his wife; he kills her and wants to murder Burattino for not having dispatched her before. Burattino commends himself to Horatio saying that pity checked him. They go off carrying the body.

ACT III

Pantalone, FABRITIO comes down the street chiding him for not going with his galleys against the Turkish galley which has been captured by the Florentines; he says that the Duke is angry; Fabritio is disturbed and does not know how to regain the Duke's favour; at this:[3]

Coviello, DORALICE still does not recognize his daughter; he is repenting his bargain and wishes to sell the slave. Pantalone buys Doralice for 50 scudi supposing her to be a Turk. They plan to give her to the Duke to regain his favour, and they go into the palace.

---

[1] In the Corsini version she gives a handkerchief.

[2] In the Corsini version he delivers a bloody handkerchief as well.

[3] In the Neapolitan version Pantalone has no scene of reproach: he buys the slave for the Duke to show him that his son has captured a Turk.

Coviello is left saying that he does not know the house where Doralice his daughter lives: he wishes to inquire and at this:

Burattino comes up the street and hears that he is looking for Doralice's house. Burattino points it out and says that he has murdered her. Coviello wants to kill him. Burattino escapes, leaving Coviello in despair over his daughter's death; at this:[1]

Franceschina comes out of the house and recognizes Coviello and makes great rejoicing. They have their scene [*azzi*] about his daughter Doralice: Franceschina says that she has gone to Horatio. Coviello tells her that she has been murdered and declares that he will have justice done. They go into the house.

Pantalone, Fabritio come from the palace rejoicing that the Turk has cured the Duchess of her gout. The Turk has revealed himself a Christian and the Duke has made him absolute governor. At this:

Doralice, COURT comes from the palace and assuming the robes of a judge prepares to give audience. All do her reverence; at this:

Coviello learning that this is the judge, accuses a certain Burattino of the murder of his daughter, crying 'Justice'; at this:

Horatio, Burattino come up the street. Burattino is arrested for the murder of Doralice: he declares that it was not he but his master Horatio who killed her. They seize Horatio and release Burattino [who claims] 100 scudi on being acquitted of the charge of homicide. Horatio confesses that he killed her because she had vowed to marry him and had been enjoyed by Fabritio. Fabritio confesses that he has enjoyed her and describes the room and produces the ring. Doralice marvels and orders Fabritio to be arrested; he is condemned to be executed as an adulterer and Horatio as a murderer. Pantalone, moved to pity, craves pardon for them both, declaring that Fabritio is not his son at all, and is not properly named Fabritio but Lutio; he explains that it was his true son who went into Spain who was called Fabritio. Horatio reveals that his name is Fabritio, that he went to Spain and called himself Horatio because of certain feuds. Lutio turns out to be Coviello's brother lost 19 years ago.[2] Doralice discovers herself alive and not violated in any way, and Fabritio, that is Lutio, clears up everything, explaining that he had not really enjoyed her but had acted thus to break off the marriage. The dead man is discovered to be Rais the Turk to whom she had given her clothes.[3] When all has been explained there is a general pardon. Horatio marries Doralice and says he will inform the Duke of all that has passed. They all enter the palace with rejoicing.

[1] In the Corsini scenario the servants first prepare the stage.
[2] Twelve years. Corsini version.
[3] In the Neapolitan scenario the General turns out to be the son of Tartaglia, an extra character.

ORACLE TO THE DUKE

Thou loving husband, though thy prayers are heard
In heaven above and thy desires known,
Yet still thy suffering wife will make her moan,
For to her ill the cure must be deferred
Until a woman, widow, wife and maid,
Shall come to her and render present aid.

LI TRE BECCHI

COMMEDIA

[*MS. Cors.* ii. 43.]

Personaggi

Pantalone

Flaminia, moglie.

_I Coviello

Cintia, moglie.

Zanni

Franceschina moglie.

Leandro Giovane.

Robbe.

Un mastello con lenzoli, una cassa da limoni, una quartarola, stoppa, foco, candela, zuppa, habito da forfante.

ATTO PRIMO

Guiel [*sic*, COVIELLO], *Cintia* fanno lazzi di Gelosia l'uno al de l'altro al fine Cintia in casa Lui resta narrando l'amore di Flam^a. moglie di Pant., e bussa da lei

Flam. fanno scena amorosa al fine le gli da l'ordine della cassa de i limoni. Cov. entra Flam. resta in qo.

Panta. le gli chiede li limoni lui promette mandarline una cassa flam. entra Pant. resta ne narra l'amore verso Fran. moglie di Zan. e bussa da lei

Fran. intende il tutto, lei dice de voler, Pant. parte lei resta in qo.

Zann. dice alla moglie che vadi à guadagna fanno molti lazzi Fran. entra lui resta narrando che lei e fastidiosa in qo.

Coviel. prega Zan. à portarlo nella cassa narrandoli il tutto e vanno per strada.

Lean. Narra l'amore verso Cintia e batte da lei.

Cinti. Udito il tutto gli dà ordine che venga vestito da furfante muto et travestito. Lei entra lui và à travestirsi.

Pant. che non puol [*sic*] piu indugiare che hormai sia hora batte da fran.

Fran. lo mena in casa et entrano con lazzi.

Zann. con la cassa esorta Coviello non parlare ne moversi et lo mette dentro in qto.

_I The underlining throughout is peculiar to the Corsini MS.

Coviel., LEAND. da furfante fingendo il muto Zan. non lo conoscendo per forza li fa agiutare à portar la cassa in qo.

Flam. Accetta la cassa Zan. lei entrano. Leandro resta e batte da Cintia.

Cintia l'accetta in casa con lazzi, et finisce l'atto primo.

ATTO SECONDO

Zann. Biasmanda flaminia per l'inganno fatto al marito et lauda fran. sua moglie di honesta lei in qo [questo] cantando sbatte i panni in casa lavando et poi vien fuori.

Fran. con la quartarola la mette in testa al marito facendo il lazzo della torta in qo.

Pant. esce di casa di Fran. ridendo e và à battere à casa sua fran. Zan. entrano. Pant. resta et chiama la moglie.

Flam. Doppo molte parole li narra il sogno del ochio e copre l'ochio bono à fran. in qo.

Coviel. Uscendo di casa di flam. ridendo della burla fatta và à battere a casa sua flam. et pant. in casa. Cov. bussa.

Cinti. fa molti carezzi a Cov. poi li narra del povero che ha in casa, in qo.

Lean. Travestito con la zuppa Cov. bravandoli entra in casa con Cintia. Leandro doppo haver riso della burla visto venir Zanni si finge di novo muto.

Zann. Doppo alquante burle riconosce Lean. et li narra la cosa seguita in casa di Pant. e Lean. narra di Cov. ridendo entra Zan. resta in qto.

Pant. Zan. li narra la burla del forfante. Pant. narra à lui quella della quartarola, et Zan. in ultimo quella della cassa di limoni et entra Pant. resta in qo.

Coviel. Pant. li narra la burla del forfante et facendo li lazzi del becco gridano insieme e finisce l'Atto Secondo.

ATTO TERZO

Fran. Per farsi imprestar un mastello da far bucata batte da

Cint. Glilo promette, et che li dara de panni da lavare, et la mena in casa

Pant. che vol tornar di novo da fran. che gli è piaciuta in qto.

Fran. con il mastello e panni. Pant. gli narra l'intento suo, lei lo fà entrare nel mastello e lo copre con panni in qo.

Zan. li è accorto del tutto che uno è nel mastello poi fatti molti lazzi di buttar li panni nella caldara che bulle porta dentro il mastello, e tornato fori di à Fran. volere andare al paese lui [lei?] allegra và in casa Zan per strada.

Covie. che essendoli riusciuto bene una volta vol procorare un altra
e batte da

Flam. Inteso il suo volere lo accetta di novo, et lo mena in casa

Lean. fa il simile [con Cintia].

Cint. quale lo abraccia et mena in casa di nuovo.

Zan. Vien per chiarirsi della Moglie si accosta alla sua porta et
senti far carezze e batte con furia.

Fran. intendendo che Zan. vol. abrugiar la casa li fa portar fuori il
mastello con li panni poi lassa dar fuoco alla casa facendo rumore

Pant fuori esce dentro alli panni del mastello in qto.

Tut fuori abracciati curono al rumore del fuoco in camera. Lean.
accorda Tutti che uno l'ha fatta al altro rendono à ogni uno la sua
moglie del che finalmente tutti contenti entrano e finisce la comedia.

THE THREE CUCKOLDS

A COMEDY

[*MS. Cors.* ii. 43, *compared with Magliabechiani scenario.*[1]]

Dramatis Personae

Pantalone.

Flaminia, his wife.   *Lucinda.*

Coviello.   *Ubaldo.*
Cintia, his wife.   *Ardelia.*

Zanni.   *Cola.*
Franceschina, his wife. *Columbina.*

Leandro, a young man.   *Ottavio.*
      Valerio.
      Stoppino, servant.

Properties.

A washing basket[2] with sheets; chest for lemons; cask; tow; fire;
candle; broth; dress for a rogue.

ACT I

Coviello, Cintia have their scene of reciprocal jealousy. Cintia
goes in and leaves Coviello to disclose his passion for Flaminia, the
wife of Pantalone; he knocks at her door:

[1] Comparison with *Li Tre Becchi* which is reprinted from the Florentine MS. by Bartoli shows that beyond the adjustments needed for the extra lover which entail more tricks on the old husbands, the scenari are substantially the same.

[2] 'Mastello', by its use here might well be rendered by 'buck-basket'.

Flaminia appears. They have their love scene and in the end she tells him about the chest of lemons. Coviello goes in, Flaminia stays; at this:

Pantalone is asked to provide her with lemons; he promises to send them in a chest. Flaminia goes in. Pantalone is left to disclose his love for Franceschina, Zanni's wife; he knocks at her door:

Franceschina hears everything and declares that she favours Pantalone; he departs, she remains; at this:

Zanni tells his wife to go to work; they have many antics. Franceschina goes in and he stays saying what a nuisance she is; at this:

Coviello asks Zanni to carry him in a chest and explains everything. They go off down the street.

Leandro declares his love for Cintia and knocks at her door:

Cintia hears everything and instructs him to come dressed as a rogue, dumb and disguised. She goes in and he departs to dress up.

Pantalone can wait no longer and says that at last it is time; he knocks for Franceschina.

Franceschina leads him into the house and they have their antics over the entrance.

Zanni, COVIELLO with the chest exhorts Coviello not to speak or move; he puts him inside; at this:

Leandro as a dumb beggar is forced to shoulder the chest by Zanni who does not recognize him; at this

Flaminia receives the chest. Zanni enters. Leandro is left and knocks for Cintia.

Cintia receives him into the house, they have their scene and the act ends.

ACT II

Zanni blames Flaminia for the trick played on her husband and congratulates himself on the honesty of his wife Franceschina; meanwhile she is heard within singing and slapping up and down with the washing; then she comes out.

Franceschina appears with the cask which she puts over her husband's head, playing the trick of the tart; at this:[1]

Pantalone comes out of Franceschina's house grinning, he goes to knock at his own home. Zanni and Franceschina go in. Pantalone is left calling his wife.

Flaminia with much circumstance recounts the dream of the eye and makes him hide his eyes from Flaminia; at this:

Coviello comes out of Flaminia's house laughing at the trick. He goes to knock at his own. Pantalone and Flaminia go in; Coviello knocks.

---

[1] Probably she promises him a tart if he will keep the cask over his head; he bargains and meanwhile the lover slips out.

Cintia makes much of Coviello and caresses him, and then tells him of the poor beggar she has in the house; at this:

Leandro disguised comes in with some soup. Coviello scolds and goes into the house with Cintia. Leandro laughs at the hoax and seeing Zanni approaching pretends to be dumb again.

Zanni after several jokes recognizes Leandro and tells him what has been going on in Pantalone's house. Leandro tells him what has happened at Coviello's and goes in laughing. Zanni stays; at this:

Pantalone learns from Zanni the jest of the rogue. Pantalone tells him the jest of the cask and Zanni in the end tells about the lemon-chest and goes in. Pantalone is left; at this:

Coviello is told of the hoax of the rogue; they have their scene together shouting 'Cuckold' at each other.

ACT III

Franceschina to borrow a buck-basket knocks for

Cintia who promises to give it her with the washing and takes her into the house.

Pantalone wishes to return to Franceschina who had pleased him; at this:

Franceschina comes with the basket and the clothes. Pantalone explains his intentions and she makes him get into the basket and covers him with clothes; at this:

Zanni aware of all that is going on and knowing there is someone in the basket has many antics about throwing the clothes into the copper and boiling them. He carries in the basket and coming out again tells Franceschina that he is going into the country. She is delighted and goes into the house. Zanni goes down the street.

Coviello after his former success wishes to try again, he knocks for

Flaminia who hears his wish and receives him once more and leads him into the house.

Leandro, Cintia do the same; Cintia embraces him and takes him into the house again.

Zanni comes to make sure about his wife; he draws near to the door and hears caresses going on; he knocks in a fury.

Franceschina hearing that Zanni wants to burn down the house makes him carry out the basket of clothes, before he sets fire to the place. With an uproar

Pantalone comes out among the clothes in the basket; at this

All the couples arm in arm rush to the alarm of fire in the room. Leandro explains what each has done to the other and delivers over to each his proper wife with whom he is at last content. They go in and the comedy ends.

LA MAGICA DI PANTALONE

[*MS. Cors.* ii. 44.]

Personaggi [1]

Pantalone, Mago.
Trappolino, servo.

Cassandro, mercante Padre adottivo di
Cintia, figlia di Pantalone.

Franceschina serva, poi moglie di Gratiano.
Zanni, servo.

Gratiano, padre Adottivo di
Lelio, figlio di Pantalone.

Facchino.

Folletto.

Robbe.

Valige, feltro, stivali, Robbe da mangiare, libri, carafa di vino, Montagna, Buchi, Tesoro, Zappe, vanghe, Denari, carta, penna, calamaio, ampolle, scritture, code per Zanni et Trappolino, corda, fiamme, Rumori.

ATTO PRIMO

Cassan., Zann., Cintia, France., Di casa con valigie Cass. raccomanda à Zan. le donne et lo fa mastro di casa dando à tutti avvertimenti. Donne in casa. Cassandro et Zanni alla barca.

Pantal., Trappo., Carichi di libri e affannati discorreno del arte magica et alchemia. Trap. lo burla et entra e va alla finestra Pant. discorre dell'arte imparata da suo Padre imperfettamente et accenna li figli persi in qo.

Grati. Impaurito Pant: gli narra l'arte sua et del Monte et del tesoro. Grat: promette agiuto e denari partono per far lo scritto.

Lelio L'amore verso Cintia in qo.

Cintia parlano amorosamente sopra la partita di Cass: vogliono esser consorti e nel darsi la fede, in qo.

Fiamme in mezzo di loro Cintia tramortisce lui la tiene che non cada in qo.

---

[1] In the third act two personages appear, Fortunio and Pedrolino, who are not mentioned in the list.

Zann. Torna dalla barca la vede, piange e la porta in casa poi torna, e contrasta con Lelio cerca placarlo fatti lazzi Lel. entra in casa di Grat: suo padre attivo [*sic*, adottivo] Zan: chiama.

France. fuori. Zan: li brava della poca cura di Cint. Zan: entra. Fran: resta scoprendosi accesa di Lelio. Biasma Grat: innamorato di lei et pensa come ingannar Zan.

Trapp. ridendo della credulitá di Grat: fran: lo scopre il tutto, e trattano il rimedio contro Zan: per farlo impazzire Trap: promette lei via, lui resta in qo.

Panta. Grati. Con denari, leggono et sottoscrivono lo scritto e ne è testimonio. Trap. quale entra Pant: Grat. à comprar le cose necessarie per il tesoro e vanno per strada.

Trapp. Con il liquore per parlare à fran.ª bussa.

Franc. Con robba da mangiare per Trap: e mentre fanno lazzi in qo.

Zanni di nascosto beve il liquore Trapp: accortosene vengono alle mani et a pugni e finisce l'Atto Primo.

ATTO SECONDO

Lelio. Stupito della fiamma vol darsi morte, credendo morta Cintia in qo.

Franc. l'impedisce, cerca placarlo, Lui fa lamenti fran: credendosi lo faccia per lei lo vol menare in casa. Lui voler andar à finire la vita ne bocchi [*sic*, boschi ? or bucchi ?] entra. Fran: resta in qo.

Zann. facendo pazzie, lega fran: con una corda e parte Fran: pentita del male fatto à Zan: resta pensando al rimedio in qo.

Cintia la slega e si querela con Amore per la fiamma e consolandosi l'una l'altra entrano.

Panta, Grati. Con robbe per il tesoro doppo lazzi entrano in casa a pigliare altri ordegni da cavare.

Lelio, Zann. Contrastando insieme per le donne Zan: doppo molte pazzie vol menar Lel: in casa per forza Lelio parte per forza Zan. resta retirandosi in qo.

Panta., Grati., Trapp., Facchi. Con ordegni magici et fermi a piedi del monte mormorano alcune note in qo. Zan: si vol intermettere. Pant: per incanto lo fa quietare e doppo alcuni suffomigi scarpellano la montagna dalle sui botte escono

Fiamm. Scaturiscono dal Monte, doppo vengono tenebre, et si odono strepiti e segni diversi, si apre la voragine loro si riparano facendo tutti l'offitio loro commessoli doppo Panta: et Grat: si battano nella voragine li altri restano in qo.

Folle fatti lazzi piglia Trap: quale si attacca à Zan: e tutti cadono nella voragine venendo una gran fiamma e finisce l'atto secondo.

ATTO TERZO

Panta., Grati., Zann., Trapp. Doppo molti rumori escono dalla voragine con il tesoro et con diverse ampolle de senni de particolari. Zan. ritorna savio ma insieme con Trap: gli è nato una coda per esser con troppo ardire scesi nella voragine e tutti entrano à riposarsi da Pant: non accortiti delle code.

Lelio. Meravigliato di tanti rumori intesi vedeno nuove fiamme dalla voragine pensando prodigij per Cintia gli prega dal Cielo piu beata vita e si rittira in qo.

Zann., Trap. Burlandosi l'uno del'altro della coda. Lelio gli fa accorgere che l'hanno tutti dua. Trap. narra del centro, e Zan. il senno ricuperato Lelio vedendo venire il Padre si ritira loro restano lamentandosi in qo.

Panta., GRATIA. Promette cavarli le code e fanno portare a casa di Gratiano la parte del tesoro Pant: dice di Lelio et Cintia sui figlioli persi, et la nova hautane per arte magica che stanno nel paese.

Lelio che had udito il tutto si scopre et si riconosce per figlio di Pant. quale dice à Grat: che Frances: è sua moglie et Grat: afferma la perdita di lei vanno à ritrovar Cintia in qo.

Cassa., Fortu. Con una valige fanno molti lazzi Cass: bussa e non è riconosciuto in casa li altri stanno à sentire da parte.

Zann. fuori gli scopre ogni cosa del seguito in casa Cass: in collera chiama le donne.

Cintia, Fran., Pedro, Tutti Vengono fuori Pant. riconosce per figlia Cintia placa Casandro e narrandoli il tesoro trovato la dota di dieci mila scudi e gli la da per moglie. Poi Grat: riconosciuto fran: per sua moglie se la repiglia Pant: promesso da vivere à Zan: e Trap: gli fa perdonare da tutti e finisce la Commedia.

THE MAGIC OF PANTALONE

[Translated from MS. Cors. ii. 44.]

Dramatis Personae

Pantalone, a magician.

Trappolino, his servant.

Cassandro, merchant, adoptive
  father of

Cintia, daughter of Pantalone.

Franceschina, her maid, later
  wife of Gratiano.

Zanni, servant.

Gratiano, adoptive father of

Lelio, son of Pantalone.

Porter.

Folletto.

Properties.

Valises; felt hat; boots; food; books; decanter of wine; mountain; caves; treasure; spades and shovels; money; paper, pen; inkstand; jars; scripts; tails for Zanni and Trappolino; cord; flames; noises.

ACT I

Cassandro, Zanni, Cintia, Franceschina from the house with valises. Cassandro entrusts the women to Zanni and leaves him master of the house, telling him to take precautions. The women go into the house: Cassandro and Zanni to the boat.

Pantalone, Trappolino loaded with books and breathless; they discuss alchemy and the art of magic. Trappolino jeers at him, goes in and comes to the window. Pantalone discourses on the art which he has picked up imperfectly from his father; he mentions his lost children; to him:

Gratiano in a fright. Pantalone tells him of his art, of the mountain and the treasure. Gratiano promises help and money and goes off with him to make out the bond.

Lelio announces his love for Cintia; to them:

Cintia they talk as lovers and mention Cassandro's departure. They wish to marry and pledge themselves to each other; at this:

Flames part them, Cintia faints, he prevents her from falling; at this:

Zanni returning from the ship sees her; he weeps and carries her into the house, and then comes back to quarrel with Lelio who tries to placate him. They have their little scene. Lelio goes into the house of Gratiano his adoptive father. Zanni summons

Franceschina and scolds her for not taking care of Cintia; he goes in. Franceschina is left to disclose her love for Lelio. She speaks ill of Gratiano who is in love with her and ponders how to deceive Zanni.

Trappolino laughing at Gratiano's credulity; Franceschina discloses everything and they discuss how to make Zanni mad. Trappolino promises; she goes away and he is left; at this:

Pantalone, Gratiano with money, they read and sign the bond: Trappolino is used as a witness; he goes in. Pantalone and Gratiano go off down the street to buy what is needed for the treasure.

Trappolino with the draught comes to talk to Franceschina, he knocks:

Franceschina comes with food for Trappolino; meanwhile they have their antics; at this:

Zanni on the sly swallows the draught. Trappolino realizes what has happened, comes to blows with him and finishes the first act.

ACT II

Lelio stupified by the flames wants to kill himself supposing that Cintia is dead; at this:

Franceschina holds him back and tries to soothe him. He laments. Franceschina, thinking that it is for her sake, tries to lead him into the house. He wants to end his life in the woods [or caves], and goes off. Franceschina is left and to her

Zanni acting the madman binds her with a cord and departs. Franceschina, repenting the harm done to Zanni, is left thinking of a remedy; at this:

Cintia unties her and accuses Love as the cause of the fire. They go in consoling each other.

Pantalone, Gratiano with equipment for the treasure, after antics go into the house to fetch other tools for digging.

Lelio, Zanni arguing together about the women. After many lunacies Zanni tries to force Lelio into the house. Lelio wrests himself free and goes away. Zanni withdraws; at this:

Pantalone, Gratiano, Trappolino, Porter come in with the apparatus for their magic. They halt by the mountain muttering something; Zanni tries to interfere: Pantalone quiets him with a spell, and after certain fumigations they hew at the mountain; at their strokes

Flames issue forth; darkness follows; howlings and portents are heard. The gulf opens. They approach, each playing the part committed to him. When Pantalone and Gratiano have thrown themselves into the gulf, the rest remain; at this:

Folletto has his antics and seizes Trappolino, who clings to Zanni and all fall into the gulf. There comes a great flame to finish the second act.

ACT III

Pantalone, Gratiano, Zanni, Trappolino after many rumblings issue from the mountain with the treasure and with jars containing the wits of various people. Zanni returns in his right mind but both he and Trappolino have acquired tails for being too bold in venturing down the gulf. All go to rest themselves in Pantalone's house, unaware of the tails.

Lelio astonished at such an uproar and seeing fresh flames issuing from the gulf supposes it is some prodigy connected with Cintia; prays heaven for a happier life and retires; at this:

Zanni, Trappolino each jeering at the other's tail. Lelio shows them that both are afflicted. Trappolino describes the centre [of the earth?]; Zanni relates how he recovered his wits. Lelio seeing his father approach, retires. They are left lamenting; at this:

Pantalone, GRATIANO promises to rid them of the tails and gets them to carry part of the treasure into Gratiano's house. Pantalone talks of Lelio and Cintia, his lost children, and says that through his magic art he has had news that they are in this country.

Lelio who has overheard all this presents himself and is recognized as the son of Pantalone, who tells Gratiano that Franceschina is his wife. Gratiano acknowledges her loss. They go in to find Cintia; at this:

Cassandro, Fortunio with luggage have their scene. Cassandro knocks and is not recognized at the house. The rest stand aside to listen.

Zanni comes out and tells him all that has happened at home. Cassandro is angry and calls for the women.

Cintia, Franceschina, Pedrolino, all come out. Pantalone recognizes his daughter Cintia, placates Cassandro by telling him about the treasure and gives her with a dowry of ten thousand scudi to be his [Lelio's ?] wife. Then Gratiano recognizes Franceschina as his wife and takes her back. Pantalone promises to support Zanni and Trappolino and begs a general pardon for them.

LI DUI SIMILI DI PLAUTO

COMMEDIA

[*MS. Loc.* i. 26; *compared with Cors.* i. 11.]

Personaggi

1. Pantalone.
2. Flavia figlia.
3. Silvio marito �️
4. Capitano fratello⎭ simili.   *Genero.*
5. Zanni ⎫
6. Burattino⎭servi.   *Sardinello.*
7. Hortentia Corteggiana.
8. Franceschina, serva.
9. Hoste.   *Coviello.*
10. Olivetta moglie.
11. Medico.   *Galeno.*

La Scena si finge Fano.

Robbe.

2 habiti simili et barbi; veste, anelli, collana; insegna di hosteria; una valigia; insegna di hosteria; bicchiero et vino.[1]

ATTO PRIMO

Silvio, ZANNI di casa dice essere innamorato di Hortentia corteggiana et haverli promesse una veste, una collana et 2 anelli et non haver denari et non haver robba à mandarli, dice à Zan. che trova qualche inventione per levar la robba di mano di Flavia sua moglie Zan. lo dissuade lasciar andar la corteggiana. Alla fine per li prieghi di Silvio dice haverli trovato l'invenzione che certi dovesti [*sic*] fare una commedia bellissima et che Flavia dirà che volerci venisse et che noi di haverli promesse alli recitanti una veste, collana et anelli. Silvio dice s'ella dicei voler venire dice haverli promessi fanno azzi di si, et del no, et batteno in qo.

Flavia di casa intende il tutto, lei ricusa et non voler andare alla commedia per non li dare le vesti, alla fine per li prieghi di Silvio gli da il tutto che segli portino quanto prima fanno azzi. Flavia in casa. Sil. e Zan. alegri, batteno in qo.

[1] The Corsini list adds: una scuffia, habiti per vestire i Cane. [Zanni ?]

Hortentia, FRANCESCHINA di casa riceve da Silvio le vesti, la collana et anelli, ringraziandolo fanno compimenti Hort. poi l'invitta à desinare seco. Sil. promette andarsi. Hort. Frᵃ. in casa. Sil. Zan. parteno per strada.

Pant. dice venir dalla villa per una lettera che li ha mandata Flavia sua figliola, dice le lodi della villa, batte per intendere quello che vogli la figliola in qo.

Flavia di casa intende da Pant. haver riceuto la sua lettera, et esser venuto dalla villa per intendere quello che ella ha bisogna, meravigliandosi per haverla lasciata Silvio suo genere. Fl. dice male del marito che lo sprega tutta la robba che va à puttane et Hosterie. Pant. meravigliandosi dice che remediarà. Fl. in casa. Pant. dice voler andare à cercar Sil. parte per strada.

Capitano, BURATTINO di strada di viaggio dice venir di Spagna quale vi andò da piccolo, et haver un fratello in Bologna sua patria, fanno azzi alla fine dicono allogiare, batteno in qo.

Hoste dall'hosteria fa azzi con li forastieri dicendo della bontà di vini et della sua hosteria chiama.

Olivetta di hosteria acarezza li forastieri piglia la valigia facendo azzi con Burattino tutti entrano nell'Hosteria. Cap. resta dice voler andar per la città per vedere come è bello il paese et il dentro della città, in qo.

Hortentia di casa che aspettar Sil. à desinare seco. Vede Cap. crede che sia Sil. lo invitta à desinare per essere à l'ordine il tutto. Cap. meravigliato per non cognoscere la donna la ringrazia della cortesia, al fine essendo importunato delle preghiere di Hort. accetta l'invitto, et entrano in casa.

Hoste, Olivetta, Burattino dall'hosteria gridano à Burat. haver messo una decina di candele nelli Tavoli et per voler buttare con Olivetta sua moglie lo bastonano. Burat. per strada. Oliv. Host. in casa.

ATTO SECONDO

Capitano, HORT. di casa si licenzia facendo compimenti et rendendo gratie delle cortesie ricevuti. Hort. li da le vesti, la collana et l'anelli accio lo facci accomodare. Cap. piglia il tutto dicendo che la servirà. Hort. in casa. Cap. meravigliandosi di tante cortesie, dice non cognoscerla, batte in qo.

Hoste dell'hosteria riceve le robbe del Cap. che le custodisca. Hoste fa azzi et entra. Cap. resta et dice voler andare per la città in qo.

Pant. di strada haver cercato Silvio, et non trovatolo vede Cap. si crede che sia Sil. li brava del suo mal vivere, et del suo cattivo essere et mali portamenti con Flavia. Cap. lo ingiuria dicendoli ruffiano, et da li delle mentite et parte per strada. Pant. resta et si meraviglia che sia fatto si insolente, in qo.

Silvio di strada li vede Pant. l'abbraccia li fa carezze ralegrandosi dal ritorno dalla villa, et rendoli gratie dal avertimento datoli. Pant. si meraviglia come puoco avanti era si tutto il contrario. Pant. l'arricomande Flav. lui volergli bene, et esserli cara. Sil. parte per strada. Pant. resta meravigliandosi della prima volta che li parlò Sil. et si bestialemente et poi si humanemente, in qo.

Cap. di strada in collera che le gente lo burla. Pant. lo esorta di tener conto del suo [*sic*] moglie et della casa. Cap. in colera li dice villanie et non haver moglie, ma lui essere un becco, parte per strada. Pant. fa meraviglie et dice esser matto et voler andare à trovare un medico, et parte per strada.

Silvio, Zanni di strada dicono volere andare à Hort. à pranzo, quale li deve aspettare, batteno in qo.

Hortentia, FRANC. di casa intende come è venuto Sil. et Zan. per pranzar con loro. Scacciano via Zan. dicendo che Sil. vi è stato à pranzo solo con esse sero [seco?] Zan. in casa per chiarirli et torna fuori piangendo con dire che è sporecchiata la tavola et mangiato ogni cosa. Sil. grida con le donne per non essersi stato fanno azzi et contrasta dicendoli delle robbe donato, che in premio cosi vien mal trattato da loro. Hort. dice di lui che dopo d'haver mangiato et si hauto le robbe faccia di quella maniera, fanno parole insieme. Sil. et Zan. in collera parteno per strada. Hort. Frª. restano meravigliati di Silvio che faccei di quella maniera che li nega il tutto, in qo.

Capitano di strada Hort. li dimanda le robbe dateli, et perche facci così et stia in collera con esso lei Cap. dice non stare in collera, et che le robbe s'andrà a pigliare et [che le?] parteno per strada. Hort. Frª. restano meravigliate in qo.

Silvio di strada dice voler andare in casa vede Hortª. quale li dimanda si ha portato le robbe. Fanno di nuova romore. Sil. in collera parte per strada. Hort. Fr. restano in qo.

Capitano di strada Hort. grida per conto delle robbe Cap. facendoli buone parole con dirle che quanto prima gli le porterà. Hort. Fr. in casa. Cap. resta in qo.

Zanni di strada vede il Cap. si crede che sia Sil. il suo padrone, li dimanda il salario che deve. Cap. dice non cognoscerlo, Zan. meravigliato che neghi questo che li farà dice dalla sua moglie istessa che l'ha servito, batte in qo.

Flavia di casa vede Cap. si crede che sia Sil. suo marito, li dice che paghi Zan. Cap. la burla di poi concede à Zan. che dormi con Flavia, et che sconti il salario. Zan. contento con Flavia entra in casa. Cap. parte per strada.

Silvio di strada sopra il mal trattare di Hort. et del suo mal procedere, in qo.

Burattino di strada vede Sil. si crede che sia il Cap. suo padrone, li dice che vadi dal hoste, et che li facei dar le robbe per haverci lui gridato, et che l'aspetta al hosteria del Sole. Burat. dice che farà il tutto. Burat. parte per strada. Silvio meravigliato dice voler provare il tutto batte in qo.

Hoste dall'hosteria vede Sil. si crede il Cap. li porta fuori tutte le sue robbe facendo conto, Silvio li paga. Hoste in casa. Silvio meravigliato con le robbe batte in qo.

Zanni dalla fenestra si lamenta con Silvio che Flavia sua moglie non vuole dormire con lui, et che vuole il salario. Sil. li brava Zan. fa la scommessa che lui haverli ordinato, che ci darmi [*sic*] per scontare il salario che il tutto li dirà Flavia in qo.

Flavia di casa dice in faccia di Silvio come lui s'è contentato che Zan. dormisse con lei per scontare il salario. Sil. si meraviglia et dice non esser vero. Sil. li restituisce le robbe alla moglie. Zan. si meraviglia fanno la scena di donare le bastonate et tutti entrano in casa.

Pant., *Medico* di strada dicono voler medicar Sil. quale crede che sia pazzo, che non sta in proposito, in qo.

Silvio di casa in villa Pant. à desinare per esser hora entra in casa. Pant. dice che Sil. sta in cervello et li certia il medico che parte per strada. Pant. resta in qo.

Capitano di strada vede Pant. vien a rumore con esso lui. Pant. chiama il medico in qo.

Medico di strada Cap. in collera parte per strada. Pant. dice a Medico che li torna la frenesia di nuovo a Silvio, pero bisogna curarlo, in qo.

Silvio di casa di nuova invittar Pant. à desinare. Medico li tocca il pulso quale li trova buono et sano. Sil. meravigliato entra in casa. Medico si licentia parte per strada. Pant. resta in qo.

Capitano di strada di nuova vengono a parole con Pant. ingiurandolo Pant. chiama in qo.

Medico di strada vuole toccare il polso al Cap. credendolo Silvio. Cap. bastona tutti et parteno per strada.

ATTO TERZO

Cap. di strada meravigliato dello successo dice voler pigliar le sue robbe, batte in qo.

Hoste dall'hosteria intende il Cap. voler le sue robbe lui dice haverle date. Fanno parole, Cap. in collera dice voler andare alla giustizia parte per strada. Hoste resta meravigliato in qo.

Silvio di strada, Hoste si crede che sia il Cap. li dice se lui ha hauto le robbe. Sil. dice di si, fanno azzi. Silvio parte per strada. Hoste meravigliato in qo.

Cap. di strada dice voler le sue robbe fanno parole. Hoste che lui istesso l'ha confessato di haverle haute. Cap. nega in collera parte per strada. Hoste resta in qo.

Silvio di strada dimandato dell'hoste delle robbe, lui confessa haverle haute in qo.

Pant. di strada si ritira se Silvio sta in cervello. Hoste li dice che stia per testimonio. Pant. si ritira d'una parte. Silvio di nuova confessa haver ricevuto le robbe et parte per strada. Hoste Pant. restano in qo.

Cap. di strada dimanda al'hoste le robbe sue con felle parole, et con amorevolezza. Hoste in collera chiama il testimonio. Pant. essendo stato da parte dice haver udito il tutto che lui ha confessato. Cap. in collera entra nell'hosteria dicendo volerle per forza. Hoste Pant. dietro entrano nell'hosteria.

Silvio di strada meravigliato delle stravagante che li succedono et delle robbe haute in qo.

Pant. dall'hosteria dice haver riserrato Sil. in una camera et voler andare trovar il medico, vede Sil., si meraviglia dubita che non sia un spirito. Al fine Mag.co. [i.e. Pantalone] li parla meravigliandosi come sia uscito dall'hosteria. Sil. fa meraviglia l'uno l'altro si sente romore nell'hosteria et li caccia mano la 'spada' in qo.

Capitano, HOSTE, OLIVETTA dall'hosteria con la spada sfoderata gridando volerle sue robbe, tutti [s'intramettono] in mezzo. Pant. meravigliato non saper cognoscere qual sia Silvio suo genero fa meraviglie in qo.

Zanni, Burat. di strada Zan. non saper cognoscere qual sia Silvio suo padrone, Burat. non saper cognoscere qual sia il Cap. suo padrone. Hoste non saper cognoscere qual sia quello che li diede le robbe et le veste, non saper cognoscere quello che entrò nell'hosteria. Tutti facendo azzi stanno meravigliati in qo.

Hortentia, Franceschina di casa fanno il simile non cognoscono qual sia Silvio, fanno azzi alla fine chiamano, in qo.

Flavia di casa non saper cognoscere qual sia Silvio suo genero fa azzi con l'uno, con l'altro. Alla fine si scopre il Cap. esser fratello di Sil. facendo allegrezze il Cap. sposa Hortentia et Zan. Franc.

THE DOUBLES ACCORDING TO PLAUTUS

COMEDY

Corsini.

Dramatis Personae

 1. Pantalone
 2. Flavia, his daughter   (Mulier)
 3. Silvio, her husband ⎫   (Menaechmus)
 4. Captain, his brother ⎰   (Menaechmus the ⎫ Doubles   *Son-in-law*
                                 traveller) ⎰
 5. Zanni   ⎫ servants   (Peniculus)
 6. Burattino ⎰   (Messenio)   *Sardinello*
 7. Hortentia, courtesan   (Erotion)
 8. Franceschina, her maid   (Ancilla)
 9. Host   *Coviello*
10. Olivetta, his wife
11. Doctor   (Medicus)   *Galeno*
                              (Cylindrus, the cook)
                              (Porters)[1]

The scene represents Fano.

Properties.

Suits and beards to match for the doubles; a dress, rings, a collar; inn-sign; valise; glass of wine.[2]

ACT I

Silvio, ZANNI comes from the house announcing that he is in love with the Courtesan Hortentia and has promised her a dress, a collar, and two rings, but has neither money nor goods to send her. He tells Zanni to find some contrivance to filch the things from Flavia his wife. Zanni tries to persuade him to leave the Courtesan alone, but at length with Silvio's pleading he says that he has thought of a plan. Flavia is to be told of a most excellent comedy which is to be presented; when she says that she wishes to go to it, he is to explain that he has promised to lend the players a dress, a collar, and rings. Silvio asks what is to be said if Flavia really wants to come; he is told to repeat that it is a promise; they have their antics of 'Yes' and 'No', and knock; at this:

Flavia from the house hears all this; she refuses and does not want to see the comedy so that she need not give them the clothes. In the end, after Silvio's pleading she relents and tells him to take the things

[1] In brackets are given the corresponding characters in Plautus's play.

[2] The Corsini list adds: a head-tire; clothes for Zanni.

and return them as soon as possible. They have their little scene [*azzi*] and Flavia goes into the house leaving Silvio and Zanni delighted; they knock and at this:

Hortentia, FRANCESCHINA from the house receives the dress, the collar, and the rings from Silvio, thanking and paying him compliments. She invites him to dine with her and Silvio accepts. Hortentia and Franceschina go in; Silvio and Zanni go down the street.

Pantalone announces that he has come in from the country in answer to a letter sent him by his daughter Flavia. He praises the country, and knocks to find out what his daughter wants with him; at this:

Flavia from the house hears that Pantalone has had her letter and has come in from the country to know what is the matter. He is surprised that Silvio his son-in-law should have left her alone. Flavia grumbles about her husband for wasting their substance and frequenting courtesans and taverns. Pantalone is shocked and says that something must be done. Flavia goes into the house. Pantalone says he will look for Silvio and goes down the street.

Captain, BURATTINO down the street arriving as from a journey; he says he has come from Spain where he has been since a child, and that he has a brother in Bologna, his native city. They have their by-play together and want to find a lodging; they knock; at this:[1]

Host from the inn has his scene with the strangers announcing the excellence of the wines and the accommodation, he calls

Olivetta from the inn, she caresses the strangers, takes the valise, playing about with Burattino; all go into the inn, leaving the Captain, who says he will go and explore the city, observing how beautiful both it and its surroundings are; at this:[2]

Hortentia comes from the house saying that she expects Silvio for dinner; she sees the Captain and thinking it is Silvio, invites him to come and dine; not knowing the lady he thanks her for her kindness, and in the end, overcome by Hortentia's entreaties, accepts the invitation and they go into the house.

Host, OLIVETTA, BURATTINO comes from the inn shouting at Burattino for having put about ten candles on the table and for carrying on with his wife Olivetta. They beat Burattino, who goes off down the street; they return into the house.

ACT II

Captain, HORTENTIA from the house takes his leave, paying her compliments and thanking her for the kindness which he has received.

[1] Corsini: when they have had their 'lazzi' with the luggage.

[2] In the Corsini version it is here and not at his first entrance that the Captain tells his story.

Hortentia gives him the dress, the collar, and the rings, so that he may have them altered to suit her. The Captain takes them all, promising to do her this service. Hortentia retires, leaving him astounded at her favours; he has no idea who she may be; he knocks and at this:

Host from the inn takes the Captain's things into his charge, after his antics the host goes in. The Captain says he will explore the city; at this:

Pantalone comes down the street looking in vain for Silvio; seeing the Captain he takes him for his son-in-law, and scolds him for his loose living, his shocking habits, and ill treatment of Flavia. The Captain abuses him, calling him a pander and giving him the lie. He goes off down the street leaving Pantalone amazed that he should have become so insolent; at this:

Silvio coming up the street[1] sees Pantalone, he embraces and caresses him, welcoming his return from the country and thanking him for the warning given him. Pantalone is surprised that a few moments ago he had behaved so differently. He commends Flavia to his care; Silvio assures him of his affection and promises to cherish her. He goes off down the street, leaving Pantalone marvelling that at first he had been so brutal and afterwards so civil; at this:

Captain comes up the street furious with the people who are joking with him. Pantalone exhorts him to have some regard for his wife and his house. The Captain flies into a temper and abuses him, saying he has no wife and calling Pantalone a cuckold. He leaves Pantalone astounded, and sure that he is mad he goes off to find a doctor.

Silvio, Zanni come up the street remarking that it is time to go to dine with Hortentia who must be waiting for them; they knock and at this:

Hortentia, Franceschina from the house hear that Silvio and Zanni have come to dinner. They turn Zanni away saying that Silvio has already dined there alone. Zanni goes in to find out for himself and comes out weeping, saying the plates are dirty and everything is eaten. Silvio shouts to the women that he has never been there, they take their part in the dispute, reminding him of the things that they gave him, and grumbling that this should be the only thanks that they get. Hortentia describes his behaviour after dinner and argues with him. Silvio and Zanni go off down the street in a rage, leaving Hortentia and Franceschina amazed at his behaviour and denial; at this:

Captain appears up the street, Hortentia inquires about the things which she gave him, and asks why he was angry with her. He insists that he is not angry at all, and departs to fetch the things, leaving Hortentia and Franceschina bewildered; at this:

[1] Corsini: 'from the same side'.

Silvio comes up the street on his way home; he sees Hortentia who asks him whether he has brought her possessions. They quarrel noisily, and Silvio departs in a temper, leaving Hortentia and Franceschina; to them comes

Captain up the street, Hortentia screams at him demanding her goods. The Captain speaks her fair, and says he will bring them as soon as possible. Hortentia and Franceschina leave him and go into the house; at this:

Zanni from the street sees the Captain and takes him for his master Silvio; he demands the wages due to him. The Captain says he does not know him. Zanni astonished at this reminds him of his own wife whom he serves; at this:

Flavia comes out of the house and supposing it is Silvio her husband tells him to pay Zanni. The Captain jokes with her and then allows Zanni to bargain that he shall sleep with Flavia instead of having his wages. Zanni agrees and goes into the house with Flavia; the Captain goes down the street.

Silvio comes up the street complaining of Hortentia's ill treatment and misbehaviour; at this:

Burattino from the street sees Silvio and takes him for the Captain, his master; he tells him to go to the innkeeper and make him hand over his goods because he has had a row with him, he is to wait for him at the sign of the Sun. [Burattino promises to do all this][1] and goes out. Silvio remains mystified, determined to follow this up; he knocks, at this:

Host from the inn sees Silvio, and mistaking him for the Captain hands over all his possessions and makes out the bill, which Silvio settles. The Host retires into the inn leaving Silvio amazed in possession of the goods; he knocks and at this:

Zanni from the window complains to Silvio that his wife Flavia will not sleep with him; he demands his wages. Silvio scolds him and Zanni bets him that Flavia will support him when he says that this was the bargain; at this:

Flavia from the house tells Silvio to his face that he had agreed to let Zanni sleep with her instead of paying him his wages. Silvio is astounded and says it is not true. He restores his wife's property. Zanni is astonished; they have the scene of the thrashing and all go into the house.

---

[1] I have bracketed this direction which turns the sense of the passage and suggests that Silvio is giving orders to Burattino mistaking him for Zanni. There is no further indication that the servants are also doubles in this scenario and as a direction for the man's acquiescence to his master's orders the phrase is so common that it may well have slipped in unconsciously while Loccatelli composed or copied out this monotonously confusing plot.

Pantalone, the Doctor from the street say that they wish to examine Silvio, who must be mad and cannot talk sense; at this:

Silvio from the house invites Pantalone to dinner which is now ready. The Doctor feels his pulse which he finds steady and regular. Silvio is surprised and goes in. The Doctor takes his leave and goes down the street: Pantalone remains; to him:

Captain comes down the street and again has words with Pantalone, abusing him. Pantalone calls for

The Doctor to return, he counts the Captain's pulse, mistaking him for Silvio. The Captain cudgels them both and they go off down the street.

ACT III

Captain amazed at what has happened goes to fetch his possessions; he knocks and at this:

The Host from the inn hearing that the Captain has called for his things tells him he has had them already. They argue and the Captain in a rage swears he will go for the justice. The Host is left dumbfounded; at this:

Silvio comes up the street and is mistaken for the Captain by the Host, who repeats that he has had his things. Silvio acknowledges them, and after their scene [*azzi*] he departs, leaving the Host to marvel; at this:

The Captain comes up the street and demands his things and argues. The Host protests that he has just admitted to having had them. The Captain denies it and goes off in a rage. The Host remains; at this:

Silvio reappearing in the street is questioned by the Host concerning the things and admits he has had them; at this:

Pantalone comes down the street to find out if Silvio is in his right mind. The Host tells him to wait there as a witness, Pantalone stands to one side and again Silvio acknowledges the goods and goes out. The Host and Pantalone are left; at this:

The Captain comes up the street demanding his possessions from the Host with threats and abuse.[1] The Host in a fury summons Pantalone from his corner to act as a witness. The Captain goes in swearing he will have his things by force, the Host and Pantalone follow.[2]

Silvio comes down the street marvelling at the extraordinary events and at the recovered goods; at this:

Pantalone comes from the inn announcing that he has locked

---

[1] 'con felle parole et con amorevolezza': I have taken it that Loccatelli intended some word connected with 'amaro, bitter', but it is impossible that 'amorevolezza' is correct and that the Captain tried to coax the Host when threats failed.

[2] In the Corsini version Pantalone does not go in but meets Silvio in the street and takes him for a ghost.

Silvio into a room and is off to find the Doctor. He sees Silvio and is dumbfounded, supposing he is a ghost. At last he addressed him, marvelling how he could have got out of the inn. Silvio is equally taken aback: hearing a disturbance within they draw their swords; at this:

Captain, HOST, OLIVETTA comes from the inn with a drawn sword shouting that he will have his goods; all rush between them. Pantalone, at a loss to know which is his son-in-law, Silvio, shows his bewilderment; at this:

Zanni, BURATTINO from the street is unable to identify his master Silvio, and Burattino cannot tell which is the Captain. The Host does not know who gave him the goods and the garment, nor who went into the inn; all are left astounded, playing their various antics; at this:

Hortentia, Franceschina from the house behave in the same way, not knowing which is Silvio; they have their scene and finally call

Flavia from the house; she cannot recognize her husband, and tries first one and then the other. At last they discover that the Captain is Silvio's brother, and making merry he marries Hortentia and Zanni takes Franceschina.

ZANNI INCREDIBILE CON QUATRO SIMILI

COMEDIA

[*MS. Correr* no. 21.]

Persone

Magnifico.
Silvia figlia.
Argentina serva.

Dottore. [Coviello]
Furtunio figlio.

Lavinio della citta⎫
Lavinio forestiero⎭ fratelli simili.

Flavia cortigiana.

Zanni della citta⎫
Zanni forastiero⎭ fratelli simili.

Roma

Robbe.

Abbitto per travestire Mag. Abbito da travestire Lavinio. Borsa con denari uno anello bastone da bastonare.

ATTO PRIMO

Mag. cov. asortando Cov. a lassar le cortigiane e prender moglie, lui che vol prima maritar Furtunio suo figlio. Mag. che gli da Silvia sua figlia. Coviello si contenta e parte per dar la nova all'figlio. Mag. batte

Argentina passa molti lazzi, con il mag. poi fa chiamare

Silvia lui averla maritata con Furtunio, lei che se sente male lo prega aspetare otto giorni. Mag. contento va trovar Coviello per fare tratenere. Silvia dice Argentina l'amore che porta à Lavinio qual si trova fora in villa, vole avisarlo et entra à scriverle una lettera, Arg. narra l'amor di Zan. che la goduta in qo.

Zanni che le facende di douana vanno male fanno lazzi di gelosia con Arg. Zan. che non la crede e la manda in casa in qo.

Mag. l'amor della cortigiana che per questo asortato Coviello lasciarla vede Zan. gli fa festa gl' dona denari e lo prega aiutarlo con la cortigiana, e che se lo fare vol che vadi in casa sua a stare. Zan. promette di aiutarlo ma che non gli crede che lo toglia in casa. Mag. promette e via Zan. resta in qo.

Flavia di casa lo prega a portar un anello a Lavinio che come torna gli donara dieci scudi, lui con lazzi che non lo crede tol l'anello gli promette lei in casa, lui resta in qo

Cov. Che a visto parlar con Flavia gli adimanda di chi parlavano Zan. che sa lui essere inamorato di lei che parlava di lui et che lei gli vol bene. Cov. alegro gli dona denari e lo mena con lui per comprar robbe di apresentarla via.

Lavinio Forastiero di viaggio voler trovar alogiamento in qo

Silvia di casa lo saluta lui che non lo conosce lei chiama

Arg. dice che Lavinio la conosce gli grida, lui con firma di Non averla mai vista. Silvia bravandogli entra. lui che deve essere qualche cortegiana va via. Arg. resta dicendo che allmeno [*sic*] il suo Zan. non fa cosi in qo.

Zanni Forastiero essere arivato in questa città voler trovare una osteria. Arg. lo chiama lui si meraviglia lei l'accarezza lui che non la conosce, lei dice che l'ingravidata lui gli da una mentita, lei gli da un schiaffo et entra lui piangendo parte facendo finir l'atto.

ATTO SECONDO

Lavinio della città dice esser stato in villa vol veder Silvia in qo.

Silvia alla finestra, lui la saluta lei gli brava scacciando entra, lui resta sospeso non sapendo la causa in qo.

Zanni domanda per che sta adolerato, lui gli dice il tutto Zanni che lassi fare à lui che Arg. gli vol bene e batte.

Arg. dice delle villanie à Zanni, lui il suo Lavio [lazzo?] non te lo detto che non ti credo, lei lo scaccia et entra. Lav[in]io lo burla Zan. disperato parte Lavinio resta in qo.

Furt. che suo padre l'a maritato con Silvia ma lui non la vole, fanno scena di amicitia, Furt. gli dice del parentato Lav. via. Furt. resta in qo.

Cov. gli dice che se metti all'ordine per piglia[r] Silvia lui che non la vole e parte. Cov. resta in qo.

Mag. lo prega à tardar le nozze lui si contenta e via. Mag. che non sa che abbia fatto Zan. con la cortegiana in qo.

Zan. Forastiero sopra il successo Mag. se à fatto l'imbasciata [?] lui che non è rufiano Mag. bravandogli via in qo.

Lavinio se a parlato con Silvia. Zan. che non la conosce. Lav. gli brava e via, lui resta confuso in qo.

Flavia di casa se a dato l'anello a Lav. Lui che non la conosce, lei gli ingiura dicendo che lo fara bastonare. Zan. so[s]petto via, lei resta in qo.

Furt. se gli scopre amante lei doppo parole si contenti, purche bastoni Zan. Furt. gli promette, lei entra, lui via

Mag. stupito che Zan. dice non lo conosce in qo.

Zan. della città Mag. gli brava per che a detto che non lo conos[c]eva. Zan. con il lazzo che non ti crede se non a mai parlato con lui ma adesso lo vol servire e batte.

Flavia l'ingiuria chiamandolo ladro et entra lui resta confuso in questo che lui è un bravo rufiano Zan. dice che vol la godi per forza gli ordina che si travesti e finghi esser servitore di Lavinio e la meni nel suo apartamento da basso Mag. va avestirsi [*sic*] lui resta in qo.

Lavinio visto Zan. domanda se lo conosce, lui di sì, Lav. pocho avanti non lo conosceva. Zan. che vol che entri da scala e che la Cortegiana è inamorata di lui, e Mag. della Cortegiana gli da ordine che vadi à travestirsi che lui lo mettera in casa del Mag. a ciò non sia conosciuto, lui va à travestirsi. Zan. resta in qo.

Furt. visto Zan. lo bastona, et fanno finir l'atto secondo.

ATTO TERZZO [*sic*]

Zanni che vole avisar Silvia batte

Arg. gli brava poi si pacificano fanno pace, e fa chiamare qo.

Silvia lui gli dice come Lav. venira travestito donne alegre via. Zanni dolendosi delle bastonate parte.

Mag. da servo fa il cenno e batte da

Flavia Mag. dice esser servitore di Lav. che la mandata à torre che vadi da lui per che se sente un pocho male in qo.

Lavinio Forastiero lei vistolo dice potete venire in casa senza che voi mandasti il servo, lui che non a servo e che non lo conosce, ne lei ne lui, Mag. fugge, lei entra in colera, lui resta in qo.

Coviello lo crede quello della città gli dice della moglie lui dice esser forastiero vinuto per trovare un suo fratello e scopre il tutto. Lav. via. Cov. batte da la Cortegiana in qo

Mag. sente il tutto da Cov. si scopreno rivali poi si accordano di stare à quello che vora lei e batteno.

Flavia inteso il tutto per burlarli gli dice che chi venera meglio vestito quello sara il suo moroso [*sic*], loro via lei entra.

Zan. sopra l'ordine dato à Lav. et à Silvia in qo.

Furt. lui se lamenta delle bastonate lui che e stata Flavia che gli a fatto dare per che negava l'anello lui che non l'a mai negato dice che gli lo vol restituir e batte.

Flavia perdona à Zan. qual gli dice che Lav. è inamorato di Silvia lui acetta Fortunio et entrano tutti incasa.

Zanni sopra le disgratie occorse vol vedere se trova il fratello in qo.

Lavinio gli dice che chiami Silvia, lui che non è rofiano, lui gli vol dare lui che non lo conosce Lav. gli vol dare lui grida in qo.

Silvia di casa con

Argentina vogliono aiutar Zan. in questo Zan. scopre venir di fora et esere fratello di Zanni della città. Sil. si ralegra è [*sic*] sposa Lav. in qo.

Flavia, Furt. Senteno il tutto mandano Zan. in casa à trovar il fratello lui va, poi torna e fatto li lazzi in qo.

Lav. Forastiero fa l'istesso va a conoscere il fratello poi torna in qo *Cov.* vistito [*sic*] stravagante in qo.

Mag. vistito stravagante tutti li burlano alla fine si scopre il tutto e fanno finire la comedia.

THE UNBELIEVING ZANNI AND THE FOUR ALIKE

COMEDY

Dramatis Personae

Magnifico.
Silvia, his daughter.
Argentina, the maid.

Doctor (Coviello).
Furtunio, his son.

Lavinio, citizen ⎱ brothers and doubles.
Lavinio, traveller ⎰

Flavia, a courtesan.

Zanni, citizen ⎱ brothers and doubles.
Zanni, traveller ⎰

Properties.

Disguise for the Magnifico; traveller's clothes for Lavinio; purse of money; ring; stage stick.

ACT I

Magnifico, coviello comes in exhorting Coviello to leave courtesans and take a wife: he says that first of all he wants to marry off his son Furtunio. The Magnifico proposes his daughter Silvia: Coviello agrees and goes to inform his son. The Magnifico knocks.

Argentina has many tricks [*lazzi*] with the Magnifico and then calls

Silvia, he tells her she is to marry Furtunio. She complains that she does not feel well and is granted eight days grace. The Magnifico goes in search of Coviello to make the arrangements. Silvia confides to Argentina her love for Lavinio who is away in the country. She wishes to warn him and goes in to write a letter. Argentina discourses on her love for Zanni and says that he has enjoyed her; at this:

Zanni grumbles that business with the customs officials [*di douana*] has gone badly. They have their scene of jealousy; Zanni says he does not believe her and sends her into the house; at this:

Magnifico discloses his passion for the Courtesan and admits that this was why he had advised Coviello to let her alone: he sees Zanni and bribes him to help with the Courtesan, promising that if he is successful he will take him into his service. Zanni promises to help but refuses to believe that he will be received into the house. The Magnifico promises and goes out leaving Zanni, at this:

Flavia from the house begs him to take a ring to Lavinio, offering him 10 scudi on his return; Zanni with his trick of not believing it takes the ring; she gives him her word and goes in; he remains, at this:

Coviello who has seen him talking with Flavia asks Zanni of whom they were speaking. Zanni, who knows that Coviello is enamoured of her, tells him that he was the subject of their conversation and that she is fond of him. Coviello is delighted and gives him money, taking him along to buy presents for the Courtesan.

Lavinio the stranger as from a journey searches for a lodging; at this:

Silvia from the house bids him 'Good-day'; he says that he does not know her; she calls

Argentina who says that Lavinio knows her; she shouts to him. He insists that he has never set eyes on her. Silvia retires reproaching him. He thinks that she must be some courtesan and goes away. Argentina is left saying that at least her Zanni would not behave like this; to them:

Zanni the traveller announces that he has just arrived in the city and is looking for an inn. Argentina calls to him; he is surprised. She caresses him and he says he does not know her. She tells him she is with child by him; he gives her the lie; she strikes him and goes in. He goes out weeping and ends the first act.

ACT II

Lavinio the citizen says that he has been away in the country and wishes to visit Silvia; at this:

Silvia appears at the window: he salutes her. She reproaches him and dismisses him. He is left anxious not knowing the reason; at this:

Zanni asks why he is so worried; he explains what has happened. Zanni tells him to let him settle it all, and says that Argentina is a friend of his; he knocks:

Argentina abuses Zanni; he replies with his trick of 'Didn't I tell you I didn't believe it?' She dismisses him and goes in. Lavinio teases him and Zanni departs in despair, leaving Lavinio; at this:

Fortunio announces that his father has engaged him to marry Silvia but that he is unwilling. They meet as friends and have their scene. Furtunio tells him about the proposed match. Lavinio begs him not to have her, Furtunio promises. Lavinio goes out leaving Furtunio; at this:

Coviello tells him to be prepared to have Silvia, Furtunio says he does not want her and goes out. Coviello is left; at this:

Magnifico asks him to put off the wedding for a little; he agrees and goes off. The Magnifico wonders what Zanni has been able to do for him with the Courtesan; at this:

Zanni the traveller commenting on his adventure meets the Magnifico who asks him what of the embassy. He retorts that he is not a go-between. The Magnifico upraids him and goes out; at this:

Lavinio asks him if he has spoken with Silvia. Zanni says he does not know her. Lavinio reproaches him and leaves him bewildered; at this:

Flavia from the house asks if he has given the ring to Lavinio. He declares that he does not know her. She abuses him, threatening to have him beaten. Zanni goes out nervously; she remains; at this:

Fortunio presents himself as a lover; after talking a while she is satisfied with him on condition that he will beat Zanni. Furtunio promises; she retires and he goes out.

Magnifico is amazed that Zanni should say that he does not know him; at this:

Zanni the citizen is scolded by the Magnifico for denying him. Zanni with his trick of 'I don't believe it', says that he has never spoken to him until now but that he is at his service; he knocks:

Flavia abuses him, calls him a thief and goes in again. He is left puzzled. The Magnifico says he is a fine pander. Zanni swears that he shall enjoy her by force, and instructs him to disguise himself and pretend to be one of Lavinio's servants, and says he will lead him into one of the rooms on the ground floor. The Magnifico goes out to dress, leaving Zanni; at this:

Lavinio sees Zanni and asks whether he knows him. Zanni says 'Yes'. Lavinio objects that he had not done so a little while ago.

Zanni says he wants him to go to Silvia, and tells him that the Courtesan is in love with him and the Magnifico with the Courtesan. He instructs him in a disguise which will get into the Magnifico's house without being recognized. He goes to dress up. Zanni is left; at this:
Furtunio sees Zanni, beats him and finishes the second act.

ACT III

Zanni, wishing to warn Silvia, knocks.
Argentina scolds him; after a little they make it up and call
Silvia and tell her that Lavinio will come disguised. The women go out overjoyed. Zanni departs grumbling about the beating.
Magnifico as a servant makes the signal and knocks for
Flavia, to whom he announces himself as one of Lavinio's men sent to fetch her to him because he feels unwell; at this:
Lavinio the stranger appears. She catches sight of him and says 'So you are able to come to the house without sending a servant'. He says he has no servant and does not know her, nor she him. The Magnifico runs away, she enters indignant; he remains; at this:
Coviello takes him for Lavinio the citizen and tells him of his wife. He explains that he is a stranger in search of his brother and makes everything clear before he goes out. Coviello knocks for the Courtesan; at this:
Magnifico hears all this; he and Coviello find that they are rivals and finally agree to leave the choice to the Courtesan; they knock.
Flavia hears everything, and to play a trick on them says she will have as her lover the one who comes a-wooing the more finely dressed. They go away; she goes in.
Zanni comments on the instructions given to Lavinio and to Silvia; at this:
Furtunio appears; Zanni complains about the beating; Furtunio explains that it was given him by order of Flavia because he had denied having received the ring. He protests that he never denied it and says that he will restore it now; he knocks:
Flavia forgives Zanni, who tells her that Lavinio is in love with Silvia; she accepts Furtunio and both go into the house.
Zanni discussing the accidents that have befallen him, wants to see if he can find his brother; at this:
Lavinio tells him to call Silvia: he says he is not a go-between. Lavinio tries to beat him. He swears that he does not know him. Again Lavinio makes for him; he shouts; at this:
Silvia from the house with
Argentina want to help Zanni, and at this Zanni explains that he is a stranger and the brother of Zanni the citizen. Silvia is delighted and pledges herself to Lavinio; at this:

Flavia Fortunio, hear all this; they send Zanni into the house to find his brother; he goes in and then comes out again playing his antics; at this:

Lavinio the stranger does the same; he goes in to meet his brother and then returns; at this[1]:

Coviello, appears absurdly dressed; at this:

Magnifico, appears absurdly dressed. All jeer at them and in the end everything is cleared up and they finish the comedy.

[1] The alternate appearances are evidently arranged for the sake of economy; the same actors take the parts of the twins.

PASTORALS

IL MAGO

PASTORALE

[*Cors.* i. 13.]

Personaggi

Pantalone

Coviello servo

Gratiano

Bertolino

Filli

Amarilli

Fausto

Selvaggio

Mago

Diavolo

Leone.

Robbe.

Fonte, Tempio, grotta, scena, robba da mangiare, maccaroni per spiriti. Pomaranci, pignatta con acqua, farina, scala, corda, Bachetta, libbro, Leone, fiamme.

ATTO PRIMO

Pant. Il Naufragio la perdita di Cov: Grat: e Berto: fa l'ecco in qo.

Covie. Di dentro poi fuori haver fame in qo.

Berto. Di dentro chiama poi fuori haver fame, si rallegrano insieme vedono il Tempio entrano, doppo haver chiamato e fatto l'ecco, che risponde nel Tempio.

Pastor, Ninfe cantando in giri pastorali vanno al tempio per fare le offerte in qo.

Buffon. da Giove, Mercurio, e Cupido ricevono la robba. pastori via loro sedono à mangiare, e burlando li Dei in qo.

Spiriti li bastinano, tutti via.

Mago. Haverli mandato lo spirito di Filli sua figlia innamorata di

Selvaggio che non l'ama, volere agiutare à burlare li Pastori forastieri chiama

Filli l'esorta ad esser patiente, et li promette agiuto, che consiste nelli frutti e via. Lei sopra di cio in qo.

Pantal. La salutano, la pregano che li dia uno di quei frutti loro battono si fa la burla della Pignatta Lei via Cov: dietro Panta. resta confuso in qo.

Grati. chiama poi fuori e dice della libraria si vole in qo.

Amari. La crudeltá di fausto loro la pregano, lei che un solo vol contentare li fa la burla del legarli li occhi, e via in qo.

Coviel., Bertol. si abbraciano, con li due cecati, fatti lazzi, si scoprono e partino burlati.

Filli, SELVA. Pregando Selvag. lui parla di mangiare, lei di amore in fine per che l'ami entra nella grotta del padre, et li porta Maccaroni. lui mangia e vol partire. Lei va per altra robba Lui mangia et parte per fuggire lo stimolo.

Panta., Coviel. escono affamati in qo.

Filli con il libbro haverlo rubbato al Padre per sodisfare al suo Selvaggio lo va cercando, e chiama. Buffoni rispondano.

Panta., Coviel. domandano à Filli che vol fare del libbro; lei il tutto. Loro le lo domandano in prestito insegnandoli Selv. che è al fonte delle Olive. Lei via dandoli il libro loro fanno il lazzo esce robba et mangiano in qo.

Grati., Bert. uno da una parte et l'altro dal altra gli rubbano il mangiare in fine dal libro escono fiamme in qo.

Diavo. Li battono loro impauriti fuggono. Diav. portano il libro nella grotta e finisce l'atto Primo.

ATTO SECONDO

Selva. Morto di fame in qo.

Panta. fuori Sel: lo crede un animale lo vole uccidere con un bastone. Pant. se ne accorge e fugge. Selv. dietro

Fausto contando l'amore di filli, et l'odio di Amarilli in qo.

Amar. lo prega, lui la scaccia. lei via dicendo che se ne pentira lui resta in qo.

Filli Sopra Selv. Faus: la prega, lei lo scaccia lui via. lei resta in qo.

Panta. Si duole delle burle riceute con lei. Lei che bisogna cogliere quei frutti con mano, et del libbro che non lo seppero adoprare in qo.

Grat. vol sforzarla, lei chiama in qo.

Diavo. Li lega, e via. Loro le barzellete in qo.

Selva. li slega con il patto del mangiare. loro fuggono lui dietro dicendo morirsi di fame.

Amar. Con cesto per offerire alli Dei per ammollir fausto in qo.
Covie., Berto. La pregano, lei la burla del ligarli le braccia e parte si [?con] soliti lazzi in qo.
Mago. Si scioglie et ammonisce et incanta la fonte al rumore in qo.
Filli Lui che havera il suo intento quel giorno, et parte lei resta in qo.
Panta., Grati. fuori lei che secondo le costume d'Arcadia per esser forastieri bisogna prima dormire, e chi fará piú bel sogno quello sia suo sempre loro dormono lei via in qo.
Diavol., Leone se li mettono a piedi loro si destano uno si alza l'altro si abassa piu volte, in fine Diavo. li bastona e finisce il secondo.

ATTO TERZO

Fausto Canta, beve, et dorme in qo.
Amar. Lieta per che Mago gli ha predetto al Tempio la sua felicità. Vede Fausto l'accarezza, lui si desta, e via à godersi in qo.
Panta., Coviel. Con scala per cogliere li pomi Cov. sale Pant. tiene la scala fanno lazzi in qo.
Diavol., Leone fuori loro impauriti. Cov. fa la cascata e fugge con Pant. Leone e Diav. li seguono.
Filli Disperata, stanca si adorme in qo.
Berto. La vol godere fa piu lazzi in qo.
Diavol. lo mena nella grotta.
Coviel. il simile del simile.
Pantal. il simile del simile.
Grati. il simile del simile.
Selvag. Stanco et assetato, beve, vede la Ninfa la desta si abbracciano tutti fuori ringratiano il Mago, e finisce la Pastorale.

THE MAGICIAN

PASTORAL

[*MS. Cors.* i. 13.]

Dramatis Personae

Pantalone	Fausto
Coviello, his servant	Selvaggio (that is, the wild
Gratiano	man)
Bertolino	Magician
Filli	Demon
Amarilli	Lion

Properties.

Fountain; temple; grotto; the scene; food; macaroni; [clothes] for the spirits; apples and oranges; cauldron with water; flour; ladder; a cord; a rod; book; lion; flames.

ACT I

Pantalone relates the shipwreck and the loss of Coviello, Gratiano, and Bertolino; he plays with the echo; at this:

Coviello from within and then on the stage announces his hunger; at this:

Bertolino calls from within and emerging says he is hungry. They are delighted to find each other; discovering the temple they enter, first calling and finding the echo which answers them from within.

Shepherds, nymphs singing in rustic groups go towards the temple to make their offerings; at this:

Buffoons dressed up as Jove, Mercury and Cupid receive the offerings. The shepherds depart and they begin to eat, mocking at the Gods; at this:

Spirits cudgel them, and all go out.

Magician explains that he has sent the spirit to his daughter Filli who is in love with Selvaggio who does not love her. He wishes to help the strangers to play tricks on the shepherds;[1] he summons

Filli and urges her to have patience; he promises to help her by means of the fruit. He goes out. She is left musing on this; to her:

Pantalone, Coviello who accost her and beg her to give them one of the fruits. They beat them and play the joke of the cauldron. She goes out followed by Coviello. Pantalone is left confused; at this:

Gratiano calls and presently enters. He discourses on his library if he wishes, at this:

Amarilli complains of Fausto's cruelty; they implore her. She says that there is only one person who can content her, and plays the trick of binding their eyes and departs, at this:

Coviello, Bertolino embrace the two who are blindfolded, they have their antics together and discovering each other they go away tricked.

Filli, SELVAGGIO implores Selvaggio. He is speaking of food, she of love. At last she goes into her father's grotto to fetch him macaroni to make him love her. He eats it and tries to depart. She goes to find more food; he eats and makes off to avoid her chiding [*lo stimolo.*]

Pantalone, Coviello emerge famished; to them

---

[1] 'a burlare li Pastori forastieri': the phrase is ambiguous; there are no 'foreign shepherds' and it is impossible to say whether the Magician wishes the strangers to trick the shepherds or vice versa.

Filli with the book which she has stolen from her father to please Selvaggio: as she is looking and calling for him the buffoons answer her.

Pantalone, Coviello ask Filli what she is going to do with the book. She tells them everything; they ask her to lend them the book informing her that Selvaggio is at the fountain by the Olives. She gives them the book and departs. They play the trick, the food appears and they eat, at this:

Gratiano from one side

Bertolino from the other steal the food. In the end flames issue from the book; at this:

Demons beat them; they run away terrified. The demons carry the book into the grotto.

ACT II

Selvaggio dying of hunger, at this:

Pantalone comes out, Selvaggio takes him for an animal and tries to kill him with a cudgel. Pantalone realizes what is happening and runs away with Selvaggio after him.

Fausto recounting his love for Filli and his hatred of Amarilli; at this:

Amarilli implores him, he drives her away. She goes out saying that he shall rue it, he remains; at this:

Filli talking about Selvaggio; Fausto implores her; she drives him off; he goes out, she remains; to her

Pantalone complains of the trick played on him. She says that he must pick this fruit by hand; and tells him about the book. They do not know how to use it; at this:

Gratiano tries to force her; she cries out; at this:

Demons bind them; they have their gambols; at this:

Selvaggio releases them and bargains for food. They run away with him after them saying that he is perishing of hunger.

Amarilli with a basket as an offering for the Gods that they may soften the heart of Fausto; at this:

Coviello, Bertolino implore her; she plays them the trick of binding their arms and goes away. They have the usual antics; at this:

Magician unties and warns them; he charms the fountain; at the noise there enters

Filli He says that she shall have her wish to-day and goes out. She remains and to her

Pantalone, Gratiano come out. She tells them that according to the Arcadian custom with strangers, they must first go to sleep and then whoever has the more beautiful dream shall be hers for ever. They sleep and she leaves them.

Demons, Lion lie down at their feet; they wake and get up and fall down alternately several times; in the end the demons cudgel them.

ACT III

Fausto sings, drinks, and sleeps; to him:

Amarilli delighted because the Magician has foretold that she shall find her happiness at the temple. She sees Fausto and caresses him; he wakes up and they go off to sport with each other; at this:

Pantalone, Coviello come with the ladder to pick the apples. Coviello mounts and Pantalone holds the ladder: they have their antics; at this:

Demons, Lion appear; they are scared; Coviello has a fall and runs away with Pantalone, the Lion and the demons in pursuit.

Filli desperate and tired out goes to sleep; to her:

Bertolino tries to enjoy her and plays other tricks; at this:

Demons take him off into the grotto.

Coviello the same with the same result,

Pantalone the same with the same result,

Gratiano the same with the same result.

Selvaggio weary and thirsty, drinks; he sees the nymph and wakes her. They embrace. All come forward to thank the Magician and finish the pastoral.

LA MAGA

PASTORALE

[*MS. Cors.* ii. 8.]

Personaggi

Giove

Maga

Spirito

Uranio⎱ Pastori
Sireno ⎰

Clori⎱ Ninfe
Filli ⎰

Pantalone

Gratiano

Coradellino

———

Zanni

Choro di Ninfe e Pastori.

Robbe.

Raggio, Zagnella Bastone, corde due Vestighe, Scala Un piatto de' Maccaroni. Grotta sasso che si apre, Albero che cade frutti, fuochi artificiali, fonte.

ATTO PRIMO

Pasto., ninfe. Tratteno la malvagita della Maga, e pregano Giove.

Giove Dal Cielo promette soccorrerli, loro gli rendono gratie e partono cantando. Giove chiama la Maga.

Maga. Intende da Giove che ritorni ciascuno nel suo essere lei promette Gio. si ritira lei fa suoi incanti poi dice che in breve ciascheduno ritornera nella sua forma e parte.

Panta. che ha persi tutti li amici in qo.

Corad. fuori da un sasso, e non saper dove si trovi in qo [questo] si riconosce con lui fatti lazzi parteno.

Urani. L'amor di Clori e non saper dove si trove in qo.

Filli fuori d'un Albero maravigliata vede Uran. lo saluta, lui gli risponde in qo.

Clori fanno la scena contraria in terzo Clori si parte. Uranio la segue filli resta in qo.

Siren., la prega. Lei lo scaccia e parte lui disperandosi la segue.

Maga che per non contradire à Giove ha fatto il tutto ma per pigliarsi piacere vole incantare li frutti l'incanta et entra.

Grati., Zann. Allegri che sono ritornati nella sua forma vanno per pigliare delli frutti si spaventano e fuggono per la scena in qo.

Panta. Li riconosce va per pigliare un frutto [ch]e crepa Grat. fugge loro restano in qo.

Maga loro gli domandano da mangiare lei li fa portare da uno spirito un piatto di maccaroni et entra loro restano mangiando in qo.

Corad. Li vede et si accorta e mangia ancor lui crepa il piatto tutti fuggono finisce l'Atto Primo.

ATTO SECONDO

Urani Si lamenta di Clori in qo.

Voce lo esorta à vivere in speranza lui parte.

Clori, FILLI. Travagliata per l'importunità delli Pastori in qo.

Gratia., Pant. Li salutano Ninfe gli fanno la burla e partono loro confusi vanno via fatti lazzi.

Maga. Non esser ancor satia di noiare li bifolchi e voler fare il simile con li pastori e Ninfe incanta il fonte e parte dandoli virtù di cambiare l'amor in odio, et l'odio in amore.

Sireno. Del ostinatione di filli in qo.

Panta., FILLI. Prega Filli che lo contenti, lei ricusa, lui vol sforzarla. Sireno corre per soccorrerla Pant. fugge. Lei scaccia Sire. e parte. lui si dispera.

Voce esorta a non uccidersi lui confuso parte

Cora., Zann. Lamentandosi della maga in qo.

Pantal. Li vede si accordano andare insieme in qo.

Clori, Filli fuori loro le vogliono sforzare Ninfe gridano in qo

Urani, Sireno li legano alli albori Ninfe via Past. non le vedono partono per trovarle loro legati restano facendo barzellette in qo.

Spiriti. Li bastonano e finisce l'Atto Secondo.

ATTO TERZO

Clori, Filli. Stanche si riposano, al fonte bevono, e si adormentano in qo.

Uran., Sireno. Vedono le Ninfe le risvegliano e le trovano benigne e si abbracciano e partono tutte

Panta., Grati. Che hanno presentito che chi vole agiuto ricorre a Giove in qo.

Zann. Intende il tutto e pregano Giove in qo.

Giove promette rimediare, et si ritira, loro restano Grat. che vole andare al porto e parte in qo.

Clori, Filli, Uranio, Sireno intendono il tutto dai Bifolchi in qo.
Voce. Canta di dentro in qo.
Fulmi. Da nella Grotta, e cade loro maravigliati
Corad. Liberato fanno lazzi Pastori promettono agiutarli e li menano alle loro capanne per darli da mangiare e finisce la Pastorale.

THE ENCHANTRESS

A PASTORAL

[*MS. Cors.* ii. 8.]

Dramatis Personae

Jove
Enchantress
Spirit
Uranio ⎱
Sireno ⎰ shepherds
Clori ⎱
Filli ⎰ nymphs
Pantalone
Gratiano
Coradellino
Zanni
Chorus of nymphs and shepherds

Properties.

A ray of lightning; sausage; cudgel; cords; two bladders; a ladder; plate of macaroni; grotto; rock to open; tree to drop fruit; artificial fire; fountain.

ACT I

Shepherds, nymphs discuss the malice of the enchantress and pray to Jove.

Jove from the sky promises to help them; they thank him and go out singing. Jove summons the enchantress.

Enchantress learns from Jove that each must be restored to his own shape; she promises. Jove retires. She makes her spells, and then says that soon each shall return to his own shape. She goes out.

Pantalone announces he has lost all his friends; at this:

Coradellino emerges from the stone and does not know where he is; at this they recognize each other and having played their antics they go out.

Uranio relates his love for Clori: he does not know where to find her; at this:

Filli emerges from a tree and is astonished to see Uranio; she speaks to him and he replies; at this:

Clori comes in; they have a scene of bickering in three parts. Clori goes out with Uranio following her. Filli is left.

Sireno implores her. She pushes him away and goes out. He follows in despair.

Enchantress says that rather than disobey Jove, she has done all that he commanded, but that for her own amusement she will charm the fruit. She casts a spell and retires.

Gratiano, Zanni, delighted to have returned to their own shapes, attempt to pick the fruit: they are scared and rush about the stage; at this:

Pantalone recognizes them; he goes to pick a fruit and it bursts. Gratiano runs away; they are left; at this:

Enchantress appears; they ask her for food. She causes a spirit to bring a dish of macaroni, and goes in. They are left eating; at this:

Coradellino spies them; he comes up and begins to eat too. The dish cracks and all run away ending Act I.

ACT II

Uranio, grieves about Clori; at this:

A voice encourages him to live in hope. He goes out.

Clori, Filli troubled by the importunity of the shepherds; at this:

Gratiano, Pantalone salute them. The nymphs play a trick on them and go out. They are left confused and having had their antics, depart.

Enchantress is not yet satisfied with molesting the peasants and wishes to do the same to the nymphs and shepherds. She enchants the fountain giving it the power of turning love into hate and hate into love; she goes out.

Sireno comments on Filli's obstinacy; at this:

Pantalone, FILLI implores Filli to gratify him; she refuses; he tries to force her. Sireno runs to her rescue. Pantalone flies. She drives off Sireno and goes out. He despairs.

A voice exhorts him not to kill himself; he goes off confused.

Coradellino, Zanni bewailing over the enchantress; to them:

Pantalone sees them; they agree to go about together; at this:

Clori, Filli come out; they try to force them; the nymphs call out; at this:

Uranio, Sireno bind them to the trees; the nymphs depart unnoticed by the shepherds who go out to find them. The others are left tied up singing their madrigals; at this:

Spirits cudgel them and finish the second act.

ACT III

Clori, Filli tired out, rest themselves and drink at the fountain. They fall asleep; at this:

Uranio, Sireno spy the nymphs and wake them; they find them kind and embracing them all go out.

Pantalone, Gratiano have a feeling that whoever wants help should turn to Jove; at this:

Zanni hears all this, they pray to Jove; at this:

Jove promises to set everything right and retires. They remain; Gratiano says that he wishes to go to the haven and departs; at this:

Clori, Filli, Uranio, Sireno learn all that has taken place from the peasants; at this:

A voice within sings; at this:

Lightning strikes the grotto which falls in. They are amazed:

Coradellino set free performs his tricks. The shepherds promise to succour them and lead them off to their huts to give them food and conclude the Pastoral.

PROTEO

FAVOLA PASTORALE

[*MS. Loc.* i. 41 *and Cors.* i. 45.]

Personaggi

1. Il Dio Proteo.
2. Fausto, figlio Pastore.
3. Selvaggio, pastore.
4. Zanni.
5. Nespola, moglie.
6. Zannolino figlio
7. Clori⎫
8. Filli ⎬ Ninfe.
9. Pantalone.
10. Burattino, servo.
11. Diavoli.
12. Diana.

La Scena si finge Arcadia

Robbe.
Mazzo di fiori, feltro, stivali, urinale, fiore dipinto, la burla della mano, tavola con robbe da mangiare, corda, conca marina, cinte tre d'una sorte, orso, leone, toro, Oraculo di Diana ò sua Voce.

ATTO PRIMO

Fausto, Selvaggio di A. discorrendo fra essi che l'uno deve cedere a l'altro l'amore di Filli, atteso che il Fausto è il maggior di tutta Arcadia, et figliolo di Proteo Dio Marino, quale gia dominava tutto quel paese. Selvag. non volerli cedere per rispetto d'un presente di fiori riceuto da lei: narrando li significati de fiori vengheno alle mani che si vogliono dare, in qo.

Zanni di C. si mette in mezzo intende le loro questioni dice, che vadino da Filli, alla quale dettali la causa de loro controversie, et rumori, lei debbia dare la sententia di chi lei voglia essere, essi contenti parteno per strada C. Zanni dice esser molti [anni] che si ritrova in Arcadia, et fa mercantia di case [?cascie], pelli, lane, et corne in quantità et ogni due anni venir Pantalone à comprarle, che li lessa 2,000 scudi alla volta, et esser ricco, haver moglie quale è Nespola desidera haver figliolo per lasciar li dopo la morte sua robba in qo.

Clori di D. dice essere amata da molti pastori della Arcadia, lei non voler nisuno per esser dedicata à Diana. Zanni la saluta dicendoli voler fare un figliolo con lei per lasciarli tutta la sua robba essendo che la sua moglie è sterile. Clor. lo burla poi li fa tirare una cordella dicendo se non rompe che farà quello che lui vuole tirono la cordella, si rompe Zan. cade in terra maledisce Clor. et parte per strada A. Clori resta in qo.

Filli di E. dice esser servata a Diana si ralegra con Clor. lodando le loro castità, et delle persecutione, et seguito de' pastori, et che non potrebbe vivere, dice Filli, se non fosse l'arte, che lei apprese dal mago suo padre detto Sabino, che con quella si cangia in varie forme, in qo.

Fausto, Selvaggio di B. narrano à Filli le loro contraverzie, et liti. Filli dice non volere alcuno di loro, essi pregono Clor. ad ricettar l'amor loro. Clor. li discaccia et parteno per strada D. Pastori vogliono sforzar Filli havendola metta [?messa] in mezzo. Filli vedendo non scappare prega li dei infernali che la mutino in altra forma et cotendo si tramuta in fiore. Sel. face disperati. Fanno lamenti et parteno per strada C.

Pantalone, Burattino di A. con stivali, feltri venir di viaggio dicono del prospero camino, et esser venuti per torre la mercantia da Zan. di pelle, lane, e corni. Burat. si ralegra piacendoli la novità del paese per non esservi mai stato. Pant. l'avisa star in cervello di non fare cosa che dispiacera alli dei perche puniscono severamente et quando si caga di non d'herba dimenta [*sic*], avisandolo di molte cose che deve osservare per non far sdegnosi li dei, fanno azzi, in qo.

Zanni di D. meravigliato che Pant. non venghi à pigliar la mercantia essendo di già parti li due anni, dubita che sia morto. Alla fine vede Pant. Fanno allegrezze si rallegrano assieme, facendo azzi di poi ordina à Burat. per esser novità del paese, che avertisce di non tocchare cosa alcuna del luoco senza licenza delli dei, in qo.

Filli di E. di haver burlato Sel. et Fausto essendosi tramutata in fiore. Zan. e Pant. vogliono burlar con lei; fanno azzi alla fine dice volerli fare una gratia che dimandi quello che desidera. Zan. voler fare un figliolo. Filli gli lo promette dicendoli che pigli dell'orine della moglie, et sua, et la sotterare [*sic*] che in una notte li nascerà un figlio. Zan. va a pigliare un orinale nel quale discende essere del piscio di Nespola, sua moglie, et suo con azzi lo sottera. Filli chiamando li dei infernali fingendo far scongiuri li dice che passata la notte vi troverà un figliolo bello è nato soscavando la terra. Filli parte per strada C. Zan. rallegrandosi del figliolo che nascerà porte fuori robbe da mangiare ordinando che non lo tocchi niente se prima non li dimanda licenza alli dei. Burat. se ne burlerà vuol mangiare et corre fiore, dicando che non ha che fare con li Dei, et non li cognosce, in qo.

Diavoli da diverse strade, bastonano tutti, et fuggono per strada.

ATTO SECONDO

Pant., Burat., Zann. di A. lamentandosi delle bastonate delli Diavoli Zan. dice haverli avisati che non tocassero niente senza licenza delli Dei; di poi dicono voler vedere s'è nato il figliolo che Filli li promesè far nascere dal piscio suo, et da sua moglie; cavano la terra in qo.

Zannolino scappa fuori dalla terra tutti fanno meraviglie et si ralegrano chiama in qo.

Nespola di E. intende esser nato il figliolo Zannolino fa allegrezze et tutti ballano. Zanolino dice voler mangiare et perche non fanno presto li bastona, Zan. fa azzi che bastona il padre ordina che il sia dato da mangiare. Nespola Zannolino entra per E. Essi restano et discorrono intorno le mercantie che habia fatto più abondanza et buona raccolta, in qo.

Clori di B. intende di Pant. et l'altri che vuole che li contenti; lei li discaccia; essi li vogliono far forza, con la legono ad un arbore facendo azzi che non la vogliono [?sciogliere] se non li contenta, lei si lamenta, et grida in qo.

Selvaggio di D. [?non] voler piu amar Filli ode Clor. che si lamenta et li [strati] che li fanno lui li bastona ingiuriandoli. Pant. Burat. Zan. fuggono via per la strada E. Selv. scioglie Clori et la prega a gradir l'amor suo comandandola[?] et haverla liberata dalle mani di quelli facendola certa[?] di lasciar andar Filli havendo hauto risposta dell'oracolo, che lui la debbia lasciare. Clor. dice che prima che lei accetti l'amor suo voler andare all'oracolo di Diana per haver consiglio d'accordo parteno per strada A.

Fausto di strada B. disperato et dolendoso di Filli non trovandola, et haverla perduta, chiama il padre che l'aiuti, et lo consigli, facendo dolmenti [?lamenti] in qo.

Proteo della buca lo consiglia a lasciar Filli perche da lei si havrebbe un figlio maggior di lui, Fausto non li curare, ne meno dimorire, et torna di nuovo à ripregare il padre che l'aiuti, et consigli di quello che deve fare. Proteo di nuova lo torna à riprendere di lasciar Filli. Alla fine mosso delli prieghi dice che volendo haver Filli bisogna che lui li leghi il braccio manco dandoli una cinta. Proteo entra nella buca Fausto piglia la cinta, allegro per haver Filli parte per strada E.

Pant., Zan. di A. dicono della ninfa, et delle bastonate haute, ne voler piu Ninfe per li pericoli, in qo.

Zannolino di E. bastona Pant. et Zan., dicendo che vuol mangiare che essi non gli danno a mangiare. Zan. lo placa dicendoli che li fara li maccaroni, in qo.

Leone di C. Pant. et Zan. si spaventano et si ritirano da parte. Leone combatte con Zannolino il quale lo uccide. Tutti allegri per haver ammazzato il leone porteno strascirando [sic] il leone nella grotta per strada D. Pant. per trovar Burat. per E.

Filli di B. dice esser stata a caccia, et esser stracca, volersi riposare vi colga per dormire in qo.

Burat. di A. cerca Pant. vede Filli dormendo fa azzi sopra le sue bellezze si mostra acceso d'amore la vorria godere ma dubita. Alla fine dice cosi dormendo la goderà, et s'impregnerà in sogno se li colga a canto volendola godere. Filli si sveglia spaventata grida chiamando li dei infernali in suo aiuto, in qo.

Diavoli di strada portano via Burat. quale gridando parteno per la strada C. Filli entra per strada A.

ATTO TERZO

Diavoli delle strade buttando fiamme saltando gridano in qo.

Pant., Burat. di A. Burat. si lamenta del Paese delle burle, et non volersi piu stare. Diavoli si metteno fra le gambe di loro; essi spaventati gridano facendo paure, in qo.

Zannolino, ZANNI di E. con una mazza combatte con li diavoli, li quali alla fine ammazzano Zannolino. Diav. parteno per diverse strade. Essi alla fine si ralegrano che esser [sic] morto per esser fastidioso, che bastonava tutti et sempre mangiava, et poi per esser nato di piscio dicono volerlo sotterare in un cagatore, et lo portano via per strada D.

Filli di C. dice non haver potuto riposare per esser stata conturbata da gente, dice voler riposare si colga per dormire, in qo.

Fausto di B. dice esser stato cercando Filli, ne haverla trovata per far quel tanto che l'ha detto il suo Padre Proteo. Fa lamenti: alla fine la vede che dorme s'avolta et la lega per il braccio et volendola abbracciare si sveglia fuggendo si trasforma in qo.

Orso saltando et passeggiono si trasforma in qo.

Toro facendo il medesimo del toro [? orso] si trasforma in qo.

Leone doppo haver fatto alcune passeggiate Fausto tutto meravigliato per veder questi trasformazioni non si vuol partire per haverli promesso Proteo che lui l'havrebbe: alla fine il leone si trasforma et torna nella medesima effigie di Filli come prima. Fausto meravigliato si scopre pregandola che l'accetti il suo amore lei promette voler esser di lui con patto che lui dimandi à Diana se li contenta lui volerlo fare in qo.

Clori, Selvaggio di C. dicono venire a l'oracolo per haver risposta di quello che si contenta et si facci. Fausto si pone inginocchione pregando la dea Diana. Sel. fa il medesimo in qo

Diana li da risposta che Clori debbia pigliar per suo sposo Selvaggio et Filli debbia pigliare Fausto, facendo allegrezzo in qo.

Pant., Burat., Zan., Nesp. di E. di haver interrato Zannolino et della sua insolenzia. Zan. allegro esserli morto dice non voler piu figliolo havendo provato quanto siano fastidiosi, intendeno delle nozze delli pastori fanno allegrezze tutti vanno per far le nozze per strada.

SELVAGGIO A DIANA

Santa triforma Dea, Casta Diana
Del gran lume si degna sorella
Che in ciel risplendi, piu d'ogni altri stella
Con la risposta il nostro male hor sana.

FAUSTO A DIANA

Di Giove et di Latona, o Casta figlia
Che in Cielo, in terra, e nell'inferno ancora
il tuo nume divino ciascuno honora
Qual che dobbiamo far, hor ne consiglia.

RISPOSTA DI DIANA À LI PASTORI

Poi che un sol parer Ninfe, e Pastori
Venite, a rivenir [sic] mio sacro altare
Per pregar fin a vostri gravi ardori
e per saper quanto debbiate fare
Selvaggio piglierai la bella Clori
e Filli Fausto disceso dal mare
Ocean di Leto à cui fu Proteo figlio
et questo è mio voler, quest' è il consiglio.

PROTEUS

A PASTORAL

[*Translated from MS. Loc. i. 41 and compared with Cors. i. 45.*]

Dramatis Personae

1. The God Proteus.
2. Fausto, his son, a shepherd.
3. Selvaggio, a shepherd.
4. Zanni.   *Pettola.*
5. Nespola, his wife.
6. Zannolino, her son.   *Pettolino.*
7. Clori ⎱
8. Filli ⎰ nymphs.
9. Pantalone.
10. Burattino, servant.   *Trappolino.*
11. Devils.
12. Diana.

Properties.   The scene represents Arcadia

Bunch of flowers; felt-hat; boots; urinal; painted flowers; the trick of the hand; table with food; cord; sea-shell; three girdles to match; bear; lion; bull; Oracle of Diana or her Voice.

ACT I

Fausto, Selvaggio from A discussing which of them ought to cede the love of Filli to the other. Fausto is the foremost Arcadian and the son of Proteus the God of the Sea who formerly was lord of these parts, but Selvaggio is not willing to give up the nymph because of a present of flowers received from her lately. They recount the meaning of flowers and after some conversation they quarrel and come to blows; at this:

Zanni from C coming between them learns their dispute and tells them to go to Filli who, when she has been informed of the reason of their quarrel, should be the one to decide. They agree and go out by C. Zanni relates that he has been in Arcadia a long time; he deals in cheeses, hides, fleeces, and horns, wholesale, and every two years when Pantalone comes to buy he leaves 2,000 scudi at a time. Zanni is rich; his wife is called Nespola; he is anxious to have a son to whom he may bequeathe his possessions; at this:

Clori from D says that she is wooed by many of the Arcadian shepherds but will have none of them because she is vowed to Diana. Zanni accosts her saying that he would like a son by her for his heir since his own wife is barren. Clori mocks him and then makes him pull her little cord, promising that if it holds she will do whatever he wishes. They tug at the cord which breaks; Zanni tumbles over cursing Clori; he goes out by A leaving the nymph; at this:

Filli from E says she serves Diana; she and Clori rejoice together over their chastity, recounting the persecution and pursuit of the shepherds. Filli declares that she could not live were it not for the art of metamorphosis taught her by her father, the magician Sabino; at this:

Fausto, Selvaggio from B narrate their controversy and contention to Filli who says that she does not want either of them. They implore Clori to return their affection but she pushes them away and goes out by D. The shepherds try to force Filli getting her between them; seeing there is no escape, she prays to the Gods of the world below to change her shape and forthwith she is turned into a flower.[1] Selvaggio despairs and lamenting together they go off by C.

Pantalone, Burattino from A wearing top-boots and felt hats as travellers, describe their excellent journey and say they have come to collect from Zanni the merchandise of hides, fleeces, and horns. Burat-

---

[1] No exit is assigned to Filli, but later she comes in by E. Perhaps the flower was thrust in from the wings as she slipped out and was later withdrawn.

tino is delighted with the country for this is his first visit. Pantalone warns him to keep his wits about him for fear of giving any offence to the Gods who punish severely: he is not to injure the grass with his dirt and is cautioned against many things which might annoy the powers. They have their antics; at this:

Zanni from D is surprised that Pantalone has not appeared to collect his merchandise; the two years are completed and he fears he may be dead. At last he spies Pantalone and gives him a cordial welcome; they have their scene together and then instruct Burattino who is new to these parts that he must not do anything without leave of the Gods; at this:

Filli comes from E talking of the way in which she has cheated Selvaggio and Fausto by her transmutation into a flower. Zanni and Pantalone want to joke with her and at length she will do each a favour if he will ask it. Zanni wants a son. Filli promises and tells him to take some of his wife's urine and his own and bury it, and says that in one night a son shall be born to him. Zanni goes in to fetch a urinal containing some of his own and Nespola's urine and has his antics of burying it. Filli invokes the Gods below and pretends to make an incantation; she tells him to dig in that spot the next morning and he will find a fine son, new-born. Filli goes out by C. Zanni, delighted at the prospect of a child, brings food, warning them not to touch it without first asking leave of the Gods. Burattino, mocking, wishes to eat and to gather flowers; he says he has no dealings with the Gods and does not know them; at this:

Devils rush from several entrances and cudgel them all until they run away.

ACT II

Pantalone, Burattino, Zanni from A come in moaning over the beating from the devils; Zanni says that he had warned them not to touch anything without leave from the Gods. They say that they want to find if the son promised by Filli is born yet. They dig and at this:

Zannilet comes up from the ground; all are delighted and amazed. Nespola is summoned; at this:

Nespola from E hears that the son, the Zannilet, is born. She rejoices and all begin to dance about. The Zannilet demands food and because they do not bring it quickly he beats them. Zanni has his antics showing them he is flogging his father and tells them to give him something to eat. Nespola takes in the Zannilet by E. They remain discussing the excellence and abundance of the produce; at this:

Clori from B learns that Pantalone and the others want her to gratify their lusts. She drives them away. They attempt to force her, tying her to a tree and saying that she must stay there until she consents. She bewails and calls out; at this:

Selvaggio from D announces that he will cease wooing Filli. He hears Clori's cry and their threats and beats and scolds them. Pantalone, Burattino, and Zanni make off by E. Selvaggio releases Clori and implores her to content his passion now that he loves her and has rescued her from their clutches. He swears he will give up Filli, being warned by the Oracle not to interfere with her. Clori says that before she can accept him as her lover she must consult the Oracle of Diana for counsel and permission; she goes out by A.

Fausto from B despairs and laments that he cannot find Filli; he has lost her and calls on his father to help and advise him. As he makes his complaint

Proteus appears from the cave and counsels him to leave Filli lest he have by her a son who should prove greater than himself. Fausto swears he does not care and cannot delay; he turns once more to his father begging him to assist and advise him. Again Proteus warns him to leave Filli, but at last, moved by his son's petitions, he tells him that if he wishes to have Filli he must tie up her left arm and he gives him a girdle. Proteus retires into the cave. Fausto goes off by E delighted with the girdle and the prospect of having Filli.

Pantalone, Zanni from A talk about the nymph and the beating they have had; they want no more nymphs, they are too dangerous; at this:

Zannilet from E beats Zanni and Pantalone, demanding food and saying that he is starved. Zanni pacifies him saying that he will get him some macaroni; at this:

Lion from C scares Pantalone and Zanni who rush to one side. The lion fights with Zannilet and is killed. All are delighted at the slaughter of the lion and drag it into the grotto by D. Pantalone goes out by E. to look for Burattino.

Filli from B says she has been hunting and is weary; she wishes to rest and sleep; at this:

Burattino from A in search of Pantalone spies Filli sleeping; he has his tricks admiring her beauty and showing his love for her; he wants to enjoy her but is nervous. At length he says that he will enjoy her and get her with child as she sleeps. He lies down at her side wishing to take his pleasure. Filli wakes frightened and calls on the Gods below to aid her; at this:

Devils carry off Burattino yelling by C. Filli goes in by A.

ACT III

Devils from the wings throw out flames, they leap and yell; at this:[1]

Pantalone, Burattino come from A. Burattino complains of the country and its jokes; he wants to get out of it.

[1] In the Corsini version the devils want to eat Pantalone.

The devils come between the legs of the buffoons who are terrified and scream with fright; at this:

Zannilet, ZANNI from E fights the devils with a cudgel and is slain. The devils go off by different ways, leaving the others congratulating themselves on the child's death. They agree that he had only been a nuisance, beating every one and always eating; since he was born of piss they decide to bury him in a privy and carry him out by D.

Filli from C says she has been disturbed and unable to rest; she lies down to sleep; at this:

Fausto from B comes in search of Filli; so far he has not been able to carry out the instructions of his father Proteus. After lamenting for a while he sees her lying asleep and drawing near binds her by the arm and tries to embrace her. She wakes and escaping transforms herself first into

A bear after leaping and prowling she changes next into

A bull after the same performance into

A lion roaming to and fro to the astonishment of Fausto who will not leave her because of what Proteus has promised. At last the lion changes back into Filli's own shape. Fausto is amazed and begs her to accept his love. She promises to be his if Diana will consent; he agrees; at this:

Clori, Selvaggio from C say that they have come to consult the oracle to inquire what it wishes them to do. Fausto and Selvaggio kneel praying to Diana; at this:

Diana replies that Clori is to take Selvaggio for her husband, and Filli, Fausto. They rejoice; at this:

Pantalone, Burattino, Zanni, Nespola from E announcing that they have buried Zannilet and talking of his insolence; Zanni says he is thankful he is dead; he wants no more sons, they are too much bother. They hear of the weddings among the shepherds and all go to the marriage with merry-making.

SELVAGGIO TO DIANA

Chaste Diana, triple One,
Brightest star of all the sky,
Worthy sister of the sun,
Heal our ill by thy reply.

FAUSTO TO DIANA

Thou born of Jove and of Latona high,
Chaste Dian', who art honoured equally
In triple realm of earth and hell and sky,
Before we act we wait for thy reply.

---

[1] The changes are not so clearly defined in the Corsini version; the devils reappear instead of the bull.

DIANA TO THE SHEPHERDS

O Nymphs and shepherds since you come to-day
And with one mind before my altar pray
That all your burning passions have an end,
Seeking Diana's oracle, attend—
The lovely Clori shall Selvaggio take,
And Fausto, Proteus' son, shall Filli make
A happy bride. Lo, thus I recommend.

IL PANTALONCINO

COMEDIA PASTORALE

[*MS. Loc.* ii. 50.]

Personaggi

1. Giove.
2. Plutone.
3. Merlino.
4. Pantalone.
5. Fausto poi Horatio ⎫
6. Selvaggio poi Silvio ⎭ figli Pastori.
7. Burattino, servo.
8. Olivetta poi Calfurnia moglie di Pant.[e]
9. Zanni marito.
10. Mago.
11. Filli ⎫
12. Clori ⎭ figlie Ninfe.
13. Pantaloncino.
    Leone.
    Spiriti.

La Scena si finge Frascati

Robbe.
Sono tutte descritte nel fine della comedia.

ATTO PRIMO

Giove dal cielo con lampi, tuoni, folgori nuvole le quale apprendosi apparisce Giove à cavallo all'aquila et dice che li Pastori vuole che siano contenti per li sacrificii che li fanno batte lo scetro in qo.

Plutone dallo inferno con terremoti, catene, urli fiamme si apre l'inferno. Giove li comanda che debbia rendere l'anima al corpo di Merlino. Pluto promette fare il tutto et partono Plutone nel'inferno et Giove in cielo.

Fausto dalla strada A. dice essersi inamorato in sogno di una Ninfa ne saper chi sia ne trovarla, dice esser venuto all'Arco del desiderio per intendere chi ella sia si inginocchia per invocarlo in qo.

Burattino di C. dice esser venuto dall'Arco del desiderio per saper nuova di Pant. suo padrone quale ha smarrito, ne trovarlo, ne saper dove sia, s'inginocchia per invocarlo in qo.

Zanni di B. disperato per haver perduto Olivetta sua moglie, ne saperne nuova alcuna et esser venuto all'Arco per saper nuova di lei, s'inginocchia per invocarlo, tutti fingendo fare oratione. Fausto dimanda intendere chi sia la ninfa della quale lui s'è inamorato in sogno, in qo.

Arco apparisce con un splendore et con voce di dentro dice à Fausto che quella che lui ha veduta in sogno chiamarsi Filli et hoggi apunto la vederà in quello istesso loco dove lui è ò vero alla fonte. Fausto per ritrovarla alla fonte parte per A. Essi restano, Buratt°· invoca l'Arco dicendoli, che li dia nova di Pant°· suo padrone, et Zan. l'invoca dimandoli di Olivetta sua moglie Arco li dice che Pantalone è trasformato in Asino, et che lo troverà nel bosco poi dice che Olivetta è trasformata in Albore et che la troverà vicino alle piante nell'Ulive. Arco sparendo si racchiude Essi restano maledicono Merlion facendo azzi in qo.

Spiriti di D. ó vero uscendo dell'Arco bastonano Zan. et Buratt°· facendo romore parteno per diverse strade.

fine dell'Atto Primo

ATTO SECONDO

Mago di D. dice esser mal fortunato nelli figlioli et che una figlia gli fu tolta molti anni sono, della quale haver veduto per scientia lei esser viva, et che la ritroverà et che l'altra figlia haverla tenuta carcerata nella grotta, havendo previsto per scientia che lei doveva in certo tempo metter mano nel suo sangue, et essendo passato l'influsso haverla liberata et hora serve Diana in qo.

Selvaggio di A. sopra l'amore di filli, vede il Mago gli la dimanda per moglie lui dice servir Diana alla fine per contentar Selvagg°· dice voler vedere di farli torre marito Selvagg°· parte per C. Mago resta dice voler parlare à Filli batte in qo.

Filli di D. si lamenta con il Mago suo padre per la lunga prigionia Mago li narra la causa di poi li dice volerla maritar con Selvaggio lei ricusa maledicendo amore, et voler seguir Diana Mago li dice li piaceri amorosi esser dolci lei non curarsi in qo.

Fausto di B. dice esser stata all' fonte per ritrovar la Ninfa veduta in sogno, ne haverla trovata, vede Filli, la vagheggia poi dice esser quella che lui ha veduto in sogno. Filli lo vagheggia et si innamora di lui. Alla fine Mago intendendo Fausto esser forastiero per insegnarli il paese parteno nella grotta. Filli resta dicendo haver provato la forza d'amore in rimirar Fausto et essersi inamorata di lui fa parole in qo.

Clori di C. dice essersi inamorata d'un pastore forastiero, et andarlo cercando vede Filli fanno parole diverse. Alla fine per andare alla festa del monte Menelao, dicono volere andare insieme di compagnia in qo.

Zanni di A. dice esser stato cercando Olivetta sua moglie ne haverla mai trovata fa disperationi in qo.

Burattino di C. esser stato cercando Pant[e] suo padrone ne haverlo ritrovato ne saper quello che si farà vedeno le Ninfe fanno azzi et parte. Alla fine dopo molti azzi li fanno la burla delli pomi incantati fatti con l'acqua si bagnano Ninfe ridono et parteno, et essi burlati parteno per A.

fine dell'atto 2o

ATTO TERZO

Burattino, ZANNI, PANT. di A. mena legato Pant[e] quale è trasformato in asino dice haverlo trovato Zanni lo cavalca facendo azzi Buratt[o] ancora fa azzi dicendo povero padrone, chi li l'havesse detto che fosse diventato asino non era meglio che tu hai fossi [sic] diventato in castrone poi che non duraresti tanta farina. Zan. dice volerli dar da mangiare piglia le foglie dell'albero in qo.

Olivetta di dentro dall'albero grida; Zan. spaventato della voce riconosce esser Olivetta trasformata in albero fa azzi et parole bracciandola et bagiandola, dicendo guarda à che pericolo sta questa mia moglie che non venghi un steccalegna e la spacchi per mozzo per brugiarla, fanno diversi azzi et parole in qo.

Mago di D. intende il tutto da Zan. et Buratt[o] pregato che li faccia ritornare nel suo essere di prima Mago promette di fare il tutto et li dice che bagni Pant. cioè l'asino nella fonte et ritornerà nell'essere di prima et con medesima bagni l'albero che farà il medesimo fanno il tutto et Pant. ritorna come prima et Oliv. ancora ringratiano il Mago quale parte per C. Essi restano ralegrandosi di essere ritornati racontano le loro disgratie fanno azzi. Olivet. grida per le doglie del parto sentendosi esser vicino al partorire tutti parteno per A.

Fausto di D. dice haver trovato Filli quale è la Ninfa che ha veduta in sogno dice andarla cercando per scoprir il suo amore ne trovarla in qo.

Clori di B. haver lasciato Filli alla festa vede Fausto li scopre l'amor suo pregandolo gradire il suo amore. Selvag[o] haver collocato li suoi pensieri altrove si fa discorsi gravi e morali in qo.

Filli di B. essersi partita della festa vede Clori che parla con [Fausto] la riprende, dicendoli lasciare andare per essere suo amante. Fausto riceve l'amore di Filli discacciano con bel modo Clori quale parte per A. in qo.

Selvaggio di C. riprende Fausto dicendo lasciare l'amore di Filli essendo sua et di gia il padre havergliela promessa per moglie Fausto dice volerla lui, vengono à parole alla fine d'accordo pattiscono venire alla lotta et il perditore debbia cedere, et renunziare l'amata al Vincitore fanno la lotta Selvag. cadde in terra. Fausto essendo vincitore allegro ridendosi abbraccia Filli et parteno per D. Selvag. quieto mal contento parte per B.

Pantalone, Zan., Burattino, Olivetta di C. portano Oliv. in sedia con tutti ordegni di partorire Oliv. grida per le doglie del parto fanno azzi Burat. dice voler esser la mammane alla fine dopo molte parole et azzi Oliv. gridando partorisce in qo.

Pantaloncino nasce ballando facendo tutti festa et azzi del figlio maschio in qo.

Spirito di D. portano via il pantaloncino tutti spauriti fuggendo parteno per strada.

fine dell'atto 3°·

ATTO QUARTO

Selvaggio di A. disperato per haver perduto nella lotta con Fausto si pente essersi messo al rischio tale che non doveva farlo poi si dole di Filli dice voler dire il tutto al Mago in qo.

Mago di D. intende da Selvaggio come Filli si è messa con il pastore forastiero et haver sprezzato lui dolendosi del Mago che lui non gli li habbia data per moglie Mago si meraviglia poi dice che essendo cio vero li vuol castigare parte per A. Selvag. resta dice voler amare Clori, et lasciare andar Filli in qo.

Clori di C. dice volere lasciare andare Fausto ne volerlo più amare è pregata da Selvaggio quale lo accetta per suo amante et facendo allegrezze abbracciandosi l'un l'altro parteno per D.

Zanni, Burattino di B. con vanghe et bastoni essendosi scoperti per fratelli dicono volere amazzare Pant. essendosi accorto del figlio, che ha hauto da fare con Oliv. sua moglie, fanno azzi dell'ammazzarlo dicendo sei tu Pant. in qo.

Mago di D. disperato havendo trovato Filli con Fausto dice volerli castigare di poi intende come Burat°· et Zan. voglino ammazzare Pant. Lui li riprende dicendo che non faccino per li venire male di poi per castigare li mal fattori fa l'incanto in qo.

Leone apparisce dal circolo fatto facendo urli parte. Mago parte per C. Essi restano dicendo volere andare cercando Pant. per ammazzarlo in qo.

Pantalone di B. cercar di Buratt°· Essi lo vogliono ammazzare dicendo haver hauto da fare con Olivetta fanno romore. Leone torna facendo spavente adosso à Zanni et Burat. tutti spaventati fuggono per diverse strade.

fine dell'atto quarto

ATTO QUINTO

Mago di C. haver fatto l'incanto per castigare Filli et Fausto, et tutti gl'altri, che nel paese commettano amore in qo.

Selvaggio, Clori di B. facendo tra essi azzi di allegrezze, poi dice al Mago che non havendoli lui voluto dar Filli haver pigliato Clori della quale ne è piu contento. Mago dice haver puniti Fausto et Filli di tale errore Selvaggio prega Mago di volerli perdonare essendo che lui piu non si cura di Filli alla fine dopo molte parole et prieghi Mago si contenta perdonarli fingendo disfar l'incanto con scongiuri in qo.

Leone di D. fuggendo con urli parte per strada. Essi restano in qo.

Filli, Fausto di D. Mago li riprende dell'errore et che per amore di Selvag°· li ha perdonato altrimente li voleva castigare et che à questo effetto haveva mandato à loro il leone per farli divorrare. Essi dicono haver fatto molta difesa contro il leone, essendosi salvati sopra di alcuni alberi dimandano perdono al Mago delli errori fatti, et ringratiano Selvaggio del buono offitio fatto con il Mago. Alla fine dopo molte parole Mago li perdona et si contenta che Fausto sposi Filli in qo.

Burattino, Zanni di A. che vanno cercando Pant. per ammazzarlo in qo.

Pantalone di C. della paura hauta Zan. lo vuole ammazzare. Mago lo fa fermare riprendendo Pant. dell'adulterio Pant. si scusa che non sapeva et haverla goduta per la somiglianza che lei haveva con Calfurnia già sua moglie in qo.

Merlino dalla sepultura esce fuori et dice come Plutone ha reso l'anima al suo corpo per ordine di Giove il quale per li sacrificii loro haverlo mandato, acciò che lui li facci palesi li errori quali essi sono, e dice come Pant[e]· è marito di Olivetta ciò Calfurnia quale per fortuna si credevano che l'uno fosse morta l'altro et non haver commesso adulterio, ma esser sua moglie et che Selvaggio et Fausto sono fratelli figlioli di Pant. li quali piccoli li furno rubbati, et di poi per diverse occassione lontanandosi l'uno dall'altro sono capitati nel Paese, et che Clori è figlia del Mago già un tempo fa rubbatali, Merlino havendo detto il tutto entra dentro alla sepultura essi restano meravigliati fanno allegrezze in qo.

Olivetta di A. fuggendo per tema di Zanni per l'adulterio, alla fine intende che Pant. suo primo Marito non è morto, et si riconoscono insieme et fanno allegrezze et poi riconoscono Fausto et Selv. cio è Silv. et Horatio per loro figlioli fanno tutti allegrezze. Clori sposa Selvaggio cio è Silvio, et Fausto cio è Horatio sposa Filli. Mago dice haver nella grotta il Pantaloncino e farlo nutrire et haverlo fatto levar via per tema che Zan. non lo uccida, havendolo conosciuto non esser suo figlio. Tutti lodano il Mago ringratiandolo delli beneficii et delli pericoli dalli quale per mezzo suo sono stati liberati, Mago dice non voler essercitar piu quell'arte ma voler vivere insieme con loro butta via la verga et il libro ringratiando tutti Giove dichiarando la favola danno fine à l'opera.

fine della Comedia

Robbe.

Sepultura di Merlino, che si apre; Alberi con frutti finti con l'acqua per far la burla; Aquila, folgori, lampi, et tuoni, nuvole et Cielo che si apre per Giove; Catene, terremoti, fiamme et inferno che si apre per Plutone; Arco del desiderio, che si apre; Fonte d'acqua; Habito e maschera d'asino per Pant^e.; Albero acconcio di star vi dentro per Olivetta; Sedia et altre robbe da partorire; Zappe et bastoni da Bastonare; Libro et verga per il Mago.

Di Merlino chi fosse et altre cose di esso si legge in Orlando Furioso al canto 33, stanza 9.

PANTALOONLET

PASTORAL COMEDY

[*MS. Loc.* ii. 50, *collated with the two variants in MS. Cors.* ii. 16 and 20.[1]]

Dramatis Personae

	Loc.	Cors. ii. 16.	Cors. ii. 20.
1.	Jove.		
2.	Pluto.		
3.	Merlin.		
4.	Pantalone.		
5.	Fausto, later Horatio ⎱ his children and	Edipo.	
6.	Selvaggio, later Silvio ⎰ shepherds.	Pettola.	
7.	Burattino, servant.		Pasquarello.
8.	Olivetta, later Calfurnia, wife of Pantalone.	Ricciolina.	
9.	Zanni, her husband.	Trappolino.	
10.	Magician.		
11.	Filli ⎱ his children, nymphs.		
12.	Clori ⎰		
13.	Pantaloonlet.	Pettolino.	
14.	Lion.		
15.	Spirits.		

The scene represents Frascati

Properties.

Merlin's tomb made to open; trees with artificial fruit containing water for the trick; eagle; thunder, lightning, and flashes; clouds and a heaven to open for Jove. Chains, earthquakes, flames, and a hell to open for Pluto; the (rain)bow of desire to unfold; fountain of water; garment

---

[1] Cors. ii. 20 is also arranged in 5 acts: ii. 16 in 3.

and mask of an ass for Pantalone; suitable tree to accommodate Olivetta; chair and other necessities for the birth; spades and cudgels for beating; book and rod for the Magician.[1]

(Note in Loccatelli. Concerning Merlin, who he was and the other things that he did, may be read in *Orlando Furioso*, canto 33, stanza 9.)

ACT I

Jove from heaven with lightning flashes and thunder. The clouds fly open and Jove appears astride the eagle and announces that he is willing to content the shepherds because of the sacrifices that they offer him. He strikes with his sceptre; at this:

Pluto from hell which opens with earthquakes, chains, howls, and flames. Jove commands him to restore his spirit to Merlin. Pluto promises to perform everything. Jove and Pluto are borne away to heaven and hell.

Fausto by entrance A says that he has fallen in love with a nymph in a dream; he does not know who she is or where to find her; he says he has come to the Bow of Desire to find out who she may be; he kneels down to invoke it; at this

Burattino from C says that he has come to the Bow of Desire for news of his master Pantalone, whom he has lost: he does not know where to find or to look for him: he kneels down to invoke it; at this:

Zanni from B, despairing at the loss of his wife Olivetta; he has no news of her and has come to the Bow to hear of her; he kneels to invoke it.[2] All pretend to make orations; Fausto asks to know who is the nymph with whom he has fallen in love in his dream; at this:

The bow appears with radiance[3], and a voice from within tells Fausto that she whom he has seen in sleep is called Filli, and that on this very day he will find her exactly on that spot where now he is, or else at the fountain. Fausto, to find her at the fountain, goes out by A. They are left. Burattino calls upon the Bow for news of his master

---

[1] More briefly given in Cors. ii. 16 as, Heaven, hell, tomb, tree, bladders, flames, food, canes with resin on them, requisites for the birth-scene. Loccatelli's more detailed list is given after the plot.

[2] In the Corsini version (16) Trappola has lost his wife and is now enamoured of another nymph; he plays with the echo. Clori and Amarilli, companion shepherdesses, come in; Trappola has his antics and tries to molest them. Edipo enters and beats Trappola who runs away. Edipo discloses his love for Clori; she rejects him but wishes to turn his affections towards Amarilli; he is unwilling. Clori goes out to avoid Edipo, he follows to avoid Amarilli. Pantaloon, Fausto, and Trappola meet and recognize each other at the Bow. The Magician instructs them how to invoke its aid. The mountain opens and answers them. When it is shut they abuse it and at this it reopens and lets out devils who beat them.

[3] In Cors. ii. 20, the Bow appears with a noise and the Magician is in attendance to instruct the suppliants how to proceed.

Pantalone, and Zanni asks about his wife Olivetta.[1] The Bow says that Pantalone has been transformed into an ass and is to be found in the wood, and that Olivetta is turned into a tree and is to be found near the olive plantation. The Bow closes and disappears. They are left cursing Merlin and playing their antics; at this:

Spirits from D, or else coming out of the Bow, cudgel Zanni and Burattino, and making an uproar they depart by different ways.

ACT II

Magician from D says that he has been unlucky with his children:[2] many years ago one daughter was stolen from him and he has learnt by his art that she is alive and that he will find her; the other daughter he keeps imprisoned in the grotto, having foreseen by his art that at a certain time she will dip her hand in his blood. Now that the influence has passed he will release her to serve Diana; at this:

Selvaggio[3] from A talks of his love for Filli. He sees the Magician and demands her for his wife. It is objected that she serves Diana. At last to content Selvaggio her father agrees to try to persuade her to take a husband. Selvaggio goes out by C. The Magician is left remarking that he wishes to speak to Filli; he knocks; at this:

Filli from D laments her long imprisonment. The Magician explains the reason and then says that he wishes her to marry Selvaggio. She refuses and abuses love and prefers to follow Diana. The Magician describes the sweet delights of love; she does not care; at this:

Fausto from B says that he has been at the fountain to look for the nymph of his dream but has not found her. He sees Filli and admires her and then declares that it was she whom he saw in his sleep. Filli sees him and falls in love.[4] At last the Magician learns that Fausto is a stranger; he takes him into the grotto to tell him about this country. Filli is left saying that she has learnt the force of love at the sight of Fausto and has lost her heart to him; she continues to talk to herself, at this:

Clori from E announces that she is in love with a strange shepherd and has come in search of him. She sees Filli and they have some conversation; they agree after a while to go together to the shepherds' festival on Mount Menelaus [*sic*].

---

[1] In Cors. ii. 20 Filli, Olivetta, and the Magician enter and declare their whereabouts.

[2] In Cors. ii. 16 the Magician explains that in accordance with the prayers of the shepherds Jove has restored the spirit to Merlin's body, thereby threatening his dominion. He tells of the Chimera which destroys all those who disobey him but prophesies that when Merlin comes he will destroy it. Clori consoles her father.

[3] In Cors. ii. 20 Selvaggio is represented as a rich shepherd.

[4] Cors. ii. 20 Filli begs her father to take him into their home.

Zanni from A says that he has been looking for his wife Olivetta and has so far been unable to find her; he is in despair; at this:

Burattino from C has been looking for his master Pantalone and has not found him; he does not know what to do. They spy the nymph and have their antics.[1] At length after much by-play and banter they serve them the trick of the enchanted apples and soak them with water; the nymphs go out laughing and the rest hoaxed depart by A.

ACT III

Burattino, ZANNI, PANTALONE[2] from A leads in Pantalone as an ass bound, and says he has discovered him. Zanni mounts with antics. Burattino also has his tricks saying, 'Poor old master, who would have said that you would become an ass? It would have been better if you had been a wether, then you would have had to bear less flour.'[3] Zanni, wanting to give him some food, picks leaves off the tree; at this:

Olivetta shrieks from inside the tree. Zanni is frightened but recognizes by the voice that the tree is Olivetta; he has his patter and antics of embracing and kissing her, saying, 'Look at the risk that my wife runs of being chopped up for firewood'. They play various tricks and quip each other; at this:

The Magician from D learns everything from Zanni and Burattino and is besought to turn them to their former shapes. He promises to do all this and instructs them to bathe Pantalone (that is the ass), in the fountain and he will be restored to his proper likeness, and to water the tree from the same fountain for the like result. They do all this and Pantalone and Olivetta return to their own shapes and thank the Magician who goes out by C. They are left delighted at their transformations; they recount their misfortunes and play their tricks. Olivetta cries out at the pangs of child-birth; the time of her delivery is near; all go out by A.[4]

Fausto from D says that he has found Filli, the nymph whom he saw in his dream; he is looking for her to disclose his love for her but cannot find her; at this:

[1] In Cors. ii. 16 the buffoons try to steal food from the nymphs who trick them and run away; devils from within scare them. The Magician tells them not to be afraid of the way in which Merlin has transformed their companions; he instructs them to bathe the ass in the river and promises to return as soon as they need him. Pantalone goes off and comes back with the devils. Trappola wishes to pick the apples.

[2] In Cors. ii. 20 Zanni does not appear.

[3] Professor Foligno points out a possible equivocation: the phrase 'poiche non duraresti tanta farina' expects 'fatica', but Burattino changes it to 'farina'.

[4] In the Corsini version (ii. 16) Olivetta says that she is with child by Pettola and that this was the reason of her transformation. Trappola fetches a midwife. There is no mention of the arrival of the child. This episode ends the second act in this three-act play.

Clori from B has left Filli at the festival. She sees Fausto and discloses her love for him, imploring him to gratify her passion. Selvaggio [*sic*, Fausto] says that his thoughts are elsewhere; they hold grave and moral discourse; to them:

Filli from B has come away from the pastoral; she spies Clori talking to Fausto and reproves her, telling her to leave her lover alone. Fausto receives Filli's advances and they drive away Clori politely; she goes out by A; at this:

Selvaggio from C reproves Fausto, telling him to stop loving Filli who belongs to him, for already her father has promised her to him as his wife. Fausto says that he wants her; they begin to quarrel.[1] In the end they bargain to wrestle, and the loser must cede and renounce the lady to the winner; they wrestle and Selvaggio is thrown. Fausto, delighted to have won, laughs at him, embraces Filli and they go off by D. Selvaggio subdued and ill-content goes out by B.

Pantalone, Zanni, Burattino, Olivetta from C carrying in Olivetta in a chair with all the requisites for the child-birth. Olivetta cries out with the pains of travail. They have their antics. Burattino wants to be the midwife. At last after much banter and by-play Olivetta cries out and brings forth

The Pantaloonlet who is born dancing; all make merry with antics over the boy; at this:

Spirit from D whisks off the Pantaloonlet; all run away terrified.

ACT IV

Selvaggio from A, desperate at the loss of the wrestling-match with Fausto, repents the risk and grieves for Filli; he resolves to confide everything to the Magician; at this:

The Magician from D learns from Selvaggio that Filli has gone off with a strange shepherd and has jilted him; he complains that the Magician has not given her to him as his wife; the Magician is astonished and says that if this is true he will punish them; he goes out by A. Selvaggio is left announcing that he will love Clori and forsake Filli; at this:

Clori from C says that she will let Fausto go and will show him no more affection. She is approached by Selvaggio and accepts him as her lover; embracing each other and rejoicing together they depart by D.

Zanni, Burattino from B with spades and cudgels have discovered that they are brothers. They are going to murder Pantalone because

---

[1] In Cors. ii. 16 the Magician intervenes saying that neither shall have her.

[2] In Cors. ii. 16 when the little Pettola is born Pantalone wants to kill it, but the Magician dissuades him and gives him the canes, telling him that they will become beautiful. Pantalone and Trappola try to force Amarilli and Clori, who blow through the canes and laugh at them.

they have found out that he has had to do with Olivetta. They have their antics of killing him, shouting 'You be Pantalone'; at this:

The Magician from D desperate at finding Filli with Fausto; he declares he will punish them. He learns that Zanni and Burattino are bent on murdering Pantalone. He reproves them, warning them to do no harm in future. To punish the evil-doers he makes a spell; at this:

Lion appears from the circle which he has described and after roaring departs. The Magician goes out by C. They are left saying that they want to look for Pantalone to kill him; at this:[1]

Pantalone from B in search of Burattino. They want to kill him, and accuse him of meddling with Olivetta. They make an uproar; the lion returns behind Zanni and Burattino and terrifies them. All, scared, run off in different directions.

ACT V

The Magician from C has made an incantation to punish Filli and Fausto and all who are love-making in these parts; at this:

Selvaggio, Clori from B with gambols of joy among themselves.[2] They tell the Magician that since he was unwilling to give Selvaggio Filli he has taken Clori instead and is the more content. The Magician says that he has punished Filli and Fausto for their error. Selvaggio begs him to forgive them now that he no longer cares for Filli. At last after many arguments and petitions the Magician agrees to pardon them and makes a show of undoing the spell with conjurations; at this:

Lion from D runs over the stage roaring. They remain; at this:

Filli, Fausto from D. The Magician reproves them for their fault and says that for love of Selvaggio he has pardoned them when otherwise they were to have been punished and devoured by the lion. They recount how they defended themselves and escaped up some trees. They ask the Magician's pardon for their faults and thank Selvaggio for his good offices with the Magician. In the end after much talking the Magician forgives them and allows Fausto to marry Filli; at this:

Burattino, Zanni from A say that they are in search of Pantalone to kill him; at this:

Pantalone from C comments on the fright he has had. Zanni offers to kill him. The Magician holds him back and reproves Pantalone as an adulterer. Pantalone apologizes and says that it was committed in ignorance and that he had enjoyed her by mistake for his wife Calfurnia; at this:

---

[1] In Cors. ii. 20 there is an extra scene in which Devils bring food and make an uproar.

[2] In Cors. ii. 20 the Magician says that he repents sending the lion and dismisses them.

Merlin[1] emerges from the tomb, announcing that Pluto has restored life to his body at the command of Jove who was moved by the sacrifices; he has come to clear up all the confusion. He declares Pantalone to be the husband of Olivetta, alias Calfurnia; they by chance believed each other to be dead; Pantalone is thus relieved of the charge of adultery. Selvaggio and Fausto are discovered as brothers, the children of Pantalone from whom they were stolen as babies; fortune had separated them but brought both into this country. Clori is found to be the daughter who was stolen from the Magician. When Merlin has finished his revelations he retires into the tomb leaving all delighted and amazed; at this:

Olivetta[2] runs in from A for fear of Zanni and the adultery. When she realizes that Pantalone, her first husband, is still alive she greets him joyfully; in Fausto and Selvaggio they discover their sons Silvio and Horatio with great jubilation. Clori marries Selvaggio, alias Silvio; and Fausto, alias Horatio, marries Filli. The Magician announces that in the grotto he is nourishing the Pantaloonlet whom he has taken for fear Zanni should kill him knowing that he was not his child. All praise the Magician and thank him for his kindness and for saving them from so many dangers.

The Magician says that he does not wish to practise his magic art any longer but instead he will live with them; he throws away his rod and his book and thanking Jove and unravelling the story they end the play.

[1] According to Cors. ii. 16 the tomb opens with an explosion. Merlin recounts the adultery committed by Pettola and Ricciolina and says that they have been punished sufficiently. He blames the Magician for bringing evil to Arcadia and orders that no one shall marry and says that he will explain how they may rid themselves of the Chimera.

[2] The last scene is not described in Cors. ii. 20.

THE MADNESS OF FILANDRO

PASTORAL COMEDY

[*Translated from MS. Loc.* ii. 4, *and compared with 'La Pazzia di Dorindo',*
ibid. ii. 5. *Reprinted by Neri.*]

Dramatis Personae

1. Gratiano.	*Tartaglia.*
2. Filandro } his children.	*Dorindo.*
3. Lidia	*Erminia.*
4. Coviello.	
5. Florindo } his children, shepherds.	*Filandro.*
6. Biagino, later Clarice	*Licori.*
7. Nespola, countrywoman.	
8. Zanni, rustic.	
9. A Shepherd.	*Pantalone.*[2]
10. Satyr.[1]	

The scene represents Arcadia

Properties.

Dress of a nymph for Coviello; a suitable tree-trunk with roots; stage-sticks; two long canes for the joke; a plate of macaroni; traps; a cat; nets, and other hunting-gear.

ACT I

Filandro, BIAGINO from A. He relates how some time ago in Naples he fell in love with a girl called Clarice; they left Naples together; the ship split, Clarice was drowned and he, by chance, found himself in Arcadia. He weeps for the death of Clarice and can never care for any other woman. Filandro leaves by B. Biagino remains, disclosing that she is a woman, Clarice herself whom Filandro supposes to be drowned; she is disguised as a man for safety's sake and dare not discover herself even to Filandro with whom she is settled as a herdsman. She prays Love to make all plain, so that she may be recognized. She goes out by C.

Coviello, Zanni from D with traps, dogs, and nets to go hunting.[3]

---

[1] Neri prints 'servo' in mistake for 'satiro'.

[2] At the end of the *Pazzia di Dorindo* there are given the choruses for the extra shepherdesses and nymphs.

[3] Loc. ii. 5 opens with the scene between Zanni and Coviello. When Licori tells her story she says she has escaped from pirates.

They have their scene. Coviello explains that because of certain feuds he and his son Florindo have retired to Arcadia. Zanni has escaped from the galleys and is a fugitive there. At length they agree to hunt. Zanni has his antics of imitating the cat with eyes like an owl that catches birds with its claws. Coviello does the trick of the broccoli that the Neapolitan birds come to peck. They spread the nets, whistling, and withdraw with by-play. At this:

Satyr from C speaks of his passion for the nymph Lidia, and laments to himself about love. Coviello and Zanni have their tricks pretending that this is a red-cap, a hooded lark, a boar, a big eagle, a little bat, a cuckoo, a screech-owl, and saying they will hunt it down.[1] In the end the Satyr gets entangled in their nets, and making a noise as he breaks and tears them he runs away by D. Zanni and Coviello are left despairing that such a fine fat beast should have escaped them; they agree to set another snare and depart by A.

Florindo from C enlarges on his love for the nymph Lidia and the hatred with which it is returned; he complains of her cruelty; to him:

Nespola from B hears of Florindo's love for Lidia; he begs her to help him to win the favour of the nymph. Nespola promises to manage everything. Florindo goes off by D. Nespola stays to reveal her love for Biagino the herdsman of Filandro; at this:

Lidia from A talks of her love for Filandro and of his neglect.[2] Nespola advises her to love Florindo and tells her of his passion. Lidia does not wish to love any one but Filandro; they have their dialogue and by-play together; at this:

Satyr from D discloses his passion for Lidia begging her to love him, and satisfy his desire; he wishes to lead her to the grotto. Lidia, afraid of the Satyr, promises to do whatever he wishes, but first with fair words she begs him to let himself be bound, after the custom of Arcadia, symbolizing the ties of Love. After a while the Satyr is coaxed into letting her bind him, and she ties him with his hands behind a tree, mocking and jeering at him. From within comes the cry of, 'Wolf, wolf'. Nespola and Lidia go off by B. The Satyr, desperate and furious, hears the cry of 'Wolf' and is afraid lest the wolf should devour him; in his fury he bursts his bonds with his efforts; at this:[3]

Shepherds from D yelling 'Wolf', run after the Satyr with sticks and cudgels and chase him off with beatings by A.

---

[1] The 'azzi' are given in more detail in ii. 5. Coviello whistles and says it is too early for Twelfth Night when the animals talk; Zanni insists it is a rare bird from the desert islands.

[2] Erminia remarks that she has lived many years in Arcadia in the service of Diana.

[3] In ii. 5 this scene is deferred until Act III. The Satyr gives the nymph a horn which will summon him should she ever find herself in distress.

ACT II

Gratiano from A marvels at the country, not knowing where he may be. He relates how he has been brought there by a storm at sea, and has his antics to show that he is perishing of hunger. He does not know whether beasts or men inhabit this place; at this:

Coviello, Zanni from C, playing their tricks over the hunting. Gratiano has his antics about Zanni saying that he does not know whether it is a man or a beast; it has a head, he says, and legs, but so has an ass. Finally he determines to ask for information about the country. Given to understand that it is a land where no one ever eats he pretends to run to and fro asking the way back to Bologna because he is starving. At last after many tricks Coviello takes him on as a swineherd. Gratiano and Zanni go out by D. Coviello is left talking of his love for Lidia; at this:

Nespola from B hears of Coviello's love for Lidia and is besought to help him. Nespola tells him about the nymphs' festival, and suggests that he should go among them dressed as a nymph and, mistaken for a woman, he will be able to enjoy Lidia. After some misgivings Coviello decides to dress up as a nymph; he goes out by D. Nespola is left saying that she has mocked Coviello and wants to play a joke on him; at this:

Biagino from A comes looking for Filandro and is told of Nespola's passion. They have their scene together. [Nespola] wishes to tell him about the joke but he will not listen to her and goes out by C. Nespola, despairing over Biagino's cruelty, departs by D.

Lidia from C says that she has escaped from the hands of the Satyr thanks to her trick; she is looking for Nespola to go to the festival of the nymphs; she speaks of her love for Filandro; at this:

Florindo from B discloses his love for Lidia; she dismisses him and refusing to listen goes out by A. Florindo is left despairing at her cruelty and complaining of his misery; he departs by C.

Coviello from A dressed as a nymph plays his tricks, and says that he is going to the nymphs' festival to find and enjoy Lidia his beloved. He practises walking and talking like a girl and says he is afraid the God Priapus will be enamoured of him as a woman; he would rather not be turned into a tree because he would be no good for anything but firewood; at this:

Satyr from D sees Coviello and takes him for the nymph Lidia; he seizes her, swearing to have his revenge, and telling her it will not avail that she has stained her face as a disguise.

Coviello appeals to him and tells him who he is. At last they come to blows; the Satyr falls down, Coviello escapes by C. Satyr lamenting his fall goes off by B to look for the nymph.

Filandro, BIAGINO from D bewails the death of his beloved Clarice; he can never be happy again. Biagino advises him to cheer up, to forget Clarice's death and turn his affections elsewhere. At last Filandro makes up his mind to forget Clarice, since it seems foolish to live weeping for the dead. He decides to love one of the nymphs to take his attention from Clarice; at this:

Lidia from A discloses her love for Filandro and begs for some return. Assured of the nymph's affection, Filandro promises to love her and gives his word that since Clarice is dead he will cherish her in her stead. Lidia, confident in Filandro's love, goes off by C. Filandro and Biagino remain. Biagino reminds him of Clarice so soon forgotten; she died for love of him, he has now fallen in love with another woman. Filandro repents his error and loses his wits and goes crazy; he departs by B tearing his clothes. Biagino is left in despair at having caused all this; she wants to put an end to herself and presses the dart against her breast moaning; at this:

Nespola from D stops Biagino from killing herself. In a round-about way she at last learns all that has happened, how Filandro has lost his wits, that Biagino is a woman and in love with Filandro who supposes she is dead and all the rest of the story. Nespola promises to cure Filandro's madness with a medecine; they go off by B.

Zanni, Gratiano from C with a plate of macaroni, playing their tricks and wrangling who ought to be the first to sample it. One says he put in the flour, the other the cheese; they make an uproar; at this:

The shepherd from D hears the dispute and quarrelling and says he will measure them, so that he who is the bigger and fatter may have the larger helping. They agree to his proposal. The shepherd plays the trick of tying their right hands to the sticks, and departs. They are left mouthing at each other and at last they begin to quarrel; at this:

Satyr from A beats them and they go out in opposite directions making a shindy.

ACT III

Lidia from A speaks of her happiness in the certainty of Filandro's affection; she will go in search of him; at this:

Satyr from C seizes her by the hair and to revenge himself for the outrage done him ties her to a tree and leaves her as a prey for wild beasts, going off by D. Lidia is left bewailing her misfortunes, as she laments

Coviello comes from B, talking of his fear of the Satyr. He has discarded his disguise and will never run such a risk again. He sees Lidia and learns that she was bound by the Satyr; he bargains for a kiss before he releases her; she refuses and he pretends to desert her. At last, angry that she will not kiss him, he departs by A. Lidia is left lamenting her misfortunes:

Zanni, Gratiano come in by C, unbraced and talking at random drunkenly. Lidia begs to be untied; they jeer and have their antics, wanting to make water against her; at this:

Filandro from D, ungirt, talking wildly, has his antics with them. Lidia asks for help; they talk nonsense. At length after much gibberish as Zanni and Gratiano are stooping Filandro takes Zanni, and Zanni Gratiano by the leg and they drag each other out by A. Lidia is left bound bewailing her misfortunes, saying she has been mocked and abandoned by all. She implores heaven to help her; at this:

Florindo from C, complaining of Lidia's hardness finds her bound. Amazed at such cruelty he looses her and offers his services beseeching her for some love in return. Lidia, seeing the courtesy of Florindo and the unkindness of all the others, accepts him for her lover and husband, promising to love him faithfully and grant all he may desire. They go off together by A rejoicing.

Filandro, BIAGINO, NESPOLA from C, cured, says he no longer remembers his frenzy; they recount his blunders and the origin of his lunacy. Filandro begins to weep remembering Clarice. Nespola declares she is not dead. They marvel and have their by-play until finally Biagino reveals that she is Clarice and has gone about in this disguise not daring to discover herself. Filandro recognizes her and rejoices; at this:

Coviello, GRATIANO, ZANNI from B scolds them for the damage done, the upsetting of the rennet for the cheese and their drunkenness. They excuse themselves protesting that they do not remember it; they have their antics showing their surprise; at this:

Florindo, Lidia, from C rejoicing. Coviello learns that Florindo has taken Lidia to wife, and wishes to know who she may be. After a while she says that she was lost at sea; she does not know more than her father's name which was Gratiano. At last Gratiano recognizes Lidia as his daughter and Filandro as his son. Biagino, that is Clarice, is found to be the daughter of Coviello. With great rejoicing Florindo marries Lidia, Filandro Clarice, and Zanni Nespola. They depart making merry.

THE GREAT MAGICIAN

A PASTORAL COMEDY

[*MS. Loc.* ii. 21, *and Cors.* i. 5.[1]]

Dramatis Personae

1. Elisabatto, Magician.
2. Captain.
3. Pantalone } strangers.
4. Gratiano
5. Burattino, servo.   *Sardinello.*
6. Clori, later Hortentia } children of Gratiano.   *Silvio.*
7. Elpino, later Lelio
8. Filli, later Flavia } children of Pantalone.   *Lelio.*
9. Sireno, later Silvio
10. Zanni, a peasant, later servant to Pantalone.
11. Filippa, later servant to Gratiano.   *Franceschina.*
12. Old Woman.
    Nymphs.   *Coviello (extra)*[2]
    Spirits.

The scene represents Arcadia

Properties.

Temple of Bacchus to open, fountain, grotto, fiery gulf to open, meat and drink. Masks for an ass, a frog, and other transformations, a tree suitable for Filippa, skins for the flogging of the old woman, arms, two garlands of flowers, fires, swords, and gear for the Morris.[3]

ACT I

Sireno, Elpino from A discuss their love-affairs and tell how they won their ladies, each extolling the qualities of his own. Sireno enlarges on the charms of Filli, Elpino on the charms of Clori, at length after

---

[1] It will be seen from the following collation that for once the Corsini version is ampler than Locatelli's. Although the hints which it affords of incidents, *motifs,* and gestures suggesting to English readers a comparison with *The Tempest* give it a peculiar interest, it has seemed wiser to carry out the original plan of taking Locatelli's version as the basis for translation, giving full details of the variations in the notes.

[2] No list of characters is given in the Corsini MS., but with the exception of the changes noted above and the extra buffoon Coviello they correspond even to the name of the Magician.

[3] The list of properties is given at the end of the Corsini scenario: hunting-tackle, a plate of macaroni, two ladels (*mescole*), two handkerchiefs, two little pumpkins are extra.

talking for some time Elpino goes out by D to give directions for some pastoral festivities. Sireno is left saying that he will go in search of Filli; at this:

Zanni the peasant from B learns that Elpino is off to look for Filli. Zanni cautions him to abandon love-making for fear of the Magician who has forbidden it altogether[1]. Sireno does not care; when they have had their scene he goes off by E. Zanni stays to tell how he had been shipwrecked in Arcadia[2] and had brought with him his master's children who have grown up as shepherds; he is a peasant; he describes the country and when all is said goes out by D.[3]

Pantalone Gratiano, Burattino from C hallooing.[4] Pantalone is the first to enter; they call out directions to each other raising their voices and playing their tricks. Then Gratiano, and after him Burattino come on saying that they have been wrecked and are lost in these woods. They show their delight at meeting again and declare that they are famished and do not know what to do; seeing the temple they kneel down and call upon the name of Bacchus; at this:

Bacchus appears from the temple as a God; the strangers explain their plight; they are perishing with hunger, and beg for food. Bacchus directs them to sacrifice and he will supply their need. He disappears and the strangers are left not knowing what to do. They have their tricks over the replies which they cannot interpret; at last after much talking they go off by A.[5]

[1] Zanni is forbidden to explain the reason why love-making has been banned (Corsini).

[2] In Locatelli's MS. the following words are cancelled: 'and Filippa his wife who died a few months ago'.

[3] The Corsini version provides an extra scene with Coviello who swaggers in; he and Zanni salute each other in country fashion and dispute which is the nobler animal, a billy-goat (*becco*) or a wether; also whether it is better to plough or to dig; they run races together. Zanni trips Coviello and makes off.

[4] Locatelli's 'fanno azzi delle voci' is expanded in the Corsini version. Pantalone calls for his shipwrecked companion and is answered by Coviello as he lies on the ground; Gratiano shouts from a distance, Sardinello from still further. When Pantalone arrives he helps Coviello up and asks for aid and information about this country. Coviello wants to know how he came to Arcadia. Pantalone gives an account of the wreck and at this point Gratiano shouts and hallooes. Pantalone and Coviello raise their voices and answer him in rhymes; Sardinello does the same. Gratiano and Sardinello both give an account of the wreck. Coviello tells them to wait and he will bring them some refreshment, intending to play the spy and inform the Magician of the arrival of the strangers. Pantalone, Gratiano, and Sardinello hug each other for joy at their escape from the tempest; they kneel down in front of the temple.

[5] Again the Corsini version is more explicit: Bacchus appears with dancing and singing and the strangers ask for food. Bacchus directs them to go three times round the Mount near by, to smile sweetly three times towards the East, to weep thrice towards the West and to display three times to the sun, now at its height in the heaven, the most beautiful and noble part of the body. They pay him reverence and again implore him for meat and drink. The

Magician from D recounts his powers and his wisdom; he says that he has foreseen that he will lose all if he cannot find the necessary remedy;[1] he comments on the arrival of strangers in Arcadia, fearing lest they find out who they are through Zanni; he speaks of the love-making among the shepherds and to make all safe weaves spells, drawing circles and conducting other ceremonies. He makes the first spell against the mingling of bloods and calls upon the infernal powers to execute his commands; as he strikes with his rod

Spirits from D appear with flames and dance in bearing two garlands of grass and flowers. They place them in the circle and depart. The Magician takes the garlands and explains that they have the opposite properties of causing love and loathing. He hangs them on the branches and then for greater safety contrives a spell to make Zanni tongue-tied. This is the second incantation; invoking the Gods below, he strikes on the ground with his rod and there is heard

A voice from within singing the spell for the dumbness of Zanni, while the Magician repeats 'Tongue of Zanni, be still'. After this the Magician considers it necessary to protect himself against Filippa, and he makes the third incantation, invoking as before and striking the ground with his rod.

The voice within sings the spell for Filippa. To secure himself against the strangers who have arrived the Magician makes the fourth incantation invoking as before and striking with his rod.

The voice within sings the spell for the strangers[2] and the Magician makes a knot in his girdle for each incantation. When all is completed he leaves by C.

Clori, Filli from B discuss their love-affairs, each praising her own

temple closes to the sound of muted instruments. They are left to discuss and interpret the Oracle and each experiments with laughing and weeping; arguing over the part of the body they go out.

[1] Locatelli's gist is clear but the phrasing is slightly ambiguous; the Corsini version makes all plain. The Magician explains that the Fates have decreed that his power shall come to an end by means of strangers and the mingling of bloods and on that very day all his spells will be shattered.

[2] The Corsini version gives the precise conditions of the spell. If ever, by accident or design, Zanni should breathe the names Pantalone, Lelio, or Flavia, he is to be struck dumb on the spot and unable to recover his speech until he shall see and not see his master at the same time. If ever Franceschina, who has also been cautioned to secrecy, should forget herself in conversation with the strangers as they eat or lodge with her, instantly she shall be turned into an object which has no power of speech, and be unable to return to her former state until some part of her body, no matter what, shall come between the teeth of a creature which is both man and not man at the same time. The strangers are enchanted so that as soon as they touch food or drink they suffer transformation and will be unable to regain their proper shape except by the hair of a stranger (*pelo di gente straniera*).

lover; they hold grave and moral discourse; Clori commends Elpino, and Filli Sireno; at length after much conversing[1] Filli goes out by D. Clori stays talking of Love; at this:

Captain from A reveals his love for Clori; he lives with the Magician and comments on his own power, swaggering and declaring after a while that he wishes to enjoy the girl. Clori, afraid of him, tells him to go into the grotto where she will come to him in a little while so that no one need be aware of what is happening. The Captain goes into the grotto by D.[2] Clori is left commenting on the malevolence of the Magician and saying that she has deceived the Captain to be rid of him; at this:

Old woman, ZANNI runs in from C calling her lost pig. Zanni runs behind to help and asks Clori if she has seen it. Clori says she will play a trick on the Captain and tells the old woman that she saw the pig go into the grotto. The old woman thanks her and goes into the grotto to find the pig leaving Clori inquiring of Zanni whether he has heard of the arrival of some strangers and what their condition may be. Zanni says he has heard that Pantalone is among them and as soon as he has pronounced the name he is struck dumb. Clori wants further information. Zanni makes signs that he cannot speak; at length after much talk and gesticulation Clori imagines that he is playing a trick on her and goes out by B. Zanni is left amazed at his dumbness and making signs to himself; at this:

Captain, OLD WOMAN from D embraces the old woman mistaking her for Clori saying that he has enjoyed her in the grotto. He makes love to her. Zanni pretending to be dumb laughs at the Captain who scolds the old woman as soon as he is aware of her. At last after much banter and by-play they hoist the old woman on to Zanni's back and give her a flogging. Making an uproar they leave by different ways.[3]

The end of Act I

[1] The Corsini version directs them to the well-worn themes: whether it is possible to have love without its pain; whether it is better to love or to hunt.

[2] In the Corsini scenario the Captain arrives while the nymphs are still together. He tries to molest Clori who is defended by Filli. He defies the nymphs who flourish darts as he attempts to make love to them. As the Captain draws back he trips and Clori escapes unobserved. Filli points in the opposite direction and the Captain goes off in pursuit leaving Filli to comment upon his evil ways.

[3] The end of the first act is rearranged in the Corsini version:

Zanni and Coviello, once more friends, come in to order the strangers to hunt and bring the spoil to the Magician. Talking of the strangers Zanni asks Coviello how they were dressed. Coviello describes their garments. Zanni sighs and names Pantalone his master and becomes mute. Coviello has his tricks with the dumb man. As they carry on together Filli retires to rest herself; Coviello spies her and points her out to Zanni; they make signs of wanting to enjoy her and tempt her with words. She rids herself of them by sending them for food and promising to wait for them

ACT II

Pantalone, Gratiano, Burattino from A have their antics of hunger; they say that they have done all that Bacchus commanded and continuing their tricks they say that they will call on the name of Bacchus for food; at this:

Captain from B catches sight of the strangers and boasts and threatens; they show signs of fear. The Captain informs them that they may not rest or eat until they have hunted and brought tribute to the Magician, the lord of this place. They protest making gesticulations unwilling to give him anything. In the end, frightened by the Captain's threats, they go out by D to hunt.[1] The Captain admits that he is afraid of the strangers and will refer everything to the Magician; he leaves by C.

Sireno from A praises the charms of his Filli and enlarges on his affection; he is looking for her, but cannot find her. He sees the Magician's garlands hanging up and takes the one which causes loathing; admiring its beauty he puts it on his head; immediately he begins to hate Filli and does not want to have anything more to do with her; he makes speeches of scorn and hatred; at this:

Filli from B comes up to Sireno with joy, caressing and speaking lovingly to him. Sireno talks to himself, making contrary speeches about hatred and takes no heed of her. They talk at cross purposes. At length after a long conversation Sireno, unwilling to listen to Filli any longer, goes out by D and lets the garland drop. Filli is left astounded at his cruelty; she laments and despairs and then picks up the garland

in the grotto. They go out. The old woman comes in shouting for her pig. Filli takes her chance and comforts the old woman by promising her a pig from her own stock if she will go into the grotto and wait for the two peasants who will bring fine things to her if she will let them have their own way. The old woman consents cheerfully and goes into the grotto. Filli departs laughing at the hoax. Zanni and Coviello rush back congratulating themselves on having stolen a basket of food from a shepherd who was asleep near by. They have their scene of quarrelling who shall be the first to meet the nymph in the grotto. Zanni wants the honour, Coviello shouts and chases him from the entrance; at this the Captain appears and subdues them with his threats; after many lies they inform him respectfully of the real

cause of their dispute. The Captain supposes it is Clori in the grotto since he cannot understand how she had eluded him so quickly a little while ago. He orders Coviello and Zanni to stand on guard. Zanni responds with his dumb gestures. The Captain gathers himself together (*prende gusto*) and at last goes in. Coviello and Zanni remain outside with antics of rage and despair. The Captain reappears quite delighted recounting the delicacy and sweetness of the nymph; he wishes to lead her out, but when he sees the old woman he realizes his mistake. Coviello and Zanni jeer and beat the old woman, making an end to the first Act.

[1] In the Corsini version they try to excuse themselves as lacking hunting-tackle but are told that this will be provided at the Captain's dwelling.

saying she will wear it for love's sake. As soon as she puts it on her head she begins to hate Sireno and declares that now he means nothing to her and that she does not want his garland. Throwing it on the ground she goes out by D.[1]

Gratiano from A has been hunting and has lost his companions; he is tired and hungry; after some antics

Clori comes in by B looking for her lover Elpino. Gratiano has his antics with her and seeing the garland which causes love hanging on the bough he takes it down and puts it on Clori's head. Immediately she begins to make love to Gratiano and they have an amorous scene. Gratiano sees the garland which causes hatred lying on the ground; he puts it on and suffers from the contrary effect of hatred. They have their tricks and discourses, Clori of love and Gratiano of hatred; as they talk there enters

Elpino from C. He stands aside watching all that takes place and is amazed at Clori; in despair at her behaviour he departs by C. They remain while they have their antics. The garlands fall off and they return to their proper senses. Clori, ashamed of herself, goes out by D. Gratiano stays amazed at the nymph who has tricked him but admitting that he had provoked her by his behaviour in the first instance; at this:

Pantalone from B has lost his companions; he sees Gratiano and learns all about the nymph; they have their tricks and patter: at last they say they have lost Burattino and are famished. They declare that they have done as Bacchus commanded and kneeling down they call upon him demanding food; at this:

The fountain in the temple of Bacchus throws out food. Gratiano gathers it up into a shell. Pantalone eats within by the fountain and turns into a mule; when at last Gratiano sees him in this shape he rushes off in terror by C. Pantalone runs after him.[2]

Filippa from B relates how she came to this country, how the pirates had snatched from her the children in her care and she herself had chanced upon this country; at this:

Burattino from C, having lost his masters, sees Filippa and tells her his situation; they have their scene together and after a while spying the eatables agree to have a meal. In the end as Burattino begins

[1] The Corsini version adds the extra detail that Filli throws away a bunch of flowers, the gift of Sireno, and describes the garland as falling off as she hurries out.

[2] According to the Corsini direction Pantalone retires behind some bushes to eat and is transformed into an ass while Gratiano holds the attention of the audience by his gobbling. An extra episode with Coviello is inserted: Coviello finds the eatables that Pantalone has left; he conceals them so that he may enjoy them later with his beloved. He puts the food in one place and the flasks in another where they will be cooler and better hidden.

to eat and drink he changes into a frog and as Filippa eats she becomes a tree. Burattino goes off by C; at this:[1]

Magician from D[2] sees all and rejoices that his spells have taken effect, he then picks up the garlands and strikes on the ground with his rod; at this:

Fiery gulf opens with flames. The Magician throws in the garlands; the gulf closes. The Magician attends to the other concerns by making a new incantation, calling on the Gods below to answer his prayers.[3] He strikes with his rod; at this:

A voice from within sings the spell against the strangers so that when they come to the field of gold they may be tormented more horribly than before.

Zanni from B makes signs to the Magician, kneeling down and pointing to his useless tongue; at last the Magician puts his rod to his mouth and Zanni's speech returns;[4] he thanks him for all he has done.

Gratiano from C brings his kill to the Magician, begging for something to eat.[5] At length the Magician grants this favour and strikes with his rod.

Spirits from D bring food and carry off the Magician by D. Gratiano and Zanni are left and begin to eat playing their antics; at this:

[1] The scene is differently arranged in the Corsini version to fit in with the previous entrance of Coviello (see n. 2, p. 653). Franceschina watches Coviello hiding the food and plans to serve a trick on him when he has gone. She takes no notice of his salutations, he threatens her and she calls out; the Captain comes to her call first shouting from within and then wishing to know the reason for her cries. Franceschina accuses Coviello and Coviello Franceschina. The Captain establishes the conditions of a formal peace to which Coviello and Franceschina assent. Coviello goes off to find his beloved, grumbling at Franceschina and calling her ugly. The Captain talks to Franceschina about Clori. He leaves her regretting her lot and recounting how she was robbed. She is interrupted by the entrance of Sardinello.

[2] In the Corsini version the frog is still on the stage rolling the flask to and fro. At the entrance of the Magician it takes fright and jumps into the fountain; the tree withers up.

[3] The Magician prepares against the possible recovery of those who have been transformed by enchanting the field of gold by which they are sure to pass so that they shall only be released from its horrible torments by the bite of an animal that has no teeth.

[4] According to the Corsini scenario Zanni's recovery is due to the sight of the ass, a result which amazes him but is in accordance with the spell for now he both sees and does not see his master at the same moment. The ass takes fright at the Magician and makes a noisy exit.

[5] According to the Corsini scenario Gratiano and Zanni, half dead with hunger, implore the Magician for food; given their choice they decide to have a plate of macaroni. The Magician causes the devils to appear as nymphs; they dance in with the dishes. The ass and the frog make separate and sensational entrances. The ass is beaten and the frog jumps in and out of the fountain. In the end the animals get the better of Gratiano and Zanni who return to find the plates full of seed; they break the plates over their heads.

Pantalone, Burattino from C, the one as a mule, the other a frog; they begin to eat, playing tricks and making an uproar. After the joke they escape in different directions.

The end of Act II

ACT III

Magician from A says that looking into the future he foresees the destruction of his rule unless he can counter the evil which has come upon him. He makes spells and conjurations drawing circles; at this:[1]

Captain from C is instructed to be on guard. The Captain boasts his prowess and diligence and asks for Clori in reward . The Magician promises he shall have her, and goes out by C.[2] The Captain leaves by B to mount guard.

Sireno from A marvels at his own rudeness towards Filli and is afraid that she may take it ill; at this:

Clori from C indignant that Elpino will no longer look at her, also marvels; she begs Sireno to approach Elpino on her behalf and tells everything that has happened. Sireno promises to help; at this:

Filli from B sees Sireno talking to Clori and suspects their confidence; she picks a quarrel with Clori. Sireno stands aside to hear what happens; at this:[3]

Elpino from D relates the inconstancy of Clori. She does not dare to approach him because of what has happened with Gratiano. Elpino talks to Filli on the same theme. Sireno, suspicious of Elpino as he speaks with Filli, accosts him. At last after a great deal of talk, the whole story comes out, all four are undeceived and agree that everything has been the Magician's doing. They confirm their loves and arrange the weddings; Filli is to marry Sireno, and Elpino Clori. First they will go to the festival prepared by Elpino and then they will tell everything to the Magician. They go out by C.

Pantalone, GRATIANO, ZANNI from B as an ass ridden by Zanni and led by Gratiano. They have their tricks, amazed that the ass is so tame; at length after much banter and by-play Gratiano, wishing to feed the ass, picks some leaves from the tree into which Filippa has been transformed. The ass eats and changes back into Pantalone; at this:

Filippa comes out of the tree and returns to her proper shape.[4]

---

[1] In the Corsini version it is precisely to-day that he fears the end of his power.

[2] The Magician returns to his enchanted room (*stanza dell'incanti*).

[3] In the Corsini version his reason is to test Filli's constancy.

[4] In the Corsini version, as the leaves of the tree are touched it shrieks and withers and Franceschina is restored, according to the conditions of the spell, for the leaves are the hair of Franceschina and thus a part of her body has come between the teeth of one who is both man and not man at the same time,

Nymphs from A playing, singing, and dancing pass over the stage on their way to the pastoral festival, inviting other shepherds and shepherdesses. As they play

Pantalone, Gratiano from B come lamed from the field of gold lamenting loudly; the nymphs jeer at them and go out by D. They are left telling each other they have hideous whiskers and are transformed. They go to look at themselves in the fountain.[1]

Burattino from C in the form of a frog goes to the fountain and frightens them. At last Burattino bathes in the fountain and returns to his former shape. Pantalone and Gratiano do likewise with the same result.[2] They marvel among themselves; in the end they decide that it has all been the doing of the Magician and determine to kill him;[3] at this:[4]

Zanni, FILLI, SIRENO from B says that[5] he wishes to give them news of their parents; they rejoice. Zanni tells Pantalone that these are Silvio and Flavia, the children entrusted to him so many years ago, and that while they were pleasuring on the sea a storm had cast them upon this coast. Pantalone recognizes and rejoices over them; he is told that they are betrothed but says this is impossible since they are brother and sister; they are glad; at this:

Filippa, CLORI, ELPINO from C informs them that their father is now in this country. She explains all to Gratiano; how his children

while the ass is changed back again because the leaves are the hide of a stranger as it was ordained. They are directed to retire behind the mount into the field of gold.

[1] There is an extra episode in the Corsini scenario: Coviello assures the Captain that he has heard that Clori has pledged herself to Elpino. The Captain is in despair and commissions Coviello to murder him. Coviello wants to know how to begin. The Captain suggests several methods; Coviello has his antics of not wanting to go. The Captain swaggers and in the end they go off together.

[2] In Locatelli's text the words 'They go out by A' are cancelled.

[3] In the Corsini version the entrances of the nymphs and buffoons are reversed.

[4] The Corsini version explains how this fulfils the spell. Pantalone and Gratiano are bitten by a frog, an animal that has no teeth, and the frog has had in his mouth the hair of strangers. Sardinello relates what happened to him as a frog; Pantalone gives them his adventures as an ass. They dispute whether it is better to be an ass or a frog; Gratiano adjudicates. Gratiano and Pantalone dispute whether it is better to be whole or maimed; Sardinello is judge. When Filli comes in looking for Clori who is expected at the feast, Gratiano, Pantalone, and Sardinello salute her and she is amused at their ridiculous manners. In the end they tempt her and she serves them the trick of the song and dance; while they contend who shall be first she slips away. Sardinello separates Pantalone and Gratiano who have come to blows. At this the Captain comes between them; they recount their differences and make him the judge. They make him hurl the club. He wins and makes game of them intending to lead them bound to the Magician. Gratiano, Pantalone, and Sardinello grow angry, and the Captain draws; Sardinello picks up the club, the Captain runs away and Sardinello plays at Hercules.

[5] Cancelled 'They are brothers', Locatelli.

were snatched from her by pirates and how she found herself in this land. Gratiano recognizes them as Lelio and Hortentia his children and all rejoice at the meetings. In the end they declare that it was by accident that they changed names and Filli marries Elpino and Clori Sireno. When they have related all that has occurred they determine to kill the Magician who has been the cause of all this.[1]

Magician from D strikes with his rod and terrifies them all. At length he declares that he has foreseen all their plans; he pardons them and gives his consent to the marriages. All rejoice and forgive the Magician.[2]

Captain from A armed, has heard that Clori is to wed Elpino; he declares he will carry her off by force and make her his. The Magician calms him and explains about the marriages; he unravels the story and puts an end to the play by making peace. (*Restore*: The Magician calls upon the infernal powers and causes spirits to appear and dance a morris.)[3]

At the opening of the Temple Bacchus says to the strangers:
Not in vain do you plead so earnestly.
Later he commands:
Circle the mountain thrice, wreathed in smiles[?][4]
Act I. Charm for Zanni, first voice.
Locked up in coldest rigour.
Act I. Charm for Filippa, second voice.
In another form, miserable and bewailing.
Act II. Charm for the strangers, first voice.
They shall incur the most grievous torments.

[1] At greater length the Corsini version describes a scene which is substantially the same but certainly owes nothing verbally to Locatelli.

[2] According to the fuller Corsini version the Magician announces that his reign is at an end now that all his spells are finished within one day; and here he explains about the garlands and the binding and loosing of the incantations which he had never imagined would come to pass. He gives his consent to the marriages. Zanni and Sardinello contend for Franceschina. She is awarded to Zanni: Sardinello plays at Hercules with the club.

[3] The final scene according to the Corsini version is arranged thus: The Captain and Coviello come in to kill the strangers and seize Clori. The Magician imposes silence and says that thus it has been ordained by the Fates; he insists on their making peace. Coviello is consoled with the spoils of the chase, which he fetches from the grotto. The Magician proposes himself as the servant of Pantalone and Gratiano who invite him to be their majordomo in Venice where all are to live together. The Captain is to be made Admiral, and Coviello is given charge of the galleys. All accept and make plans to depart on the morrow. The Magician renounces his magic art. They conclude the Pastoral with a dance.

[4] A cryptic phrase 'un riso adorno', which is elucidated by the Corsini version, see p. 649 n. 5.

THE SHIP

PASTORAL COMEDY

[Translated from MS. Loc. ii. 26; reprinted by F. Neri and compared with Cors. i. 33.]

Dramatis Personae

1. Pantalone.
2. Sireno, later his son Lelio.
3. Gratiano.
4. Elpino, later Leandro ⎫ his chil-   *Accidentally omitted from*
5. Clori, later Clarice ⎭ dren.   *the Corsini list.*
6. Zanni.
7. Magician.
8. Captain.
9. Queen.
   Bacchus.
   Love.   *Extra in the Corsini list:*
   Spirits.   *Francatrippe.*
   Jove.   *Franceschina.*
   Servant.   *A Mariner.*
                        Mars.
                        Lion.

The Scene represents [Arcadia, and a lost island][1]

Properties.

Wood; grotto; rock with squibs [*soffioni*]; fires; sea; ship; sky; clouds; ray, or lightning; dolphin; lion; fountain; swords for the morris; wine; bread; rod and book for the Magician. Two crowns or garlands; a drum to be beaten; arms for the Captain.[2]

ACT I

Pantalone, Gratiano from A announce that chance has thrown them on this coast;[3] they are lost in Arcadia perishing with thirst and

---

[1] Locatelli accidentally leaves the place blank but it is plain from the text that Neri's suggestion is correct.

[2] To these properties the Corsini version adds certain details: The rock is to be large and made of paper with tric-

trac; Devils find a place in this list instead of the lion who is here a character; oil and a basket of grain are added.

[3] According to the Corsini version they are in search of a daughter.

hunger, not knowing what to do. Seeing the temple they fall on their knees and do obeisance, calling on Bacchus to help them ere they die for want of food; at this:

Bacchus from the temple reveals himself with dance and song. They demand sustenance. Bacchus grants that all that they touch as they call upon his name shall turn into bread, wine, and other provisions. Bacchus retires and they are left to experiment; they invoke Bacchus and ask for bread, wine and other things; at this:

The fountain throws out wine, bread, and other provisions. They refresh themselves and thanking Bacchus go off by B.[1]

Elpino from C discourses on his love for Clori and her cruelty; at this:

Zanni from B learns of Elpino's passion; he has his antics about Clori, pretending at first that it is a great misfortune and then that it is nothing; finally after quips and tricks he tells him that Clori is under the Mount Parthenio.[2] Elpino goes off by D to find her. Zanni remains to comment on his love for Nespola;[3] he has his scene; at this:

Magician from A learns Zanni's love for Nespola and tells him to leave her alone or it will be the worse for him. Zanni laughs and after his antics goes off by C.[4] Magician remains saying he wishes to prepare against certain dangers which are lying in wait for some of the shepherds of this country; he makes magic, ordering the spirit to bring him two crowns; at this:

Spirit from A with two wreaths of wild flowers presents them to the Magician and disappears by A. The Magician is left describing their properties; he has enchanted them so that one when worn causes love and the other hatred; he hangs them upon two trees, that is on the branches, and goes out by C.

Sireno from B congratulates himself on the reciprocal affection of Clori; he sees the garlands, and ignorant of their power, admires their beauty and takes the one which causes hatred and puts it on; he lies down to sleep; at this:

Clori from D talks of the reciprocal love of Sireno; spying him she runs to embrace him. Sireno wakes and drives her away and making signs of loathing, flies from her. Clori holds him back; he lets fall the garland and then goes off by A. Clori is left astounded at his cruelty; at last after many lamentations she sees the crown which he has dropped, and picking it up puts it on her head and begins to hate Sireno and wishes to have no more to do with him; at this:

---

[1] Nothing is said of the fountain in the Corsini version.

[2] In a wood near by. Corsini.

[3] Franceschina, the Magician's servant. Corsini.

[4] In the Corsini version Zanni tries to interfere with the incantations and is snubbed; nothing is said of his love-affairs.

Pantalone, Gratiano from C see the nymph and admiring her offer to make love to her; she drives them off and at last after much talk and action Clori leaves by C and they follow.

Captain on the sea on a dolphin's back announces that he has come to the lost island to rescue the Queen who is in the clutches of the Magician Falsicon. He calls Mars to help and favour him; at this:

Mars from the clouds proclaims his favour and promises his help telling him to have no fear. Mars withdraws leaving the Captain to invoke Jove for his favour and assistance; at this:

Jove from the sky promises to make the Captain happy and fortunate and advises him to continue in his enterprise. The Captain thanks the Gods; Jove retires within; the Captain departs and the sea vanishes.

End of Act I

ACT II

Sireno from C says that he no longer cares for Clori but cannot understand why since she has given him no offence. He sees the garland which causes love hanging on the branch and as he puts it on his head he begins to feel affectionate towards Clori and makes speeches; at this:

Clori from B wearing the garland of hatred learns that Sireno is in love with her; he reminds her of former kindnesses; she repulses him and will not listen, showing that she hates him. In despair Sireno throws down the wreath and goes out by D. Clori stays and picks up the crown which he has flung aside; admiring its beauty she puts it on her head instead of her own, and by its power immediately she begins to love Sireno making many speeches and gestures; at this:

Elpino from A discussing Clori's rejection. Zanni offers to speak to her himself. They see her. Zanni salutes her expressing his love and his griefs. Clori accepts him as her lover and is enamoured of Zanni. At length after much talk and action Elpino and Zanni depart by A. Clori remains; to her:

Pantalone, Gratiano from D discuss the nymph's repulse. Catching sight of her they salute her addressing amorous compliments. Clori is disposed to like them and they demand a favour. She gives them the crowns; Pantalone receives the one which causes love and Gratiano the other for hating. Clori goes out by A. They are left to have their antics over the favours received. Gratiano shows signs of loathing, and Pantalone of loving her, and then Pantalone approaches Gratiano pretending to take him for a woman. Gratiano repulses him and at length after much talk and many antics as Pantalone tries to embrace him. Gratiano goes off by D with Pantalone running behind.

Captain, servant from A armed. He announces that he has disembarked and arrived at the lost island in search of the Magician Falsicon to rescue the Queen of Thessaly who lies in his power. The servant beats the drum; the Captain summons the Magician to the Tower; at this:

Magician, QUEEN on the tower says he cannot withstand his valour and is therefore obliged to restore the queen whom he had taken into his charge at the request of the King of Bœotia to whom the kingdom would fall if she were to die childless, and since he did not wish her to have any issue he had acted thus. Now, however, he is unable to resist and hands over the queen into the Captain's care. The Magician departs by D. The Queen thanks the Captain for delivering her from the hands of the Magician. At last after much talk they leave by A to go to their ship.

The end of Act II

ACT III

Elpino from A says that he is once more in love with Clori and is going to seek her out; at this:

Clori from B no longer wearing the enchanted wreath sees Elpino and repulses him. Elpino, amazed, laments her cruelty and the inconstancy of Woman, a fickle creature with no stability. At length after speaking for some time without persuading Clori to listen he goes off by D sorrowfully. Clori is left talking of her love for Sireno; at this:

Sireno from D talks to himself about the cruelty of Clori, when at last he catches sight of her and they make it up, marvelling at the accidents that have occurred, which they decide were due to the inventions of the Magician. They rejoice together; at this:[1]

Spirits from the grotto carry off Clori into the grotto. Sireno is in despair and cursing the malevolence of the Magician he calls at the door; flames of fire from the grotto scare Sireno, who goes out by A.

Zanni from B says he has taken the wreaths from Pantalone and Gratiano, having learnt that they were the gifts of Clori. He is wearing both and feels both love and loathing simultaneously; at length after talking and playing his tricks

Magician comes from the grotto and sees Zanni with both garlands; he takes them away and flings them down making conjurations with the rod; at this:

Spirits from the grotto fetch the wreaths; Zanni in a fright makes off by A. The spirits go into the grotto leaving the Magician who says that he has stolen Clori from Sireno because he is annoyed with him.

---

[1] In the Corsini scenario Clori and Sireno come in and out several times searching for each other.

He shows his wrath against the Captain for robbing him of the Queen: he makes magic conjuring the sea into a storm so that they may be wrecked. He retires into the tower.

Captain, Queen on the sea in the ship call out and bewail shouting for help in the storm, imploring the assistance of Jove; at this:

Magician on the top of the tower pretends to make magic; the ship sinks with the Captain and the Queen; the sea vanishes; the Magician retires into the tower.

Elpino from B, complaining of the cruelty of Clori and of[1] her inconstancy, is about to kill himself; at this:

Love (AMORE) from within; the voice bids him hold his hand for he is destined for happier things;[2] Elpino refrains from suicide, encouraged by the voice of Love which predicts happily for him; at this:

Sireno from C complaining of the loss of Clori and the ill-will of the Magician; at this:

Pantalone, Gratiano, Zanni from A talk of the power of the wreaths and then learn of the quarrels between the shepherds. At length Pantalone recognizes Sireno as the son whom he lost as a baby, and Gratiano finds in Elpino his long-lost child. They discuss the evil ways of the Magician and kneel to pray Jove to punish him; at this:

Magician is struck from the tower by a flash and is turned into a stone with the noise of fireworks;[3] at this:

Clori from the grotto,[4] escaping from the clutches of the Magician, is found to be the daughter of Gratiano; she is given to Sireno as his wife. All thank Jove and rejoice over the punishment of the Magician; at this:

Jove from the sky announces that he has saved the Queen and the Captain from the dangers of the sea; at this:

Captain, Queen from D thank Jove for saving them from wreck. The Captain marries the Queen and all making merry they unravel the story and wind up the play.

[1] In the Corsini version the order of the entrances from this scene onwards is slightly different: the recognition is delayed.

[2] The Voice in the Corsini version instructs Elpino how he is to turn into a fountain.

[3] The Corsini version explains that the rock is full of 'tric-trac', and bursts.

[4] According to the Corsini scenario Clori bathes in the fountain by means of 'a contrivance of silk or something of that description'.

THE THREE SATYRS

A PASTORAL

[*Translated from MS. Loc.* ii. 28; *reprinted by F. Neri and compared with MS. Cors.* i. 9.]

Dramatis Personae

1. Pantalone.
2. Filli, his daughter.
3. Gratiano.
4. Fausto, his son.
5. Coviello.   *Accidentally omitted from the Corsini list.*
6. Clori, his daughter.
7. Zanni.
8. Burattino.   *Sardinello.*
9. Magician.
   Three Satyrs.
   Shepherds.
   Cupid.

Extra: Franceschina.

The Scene represents Arcadia

Properties.

Cupid's dress for Burattino, half-hoop, big sausage, two shoes, and a riding-boot for a quiver. Equipment for Zanni as Mercury, three sausages on a spit and two shoes for wings. Jove's equipment for Pantalone, a pestle. Tree, rock to explode, whale, fountain, temple, masks of a mule and an ox; a wood; macaroni; fire; eatables; a suitable book; cords; a woman's dress for Burattino; resin; stage sticks.[1]

ACT I

Magician from the grotto declares his wisdom and power; the infernal world obeys him, spirits in the form of wild creatures serve him and perform his commands, and all things are subject to him:

Filli from A singing; she discourses on hunting. The Magician orders her to leave the chase and follow Venus whose delights are much sweeter. Filli scorns him. At length after much talking, the Magician,

---

[1] The Corsini list adds: nets; snares;   turnips; squibs; grass; garlands; apples;
three cudgels for the satyrs; a rod; two   water.

annoyed with Filli, touches her with his enchanted rod; he makes a show of invoking Pluto and transforms her into a tree, binding her with a spell so that until the tree is touched with iron she cannot be loosed. He declares that he has punished with his enchantments many other shepherds and strangers who have reverenced his person too little; he goes out by D.

Pantalone from A recounts the shipwreck and the loss of his companions; he enlarges on his misfortunes, not knowing where he is or in what country; he is afraid of being eaten by wild beasts. He calls for Gratiano, Zanni, and Burattino to see if they are in these parts. At length, when he has grumbled and talked to himself for some time, there appears

The sea on which ships and boats are to be seen. Pantalone shouts for his companions but gets no reply. The boats disappear and there arrives

A Whale. Pantalone shows signs of terror; he shouts for fear that the Whale will swallow him. The Whale opens his mouth and sends out

Burattino from the Whale's mouth. Whale and sea vanish; Pantalone and Burattino remain and at last after many antics they recognize each other and marvel together. Burattino says he has been in a little boat inside the Whale's carcass; he recounts the jokes that he played inside and believes that they account for the way in which he was thrown up. He says that if he had had a light he would have fried its liver whole. At length he offers to make water against a rock; at this:

Zanni explodes the rock and emerges. They recognize each other and make merry. He says that he has been transformed thus by an old necromancer because he would not obey him. At last they declare their hunger; they play with the echo; supposing the temple is an inn they enter with delight.[1]

Gratiano, Coviello from B[2] enlarge on the misfortune of the loss

---

[1] The opening scenes are slightly rearranged in the Corsini version: The play opens with the entrance of Pantalone calling from within the wood; he is seized by the three satyrs and rescued by some shepherds to whom he gives an account of the wreck and asks for news of his companions; all go out to make sacrifice to Jove. The Magician finds Filli asleep after her hunting; he discloses his love-torments in a song. She wakes and the Magician makes love to her with no success. He transforms her with the spell that unless she is touched by the spittal of strangers she cannot recover. He explains that he has enchanted a peasant who molested his lady in a similar way. He boasts his safety and the obedience of his satyrs. Franceschina, Gratiano, and Coviello come in together telling their adventures since the wreck. They leave before the reappearance of Pantalone who has been deserted by the shepherds who have gone to the sacrifice. As he laments the loss of his friends the whale appears on the tongue of sea and after three or four approaches finally throws out Sardinello.

[2] In the Corsini version Gratiano and Coviello enter severally, so hungry that they want to hang themselves.

of their companions, the unknown country and their hunger; they do not know how to exist. They have their quips and antics. At last they resolve to seek news of their company and find out the customs of the country so that they may be able to live. They discuss how they shall proceed and go off by A.

Fausto, Shepherds from C, playing and singing, with gifts and food to offer to the gods asking their favour. They kneel before the temple calling on the gods to be gracious to their prayers; they offer the gifts; at this:

Pantalone, Zanni, Burattino from the temple dressed as gods; Pantalone as Jove, Zanni as Mercury, Burattino as Cupid.[1] They play their parts, at first showing anger towards the shepherds; after a while they accept their gifts and hear their requests, saying that they will give a response at another time. Zanni and Burattino go into the temple again with the gifts. The shepherds leave by C. Fausto remains to declare his love for Filli, who is a follower of Diana and rejects his advances; he laments her cruelty and then explains the obligations owing to Clori for many kindnesses shown him and her love for him which he cannot reciprocate; at this:

Clori from D reminds Fausto of her love and begs him for some return; she reproaches him for the favours he has received. Fausto dare not reply and at last, not wishing to listen to her, he drives her away and goes out by A. Clori is left bewailing his cruelty and follows him out by A.[2]

Pantalone, Zanni, Burattino from the temple laughing at the joke played on the shepherds, who mistook them for the gods, and at the gifts offered to them. They bring out the food that the shepherds have given them and prepare for a meal. They explain that they have dressed up as the gods with the things found inside the temple. They congratulate themselves on the idea, and plan to cut down a tree-trunk to make a club to defend themselves should they be found out. Pantalone chops at the tree into which Filli has been transformed;[3] she is freed from the spell and at this:

Filli emerges from the tree. They are amazed and try to joke with her and invite her to share their meal;[4] at this:

---

[1] The Corsini variant explains their make-up. Pantalone carries a pestel (for a thunder-bolt); Zanni has bound two shoes to his head and two to his ankles for wings; he carries a spit wreathed with sausages for a caduceus; Sardinello has shoes for wings and a half-hoop of sausage-meat (for Cupid's bow). The illustration to the scenario of *Il Mago* makes the disguise quite clear. The shepherds ask these strange Gods to protect them from the satyrs.

[2] In the Corsini scenario Clori remains until the clowns invite her to share their meal; at this she departs.

[3] To fulfil the Corsini spell Zanni spits on the tree with the desired result.

[4] In the Corsini version they try to force her, but she escapes with the trick of blindfolding them. Three satyrs find them groping about and pretend to be the nymph; the buffoons embrace them.

Satyrs from the grotto making an uproar cudgel them all and they escape in different directions, ending the first act.

ACT II

Magician from D, discoursing on his art. He sees first the rock and then the tree disenchanted and is surprised at what has happened (that the Fates should have foreseen all so soon).[1] He wishes to punish the strangers for the damage that they do to the country. He makes spells and summons

Satyrs from the grotto. The Magician orders them to find the strangers and bring them to the grotto before they commit any more outrages. The satyrs go into the grotto and the Magician leaves by A.

Pantalone, Zanni from C, recounting their misfortunes and escape from the hands of the satyrs.[2] They have lost Burattino and shout for him; at this:

Satyrs coming out of the grotto carry off Pantalone and Zanni who make an uproar in their terror. All disappear into the grotto.

(**Filli**[3] from B discourses on hunting, the power of the Magician, and her deliverance from his enchantments. She says that she is weary and rails against love and describes the bliss of those who follow Diana. She goes to sleep by the fountain; at this:

Gratiano, Coviello from A, despairing that they are lost and have no news of their companions. They are perishing with hunger and the hardships that have befallen them. They spy the nymph asleep by the fountain and admire her, and make a pretence of enjoying her in dumb-show. They want to wake her but do not dare; they say they will enjoy her as she sleeps; they have various antics and at this:

Magician from D, aware that the strangers are about to molest the nymph, calls to them telling them to leave her alone or they shall rue their audacity. They take no notice and say they will do as they please. The Magician in a fury raises his rod and invokes Jove; he strikes on the ground and flame appears. Gratiano and Coviello frightened run

When their eyes are unbound they scream with terror and try to escape; again they are rescued by shepherds with cudgels.

[1] An ambiguous phrase, 'si maraviglia delli fati, che cosi presto hanno previsto al tutto'.

[2] They fell into the snares and the satyrs wanted to eat them.

[3] The scenes marked with a bracket have the following development in the Corsini version: Gratiano, hungry and puzzled, finds Filli and makes love to her. The Magician scolds him and turns him into a toad, enchanting it so that it cannot be transformed except by a wound from a friendly hand. Filli, railing against love and lovers, lies down by the fountain.

off by A. The Magician is left; he says that he will punish the nymph and will make her in love with herself and with the reflection that she sees in the fountain so that she will hate love. He enchants the fountain where Filli is sleeping and goes out by C); at this:

Cupid from the sky appears singing; he shoots his arrow and disappears. Filli sleeps on; to her:

Burattino from B in despair at the loss of his companions and the subsequent disasters. He does not know what to do. At last after talking and playing tricks with himself he sees Filli asleep and has his antics with her. Filli wakes. Burattino hides himself behind the fountain. Filli looking down into the water falls in love with her own face and makes love to her shadow. At length after much talking Burattino plays tricks with Filli, declaring that he has been in the fountain and making love to her. Filli shows herself enamoured of Burattino and embraces him; at this:

Magician from C learns that Filli loves Burattino and is surprised at her lack of discernment. Annoyed at her repulse he contrives a spell to turn Burattino into a woman. He summons

Satyrs from the grotto to carry off Burattino by B. Filli and the Magician remain; she is amazed and afraid of him; at this:

Fausto from B discovers his love for Filli; she repulses and will not listen to him. Fausto laments her cruelty; at this:

Clori from C discloses her love for Fausto. Fausto will not listen and drives her away, saying that it is Filli not she whom he longs for. Filli declares that she follows Diana and will not love him. Clori bewails the cruelty of Fausto, Fausto the cruelty of Filli, who to avoid listening goes off by D. Fausto to escape from Clori follows her. Clori, bewailing the hardness of Leandro [*sic*, Fausto], goes after him by D.

Pantalone, Zanni from the grotto with a book; they announce that they have robbed the Magician and by this means have got out of the grotto. They have their antics showing their fear of the spirits, the cudgellings, and the darkness. Finally they decide to open the book to try its powers. They open the book and at this:

Satyrs from D ask for orders. They are amazed to find them so obedient. Pantalone orders them to bring some braces: they are brought. Zanni orders one thing and Pantalone another. The satyrs bring and do everything that they command. In the end they ask for food and then for a plate of macaroni; they shut the book and prepare to eat. At this flames appear juggling with the book.[1] They take to their heels and go out by A and in various directions.

---

[1] 'in qo appariscono fiamme di fuoco facendosi la burla col libro'. In the Corsini scenario water also spurts up from the plates and drenches them.

ACT III

Magician SATYRS[1] from C is informed by the satyrs that the strangers have commanded them by their possession of the book. The Magician is angry at the theft and their escape from the grotto. He dismisses the satyrs and warns them to take care. The satyrs go into the grotto. The Magician is left saying that he wants to avenge himself on the strangers and to enchant the fountain so that whoever drinks of it shall be turned into a beast. He makes the incantation and goes out by D.

Gratiano, Coviello from A talk over their misadventure with the nymph and are frightened of this country. They are thirsty and go to drink at the fountain. They turn into animals, Gratiano to a mule and Coviello into an ox.[2] Gambolling and howling they go off by A.

Pantalone, Zanni from C, discussing the fright they had over the macaroni as soon as the book was closed. They are delighted with the book and say that it has the power to make the wild men obey them and bring whatever they demand. They have their antics, saying, 'I want to ask them to bring the city of Bergamo here to me'; at this:

Burattino from B in the likeness of a woman transformed by the Magician's spell plays tricks with Pantalone and Zanni who wish to enjoy him against his will. At length after many quips and antics they open the book; at this:

Satyrs from the grotto are ordered to carry off Burattino. They bear him off by D. Zanni and Pantalone are left laughing over the powers of the book; they determine to make themselves respected throughout the land; at this:

Fausto from A is informed that Pantalone and Zanni are the masters and wish to be known abroad as such. At last after much banter and many tricks Pantalone and Zanni get angry and open the book saying they will chastise him; at this:

Satyrs from D are ordered to bind Fausto, who is immediately made fast. The satyrs retire into the grotto. Fausto sees their power and commends himself to their mercy, begging to be unloosed and promising to obey their commands. Finally after many quips and antics they untie him.[3] Fausto thanks them, imploring them to help him win Filli for his bride. He says that the Magician should be punished as the cause of all the evil in this land. They promise to do all this and go off by D to find the shepherds.

---

[1] In the Corsini scenario the satyrs appear first, shuddering at the Magician's impending wrath.

[2] In the Corsini version there is also Franceschina who becomes a cow.

[3] The Corsini version describes extra tricks with the satyr and Sardinello who is brought in and out disguised as a woman.

Magician from A declares that he has foreseen the treacherous conspiracy of the strangers and the shepherds made with the help of the magic book. He prepares to counter all with spells and invokes Pluto, drawing a circle on the ground with his rod and weaving his incantations. He dances into the grotto.[1]

Fausto, Filli from C talk of their love, of the bliss of lovers, and show their content. As they discuss they wander into the Magician's enchanted circle; both begin to dance, marvelling at each other; to them:

Clori, shepherds from A, announcing that they are going to punish the Magician for the troubles which he has caused to the people of these parts. They walk into the circle and begin to dance. All are amazed not knowing what to do; to them:

Burattino, PANTALONE, ZANNI from B runs in saying that Pantalone and Zanni are trying to force him, supposing that he is a woman. They also come into the circle and begin to dance; to them:

Gratiano from C makes an uproar and howls; as he too comes into the circle he begins to dance until all are hopping about together. They marvel at the dancing animals and cannot keep still; to them:

Magician from the grotto upbraids them all for plotting against him; he had foreseen everything and demands the restoration of his enchanted book, threatening that otherwise they shall burst themselves. Still dancing they promise to give up the book if he will release them. The Magician promises to free them. Zanni restores the book with his antics. The Magician makes a spell and strikes on the ground with his rod; all stand still. He then orders Burattino, Gratiano, and Coviello to drink at the fountain so that they may return to their proper shapes. They drink and are changed; thanking the Magician they recognize each other joyfully. At last Gratiano recognizes Fausto as his son, formerly called Lelio, who was lost as a baby. Pantalone finds that Filli is his daughter Clarice; Coviello recognizes Clori as Lidia; they rejoice. Fausto marries Filli and to Clori they promise one of Pantalone's sons. They wish to set sail at once for Venice and unravelling the story they end the play with merry-making.

[1] In the Corsini version the spell is that whoever comes to the grotto shall dance himself to death. The entrances are slightly rearranged.

ARCADIA ENCHANTED

[*Translated from the Neapolitan MS.* i. 1; *compared with the*
'*Arcadia Incantata*' *in Perugia, no.* 6. *See F. Neri, p.* 87.]

Dramatis Personae.

Magician.

Silvio ⎫
Fileno ⎭ friends.   *Silvano.*

Clori ⎫
Filli ⎭ nymphs.   *Tisbe.*

Silvana, a country woman.   *Rosetta.*

Doctor, the master of

Tartaglia   ⎫
Pollicinella ⎭ servants.

Coviello.

4 spirits, priests, shepherds.[1]

Arcadia.

Scenes (*Apparenze*).

A stormy sea, with a sinking ship. Temple—Woods.

Properties at the end.[2]

ACT I

Scene I. The Woods

Magician announces the arrival of strangers and swears they shall
not go hence without his leave. He mentions the derisive way in which
the shepherds and wood-nymphs treat him. After the incantation he
departs.[3]

Stormy sea with a sinking ship

Pollicinella from the sea talking of the tempest passed, the loss
and wreck of his masters and the servants his companions; at this:[4]

Coviello from the other side repeats Pollicinella's tale; they see
each other and pretend to be afraid; at length after their tricks of

---

[1] D. Placido Adriano in casting the
scenario for the Perugian miscellany
observes that either Silvio or Silvano
might take the part of the Magician, and
both Silvio and Coviello are marked to
play the Priest.

[2] Cancelled 'per esser molte'!

[3] In the Perugian version the Magician enchants the wood and calls out the
spirits.

[4] In the Perugian scenario Lattanzio
enters first, then Coviello who thinks he
sees the ghost of Lattanzio.

touching each other they realize that they have been saved and discuss the loss of their master and companions; at this:

Tartaglia from one side and

The Doctor from the other each give an account of the loss of their company. After antics they notice each other and play the scene of being scared between the four of them; after their antics they realize that they have been saved. They recount their adventures and try to find out where they are and how they may live.

The Woods

Silvio discoursing on his love for Clori and her cruelty; at this:[1]

Clori on the cruelty of Fileno; Silvio implores her; she scorns him and leaves him to follow mournfully.

Fileno on the love of Filli and her cruelty; at this:

Filli on the cruelty of Silvio; Fileno implores her; she leaves him scorned and he goes off in despair.

Pollicinella, who has not managed to pick up anything and has lost his companions, has a scene with the echo; at this:

The priests catch sight of the stranger and caress him. He wants something to eat: they promise to satisfy him and bear him to the temple.

Clori, Filli, Silvana, hearing that a stranger is to be sacrificed at the temple, wish to go themselves and watch.[2]

The Temple

Priests, shepherds carry in the seat with

Pollicinella prepared for the sacrifice; after the procession [*scena*]

Nymphs arrive for the sacrifice. Pollicinella asks for food; they exhort him to make a good end; at this:

The Magician forbids them to make such a sacrifice and reproves the priests:[2] they are obstinate and as they persist he summons

Two spirits who beat them. All depart and the spirits carry off the terrified Pollicinella and end the first act.

ACT II
The Woods with a fruit tree

The Doctor, Tartaglia, Coviello; they have not been able to find a thing to eat and do not know where they are. They say there are many wild beasts and fear that Pollicinella is lost; at this:

[1] Some extra episodes are supplied in the Perugian version. Pascale plays the trick of the puppet which is twitched up and down to scare Pollicinella who holds the lantern. Rosetta mistakes Pollicinella for a wild beast and coaxes him to the hayrick. Coviello meets Lattanzio and they play the 'lazzo' described on f. 145 (no. 21), in which the fruit disappears, water and flames spurt up; see later Act II. The women have a scene with riddles given on f. 107 e.

[2] The Magician first sends the women away. Perugia.

Pollicinella in flight has his little scene [*sue passate*]. He is trembling with fright. They waylay him and he gives an account of all that happened in the temple; they laugh and think that hunger has driven him out of his wits. At length they notice the fruit-tree, and standing on guard for fear of the owners, they begin to pick; at this there issue

Flames; they are terrified; the fruit vanishes into the air; they try to get at it with sticks and break the pot of water and scare themselves; at this within

Silvana calls out that the shepherd Dameta has ravished her and deserted her. They see her and ask where they are and what country this may be. She tells them it is Arcadia. Silvana sees that they are strangers and makes much of them; they are enamoured of her and quarrel among themselves; at the noise

The Magician reproves their lusts; this annoys them and they try to assault him. He makes a spell and they are struck motionless; at length they implore him and he frees them, exhorts them to live honestly and goes out. They remain demanding food. Silvana takes them off to her hut to refresh them.

Fileno on the love of Filli and her cruelty; at this:

Clori implores him, he disdains and leaves her, she follows mournfully.

Silvio on his fortune; at this:

Filli implores him, he scorns her and departs, she goes away sorrowful.

The Magician enchants a garland so that whoever wears it shall resemble the beloved person; he hangs it on a branch and goes out.

Pollicinella says he has fed well and left his mates asleep; he sees the garland and puts it on; at this:

Silvio taking him for Clori implores him; he mocks him and laughs. Silvio goes away hurt and grieving; he stays.

Filli mistakes him for Silvio and implores him. He scorns her and she goes away. Pollicinella remains.

Fileno takes him for Filli, implores, is mocked and departs leaving him; at this:

Clori implores, is mocked, and departs. Pollicinella is amazed at their infatuation; at this:

The Doctor, Coviello, Tartaglia saying they have eaten and slept well but have lost their fellow, Pollicinella. Seeing him wearing the garland they take him for Silvana and ask about Pollicinella; he laughs at them and is put between them and fondled; at this:

The Magician invisible, removes the garland and puts it on each in turn; they have a scene in four parts; finally the Magician takes away the garland altogether and the four are left asking Pollicinella where he has been; at this:

Silvana salutes them; once more they are enamoured; she says they cannot all have her, but that if they agree she will belong to the one who has the best dream. They consent and lie down to sleep; she leaves them there; at this:

4 spirits lie down among them; they wake and try to rise, and end the act with noise and alarm.[1]

ACT III

Silvio, Fileno discuss their unhappy love-affairs and decide to go to the temple and beseech the Deities with gifts to soften the disdain of their mistresses; they go out.

Clori, Filli, Silvana say the same and go off to bear their gifts to the gods.

Coviello overhears all this and says he will find his companions and apprise them of everything; at this:

The Doctor, Tartaglia, Pollicinella. Coviello tells them all about the nymphs and shepherds; they go away to dress up and take their places near the temple.

Silvio, Fileno with gifts;

Clori, Filli, **and** *Silvana* with gifts go towards the temple; at this there opens

The Temple

The Doctor as Jove, Tartaglia as Venus, Pollicinella as Cupid, Coviello as the Priest. The shepherds and nymphs make their petitions and offer their gifts; the buffoons make their replies. Nymphs and shepherds go away and they begin to eat. Pollicinella becomes quarrelsome; they forbid him to talk and he leaves them. At this the temple shuts.

The Magician makes Pollicinella King of Arcadia, giving him the book, the crown and sceptre.[2] The Magician leaves him to open the book.

Spirit says 'Your pleasure, your pleasure?' Pollicinella recovers from his fright, orders a seat, dismisses the spirit, and sits down; at this:

Silvio sees him and supposing he is mad jeers; he opens the book; at this:

---

[1] The scenes in the Perugian scenario are differently arranged. After the episode of the enchanted garland, Rosetta treats the strangers to a plate of macaroni, but binds their hands; the spirits rob them. They are unloosed by Lattanzio and proceed to the temple where they play the old joke of impersonating the Gods and eating the offerings. The priests beat them.

[2] The entrance of the Magician is not mentioned in the Perugian version; Silvio finds Pollicinella posing as the king.

Spirit is ordered to beat Silvio who then begs Pollicinella's pardon and is made his secretary; at this:

Fileno does the same; they remain; at this:

Clori the same;

Filli the same;

Silvana the same; at this:

The Doctor, Tartaglia, Coviello see Pollicinella and jeer. The others tell them to respect the King of Arcadia; they mock the more until he is annoyed and opens the book.

Spirit is ordered to beat them and when this is done to bring a rope and hang them. They weep. The Spirit returns with the rope and is told to put it round their necks and string them up. They weep and implore his pardon; at this:

The Magician restrains the Spirit and takes away the rope. He tells Pollicinella that the book was not given him so that he might outrage any one, but to vindicate himself. He takes the book away, gives Clori to Silvio and Filli to Fileno, Silvana to Dameta, and ends the play.

Properties.

Five garlands of flowers; four darts; two skins; three vestments for the priests; three mitres; a stick for underpropping; a large seat with a chair in the middle; five little baskets of provisions; a tree with fruit which will disappear into the air; four costumes for spirits and shepherds; equipment of Jove for the Doctor; equipment of Venus for Tartaglia, of Cupid for Pollicinella, of a priest for Coviello; sceptre, crown, and book; a seat for reclining; stage sticks; Magician's gear; eight tric-tracs; powder for the flames; pitch torch; ship; rope.

---

[1] The Magician's part in the third act is developed more fully in the Perugian version. He comments on the quarrels among the shepherds and nymphs, explaining that they are the result of the vengeance that he is taking upon the children of Stefanello and Lattanzio. He had stolen them as infants and kept them here in Arcadia. As he goes out he must drop his book. Pollicinella picks up the book and has his scenes with the shepherds and spirits: he makes Rosetta his queen and during their love-scene Silvio, if he is taking the part of the Magician, should retire to change. When Coviello teases Pollicinella the book will not work because the Magician is standing by; at length he comes forward and discloses that he is Signor Argenio, the enemy of Lattanzio, whose father Stefanello had killed one of Argenio's brothers. In revenge he stole from Stefanello his daughters, Angela (that is Clori) and Isabella (or Tisbe), and from Lattanzio his sons, by name Flaminio, now Silvio, and Celio, now Silvano. These are now betrothed among themselves. He explains that he has sent in Silvio (or whoever is taking the part of the Magician) to prepare the feast. He makes peace with Lattanzio; Pollicinella marries Rosetta and winds up the comedy.

BIBLIOGRAPHY

The following bibliography is eclectic and should be supplemented by the special lists provided in the appendices. Books and plays of accidental interest have not been described, but reference is made in the index to the pages on which their relevance is noted and bibliographical details are given in the footnotes. For other rare pamphlets and works which lie somewhat out of my period the reader is referred to the bibliographies provided by Duchartre, *La Comédie italienne*, 1925, and supplemented by Mic, *La Commedia dell'arte*, 1927.

ADEMOLLO, A. 'Intorno al teatro drammatico italiano dal 1550 in poi.' *Nuova Antologia*, Mar. 1881.
Una famiglia di comici italiani nel secolo XVIII. 1885.
La bella Adriana e le altre virtuose del suo tempo. 1888.
'Bibliografia della cronisteria teatrale italiana.' *Gazzetta musicale di Milano*, 1888, nos. 35, 36.

AGOCCHI, G. B. Diario del Viaggio del Card^e. Pietro Aldobrandino creato legato de Latere da Clemente VIII suo zio per andare a Firenze ad effetto di sposare la Principessa Maria di Toscana con Enrico IV Re di Francia, ecc. Cominciata dalli 25 di Settembre 1600 e finisce alli tre di Aprile 1601. (B.M. MS. Add. 20018.)

'ALDEANO' (N. Villani). Ragionamento sopra la Poesia Giocosa. 1634.

ALLACCI, L. Drammaturgia. 1666, accresciuta, 1755.

AMICIS, V. DE. La Commedia popolare latina e la Commedia dell'arte. 1882.
L'imitazione latina nella commedia italiana nel secolo XVI. 1897.

D'ANCONA, A. Origini del teatro italiano. 1891.
See also *Gazzetta letteraria di Torino*, 25 July 1885, 24 Mar. 1888, 11, 18 May 1889.
'Lettere di comici.' Published 'per nozze Martini-Benzoni', 1893.

ANDREINI, F. Le bravure del Capitano Spavento. Venice, 1607, 1609, 1618, 1624. See *supra*, p. 43.
Ragionamenti fantastici. Venezia, 1612.

ANDREINI, Isabella. Lettere d'Isabella Andreini Padovana Comica Gelosa et Academica Intenta nominata l'Accesa. Venetia, 1608.
See BORGOGNI.
See App. F and Rasi, op. cit.

ANDREINI, Lelio. *See* App. B.

ANGELI, U. Notizie per la storia del teatro a Firenze nel secolo XVI, specialmente circa gli intermezzi. Modena, 1891.

APOLLONIO, M. Storia della Commedia dell'arte. 1930.

ARETINO, Pietro. Ragionamento nel quale M. Pietro Aretino figura quattro suoi amici, che favellano delle corti del mondo, e di quelle del cielo. 1538.

ARKWRIGHT, G. E. P. 'Notes on the Ferrabosco Family.' *Musical Antiquary*, iii. 220; iv. 42, 1911–12.

BARBIERI, F. 'Per la storia del teatro lombardo nella seconda metà del secolo XVI.' *Athenaeum*, Pavia, April 1914.

BARBIERI, N. *See* App. B. ✦

BARRY, L. Ram Alley, or Merry Tricks. 1611.

BARTOLI, A. Scenari inediti della Commedia dell'arte. 1880.

BARTOLI, F. Notizie istoriche de' comici italiani che fiorivano intorno all'anno 1540 fino ai giorni presenti. Padova, 1781.

BARTOLI, P. La schiava. 1602.
    See *The Mask*, ix. 13, 1923, and see App. F.

BASCHET, A. Les Comédiens italiens à la cour de France. 1882.

BASKERVILL, C. R. The Elizabethan Jig. 1929.

BAUGH, A. C. *See* HAUGHTON.

BEAUMONT, C. The History of Harlequin. 1926.

BEIJER, A. Recueil de plusieurs fragments des premières comédies italiennes qui ont esté représentées en France sous le règne de Henri III. Recueil dit de Fossard, conservé au musée national de Stockholm, présenté par Agne Beijer. Paris, 1928.

BELANDO, V. Lettere facetie, e chiribizzose. Paris, 1588.

BELGRANO, L. T. 'Delle feste e dei giuochi dei Genovesi.' *Arch. storico italiano*, serie iii, vol. 15, 1872.
    'Comici del secolo XVII. Accesi e Fedeli.' *Domenica letteraria*, anno iv, no. 1, 1885.
    See *Il Caffaro*, Genova, 1882, 22 Dec. 1886, nos. 87, 157, 171.

BELTRAME, Tina. 'Gli scenari del Museo Correr.' *Giornale storico della lett. it.* xcvii, Jan.–Mar. 1931.
    'G. B. della Porta e la Commedia dell'arte.' Ibid., ci, fasc. 3, 1933.

BERTELLI, F. Il carnovale italiano mascherato. 1642.

BERTELLI, P. Diversarum Nationum Habitus. 1594.

BERTOLOTTI, A. Artisti veneti in Roma nei secoli XV, XVI e XVII. 1884.
    'Spesiere segrete e pubbliche di Papa Paolo III.' *Atti e memorie delle R. R. Deput. di Storia Patria per le provincie dell'Emilia*, vol. iii, pte. 1.

BEVILACQUA, E. 'G. B. Andreini e la Compagnia dei Fedeli.' *Giorn. Stor.* xxiii and xxiv.

BÉVOTTE, G. Gendarme de. 'Le Festin de Pierre' avant Molière. 1907.

BOCCHINI, B. *See* App. A.

BOLTE, J. Das Danziger Theater. 1895.

BORGOGNI, G. Muse Toscane di diversi Nobilissimi Ingegneri. . . . 1594.
    Pt. 2, pp. 27–30, for verses by Isabella Andreini.
    Rime Di Diversi Illustr. Poeti de' nostri tempi. Venetia, 1599, p. 31.

BORROMEO. Sentimenti di San Carlo Borromeo intorno agli spettacoli. 1759.

BROÜWER, F. de Simone. 'Due scenari inediti del secolo XVIII.' *Giorn. Stor.* xv, 1891.
'Ancora una raccolta di scenari.' *Rendiconti della R. Acc. dei Lincei*, serie v, vol. x, 1901.

BRUNELLI, B. I teatri di Padova. 1921.

BRUNI, D. Fatiche comiche di Domenico Bruni, detto Fulvio Comico di Madama Serenissima Principessa di Piemonte. Paris, 1623.

CALLOT, J. I balli di Sfessania. See also modern reproduction by J. Kippenheuer. Potsdam, 1921.

CALMO, A. Lettere piacevoli. Ed. V. Rossi, 1888.
For comedies see *supra*, pp. 239-45.

CALVI. Il teatro popolare romano nel Cinquecento. See *Italia Moderna*, 1908.

CAMPBELL, O. J. *'Love's Labour's Lost* restudied.' See *Studies in Milton and Donne*. 1925.

CAMPOS, GIULIA. '"L'Arlichino" di Giorgio Maria Raparini (1718).' *Giorn. Stor.* cii, 3 Dec. 1933. I regret that it has been too late to incorporate in my text and notes the valuable matter contained in this study of an early eighteenth-century poem devoted to a description of the appearance, dialogue, and 'lazzi' of Arlecchino.

CAPRIN, G. 'La Commedia dell'arte al principio del secolo XVIII.' *Riv. teatrale it.* ix. 48, 145, 1905; x. 19, 1906.

'CARLETTA.' *See* A. VALERI.

CARO, A. Lettere familiare. 1572.

CECCHINI, P. M. *See* App. A and F.

CERRO, E. del. See *Natura ed Arte*, vol. xvi, Feb.–Mar. 1908.
Nel regno delle maschere. 1914.

CHAMBERS, Sir E. K. The Elizabethan Stage. 1923.
'The Integrity of *The Tempest*.' *Rev. of Eng. Studies*, i. 129, 1925.

CLEMENTI, F. Il carnovale romano nelle cronache contemporanee. 1899.

COCCHIARA, G. 'Stenterello e le Stenterellate.' *Giorn. Stor.* xcix, 1932.

COCCO, E. 'Una compagnia comica nella prima metà del secolo XVI.' *Giorn. Stor.* lxv, 1915.

COHN, A. Shakespeare in Germany. 1865.

COOKE, J. Greene's Tu Quoque, or the Cittie Gallant.

CORTE, Claudio. See *supra*, p. 366.

CORBELLI. Rime di Diversi Celebri poeti Dell'età nostra. Bergamo, 1587.

CORTESE, G. C. Viaggio di Parnaso. 1635.

CORYAT, T. Coryat's Crudities. 1611. Ed. MacLehose, 1905.

COTARELO Y MORI, E. Revista de Archivos Bibliotecas y Museos. 1908.

CREIZENACH, W. Geschichte des neueren Dramas. Halle, 1911.
The English Drama in the age of Shakespeare, trans. C. Hugon. 1916.

CROCE, B. 'Una nuova raccolta di scenari.' *Giorn. Stor.* xxix, 1897.
'Un repertorio della Commedia dell'arte.' *Giorn. Stor.* xxxi, 1898.
Ricerche ispano-italiane, ii, 1898.
Pulcinella e il personaggio napoletano in commedia. 1899.
I teatri di Napoli. Secolo XV–XVIII. 1891.
Nuove curiosità storiche. 1922.

CROCE, G. C. *See* O. GUERRINI.

DAY, John. The Travailes of the Three English Brothers. 1607.

Dieterich, A. Pulcinella, pompejanische Wandbilder und römische Satyrspiele. 1897.

DE DOMINICI. Vite de' pittori, scultori ed architetti napoletani. 1742–3.

DRIESEN, O. Der Ursprung des Harlekin. 1904.

DUCHARTRE, P. L. La Comédie italienne. Enlarged edition, 1925.

ECCARD, J. Neue Lieder, mit fünff und vier Stimmen. 1589.

ELIOT, J. Ortho-Epia Gallica. 1593.

FAINELLI, V. 'Chi era Pulcinella?' *Giorn. Stor.* liv, 1906.

FERRIGNI, P. C. ('Yorick'). La storia dei burattini. Vent' anni al teatro. Vol. i, 1884.

FEUILLERAT, A. Documents relating to the Revels at Court in the time of Queen Elizabeth. 1908.

FICORONI. De larvis scenicis. 1750.

FLAMINI, F. Il Cinquecento. 1900.

FLEAY. Biographical Chronicle of the English Stage. 1891.

FLORIO, G. A Worlde of Wordes. 1598. Queen Anna's New World of Words. 1611.

FOSSARD. *See* BEIJER.

FREEBURG, V. O. Disguise Plots in Elizabethan Drama. 1915.

GANDINI, A. Cronisteria dei teatri di Modena. 1871.

GARGANÒ, G. S. Scapigliatura italiana à Londra sotto Elisabetta e Giacomo I. 1918.

GARZONI, T. Piazza Universale. 1585.

GAW, A. 'The Evolution of the Comedy of Errors.' *Pub. Mod. Lang. Ass. of America*, xli, 1926.

GHERARDI, E. Le Théâtre italien, ou le recueil général de toutes les comédies et scènes françaises jouées par les comédiens italiens du Roi, pendant tout le temps qu'ils ont été au service. 1694 and 1741.

GOLDONI, C. Mémoires. Ed. Moreau, vol. ii. 1822.

GOZZI, C. Memorie inutili. 1797.
I contratti rotti. *Opere*, iv. 35, 1772–4.

GOSSON, S. Playes confuted in five actions. 1582.

GRAY, H. D. 'The Sources of *The Tempest.*' *Mod. Lang. Notes*, xxxv, 1920.
'Some Indications that *The Tempest* was revised.' *Studies in Philology*, xxviii, 1921.

GRAZZINI, A. 'Il Lasca.' La Strega. 1582.
Rime burlesche edite ed inedite . . . a cura di C. Verzone. 1882.

GREG, W. W. Henslowe's Diary. 1904.
Dramatic Documents from the Elizabethan Playhouses. 1931.

GUARNERIO, P. E. Articles on the Mask of Meneghino in *Natura ed Arte*, xvii. 223 and 313, 1908.

GUERRINI, O. La vita e le opere di G. C. Croce. 1879.

HARVEY, G. Foure Letters. *Collected Works*, ed. Grosart, i. 84.

HAUGHTON, Englishmen for My Money; or A Woman Will Have Her Will. Ed. A. C. Baugh, 1917.

HEYWOOD, T. Apology for Actors. 1612.

How a Man May Chuse. A Pleasant Conceited Comedy wherein is shewed how a Man may chuse a Good Wife from a Bad. 1602.

INGEGNERI, A. Della Poesia rappresentativa et del Modo di Rappresentare le favole sceniche. 1598.
See also App. A.

ISAACS, J. Shakespeare as Man of the Theatre. 1927.

'JARRO' (G. Picini). L'epistolario d'Arlecchino. 1896.

LASSO, Orlando di. Villanelle, Moresche, et altre Canzoni, a 4. 5. 6. e 8 Voci. Antwerp, 1582.

LAWRENCE, W. J. The Elizabethan Playhouse. 2nd series, 1912.
Englishmen for My Money; a possible prototype.
See *Rev. of Eng. Studies*, i. 216, April 1925.
For discussion of the relationship of *The Tempest* to the Commedia dell'arte see also *Times Lit. Sup.*, 11 Nov., 1920, and *Le lettere*, Jan. 1921.

LEVI, C. *Riv. teatrale it.* ix. 20, 1905 (Colombina).
Natura ed Arte, xvi. 250, Jan. 1908 (Brighella).
Emporium, 1919, p. 80; 1920, pp. 131, 253 (Pantalone).

LIVI, G. 'The Ferrabosco Family.' *Musical Antiquary*, iv. 121.

MADDALENA, E. Uno scenario inedito.
See App. F. Un pazzo guarisce l'altro.

MAGNIN, C. 'Teatro celeste.' *Revue des deux mondes*, xx, 1847.

MANDOSIO, P. Biblioteca romana. 1682.

MANTZIUS, K. (Trans.) A History of theatrical art in ancient and modern times. 1903.

MARRIOTTI, F. Il teatro in Italia nei secoli XVI, XVII, XVIII. Curiosità e notizie storiche corredate di molti documenti inediti. Firenze, 1874–86. MS. Magliabech, II. iii.

MARSCHALL, W. 'Das *Sir Thomas Moore* Manuskript und die englische Commedia dell'arte.' *Anglia*, lii, 1928.
Die neun Dichter des *Hamlet*. Heidelberg, 1928.

MARSTON, J. Jack Drum's Entertainment. 1601.

MARTUCCI, G. 'Un Comico dell'arte.' *Nuova antologia*, serie II, xlviii. 618 seq., 1884.

MARTUCCI, G. 'Un scenario inedito della Commedia dell'arte.' *Nuova antologia*, serie II, li. 219, 233, 1885. *See* 'Flaminio desperato', App. F.

The Mask, ed. G. Craig. The following parts of this periodical contain miscellaneous notes, sketches, and translations relative to the Commedia dell'arte:
Vol. iii, 1910–11, pp. 22, 108, 110, 126, 129, 147, 149, 161, 173, 175.
Vol. iv, 1911–12, pp. 113, 121, 199, 335, 340.
Vol. v, 1912, pp. 20, 104.
Vol. vi, 1913, pp. 33, 286, 353.
Vol. vii, 1914, pp. 53, 354.
Vol. ix, 1923, p. 13.

Maske of Flowers. 1613. *See* p. 389.

MELZI-TOSI. Bib. dei romanzi di cavalleria. 1865.

MÉNAGES, G. Le origini della lingua italiana. 1685.

MERLINI, D. Saggio di ricerche sulla satira contro il villano. 1894.

MIC, C. (Miclachevsky). La Commedia dell'arte. Petrograd, 1914, 1917, and Paris, 1927.

MICHAUT, G. Sur les trétaux latins. 1912.

MOLAND, L. Molière et la comédie italienne. 1867.

MOLMENTI, P. Storia di Venezia nella vita privata. 1906.

MONTAIGNE, Michel, Sieur de. Voyage en Italie. Ed. d'Ancona, 1895, containing also a bibliography of travel literature.

MORTIER, A. 'Ruzzante.' 1925.

MORYSON, Fynes. Itinerary. 1617. *See also* 'Shakespeare's Europe', unpublished chapters of Moryson's *Itinerary*, ed. C. Hughes.

MUNCK, E. De Fabulis Atellanis. 1840.

MURRAY, J. Tucker. English Dramatic Companies. 1910.

NAPOLI-SIGNORELLI, P. Storia critica de' teatri antichi e moderni. 1777.

NASHE, T. Works. Ed. R. B. McKerrow. 5 vols. 1910.

NEGRI, M. La pace. Venezia, 1584.

NERI, A. 'Una Commedia dell'arte.' *Giorn. Stor.* i, 1883.
'I Comici *Uniti* nel 1593.' *Fanfulla della domenica*, 4 Apr. 1886.
'Capitano Spavento.' *Gaz. letteraria di Torino*, 1886, nos. 40, 41.
'Una famiglia di comici.' Ibid., Mar. 1888.
'La Lavinia de' *Confidenti.*' *Scena illustrata*, 11, 18, May, 1889.
'Rivaltà e disside della scena.' Ibid., l. Aug., 1887.
'Fra i comici dell'arte.' *Riv. teatrale it.* xi.

NERI, F. La tragedia italiana del Cinquecento. 1904.
Scenari delle màschere in Arcadia. 1913.
'Studi sul teatro italiano antico. Le parabole'. (Scenari of the Prodigal Son.) *Giorn. Stor.* lxv, 1915.

NICHOLS, J. (ed.). Progresses and Public Processions of Queen Elizabeth. 3 vols. 1788.

NICOLL, Allardyce. Masks, Mimes and Miracles. 1931.

NOLHAC, P. de, and A. SOLERTI. Il viaggio in Italia di Enrico III, Re di Francia, e le feste a Venezia, Ferrara, Mantova e Torino. Torino, 1890.

NOVATI, F. Review of Scherillo's *La Commedia dell'Arte*. *Giorn. Stor.* v. 279.

OTTONELLI, D. Della christiana moderazione del teatro. . . . 1646.

PACICCHELLI, G. B. Schediasma juridico-philogicum . . . de larvis, de capillamentis, etc. Naples, 1893.

PAGANI, G. Del teatro in Milano avanti il 1598. See *Teatro illustrato*, 1884.

PAGLICCI-BROZZI, A. Il Teatro a Milano nel secolo XVII. See *Gaz. musicale di Milano*, 1891, nos. 34, 36, 38, 40–3.
See *La scena illustata*, 15 Oct., 1890. (Documents of the *Confidenti*.)

PASTOR, Perez. Nuevos Datos acerca del histrionismo español en los siglos XVI y XVII. 1906.

PARDI, A. Le stupende forze e bravure del Capitano Spezza Capo, et Sputa Saette. Padova, 1606. *See also* Chapter II for Braggart literature.

PELLICER, C. Tradado Histórico sobre el Origen y Progresos de la Comedia y del Histrionismo en Espagna. 1804.

PERRUCCI, A. Dell'arte rappresentativa. Napoli, 1699. Extracts from this rare book are given by PETRACCONE.

PETRACCONE, E. La Commedia dell'arte. Storia, tecnica, scenari. 1927.

PICCOLOMINI, A. La Sfera del mondo. . . . 1573.
L'Amor Costante. (1536) pr. 1540.

PORCACCHI, L. Le Attioni d'Arrigo Terzo di Francia. . . . 1574.

RACIOPI, G. 'Per la Storia di Pulcinella.' *Arch. storico per le provincie napoletane*, xv, 1890.

RAO, C. Le argute e facete lettere. Pavia, 1573.

RASI, L. I comici italiani. 1897–1905.

RE, E. 'La tradizione comica dell'imprudente.' *Riv. teatrale it.* ix, no. 2.
'Scenarii modenesi.' *Giorn. Stor.* lv, 1910.
'Commedianti a Roma nel secolo XVI.' *Giorn. Stor.* lxiii, 1914.

REBORA, P. L'Italia nel dramma inglese, 1558–1642. 1925.

REICH, H. Der Mimus. 1903.

RENNERT, H. A. The Spanish Stage in the time of Lope de Vega. 1909.

RICCI, C. Teatri di Bologna nei secoli XVII, XVIII. 1888.

RICCOBONI, L. *See* App. F.

ROSSI, N. Discorsi sulla Commedia. Vicenza, 1589.

ROSSI, V. Review of Stoppato, q.v. *Giorn. Stor.* ix. 295.
'Una commedia di G. B. della Porta ed uno nuovo scenario' (*L'Astrologo*). *Giorn. Stor.* xxviii, 1896, and *Rendiconti del R. Ist. Lombardo*, serie II, vol. xxix, 1896.
I Suppositi del L. Ariosto ridotti a scenario di commedia improvisa. Bergamo, 1895. See *Giorn. Stor.* xxvii, 1895.
See also under CALMO.

RUELENS, C. Erycius Puteanus et Isabella Andreini. 1889.

SALTINI, G. C. Carnevale Veneziani. 1584.
  See *Fanfulla della domenica*, 1881, no. 9.

SALVERAGLIA, F. (An account of the festivities in Milan, 1594.) 'Per nozze Pupilli-Kruch', 1890.

SANCHEZ-ARJONA, J. Noticias referentes à los Anales del Teatro en Sevilla, 1898. Desde Lope de Rueda hasta fines del siglo XVII.

SAND, M. Masques et Bouffons. 1860.

SANDBERGER, A. Beiträge zur Geschichte der bayerischen Hofkapelle unter Orlando di Lasso. 1894.

SANESI, I. 'Intorno a Pulcinella.' *Giorn. Stor.* lxi, 1906.
  'La Commedia', in Vallardi, *Storia dei generi letterari*, vol. ii (only 96 pages issued), [191 ...].

SANSOVINO, F. Venetia città nobilissima et singolare. 1581.

SANUDO, Marin. I diarii. Pub. 1879–1903. *See* App. C.

SARTI, C. G. Il teatro dialettale bolognese. 1894.

SAVIOTTI, A. 'Feste e spettacoli nel Seicento.' *Giorn. Stor.* xli.

SCALIGERO, C. *See* App. A.

SCHANZ, Martin von, and C. HOSIUS. Geschichte der römischen Litteratur. 1927.

SCHERILLO, M. La Commedia dell'arte in Italia. Studi e profili. 1884.
  'La Commedia dell'arte.' *La Vita italiana nel Seicento*, 1897.
  See also *The Mask*, vol. iii, 1910–11.

SCHWARTZ, I. The Commedia dell'arte and its influence on French Comedy in the Seventeenth Century. Pub. of the Institute of French Studies, Inc. New York 1932.

SENIGAGLIA, G. Capitano Spavento. 1899.

SFORZA, G. F. M. Fiorentini ed i suoi contemporanei lucchesi. 1879.
  'I comici italiani del secolo XVI e XVII e la moralità del teatro.' *Gaz. letteraria*, anno xiv, nos. 15–19.

SMALL, R. A. The Stage Quarrel. 1899.

SMITH, Winifred. The Commedia dell'arte. A Study in Italian popular comedy. 1912.
  'Italian and English Comedy'. *Modern Philology*, v. 555, April 1908.
  'A Comic Version of *Romeo and Juliet*.' Ibid., vii, Oct. 1909.
  'The Academies of the Popular Italian Stage in the XVIth Century'. Ibid., viii, April 1911.
  'The Maréchal di Biron on the Stage.' *Modern Philology*, xx, 1923.
  Anti-Catholic Propaganda in Elizabethan London. Ibid., xxviii, Nov. 1930.
  'Two Commedie dell'arte on the *Measure for Measure* story.' *Romanic Review*, xiii, 1922.
  'The Earl of Essex on the Stage.' Publ. *Mod. Lang. Ass. of America*, 1924.
  'G. B. Andreini as a Theatrical Innovator. *Modern Language Review*, xvii, 1922.

Notes on 'Aurelio, comico' in *Giorn. Stor.* xcii. 208, 1928.

Italian Actors of the Renaissance. New York, 1930.

SOLERTI, A., and D. LANZA. 'Il teatro ferrarese nella seconda metà del secolo XVI.' *Giorn. Stor.* xviii, 1891.

Rassegna bibliografica della letteratura italiana. Anno 2, p. 195, 1894. (Documents from Bolognese MSS. relating to theatrical regulations.)

SOLERTI, A. Ferrara: la corte estense nella seconda metà del secolo XVI. 1899 and 1900.

Gl'albori del melodramma. 1904.

Musica, ballo e drammatica alla corte medicea dal 1600 al 1637. 1905.

STONEX, A. B. 'The Usurer in Elizabethan Drama.' *Mod. Lang. Ass. of America*, xxxi, 1916.

STOPPATO, L. La commedia popolare in Italia. 1887.

SUMMONTE, G. A. Historia della città e regno di Napoli. 1765. See *supra*, p. 387.

TAYLOR, R. The Hog hath lost his Pearl. 1612–1613.

TINGHI, C. Diario di Ferdinando I e Cosimo II, Gran Duca di Toscano scritto da Cesare Tinghi, suo aiutante di camera, da' 22 luglio, 1622. (MS. in Bib. Nazionale di Firenze.)

TOLDO, P. 'Il teatro di Evaristo Gherardi.' *Rassegna nazionale*, anno xix, p. 607, April 1897.

'Di alcuni scenari inediti della Commedia dell'arte e delle loro relazioni col teatro del Molière.' *Atti della R. Acc. delle Scienze di Torino*, xlii. 460–82, 1907.

'A proposito d'una fonte italiana del *Tartuffe.*' *Giorn. Stor.* xxiii. 297–301.

'Gli sdegni amorosi di Frandaglia di Val di Sturla, da un MS. della Biblioteca di Rouen.' *Giorn. Stor.* lxiv. 372–85, 1914.

TRAUTMANN, K. 'Italienische Schauspieler am bayerischen Hofe.' *Jahrbuch für Münchener Geschichte*, i, 1887.

TROIANO, Massimo. Discorsi delli Trionfi, Giostre, Apparati . . . fatti nelle Sontuose Nozze dell' Ill. . . . Guglielmo . . . Duca della Baviera. . . . 1568.

See *supra*, p. 5, for bibliographical details.

VALERI, A. ('Carletta'). Chi era Pedrolino? *Rassegna bibliografica della lett. it.* iv. 94, 1896.

'Un Palco scenico del Settecento.' *Nuova rassegna*, 1893, p. 797.

'Gli scenari inediti di B. Locatelli.' Ibid., 1894, pp. 441, 523.

VARCHI, B. L'Ercolano. 1570.

VITTI, A. 'Le maschere nel teatro italiano.' *Nuova antologia*, vol. 182, May–June 1916.

WHETSTONE, G. Heptameron of Civill Discourses. 1582.

Wit of a Woman. A pleasant Comedie wherein is merily shewen: The wit of a Woman. 1604.

WOLFF, M. 'Shakespeare und die Commedia dell'arte.' *Shakespeare-Jahrbuch*, xlvi, 1910.

WOLFF, M. 'Flaminio Scala und sein Szenarium *Li tragici successi*: Ein Beitrag zur Geschichte des Stoffes von *Romeo und Juliet*.' *Archiv für das Studium der neueren Sprachen und Litteraturen*, cxxviii, 1912. (This I have not been able to examine.)

WRIGHT, L. B. 'Will Kemp and the *Travailes of the Three English Brothers*.' *Mod. Lang. Notes*, xli, no. 8, 1926.

'Juggling Tricks and Conjury on the English Stage before 1642.' *Modern Philology*, xxiv, 1927.

'Vaudeville Dancing and Acrobatics in Elizabethan Plays.' *Englische Studien*, lxiii, 1928.

YATES, F. 'English Actors in Paris during the Lifetime of Shakespeare.' *Rev. of Eng. Studies*, i. 392, Oct. 1925.

'The Importance of John Eliot's Ortho-epia Gallica.' Ibid., vii, Oct. 1931.

ZENATTI, A. 'Una raccolta di scenari della Commedia dell'arte.' *Riv. critica della letteratura italiana*, ii. 156–9, 1885.

ZERBINI, E. Note storiche sul dialetto Bergamasco. 1886.

ZUCCARO, F. Il passaggio per Italia con la dimora di Parma. 1608.

ZUCCHI, F. La Tabbaccheide. 1636.

INDEX

PRINTED IN
GREAT BRITAIN
AT THE
UNIVERSITY PRESS
OXFORD
BY
JOHN JOHNSON
PRINTER
TO THE
UNIVERSITY